The Organized Teacher's Guide to Children's Literature

The Organized Teacher's Guide to Children's Literature

Kimberly Persiani, EdD

Illustrations by Steve Springer, MA

New York   Chicago   San Francisco   Athens   London   Madrid
Mexico City   Milan   New Delhi   Singapore   Sydney   Toronto

1 2 3 4 5 6 7 8 9 10 11 12 13   QVS/QVS   1 0 9 8 7 6 5 4

ISBN   978-0-07-180063-1
MHID   0-07-180063-8

e-ISBN   978-0-07-180064-8
e-MHID   0-07-180064-6

Library of Congress Control Number 2013948158

Interior illustrations copyright © Steve Springer

McGraw-Hill Education products are available at special quantity discounts to use as premiums and sales promotions or for use in corporate training programs. To contact a representative, please visit the Contact Us pages at www.mhprofessional.com.

This book is printed on acid-free paper.

Contents

Contents

Contents

Introduction

In my 20 years of experience in working with children in the K–12 public school and private school system and in my work training teachers, I have always encouraged the use of children's and young adult literature as a key element for planning and delivering instruction in all the subject areas. This guide for children and young adults from pre-K to 12th grade explores the fantastic world of picture books as well as the lovely stories of depth and complexity found in chapter books and novels.

Reading wonderful stories is something of a lost art. When I have the opportunity to share my passion, I always hope my excitement for books comes across to all new and veteran teachers. This book gives me the chance to do just that by presenting hundreds of books that I have had the absolute joy of reading. These titles have been carefully selected to meet a myriad of themes, topics, and relevant issues for today's youth.

Over the years, publishers of many comprehensive reading and language arts programs have done a great job of connecting the various subject areas such as writing, science, history, and the arts across the curriculum to match corresponding stories and novel excerpts. However, although they do teach students "how to read," one of the most important elements often slighted in these programs as well as in the training for using these programs is teaching students a "love of reading." This is what this text hopes to accomplish: to encourage teachers to engage and teach their students a love of reading by using a wide range of books on specific themes of great interest to their students. It is more than just learning how to read or finish a book.

Because today's students are technologically connected and engaged, they don't gravitate toward the bookshelves as much as they used to. Less commonly do they pick up an interesting book for the pure pleasure of it before they grab their gaming instrument, cell phone, or tablet.

The questions are how do we get kids excited about reading? How do we get them to move away from their electronics long enough to get engrossed in a good piece of literature? And if they ultimately choose their technology at home, how can we at least get them interested in good books at school? Good books are the vehicle for cultivating a student's reading fluency and excitement about reading. Whether introducing rich literature into their lives on a daily basis, via hard copy or in electronic form, if students do not have access to books that inspire them, thrill them, and draw in their interests, they will not gravitate toward those bookshelves.

In this text, you will be introduced to a variety of important, interesting, captivating, and fun book titles. These books offer opportunities to develop unit themes, supplement existing lesson plans, and support subject-specific pedagogy while keeping the attention of students and getting them to come back for more.

This book is organized in a strategic way. Chapter 1 explains what Lexile levels are and why these are found throughout the book. The idea behind the Lexile Framework for Reading says that if we know how well a student can read and how hard a specific book is to comprehend, we can predict how well that student will likely understand the book. This gives teachers and librarians the information they need to know exactly which books will meet their students' reading levels so that books within these Lexile levels can be made available for students. Instead of offering books that "dumb down" the curriculum, decent and meaningful pieces of literature can be pulled for students.

In Chapter 2 you will read about how to set up a library. This is important so that students have a quiet and comfortable place to read in the classroom besides their own desks. This often makes reading books much more relaxing and enjoyable for young people. Additionally, knowing how to organize books for easy access is critical for making book selection less frustrating for the students.

Once the library is set up, teachers and librarians alike will want to review a variety of reading strategies so that book reading can commence. When reading with students, teachers and librarians can incorporate useful strategies from Chapter 3 to increase reading comprehension, vocabulary development, understanding, and interpretation of the theme or content. This is especially important for English language learners and students who struggle with reading, as well as a challenge for those who enjoy thinking outside the box at a higher level.

After explaining reading strategies, it is important to consider ways to group students for discussing books and chapters. Chapter 4 presents several opportunities for students to meet and share their ideas about what has been read to them or what they have read independently.

Once students have a full library of books to choose from and are prompted through reading strategies and grouping experiences, there are many ways to respond to literature, which can be found in Chapter 5. Ideas for book reports and projects are explained so that teachers and librarians can encourage students to share their comprehension of stories in fun and creative ways.

Following the opening chapters of this book are lists of titles that are recommended for all age-and-grade appropriate bookshelves. Chapter 6 on awards introduces books from the year 2000 to the current day for the Caldecott, Newbery, Coretta Scott King, Pura Belpré, and Scott O'Dell awards. In Chapter 7 you will learn about some of the most well-known authors of children's and young adult books and classic and young adult novels that come highly recommended.

This guide then continues into multicultural books, titles about character traits, and then books organized by race cultures. Many of the books in these three categories connect to the chapter on history. To finish the subject areas, books related to math and science, are presented. And since many of the major holidays occur during the school year, it is important to teach about the cultural and historical background of the holidays that schools recognize.

Last, the final chapter of this book shows how one title for each grade level can be linked across the curriculum, which will be increasingly important as the Common Core Standards (http://www.corestandards.org) are implemented. In choosing books for your library that address the previously mentioned topics, it is also important to choose titles that can be read aloud to the students as well as read by the students.

The Organized Teacher's Guide to

Children's Literature

1

Lexile Measures

· · · · · · · · · · · ·

Throughout this guide, book titles are listed beginning with the author's name, the most recent date of publication (this depends on edition number, reprint date, anniversary years, etc.), the title, the most current ISBN number (again, that number can change with a new edition), a brief summary of the book, and then the Lexile level and the appropriate grade level for the content maturity of the book. What may be new to some readers are the Lexile level designations for many of the titles. Lexile measures are valuable tools that help teachers, librarians, parents, and children select books that will provide the right level of challenge for the child's reading ability—not too difficult to be frustrating, but difficult enough to encourage reading growth.

The idea behind the Lexile Framework for Reading is that if we know how well a student can read and how hard a specific book is to comprehend, we can predict how well that student will likely understand the book. Lexile measures help a reader find books and articles at an appropriate level of difficulty and determine how well that reader will likely comprehend a text. Lexile measures can also monitor a reader's growth in reading ability over time. While the Lexile measure of a book is based on word frequency and sentence length, many other factors affect the relationship between a reader and a book, including content, the age and interests of the reader, the design of the actual book, and more. A child's grade level and reading ability are two different measures. That's why the Lexile level measures the child's ability based on reading comprehension, not grade level.

A Lexile measure is a valuable piece of information about either the difficulty of a text, such as a book or magazine article, or an individual's reading ability. A Lexile *text* measure is obtained by analyzing the text's semantic and syntactic characteristics and assigning it a Lexile measure. Usually the higher the Lexile measure, the more difficult the text is to understand. To learn whether Lexile measures are available in your area, contact your school district or state department of education. The Lexile measure is shown as a number with an "L" after it (880L is 880 Lexile).

A Lexile *reader* measure places students on the same Lexile scale as the texts. A child typically receives a Lexile measure by taking a test of reading comprehension from a variety of appropriate assessments. Numerous tests report Lexile reader measures, including many state end-of-year assessments, national norm-referenced assessments, and reading program assessments. For example, if a student receives an 880L on her end-of-grade reading test, she is an 880 Lexile reader. Higher Lexile measures represent a higher level of reading ability. A Lexile reader measure can range from below 200L for beginning readers to above 1600L for advanced readers. Readers who score at or below 0L receive a BR for "beginning reader."

When a Lexile text measure matches a Lexile reader measure, this is called a "targeted" reading experience. The reader will likely encounter some level of difficulty with the text, but not enough to get frustrated. The best way for a reader to grow is to read text that is not too hard but not too easy. Also, when considering a Lexile measure, consider a reading range around the number instead of focusing on the exact number.

The Lexile map provides examples of popular books and sample texts at various points on the Lexile scale. The examples on the map help explain text complexity and help readers identify books of various levels of text complexity.

When readers are matched with texts in their Lexile range (100L below to 50L above their Lexile reader measures), they are likely to comprehend about 75 percent of the text when reading independently. This targeted reading rate is the point at which a reader will comprehend enough to understand the text but will still face some reading challenge. The result is growth in reading ability and a rewarding reading experience, especially if high-interest books can be pinpointed within a student's Lexile range.

For more information on Lexile measures, their uses, and ways to assess students' Lexile levels, visit http://www.Lexile.com. A Lexile measure considers text difficulty only. It does not address the subject matter or quality of the text, age-appropriateness of the content, or the reader's interests. It is highly encouraged to preview all reading materials in advance for age appropriateness and high interest.

What Is a Lexile Code?

Sometimes a Lexile measure does not supply enough information to select a particular book for a particular reader. It's important that children's reading experiences are positive and successful, so choosing books that not only are at their Lexile levels but also are engaging is important to develop lovers of reading. Since a Lexile measure does not always provide a complete picture, some books are assigned an additional two-letter code that provides supplemental data about developmental appropriateness, reading difficulty, and common or intended usage.

The following guide can help determine how to use Lexile-leveled books in your planning and delivery of instruction:

- **AD (adult directed):** The book is generally intended to be read aloud to a child, rather than for the child to read it for the first time independently. Many picture books have been assigned the AD code.
- **BR (beginning reader):** The book has a Lexile measure of 0L or below and is appropriate for a beginning reader. The Lexile measure is shown only as BR, without a zero or negative number.
- **GN (graphic novel):** The book is a graphic novel or comic book.
- **HL (high-low):** The book has a Lexile measure much lower than the average reading ability of the intended age range of its readers. HL books include content of a high interest level, but they are written in a style that is easier for a struggling reader.
- **IG (illustrated guide):** The book consists of independent pieces or sections of text, such as an encyclopedia or glossary.
- **NC (non-conforming):** The book has a Lexile measure that is markedly higher than is typical for the publisher's intended audience or designated developmental level of the book. NC books are good choices for high-ability readers.
- **NP (non-prose):** The book contains more than 50 percent of nonstandard or non-conforming prose, such as poems, plays, songs, and recipes. NP books do not receive a Lexile measure.

In addition to the Lexile scores and the two-letter codes, choosing books for your students based on their reading level ability are attached to books with high interest in terms of content, while also meeting needs of both low-leveled readers and high-leveled readers. Since Lexiles are a measure of text difficulty or readability, they cannot determine the literary or informational content of a text, so it is important to consider the following aspects when adding Lexile leveled books to the classroom or school library:

- **Student interest** in the addressed topic is needed to motivate student effort toward deciphering the text (i.e., the Harry Potter series is of high interest, and many students find it worthwhile to try hard to get through the text).
- **Age appropriateness** of the topic for the student needs to be considered. The text should be neither too "immature" nor too "mature" for the age level of the student. Just because a student can read a higher-leveled book does not mean that the student should if the content is too mature for his or her age (e.g., the Twilight series for a third-grader).
- **Text support**, including features such as illustrations, size of type, captions, and sidebars, can greatly aid student comprehension of a text. This is especially important for English language learners (ELLs) and students with reading disabilities, both of whom rely on highlighted keywords, picture cues that match the text, large print, and so on.
- **Quality of text**, including its size, weight, construction, and aesthetic appeal is important.

Common Core Standards and Lexile Levels

According to Lexile.com, the Common Core Standards in relation to Lexile levels aim to ensure that all students are "on track" to be both college and career ready. Because high school graduation does not guarantee that students are ready for the postsecondary challenges that await them, and since the reading demands of college, the workforce, and life in general have remained consistent or increased over time, K–12 texts and reading tasks have decreased in complexity. Generally speaking, the result is a gap between students' reading abilities and the reading demands they will likely encounter after graduation.

With the Common Core Standards Initiative placing strong emphasis on the role of text complexity in evaluating student readiness for college and careers, the following are the Common Core Standards' three equally important components of text complexity and how Lexile measures can support them:

1. **Qualitative dimensions of text complexity, such as levels of meaning, structure, language conventionality and clarity, and knowledge demands.** Lexile codes provide more information about a book's characteristics, such as its developmental appropriateness, reading difficulty, and common or intended usage.
2. **Quantitative measures of text complexity, such as word frequency and sentence length, which are typically measured by computer software.** The Lexile Analyzer is software that measures text demand based on these two widely adopted variables.
3. **Reader and task considerations, such as students' knowledge, motivation, and interests.** Lexile levels help readers build custom book lists based on their ability and personal interests or school assignments.

Apply Lexiles Across the Curriculum

With the Common Core Standards asking teachers to link subject areas and teacher resources across the curriculum, consider the following simple ways teachers can do so:

- Use a realistic fiction or nonfiction chapter book or picture book to bring experiences of the Civil War to the history class and develop a sequence of events and discuss significant contributions to the war.
- Use the same book in English for reading, writing, and vocabulary development.

- In math this same book can be used to develop a timeline of the war, showing increments in time between significant events during the war.
- Then use it again for visual and performing arts where scripts and role plays are carried out to demonstrate an actual exchange between soldiers and politicians.

Lexile levels of theme-based books can help a teacher decide if certain books are more appropriate to be read aloud to students, read by students, used for research, and more.

Certain types of text cannot be assigned a Lexile measure because they are not prose. These include poems and plays. Additionally, for books below 100L, Lexile text measures often aren't assigned, because such books rely heavily on illustrations, rhyme, rhythm, repetition, and so on. Such access features are not accounted for in the Lexile framework and therefore are given the designation of beginner reader (BR).

References

www.Scholastic.com. (December 2012). *Lexiles: A System for Measuring Reader Ability and Text Difficulty: A Guide for Educators* MetaMetrics, Inc. http://teacher.scholastic.com/products/sri_reading_assessment/pdfs/SRI_ProfPaper_Lexiles.pdf

www.Lexile.com. (December 2012). *Common Core Standards and Text Complexity.* http://lexilc.com/using-lexile/lexile-measures-and-the-ccssi/the-common-core-and-text-complexity/

2

Setting Up Your Library

Aclassroom or school library is an important component for any classroom or school. It's most useful for supplementing your curriculum and in meeting your students' needs and interests. It takes time to build a great library, and it can be an excellent resource for both you and your students. Setting up your library can be expensive and time consuming. Take time and seek out alternative ways of obtaining books besides dipping too deeply into your own pocket to purchase them. You do want to choose books carefully; more is not always better.

The classroom library is often one of the last things considered when organizing classroom space for the year. This is especially true for a new teacher who typically inherits a classroom library from the teacher before him or her. It's even possible that the library can become a neglected corner of the room without some kind of organization. But a well-stocked, organized, high-quality classroom library can increase interest and motivation for reading, support differentiated instruction through better matching of students reading levels and English language development (ELD) levels with texts, and provide the means for the practice necessary to develop reading skills. In this chapter, you will gain tips on building and organizing a classroom library.

The Library Space

A student-friendly setup and clear organization can make all the difference in getting students going to the library and using it consistently. A visually pleasing, warm, welcoming place for students to gather is important for making them feel excited about visiting the library.

An area in the classroom or school library can be set up in a way that allows for relaxation, interaction among pairs of students, or as a gathering spot for a small group of students to share books. Soft seating areas can be created with chair pads, beanbag chairs, large pillows, and colorful rugs.

Organizing the Books

The library should be organized for students to be able to select books on their own. Theme or topic groupings and reading-level groupings help students choose appropriate books for their instructional reading level, interests, or curriculum needs. Books can be grouped in various ways. They can be organized by the developmental levels of the students in the classroom or by topics or themes such as multicultural subjects, fiction, nonfiction, insects, animals, families, fantasy, fairy tales, poetry, or informational texts. This will help students navigate the collection with ease.

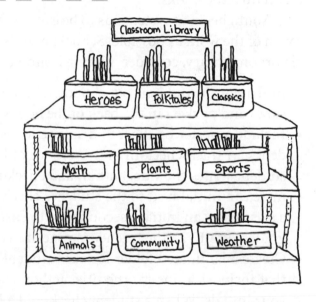

When organizing and leveling books, use whatever works best for you and your students: a numbering system, a lettering system, or even color-coded stickers to identify students' reading levels. You may want to write on the stickers to create subcategories or to identify a theme, topic, genre, or level. Be sure to mark every book in the same place so students know quickly where to look to find the identifier. Of course, you will need to teach students the organizational system of the library: how the books are displayed and why.

When organizing the books within the library, try to allow for a large number of books to be displayed with their covers visible for easy identification. Face as many books forward as possible so students can see what is available. It's always helpful if these books are related to the theme or unit that you are currently studying.

A special display section should be set aside for the books most recently read aloud by the teacher or librarian so students can explore the books on their own and support the connections made between the illustrations and their understanding of the story. Another special display could be "Teacher Recommended" and "Student Recommended" books so readers can share their favorites with others.

You may also want to include books that prepare students for upcoming themes, topics, or issues so students start to form ideas and ask questions about what they will learn. It gives struggling readers and English language learners (ELLs) an opportunity for prelearning and for more advanced readers a preview so the stories aren't as intimidating or overwhelming when they become part of upcoming lessons.

Checkout and Return

It's important to clearly establish a library checkout and return system for books. You will need to teach students how to check out books, how long they can be kept, and how to properly return the books.

Your checkout system has to be easy to manage and should rely on the students to do as much of the work as possible. School libraries likely have a policy in place already, but for the classroom library, consider making it simple.

- Add a sign-in and sign-out clipboard in the classroom library rather than using individual cards and pockets in the back of the books like most school libraries used to employ.
- Include a poster or chart to display a list with each student's name where you or the student can track check-in and checkout of books. Each time a student selects a book, the student writes the title, author, and checkout date on the poster or chart. You or a classmate can initial next to the student's checkout line, and once the book is returned, you or a classmate can initial a second time to ensure the safe return of the book. For the younger grades (Pre-K–2), the teacher may need to do this.
- Create a laminated folder for each student. Add a chart to the folder prior to lamination that includes a line for the title, author, checkout date, return date, and two sections for your initials. When a student checks out a book from the classroom library to take home, he or she completes the information on an empty line, gets your initials, and then has a designated number of days before the book needs to be returned (five days, one weekend, two weeks, etc.). Once returned, you initial again to indicate the book's safe return.

Reshelving can be another time-consuming task once books have been returned. Some ideas for making this easier could include:

- Use designated return bins like that of a public library or school library. After signing books in as "returned," the students can place the books into a return bin.
- Ask a parent volunteer or teaching assistant to reshelve the books on the day books are always due (you may want to plan this for the days you know you will have someone there to do this). You will also need to teach this person your system for organizing books.
- Engage students in this responsibility when you can. They will likely know where the books go faster than you will, as they are pretty quick at figuring out organizational sys-

tems—especially if it includes a simple concept such as labeling, color coding, or separating the books by theme, topic, or genre. Have two or three responsible students take on this task. They can do the work each morning, every Friday, or another time—whatever works best to help manage your time.

Regardless of how you set up your library space, the method you choose for organizing your books, or the system you use for checking out and returning books, teaching the students how to appropriately access and use the classroom library is crucial to the meaningful use of the library.

Summary of Library Setup and Use

- Books can be purchased or acquired from:
  - Yard sales
  - Church and community groups
  - Friends with books their children have outgrown
  - Other teachers
  - Library book sales
  - Book fair events
  - Neighborhood organizations
  - Requests for books as gifts; wish lists for family and friends
  - Monthly book-order clubs
  - Grants
  - Dollar stores and thrift stores
  - Retiring teachers and teachers switching grade levels
  - Used book stores
- Designate an area in the classroom where students can find books and read.
- Bookshelves, a rug, large pillows or a beanbag chair, and even a teddy bear or two can make a comfortable reading space.
- Plastic tubs can serve as theme or genre organizers.
- Label books on their covers with your name and room number using a permanent marker.
- Create bookshelf placeholders. When a student takes a book from the shelf and is browsing the pages, the placeholder can keep its spot on the shelf.
- Set up the book checkout. Students can then sign out books to read at home.
- Assign book reports.
  - Students can select a book of choice.
  - Primary grades can use large ziplock baggies or laminated envelopes to transport books home.
  - Students keep books for a weekend, a week, or a designated time frame.
  - Students complete the appropriate book report forms.
  - Students track their reading using reading logs.

- Organize books by theme or genre. How could you easily access a given book? What works for you? As your library grows, you can expand.
  - General: science, social science, math, and so on
  - Theme: plants, friendship, courage, multicultural, favorite authors
  - Standards: plate tectonics, volcanoes, and so on
- For lower grades, place colored stickers on books to designate their level.
  - Green: easy
  - Yellow: intermediate
  - Red: advanced
- Consider the following when choosing books:
  - Visit a bookstore and spend time with picture books if you are unfamiliar with them.
  - Select books that inspire you and that you think your students will enjoy.
  - Include a variety of authors and genres for picture books.
  - Include rich, multicultural books (picture books as well as chapter books).
  - Choose varied reading levels especially for struggling readers, English language learners (ELLs), and those who might need 5 to 10 minutes as a time filler between transitions.
  - Go beyond books and include magazines and comic books.

3

Reading Strategies

Books for children and young adults that include engaging, extended lessons are essential for every grade. They are powerful tools in teaching theme-based units that link subject areas across the curriculum. The Common Core Standards for English Language Arts and Literacy (http://www.corestandards.org) states that the following qualities characterize literate students:

1. They demonstrate independence.
2. They build strong content knowledge.
3. They respond to the varying demands of audience, task, purpose, and discipline.
4. They comprehend as well as critique.
5. They value evidence.
6. They use technology and digital media strategically and capably.
7. They come to understand other perspectives and cultures.

When incorporating the reading strategies described in this section, learners have many opportunities to engage with literature that allows for all this and more. Here are some things to keep in mind when reading a picture book or chapter book to the class:

- Introduce the book.
  - Title
  - Author
  - Illustrator
  - Copyright, or "birthday of the book"
- Use an appropriately animated voice to read the story.
- Hold the book in one hand so you can read it and the class can see the pictures.
- Exercise "wait time" at the end of each page or chapter so students can take in the illustrations and content.
- After the story or chapter, ask questions such as:
  - What was the setting of the story or chapter?
  - Who were the main characters?
  - What was the main idea of the story or chapter?
  - What was the problem or conflict in the story or chapter?
  - How was the problem or conflict resolved in the story or chapter?
  - Have students sequence the story or chapter.
- During the story ask students critical-thinking questions such as:
  - What do you think will happen next?
  - Has anything like this ever happened to you?
  - How would you handle the situation?

Strategies to Improve Reading Skills

When reading with students, the following strategies can be used to increase comprehension, vocabulary development, understanding, and interpretation. Teachers can use these questions verbatim when reading and discussing a story. Students should also be able to go back into the text and find specific support (page numbers and quotes) for their responses.

Predict

Make predictions about what will happen in the story. This strategy can be used effectively before reading and at key points in the texts, where learners discuss what might happen next or how the story might end. It should not be overused or allowed to spoil the narrative.

- What do you think will happen next or in the next chapter?
- Can anyone make a prediction about what might be coming?
- What do you think this might be about?
- Does this remind you of anything you have seen, read, or heard before?
- What kind of story do you think this might be?
- What do you think [the character] will do next?
- How do you think this will end?

Summarize

Wrap up what is happening or has happened in the story. The ability to summarize is an essential skill for the developing, fluent-comprehending reader, but it is also a skill that needs to be modeled repeatedly by the teacher. It can be broken down into parts, each of which can be emphasized in different contexts and can be practiced through a range of activities. Readers can be asked to write chapter headings, list the writer's main ideas, provide a piece from the book, or write a short review—all of these are ways to summarize the text. Ask students:

- Who can summarize what happened on this page?
- Who can summarize what happened in this chapter?
- Who can summarize what happened so far?

Visualize

Envision the story, the setting, characters, action, and so on. Tell students to close their eyes and try to see the story. Ask students:

- Can you visualize what it would be like to be there in that situation?
- Can you describe the setting?
- Can you see it?

Infer or Interpret

Derive meaning from the text. Make an educated guess as to an aspect of the story. Ask students:

- What does this mean in the story?
- How do you think the character feels?

- What is the message here?
- What is the author trying to convey?

Ask Questions

You, the students, or both can ask and discuss questions to understand the story. The key idea here is to develop an understanding in the learner that asking questions is probably more important than answering them. This is a core strategy in the development of critical thinkers, and it is important to guide learners toward the hierarchy of questions they should be asking as they read a text. Ask students:

- What questions do you have?
- What do you think . . . ?
- What does it mean . . . ?
- How is . . . ?
- Would you . . . ?
- Where and when do you think the story is set?
- Why does [character] act in this way at this particular time?
- What do you think is going through [character's] mind here?
- How do you think the author wants us to feel toward this character, event, or experience?

Reference

Students can refer to a similar situation or research an aspect of the story.

- How is this similar to what happened in . . . ?
- During this time in history what happened . . . ?
- Have you experienced a similar situation in reference to . . . ?

Clarify

Clear up any issues for understanding the story better.

- I would like to clarify . . .
- Can anyone clarify what happened?
- I am confused, what does . . . mean?

Evaluate

One aspect of reading is the process of evaluating or assessing the authenticity and credibility of a text. Readers of any age will happily tell you what they think of a text, but they will often struggle to explain why, beyond the stock responses of "it was boring" or "it was exciting." A discussion and use of open questions will determine the quality of the dialogue and outcome.

Questions to consider for the dialogue could include:

- What was the author's purpose, and to what extent did he or she achieve it?
- What was the writer's point of view?
- Was the ending of the story the most appropriate ending? Why?
- Were the characters multiculturally authentic?
- Was the story multiculturally authentic?
- Were the illustrations multiculturally authentic?

Compare and Contrast

Relate the story to another story, another character, or a similar experience. As we read a text we are constantly making connections between what we are reading and our own real-life experiences in that we draw upon our prior learning. To develop that in young readers we have to encourage them to make the links and explore those aspects of the text, which are most likely to pull out the comparisons. It is also important to explore the notion that while the text will often be a shared experience, our reactions to it may be quite different, depending on the associations we make:

- How is this similar to . . . ?
- How is it different from . . . ?
- Can we compare . . . ?
- Can we contrast . . . ?
- What are the similarities?
- What are the differences?
- Does this remind me of anything I have experienced before?
- Does this remind me of anything I have read or seen before?
- How would I have behaved in that situation? Why?
- How does this text compare with [a previous one I read]?

Cause and Effect

Look for events that bring about or result in a specific outcome.

- What caused this to happen?
- What was the effect?
- What were the actions of this character?
- What happened as a result?

Connections and Patterns

Make connections or find patterns from the story to relate to past readings and real-life experiences. More advanced or fluent readers begin to show a deeper understanding of genre or of the work of a particular author. Patterns might include elements of the plot, structure, layout, use of graphics, and so on. It also includes language patterns, the repeated use of particular words, images or symbols, and the recognition of common themes in a text or group of texts.

- What does this remind you of in yourself?
- What do you think this character or place would look like?
- Draw a map of the area where this story takes place.
- Draw a mind-map showing the main elements of the story.
- What connections can we make here?
- Use a Venn diagram to identify connections from this story to another one.

Personally Relate

Relate personally in some way to the story:

- This happened to me once . . .
- I don't like it when . . .
- I enjoy . . .

Describe

Use details to retell or describe the story:

- What is happening here?
- Identify details or examples that support the story.
- Can you describe the setting, what is happening, or how the character felt?

Author's Point of View

Interpret what the author is trying to say, or the author's opinion.

- How does the author help illustrate his or her point of view (language, events, etc.)?
- What is the author of this story trying to say?
- What does the author think about . . . ?
- How does the author get his or her point across?
- What does the author use in the story to support his or her opinion?

Author's Purpose

Determine what the author is trying to do or accomplish—entertain, inform, and so on.

- Why do you think this story was written?
- Is this fact or opinion?
- What is the author trying to accomplish by telling this story?

Sequence

Have students put the events of the story in time-order sequence.

- What is the sequence of events that happened in this story?
  - What happened first?
  - Next?
  - Then?
  - Last?

Reading Genres

There are many genres of reading, and each serves a purpose. The following is a breakdown of common reading genres. Students need to understand the differences and how to identify what genre best meets their needs for entertainment, research, information, interest, and so on.

Mystery

- Mysterious events
- Explained or revealed at the end
- Suspenseful

Realistic Fiction

- Takes place in modern time
- Here and now
- Realistic events

Historical Fiction

- Made-up characters set in historical context
- Pertains to a time in the past
- Setting real, characters fictional

Nonfiction

- True facts
- Any subject
- About people—biography

Biography

- Story of person's life
- Told by another person

Autobiography

- Story of person's life
- Told by that person

Science Fiction

- Blends scientific fact and fiction
- Futuristic technology

Myth

- Explains something
- Characters may be gods or superhumans

Drama

- Written to be acted out
- Audience

Folktale

- No known author
- Passed on through generations

Poetry

- Verse
- Creates thought and feeling
- Use of rhythm and sometimes rhyme

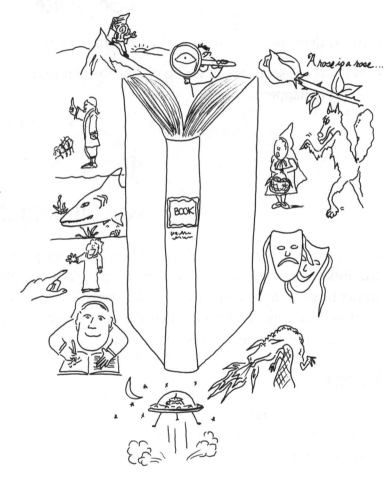

Ways to Read

There are many ways for you to read with students. It is a good idea to mix it up when you can and try different ways for managing your reading. Some methods will work best with small groups and others with the whole class. Much depends on your purpose. Are you reading with the class for information? For entertainment? To model comprehension?

Choral Reading

- "Unison reading"
- Many opportunities for repeated readings of a selected piece
- Practice in oral reading
- Excellent for poetry or rhymes
- Repeated readings of big books

Shared Reading

- Teacher reading big book or text aloud
- Students viewing or following
- Early reading strategies
- Phonemic awareness
- Model reading strategies
- Predicting
- Use of contextual clues

Independent Reading

- Students reading independently
- Practice learned strategies
- Builds fluency
- Problem-solving application

Sustained Silent Reading (SSR)

- Students reading on their own
- Independent and silent
- Individual instructional levels
- Provides practice
- Encourages reading
- Uninterrupted sustained silent reading (USSR)
- Drop everything and read (DEAR)

Guided Reading

- Teacher and student reading text together
- Reading, thinking, and talking through text
- Supports intervention
- Teaches problem solving
- Can also "echo read"
- Teacher reading and students rereading

Read Aloud

- Teacher reading aloud to class without stopping to summarize or ask questions
- Class discussion or dialogue
- Follow-up activity
- Journals, art, and so on
- Pure enjoyment

Popcorn Reading

- Teacher asks a student to begin reading aloud.
- Any willing student can start.
- When one student stops, another student continues (without teacher's direction).
- Reading continues until all have read.
- This builds responsibility to participate and offers a choice when to do so.
- Lower-grade students can pick the next reader from those who have not read yet.

Buddy Reading

- Students pair up.
- Lower-grade student pairs with upper-grade student.
- The two read and discuss story.
- They take turns reading aloud.
- Older student serves as a coach or reading mentor.

Timed Reading

- Designate the number of minutes.
- Students read twice.
- Student attempts to read further the second time.
- Note number of words per minute.
- This builds fluency.

Partner Reading

- Students in the class pair up. (Pair students with one another: high with medium and medium with low or allow students to select.)
- Take turns and assist one another.
- This showcases their skills.
- This allows for practice in nonthreatening way.
- Select a special spot to read in the room.

English Language Learners

It is highly likely you will have students in your class whose primary language is not English. These students are often categorized as English language learners (ELLs) and are required to receive English language instruction. Having books available to them that are at their instructional reading level, as well as books that are culturally relevant, is important and ought not be overlooked. Before gathering appropriate books for your classroom or school library, understanding your language learners is essential. This section offers a variety of tangible ideas and reminders for teachers to employ when using literature to bring the curriculum to life for those who are still mastering the English language. This is especially important as students begin to develop advanced skills set forth by the Common Core in which the standards define what students should understand and be able to do by the end of each grade and correspond to the College and Career Readiness (CCR) anchor standards (http://www .corestandards.org).

Consider that your school or district might already have a list of books for you to access to meet the English language development (ELD) levels of the students in your classroom or school:

- Look or ask for possible adopted support curriculum such as book titles that are already available for you to refer to in choosing appropriate books at instructional reading levels, bilingual books, multicultural books, or any combination of these relevant to your students.

- Create a progress system to track students' language development and to also use in organizing your leveled books.
- Create or locate appropriate assessments to promote students into higher reading levels with richer content.
- Check with your school's administration and other teachers to get guidelines and strategies for selecting books for your school's population.

As you research and gather materials, it is important to be familiar with the following abbreviations:

Common Acronyms and Bilingual Terms

- **ELL:** English language learner
- **ESL:** English as a second language
- **ELD:** English language development
- **SDAIE:** Specifically designed academic instruction in English
- **SIOP:** Sheltered instruction observation protocol
- **Comprehensible input:** Information delivered so it is understandable for a given ELD level

Strategies for Working with ELLs

The following lists describe the important basic aspects of Specially Designed Academic Instruction in English (SDAIE).

SDAIE

- Involves strategic instruction that layers (scaffolds) lessons to review vocabulary and concepts according to a student's needs
- Targets and narrows a book's focus, making it easier for the ELL (comprehensible input)
- Provides a useful strategy for all learners

Realia (Part of SDAIE)

- Tangible items can be used to introduce vocabulary or concepts.
- Students use any or all of their five senses to make the language, ideas, and vocabulary being introduced more tangible

Preteach/Reteach (Part of SDAIE)

- Involves preteaching a book's vocabulary or concepts
- Increases familiarity and builds background knowledge of the book's plot, setting, and so on
- Involves reteaching concepts after a book has been read for reinforcement purposes

Total Physical Response/Role-Play (Part of SDAIE)

- Total physical response (TPR) involves physically executing described actions that may be presented in a book.
- Role-playing is a good way to demonstrate key words and key concepts for new information.

Pictures (Part of SDAIE)

- "A picture is worth a thousand words."
- Picture cues can be used for vocabulary, historical references, people, and so on.

English Language Development (ELD) Levels

There are five ELD levels. These levels help you understand a student's language capabilities, which can be helpful as you choose books for various levels of readers or students. The goal is to move at least one ELD level per year, eventually being redesignated to "fluent English." The following is a simplified look at each level. If engaged in a discussion about a book or a written response related to a given title, a student would communicate according to the following:

ELD 1

- Responds nonverbally or uses a few words when responding orally
- Points to pictures to respond during discussions of stories
- Draws pictures related to the topic or story

ELD 2

- Gives verbal responses of a few words when asked for a response
- Uses yes or no responses appropriately
- Writes phrases with invented spelling and asks for help spelling words correctly or using appropriate words to answer questions correctly

ELD 3

- Gives verbal responses in short phrases (omitting words or verbs)
- Responds to the "why" questions and can elaborate
- Writes phrases or simple sentences (conventional spelling begins)

ELD 4

- Converses verbally with few errors
- Answers during class discussions
- Writes related sentences with strong vocabulary and few errors

ELD 5

- Responds verbally like a native speaker
- Participates in discussions like a native speaker
- Writes with the ease of a native speaker

Basic Fundamentals of Reading

The following is a brief overview of the basic fundamentals of reading that can assist you in preparing for the use of picture books, chapter books, and anthologies for teaching reading instruction for all students, including English language learners and students with reading difficulties. This breakdown is meant to give you some simple approaches when you use core literature to plan the curriculum and employ a variety of reading strategies.

Alphabet

There are 26 letters in the alphabet. Kindergarten and first-grade students need to understand that the alphabet has a sequence.

    A _ C _ _ F = A B C D E F   L _ N _ = L M N O

The letters of the alphabet have names and sounds. Kindergarten students generally start learning the uppercase, or capital, letters first (A, B, C). Lowercase letters (a, b, c) are introduced later.

Letters

The letters are broken down into consonants and vowels.

- **Consonants:** *b*, *c*, *d*, and so on
- **Vowels:** *a*, *e*, *i*, *o*, *u* (sometimes *y*)
  - **Short vowels:** **a**pple, **e**gg, **i**gloo, **o**ctopus, **u**mbrella
  - **Long vowels:** **a**pe, **e**normous, **i**ce, **o**at, **u**nicorn
    Long *a*: bake, pail, acorn, day
    Long *e*: Pete, feet, seat, chief, city
    Long *i*: bike, kind, cry, high, tie
    Long *o*: joke, boat, toe, show
    Long *u*: mule, unicorn

Letter Combinations and Spellings

Two or more letters create a sound. Kindergarten starts with the basic letter sounds of consonants and vowels (short vowels). First grade builds upon this adding in more complex spelling patterns. The following is a breakdown of letter patterns and spellings for common vowel and consonant sounds.

Vowels

- **Vowel digraphs:** two letters (vowels) together that make one sound (**ai**, **ay**, **oa**, **oe**, **ow**, **ee**, **ey**, **ea**, **ie**, **ei**).
- **Vowel dipthongs:** two vowels together that make a new, special sound (**au**, **aw**, **oi**, **oy**, **oo**, **eu**, **ue**, **ew**, **ui**, **ou**, **ow**).
- **R-controlled vowel sounds:** vowels followed by *r* create a new sound (**ar**, **er**, **ir**, **ur**, **or**)
- **Letter *y*:** *y* has the sound of the long *i* at the end of one-syllable words (cr**y**, m**y**, fl**y**); *y* has the sound of the long *e* at the end of words with two or more syllables (cit**y**, prett**y**, rub**y**).
- **Letter *w*:** *w* can combine with *a* and have a short *o* sound (**wa**sh, **wa**tch, s**wa**t).
- **Letters *qu*:** *qu* can combine with *a* and have a short *o* sound; *qu* is pronounced "kwah," as if it has a *w* (**squa**t, **qua**drant).

Consonants

- **Two-sounded consonants:**
  (1) *c* and *g* can be hard or soft:
    - **Soft** *c* = **c**ent, **c**ircle, **c**ytoplasm; **hard** *c* = **c**at, magi**c**, s**c**an
    - **Soft** *g* = **g**entle, **g**iraffe, **g**ym; **hard** *g* = **g**um, ba**g**, **g**rape
  (2) *s* can make an *s* or *z* sound:
    - *s* = "s" = **s**ee, pa**ss**
    - *s* = "z" = bee**s**, lo**s**e

- **Letters *x* and *q*:** these consonants have two consonant sounds combined: *x = ks, q = kw.*
- **Silent consonants:** two consonants with one silent letter (**kn**ight, **wr**ite, **rh**yme, com**b**, autu**mn**, ni**gh**t).
- **Consonant blends:** two or more consonants blended where a little of each consonant is heard.
  - *l* blends: **bl, cl, fl, gl, pl, sl**
  - *s* blends: **sm, sn, sk, sc, st, sp, sw, str, spr, spl, scr**
  - *r* blends: **br, cr, dr, fr, gr, pr, tr**
- **Consonant digraphs:** two consonants come together to make one new sound (**sh**ip, **ch**in, ba**ck**, **ph**oto, **th**in, **wh**ip, ba**tch**, lau**gh**).

Letter Sounds

These are introduced in kindergarten and carried on through first grade. Each letter has a distinct sound. When saying the letter's sound, it is important not to add a vowel: *B* is "b"—not "ba" or "buh."

A sound can be spelled with a single letter or a combination of letters. Some sounds can be represented by several letter combinations. Spelling patterns can be recognized by:

Name of the letter: *A*
Sound of the letter: "a" (**a**pple)
Spelling of the sound: **a**

Name of the letter: *A*
Sound of the letter: "a" (**a**pe)
Spelling of the sound: **a__e, ai, a, ay**

Students need to know that there can be several spellings of a single sound. For the previous example, the "long *a*" has four possible spellings. A student can be asked, "Which spelling of 'long *a*' is found in this word?" and they can respond. Give the following word as an example: *pail*

Teacher: Which spelling of "long *a*" is found in the word "pail"?
Student: The **ai** spelling.

Sounds are blended together to create words. Beginning readers start with short-vowel words.

C = consonant, **V** = vowel
CVC word = *cat*
CVCC word = *back*

Sight Words

Additionally, some common words are introduced and drilled as sight words or high-frequency words. These words don't need to be sounded out.

Common Sight Words

all	and	are	an	at	be
but	came	for	from	go	got
had	have	he	her	him	his
if	in	is	it	me	of
on	one	out	said	saw	she
so	that	the	their	there	then
there	they	this	to	up	was
we	went	were	with	you	your

Blending

Readers blend sounds together to form words. This process starts sound by sound and then builds into sound patterns or chunks as students know increasingly more patterns.

Letter by letter: **c-a-t** = **cat**
To the vowel: **c-a** = **ca** . . . **t** = **cat**
Entire word: **c-a-t** = **cat**

Word Families

Words ending in the same vowel or consonant spelling can be grouped into "families," which can facilitate blending and word recognition. Having students build word families can be a great activity. Word families also introduce rhyming patterns.

-at: cat, mat, hat, rat, sat, and so on
-ock: block, sock, rock, and so on
-ake: bake, cake, rake, snake, and so on

4

Group Strategies
for Book Discussions

Allowing students "talk time" after reading a picture book, fiction or nonfiction, or a chapter from a novel is important. It's easy for a teacher to dominate the discussion and review information from the book for the students, but real learning occurs when students can discuss what they've read and learned with one another and then draw their own conclusions. There are several ways to facilitate student discussions following the reading of a book or chapter. The first focuses on a more complex and structured strategy with literature circles, followed by a variety of techniques that are easier to manage.

Find grouping strategies that best fit your style, classroom environment, and your particular group of students in their ability to interact and engage in rich discussion. Varying these approaches will make your classroom conversations more diverse and interesting for you and your students.

Common Core Standards:
Reading, Listening, and Speaking

These reading strategies for discussing books with one another offer students many experiences in developing the College and Career Readiness Anchor Standards for the English Language Arts (ELA) Common Core Standards, especially related to reading, speaking, and listening. The K–12 broad standards that generally define the skills and understandings that all students must demonstrate for *reading* include:

1. Read closely to determine what the text says explicitly and to make logical inferences from it; cite specific textual evidence when writing or speaking to support conclusions drawn from the text.
2. Determine central ideas or themes of a text and analyze their development; summarize the key supporting details and ideas.
3. Analyze how and why individuals, events, and ideas develop and interact over the course of a text.
4. Interpret words and phrases as they are used in a text, including determining technical, connotative, and figurative meanings, and analyze how specific word choices shape meaning or tone.
5. Analyze the structure of texts, including how specific sentences, paragraphs, and larger portions of the text (e.g., a section, chapter, scene, or stanza) relate to each other and the whole.
6. Assess how point of view or purpose shapes the content and style of a text. Integrate and evaluate content presented in diverse media and formats, including visually and quantitatively, as well as in words.
7. Delineate and evaluate the argument and specific claims in a text, including the validity of the reasoning as well as the relevance and sufficiency of the evidence.
8. Analyze how two or more texts address similar themes or topics to build knowledge or to compare the approaches the authors take.
9. Read and comprehend complex literary and informational texts independently and proficiently.

The K–12 broad standards that generally define the skills and understandings that all students must demonstrate for *speaking* and *listening* include:

1. Prepare for and participate effectively in a range of conversations and collaborations with diverse partners, building on others' ideas and expressing their own clearly and persuasively.
2. Integrate and evaluate information presented in diverse media and formats, including visually, quantitatively, and orally.
3. Evaluate a speaker's point of view, reasoning, and use of evidence and rhetoric.
4. Present information, findings, and supporting evidence such that listeners can follow the line of reasoning and the organization, development, and style are appropriate to task, purpose, and audience.

5. Make strategic use of digital media and visual displays of data to express information and enhance understanding of presentations.
6. Adapt speech to a variety of contexts and communicative tasks, demonstrating command of formal English when indicated or appropriate.

Since these are only general lists for reading, speaking, and listening, visit the website at http://www.corestandards.org for more grade-level specificity for the Common Core State Standards for English Language Arts & Literacy.

Literature Circles

A literature circle is a student's equivalent to an adult book club but with more structure, creativity, and rigor. The aim is to encourage thoughtful discussion and a love of reading.

Literature circles were first implemented in 1982 by Karen Smith, an elementary school teacher in Phoenix, Arizona. One year, some of her fifth-grade students expressed an interest in reading some books Karen had been given and placed aside. She let the students use the books, and they quickly organized themselves into groups and started to discuss the novels. They were highly engaged with the books and held rich discussions without any help or instruction from her. Since then, literature circles have evolved into what they are today.

Well-run literature circles highlight student choice and occur over an extended period of time. They include several structured and unstructured opportunities for student response and interpretation and incorporate assessment and evaluation, including self-assessment and projects.

Literature circles offer students a chance to be readers and writers and to apply the literacy skills that they are learning (Schlick Noe, 2012). Literature circles are small discussion groups of students who read the same work of literature. Each member takes on specific responsibilities during discussion sessions. The circle groups meet regularly, and the discussion roles change at each meeting. When the circle finishes a book, the members showcase their literary work for the rest of the class (Daniels, 1994). Book-discussion groups typically follow a format that includes responsibility roles for a chosen book.

Literature Circle Grouping

Obviously, it's natural to want to group students by ability level, and it is certainly an option. Even students who are struggling readers can learn a lot from a book when given a chance to share a book of interest within a group, which can be a powerful tool for learning vocabulary, discussing important themes in the book, and also for increasing the comprehension process. This is especially true for students of lower reading ability levels who might not be comfortable sharing ideas if they are grouped with students of greater ability. You know your students and you know which students will benefit from being grouped with higher-level readers and thinkers.

Before organizing your groups, you may want to meet with each student to discuss the student's reading interest and reading ability. This will give you a gauge for how a student might fit within a small group of others whose reading abilities differ from the student's own.

After the meetings, the teacher can organize groups of four to five students as literature circles. It's also helpful for students if they can be grouped with at least one classmate whose reading ability is similar to their own. However, consider keeping the range of reading ability within each circle to about two grade levels so no single student is way above or below the rest.

Book Choice

While some teachers will preorganize groups in a heterogeneous way and then choose a book that he or she thinks all students will enjoy, others believe that if the goal of literature circles is to build understanding and response in collaboration with others, then student choice ought not be overlooked.

Even if the teacher is the one who decides on the groups, students should still have a part in choosing what books they read. This is where you may decide to group students into literature circles by ability so each circle can choose a book appropriate for their reading level.

Literature Circle Roles

Roles in literature circles give a thinking task to each group member. The tasks are divided among the students in each group. As the groups come together for each book meeting, students switch roles so that by the end of the literature circles "unit," each student will have the opportunity to participate in each role—sometimes several times. The idea is to eventually do away with the roles, though many teachers opt to continue using the roles to keep students on-task and to use time efficiently.

Readers who are deeply engaged with a book and eager to talk about it with others may not need the structure of roles. The roles can sometimes be restrictive and can cause disinterest for some students to take part in literature circles. You know your students best, so consider the roles to be a temporary scaffold to support students as they learn to talk about books in small groups (Daniels, 1994).

It's important that the teacher models the various roles within a small group in front of the whole class so students "see" how those roles allow the group to function. It can take anywhere from one to two weeks for students to learn how to systematically handle the group discussion.

When the students are comfortable with the format, the formal use of roles can be discontinued, and, in fact, the roles will organically take on a meaning of their own. While the roles set up a certain systematic format, teachers want to promote natural conversations as opposed to keeping them boxed in. But the roles help set the stage for these rich discussions until individual book groups feel more comfortable with one another, the book, and the roles.

Predefined roles that students take turns filling during each book group meeting include a variety of options, though the descriptions are similar. Some roles that students can take on in literature circles include:

1. **Artist:** The student in this role uses some form of artwork to represent a significant scene or idea from the reading (chapter or picture book).

2. **Connector:** The student in this role finds connections between the reading material and something outside the text, such as a personal experience, a topic studied in another class, or a different work of literature, a book, or a chapter that are unusual, interesting, or difficult to understand. The connections might relate to school, friends or family, home, or the community, or they might relate to movies, celebrities, the media, and so on. Students should also feel free to connect incidents or characters with other books that they have read. Of all the roles, this role is often the most personal in its focus.

3. **Discussion director:** The student in this role writes questions that will lead to discussion topics by the group.

4. **Discussion facilitator:** The student in this role develops a list of questions that the group might discuss about the book or the section of the novel to be discussed for that meeting. Questions should be open-ended and should not be yes-or-no questions. A student with this role asks these questions to the group to prompt discussion overall and keep the group talking and on-task. Questions that a student might ask could be: "What was going through your mind when you read this passage?" or "How did the main character change as a result of this incident?" The role leader may even read a quote or passage from the book before asking these questions.

5. **Figurative language finder:** The student in this role includes identification of various types of figurative language, such as simile, metaphor, personification, hyperbole, and idiom.

6. **Illustrator:** The student in this role draws, sketches, or paints a picture, portrait, or scene relating to the appropriate section of the book or novel. Collages from magazines, images from the Internet, and other media can also be used. The student with this role then shares the artwork with the group, explaining the passage(s) that relate to the art. Typically, students who do not like to write do very well with this role. The pictures usually generate interesting group conversations.

7. **Investigator:** Students in this role take on investigative work where background information needs to be found on any topic relating to the book. Historical, geographical, cultural, musical, or other information that would help readers connect to the novel is often researched and shared with the group. The research is informal in nature, providing small bits of information so others can better understand the novel.

8. **Literary luminary:** The student in this role points out interesting or important passages within the reading.

33

9. **Literature leader:** The student in this role writes five or more comprehension questions about the book or chapters. The group will be asked these questions, and responses should match those that the literature leader has already identified.

10. **Locator:** This role involves locating a few significant passages of text that are thought-provoking, funny, interesting, disturbing, or powerful. The quotations are copied down with properly cited page numbers. A student with this task can read the passages out loud him- or herself or ask other group members to read. Commentary and discussion will be generated from these passages.

11. **Passage performer:** The student in this role chooses a favorite passage or part of the story or chapter. After reading it aloud to the group members, he or she explains why this was chosen.

12. **Super storyteller:** The student in this role uses sticky notes to take notes on story events. The student also identifies the main character and setting of the story or that chapter. Then the student summarizes the story or chapter, including the main events, prior to sharing with the group.

13. **Wacky word finder:** The student in this role looks for two to three wacky words within the book or chapter. These words could be unknown words, words that are interesting, unusual, silly, or obscure. The student writes these words along with the page number(s), uses a dictionary to define them, and then writes a sentence using the word correctly.

14. **Word wizard:** The student in this role searches for words in a section or chapter of the book that others might not know. After challenging words are found, the student tells where they are used in the story and finds the definitions.

15. **Summarizer:** The student in this role prepares a brief summary of the reading (chapter or book) that was assigned for that day's meeting. The summary should include the main ideas or events to remember, major characters, symbols, or other significant highlights of the passage. Good summarizers are important to literature circles, as they can help their peers see the overall picture.

16. **Travel tracer:** Students in this role record where the major shifts in action or location take place in the novel for the reading section. Keeping track of shifts in place, time, and characters helps students follow important movement in the novel. Artistic students also gravitate to this role, as artwork can be incorporated into this job. The student's role is to describe each setting in detail, using words or maps that illustrate the action.

17. **Vocabulary enricher:** Students in this role record important words for that day's reading. The student usually chooses words that are unusual, unknown, or stand out in some way. The page numbers and definitions are also recorded.

The Teacher's Role

As mentioned earlier, the teacher needs to specifically teach the students how to carry out each role that he or she assigns. This usually includes four to five of the different roles introduced earlier.

When students are able to meet in their book groups and carry out their roles or routine within a literature circle on their own, the teacher can either drop out of the group or take a less hands-on approach. This is an opportunity for students to discuss literature with their peers and should allow students to explore literature together. The discussions should be facilitated by the students and not necessarily be controlled by an adult, although a teacher knows his or her students best and can gauge how much of a role to play. This is especially true if the teacher wants to use observations for assessment purposes even if this means just sitting nearby and taking anecdotal notes. It can be easily accomplished when the groups are at work together because the teacher can roam among the literature circles. This also helps keep the other students occupied while the teacher meets with one group.

Implementation Considerations

- Students begin literature circles by participating in and observing mini-lessons on how to carry out a discussion group.
- It's helpful to start students out with role sheets to assist them in taking notes on their reading, for preparing for the discussion, and for redirecting the discussion when students get off-track.
- Yellow sticky notes can be given out to assist students in recording their thoughts about the text elements.
- Clipboards may assist students in using their role sheets when groups use floor space to conduct their discussions.

Assessment and Evaluation

Most teachers assess and evaluate what students do in literature circles through a variety of means:

- **Self-assessment:** Students should be involved in assessing their own level of engagement with their book and participation with their group. Formal checklists can be used for students to keep track of their progress. These can get turned in and may even require another student's signature for confirmation and comments.

- **Peer assessment:** Students can assess their fellow group members over the course of their book meetings. As with self-assessment, checklists or other rubrics can provide scoring structure.

- **Observations:** Ongoing teacher observations and active participation in the group discussions are critical in assessing student progress both individually and in whole group. Observations and anecdotal note-taking by the teacher can meet necessary assessment criteria.

- **Conferences:** Face-to-face conferencing between the student and the teacher can help in tracking and monitoring student growth (Daniels, 1994, p. 160).

- **Portfolios:** Collections of student products, gathered and assembled in a meaningful fashion, provide the opportunity for reflection, discussion, response to the book, and display of a student's best work. Portfolios can take on many forms, ranging from writing, art, video/audiotapes, learning logs, student journals, personal responses, and so on (Daniels, 1994).

- **Tangible projects:** These projects can take the form of creative and artistic student products, from book jackets to visual media or printed forms. More conversations about the books usually arise out of sharing these projects with the group and the whole class.

- **Student artifacts:** Reading response logs, role sheets, and other process material that students have compiled over the course of the literature circle meetings also can be evaluated, providing "a rich source of insight" (Daniels, 1994, p. 164) for the teacher to assess growth and progress of students.

Review of Literature Circle Features

- The teacher offers choices, or students choose the reading materials.
- Based on book choice, small temporary groups are formed.
- Different groups read different books.
- Groups meet on a regular basis.
- Students use written or drawn notes to guide both their reading and discussion.

- Discussion topics come from the students, typically after completing work for their assigned roles.
- Group meetings are open, natural conversations but should stay focused on the book or chapter.
- The teacher serves as a facilitator, an observer, and a listener. The teacher is not usually an instructor but may step in from time to time to keep students focused and on task, especially in the early stages of learning how to keep the discussion going.
- Typically, students are given roles or jobs to complete for each group meeting.
- The teacher should model how students should carry out each role or job.
- Evaluation is by teacher observation and student self-evaluation and should also include tangible projects.
- New groups form around new reading choices.
- Discussion prompts can be given by the teacher to encourage a direction for the students' responses, such as "How does the setting affect the characters?" "What are alternative solutions to the character's conflicts in the text?" "What connections can you make with regard to the character's situation?" (Daniels, 1994).
- Groups meet regularly for consistent time periods. Students rotate through the roles.
- Students run their own discussions and remain on task.
- Each student takes a turn within his or her group.
- Everyone is a valued member.
- Students act responsibly, do their reading selections, ask good questions, construct meaning, and are respectful while group members are sharing.

While literature circles tend to take a lot of time and planning, their relevance in reading instruction is worth the effort. However, the following ideas are just as meaningful and offer the students a variety of ways to share and discuss exciting books.

Pair Share

After a whole-class read-aloud; assigned, independent reading at home; or silent reading in class, you might want students to think about a question or prompt related to the book or chapter. Have pairs meet to share their ideas. This approach provides students with immediate feedback about how to approach the question, idea, or problem presented to them with  their "shoulder-to-shoulder," "desk-to-desk," or "knees-to-knees" partner (good for low classroom volume as students can talk quietly due to close proximity). This is really powerful for English language learners who may need to dialogue with a partner in their native language or get an idea in English from their neighbor.

Peer Tutors

Peer tutoring is less threatening and intimidating especially when it is presented with new ideas. Because the peer tutor is seen as at the level of the student being tutored, ideas presented by the peer tutor may be accepted more readily than advice from a teacher. For this grouping strategy, students can work together to accomplish a task for any of the prompts, questions, ideas, or problems from the book or chapter presented to them.

Bean Bag Toss

For this strategy, when discussing prompts, questions, ideas, or problems from the book or chapter, whether it's new information, review, or extended information, students or students and the teacher can pass the bean bag to one another to offer turns for discussion. Responses can be transcribed to a chart, poster, or the like to use as reference later.

Magic Circle

When introducing prompts, questions, ideas, or problems from the book or chapter; reviewing them; and extending thoughts through discussion, students can pass the "magic stick" to one another to offer turns for discussion. Students can sit in a circle facing one another.

When a student wishes to speak he can raise his hand, and once the stick has been passed to him, he speaks about the topic. Only the student with the stick in hand can speak, while the class listens. It is important that this be monitored, and all students have an opportunity to speak if possible. Responses can be transcribed to a chart, poster, or the like to use as reference later.

Draw a Name

The name of each student is written on a craft stick and then drawn from a can or is added to individual cards from a deck of cards that can be shuffled and drawn. The teacher or an appointed student monitor draws a craft stick from the can or a card from the deck to choose a student to speak or answer a question. This student responds to prompts, questions, ideas, or problems from the book or chapter.  Names can be drawn until everyone has answered, or the sticks or cards can be replaced so students don't "check out" after they have been called on. This is also a way to create random, equitable small groups for discussion or project work. If a student is not prepared to respond, that student can call on a friend to respond in his or her place. Responses can be transcribed to a chart, poster, or the like to use as reference later.

Two, Four, Share Some More

The teacher poses prompts, questions, ideas, or problems from the book or chapter. Two students discuss this with one another for two to five minutes (as with Pair Share). After time is up, those two students join another group of two and share what they discussed in their groups of two. Finally, the group of four shares with the whole class. This can continue through a  series of prompts, questions, ideas, or problems from the book or chapter. Responses can be transcribed to a chart, poster, or the like to use as reference later.

Speed Talk or Topic Rotation

Students are placed in groups of four to six. A prompt, question, idea, or problem from the book or chapter is placed at each table. This can also be done with chart paper, and each group can rotate, adding their comments to the chart paper. The small group discusses the topic for two to five minutes. Afterward, each group rotates to the next table or chart where they have a new prompt, question,  idea, or problem to discuss. You may even want students to keep track of their responses for reference later when a discussion about each ensues after all the tables or charts have been visited. Roles can even be designated to facilitate the rotation. A recorder can record responses, a time-keeper can track time, and a facilitator can keep students on task.

Four Corners

Using chart paper, the teacher poses or shares four prompts, questions, ideas, or problems related to the book or chapter. These are posted, one in each of the four corners of the classroom along with colored chart-marking pens. Each student chooses a corner of the classroom where the topic of his or her inter-  est is displayed. This is a quick way to get together those students who have similar interests related to the chapter or book so they can have a discussion about it. Students can sit in a circle on the floor or at desks to dialogue. Responses need to be transcribed onto the available chart paper to be shared with the whole class after a reasonable amount of time (approximately 15 to 30 minutes depending on the prompt, question, idea, or problem, or if you want students to visit more than one corner). A recorder can record responses, a time-keeper can track time, a facilitator can keep students on task, and a responder can share group responses with the whole class.

References

Common Core State Standards for English Language Arts & Literacy in History/Social Studies, Science, and Technical Subjects. (December 2012). http://www.corestandards.org/assets /CCSSI_ELA%20Standards.pdf

Daniels, H. (1994). *Literature Circles: Voice and Choice in the Student-Centered Classroom.* Markham: Pembroke Publishers Ltd.

Schlick Noe, K. L. & Johnson, N. J. (1999). *Getting Started with Literature Circles.* Norwood, MA: Christopher-Gordon Publishers, Inc.

5

Responses to Literature

After reading a book aloud or after having your students read a book on their own, a good way to have them respond is by having them complete a book report or project to demonstrate their understanding of the story and its main components. Included here are ideas for responding to literature in a variety of creative ways, as well as two traditional book-report formats ranging from a few sentences for the early grades, to deeper inference and higher-level prompts for the higher grades.

Encouraging a combination of fiction and nonfiction texts allows for creativity and student choice while also meeting the Common Core Standards for English Language Arts & Literacy (http://www.corestandards.org). As noted earlier in the book, while students advance through the grades and master grade-level standards in reading, writing, speaking, listening, and language, they exhibit the following characteristics as literate individuals:

1. They demonstrate independence.
2. They build strong content knowledge.
3. They respond to the varying demands of audience, task, purpose, and discipline.
4. They comprehend as well as critique.
5. They value evidence.
6. They use technology and digital media strategically and capably.
7. They come to understand other perspectives and cultures.

All of this can be accomplished when consistently incorporating book reports and responses to literature as part of your curriculum.

Ideas for Responding to Literature: Grades K–12

- **Comic strip:** Draw a comic strip of your favorite scene or of the main idea of the story. Fold an 11-by-14-inch piece of white construction paper in half. Cut it down the middle. One sheet is enough for two students. Fold each sheet like an accordion, and develop a comic strip based on the story.

- **Diorama:** Use a shoebox or similar item to make a model of a scene or the main idea of the story.

- **Résumé:** Using what you know about one of the main characters from a story, create a résumé based on his or her personal characteristics.

- **Mini book:** Create a mini book about the story either by sequencing the plot or describing each of the characters.

- **Friendly letter:** Write a letter to one of the characters you most closely *relate* to from the story.

- **Movie poster:** Make a poster about your book as if you were introducing it to the world like a movie.

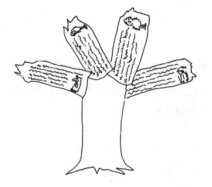

- **Character tree:** Make a character tree illustrating the characters on the tree branches with a short description of each character's role in the book.

- **Postcard:** Create a postcard you would like to send to one of the characters from the story. In it, recall the events he or she was involved in during the story and why you would like to meet the character in real life.

- **Dear Abby:** Have students write "Dear Abby" letters about a problem they are having as one of the characters in the story. They can **exchange** these with classmates who will respond to their problem.

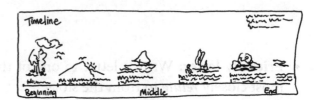

- **Timeline:** Create a timeline sequencing the events in the story. Above each entry on the timeline, illustrate the event.

- **Crystal ball:** Students predict the future for the main characters in the story, for example, Little Red Riding Hood. What happens to her in the future?

- **Wanted:** Write an ad for one of the characters as if he or she were looking for a friend. Draw upon the character's traits to describe his or her persona.

- **Obituary:** Write an obituary for one of the characters. Include lifetime accomplishments, using scenes from the book to describe the character.

- **Bookmark:** Make a bookmark addressing key elements of a book report such as plot, summary, setting, conflict, and resolution on one side. Illustrate a scene from the book on the other.

- **Take out the trash:** Students will draw and fill in a trash can with illustrations and words to describe what would be found in one of the character's trash.

Elements for Traditional Book Reports

You can use the following templates to help your students start writing book reports.

Lower-Grade Traditional Book Report

Title _____

Author _____

Illustrator _____

1. Write three sentences telling what the book is about.

2. What was your favorite part (three or more sentences)?

3. Draw a picture about the story (on the back). Include characters and setting.

Upper-Grade Traditional Book Report

Title _____

Author _____

Illustrator _____

Copyright date _____

Number of pages _____

Genre   ☐ Fiction   ☐ Nonfiction   ☐ Fable   ☐ Fantasy

           ☐ Fairy Tale   ☐ Expository   ☐ Bibliography   ☐ Autobiography

1. Describe the main characters.

2. Describe the setting.

3. Explain the conflict or problem.

4. Explain the resolution.

5. Describe your personal connection or opinion.

6. Describe the most interesting part.

7. Draw a picture of your favorite part of the story.

Award-Winning Books
for Children and Young Adults

This chapter introduces some of the most popular and recognizable awards for writing and illustrations in children's and young adult literature. The significance of each award is described as well. The lists of books go back only as far as the year 2000, so each award description includes a website link for locating book award winners prior to 2000. The books that received the award from 2000 to the present are noted after the award description.

Caldecott Medal

The Caldecott Medal was named in honor of 19th-century English illustrator Randolph Caldecott. This award is given annually by the Association for Library Service to Children, a division of the American Library Association, to the artist of the most distinguished American picture book for children.

When the Caldecott Medal was first awarded, committees often also cited other books as worthy of merit. These books were referred to as Caldecott "runners-up" until 1971 when they were named Caldecott Honor Books. Now all former runners-up are also called Caldecott Honor Books. In the following lists, the year's winner is listed first, followed by the honor books. Visit http://www.ala.org/alsc/awardsgrants/bookmedia/caldecottmedal/caldecotthonors/caldecottmedal for awards prior to 2000.

2013

Award Winner

Klassen, Jon. *This Is Not My Hat.*   ISBN-13: 9780763655990

A tiny fish knows it's wrong to steal a hat even though it fits him just right. Unfortunately, the big fish wants his hat back.   Lexile: AD340L   (Grades Pre-K–3)   F

Honor Books

Brown, Peter, text by Aaron Reynolds. *Creepy Carrots.*   ISBN-13: 9781442402973

Jasper the rabbit loves carrots, but when he sees that they are everywhere he thinks they're coming for him.   Lexile: AD410L   (Grades Pre-K–3)   F

Klassen, Jon, text by Mac Barnett. *Extra Yarn.*   ISBN-13: 9780061953385

A selfish archduke threatens to stop a little girl's transformation of a town in need of color and steals her box of magical yarn.   Lexile: AD620L   (Grades Pre-K–3)   F

Seeger, Laura Vaccaro. *Green.*   ISBN-13: 9781596433977

Children's senses will be engaged with the multiple meanings of "green."

Lexile: N/A   (Grades Pre-K–1)   F

Small, David, text by Toni Buzzeo. *One Cool Friend.*   ISBN-13: 9780803734135

On a trip to the aquarium, Elliot discovers his dream for a pet penguin. His father says "yes" when Elliot asks if he may have one, though his father was probably thinking of a toy penguin, not a real one.   Lexile: 620L   (Grades K–3)   F

Zagarenski, Pamela, text by Mary Logue. *Sleep Like a Tiger.*   ISBN-13: 9780547641034

The dialogue between a child who is not sleepy and her understanding parents, when a little girl decides she is ready to sleep, warm and strong, just like a tiger.

Lexile: N/A   (Grades Pre-K–3)   F

2012

Award Winner

Raschka, Chris. *A Ball for Daisy.*   ISBN-13: 9780375858611

Children will understand Daisy's distress when her favorite ball is destroyed by a bigger dog. In this nearly wordless picture book, Raschka explores through pictures the joy and sadness that having a special toy can bring.   Lexile: NPL   (Grades Pre-K–3)   F

Honor Books

McDonnell, Patrick. *Me . . . Jane.*   ISBN-13: 9780316045469

This is the story of the young Jane Goodall and her toy chimpanzee named Jubilee. The young Jane dreams of "a life living with and helping all animals," until one day she finds that her dream has come true.   Lexile: 740L   (Grades Pre-K–2)   F

Rocco, John. *Blackout.* ISBN-13: 9781423121909

One hot, summer night, all the power goes out. The TV shuts off and a boy shouts out for his mom. His sister can no longer use the phone, Mom can't work on her computer, and Dad can't finish cooking dinner. When they go up to the roof to escape the heat, they find the lights in stars along with many neighbors. The boy and his family enjoy being not so busy for once. Even when the electricity is restored, not everyone likes it. The boy switches off the lights, and out come the board games. Lexile: NA (Grades Pre-K–2) F

Smith, Lane. *Grandpa Green.* ISBN-13: 9781596436077

Grandpa Green was a little boy too, with a history all his own. That history remains alive in the garden that his great-grandson now tends, and a place where memories and family bonds grow strong. Lexile: 360 (Grades Pre-K–2) F

2011
Award Winner

Stead, Erin E., text by Peter C. Stead. *A Sick Day for Amos McGee.* ISBN-13: 9781596434028

In this story of friendship, a zookeeper gets sick and receives a visit from several of his animal friends. Lexile: AD760L (Grades Pre-K–2) F

Honor Books

Collier, Bryan, text by Laban Carrick Hill. *Dave the Potter: Artist, Poet, Slave.*

ISBN-13: 9780316107310

This is a story about the triumph of humanity in the face of oppression.

Lexile: AD1100L (Grades K–4) NF

Stein, David Ezra. *Interrupting Chicken.* ISBN-13: 9780763641689

Little Chicken and her papa do their best to get through a bedtime story without her interrupting. Lexile: AD300L (Grades K–3) F

2010
Award Winner

Pinkney, Jerry. *The Lion & the Mouse.* ISBN-13: 9780316013567

In this wordless version of the classic Aesop's fable, an intense lion lets a mouse live that he had planned to eat, and the mouse later comes to the lion's rescue, freeing him from a poacher's trap. Lexile: 100 (Grades Pre-K–2) F

Honor Books

Frazee, Marla, text by Liz Garton Scanlon. *All the World.* ISBN-13: 9781416985808

This book talks about things in our world, from the tiniest shell on the beach, to family connections, to the sunset in the sky. Lexile: AD380L (Grades Pre-K–2) F

Zagarenski, Pamela, text by Joyce Sidman. *Red Sings from Treetops: A Year in Colors.*

ISBN-13: 9780547014944

The colors of the seasons are brought to life through the senses of sight, sound, smell, and taste. Lexile: AD570L (Grades Pre-K–3) NF

2009

Award Winner

Krommes, Beth, text by Susan Marie Swanson. *The House in the Night.*

ISBN-13: 9780618862443

This book shows how light makes a house a home. Lexile: 60L (Grades Pre-K–2) F

Honor Books

Frazee, Marla. *A Couple of Boys Have the Best Week Ever.* ISBN-13: 9780152060206

Things didn't go exactly as planned when James and Eamon go to Nature Camp and end up staying at Eamon's grandparents' house. They spend their free time inside, eating waffles and playing video games. Lexile: AD680L (Grades Pre-K–3) F

Shulevitz, Uri. *How I Learned Geography.* ISBN-13: 9780374334994

A boy and his family are living in poverty in a new country. When the boy's father brings home a map and hangs it on the wall, the room fills with color. The boy studies it and is transported to places without leaving the room. Lexile: AD660L (Grades Pre-K–3) F

Sweet, Melissa, text by Jen Bryant. *A River of Words: The Story of William Carlos Williams.* ISBN-13: 9780802853028

Willie needed to earn a living, so when he grew up he went off to medical school and became a doctor even though he loved to write. Lexile: AD820L (Grades K–6) NF

2008

Award Winner

Selznick, Brian. *The Invention of Hugo Cabret.* ISBN-13: 9780439813785

Hugo's undercover life of living in a busy Paris train station is put in jeopardy when he meets a girl and an old man who runs a toy booth in the station.

Lexile: 820L (Grades 2–6) F

Honor Books

Nelson, Kadir, text by Ellen Levine. *Henry's Freedom Box: A True Story from the Underground Railroad.* ISBN-13: 9780439777339

Henry Brown, a slave, doesn't know how old he is. He dreams about freedom but is torn from his family and put to work in a warehouse. Eventually, he mails himself to the North and finally has a birthday—his first day of freedom. Lexile: AD380L (Grades K–5) F

Seeger, Laura Vaccaro. *First the Egg.*   ISBN-13: 9781596432727

This is a book about transformations like an egg to chicken, seed to flower, and caterpillar to butterfly.   Lexile: NPL   (Grades Pre-K–3)   NF

Sís, Peter. *The Wall: Growing Up Behind the Iron Curtain.*   ISBN-13: 9780374347017

This story shows what life was like for a child who loved to draw, wore the red scarf of a Young Pioneer, proudly stood guard at the statue of Stalin, and believed whatever he was told to believe.   Lexile: AD760L   (Grades 3–9)   NF

Willems, Mo. *Knuffle Bunny Too: A Case of Mistaken Identity.*   ISBN-13: 9781423102991

Trixie brought her one-of-a-kind Knuffle Bunny to school to show him off only to find Sonja has the same bunny. Trixie ends up with that other bunny that night after retrieving what she thought was her bunny from the teacher.   Lexile: AD690L   (Grades K–5)   F

2007
Award Winner

Wiesner, David. *Flotsam.*   ISBN-13: 9780618194575

A boy goes to the beach to collect and examine floating items that have been washed ashore. He finds bottles, toys, and varied small objects, but most important he discovers a barnacle-encrusted underwater camera.   Lexile: NPL   (Grades K–5)   F

Honor Books

McLimans, David. *Gone Wild: An Endangered Animal Alphabet.*   ISBN-13: 9780802795632

Wild animals, so rare that they're all endangered, transform each letter into a work of art. The animal characteristics such as scales, horns, and insect wings make the alphabet become animated life.   Lexile: NPL   (Grades Pre-K–3)   NF

Nelson, Kadir, text by Carole Boston Weatherford. *Moses: When Harriet Tubman Led Her People to Freedom.*   ISBN-13: 9780786851751

This is the story of Harriet Tubman, the Moses of her people, who guided enslaved Africans along the Underground Railroad. This book talks of her first trip, how she became free, and what inspired her to escort hundreds of slaves to freedom.

Lexile: AD660L   (Grades K–5)   NF

2006
Award Winner

Raschka, Chris, text by Norton Juster. *The Hello, Goodbye Window.*

ISBN-13: 9780786809141

The kitchen window at her grandparent's house is a window that shows everything important for a little girl while she sees the many surprises that define childhood.

Lexile: 760L   (Grades Pre-K–3)   F

Honor Books

Collier, Bryan, text by Nikki Giovanni. **Rosa.**   ISBN-13: 9780312376024

This is a tribute to Rosa Parks as a celebration of her courageous action and the events that followed.   Lexile: 900L   (Grades K–6)   NF

Muth, Jon J. **Zen Shorts.**   ISBN-13: 9780439339117

Stillwater, a giant panda, moves into the neighborhood and tells astonishing tales.

Lexile: 540L   (Grades Pre-K–3)   F

Prange, Beckie, text by Joyce Sidman. **Song of the Water Boatman & Other Pond Poems.**   ISBN-13: 9780618135479

This collection of poems takes a closer look at ponds and wetlands.

Lexile: NPL   (Grades Pre-K–3)   NF

Priceman, Marjorie. **Hot Air: The (Mostly) True Story of the First Hot-Air Balloon Ride.**

ISBN-13: 9780689826429

The first hot-air balloon is meant to take off but noises are coming from the basket.

Lexile: AD690L   (Grades 1–5)   F

2005

Award Winner

Henkes, Kevin. **Kitten's First Full Moon.**   ISBN-13: 9780060588281

On the night of the full moon, Kitten is hungry, curious, brave, fast, and persistent.

Lexile: 360L   (Grades Pre-K–2)   F

Honor Books

Lehman, Barbara. **The Red Book.**   ISBN-13: 9780618428588

The Red Book crosses oceans and continents taking a girl into a world of possibility, where a friend she's never met is waiting.   Lexile: NPL   (Grades Pre-K–3)   F

Lewis, E. B., text by Jacqueline Woodson. **Coming on Home Soon.**   ISBN-13: 9780399237485

A young girl's mother must go away to Chicago to work during wartime, leaving the girl and her grandma behind. They find strength in each other while waiting for the letter that says her mother will be coming home soon.   Lexile: 550L   (Grades 1–5)   F

Willems, Mo. **Knuffle Bunny: A Cautionary Tale.**   ISBN-13: 9780786818709

When Trixie, Daddy, and Knuffle Bunny take a trip to the Laundromat, they come upon an adventure that takes a turn when Trixie realizes somebunny has been left behind.

Lexile: 120L   (Grades Pre-K–2)   F

2004
Award Winner

Gerstein, Mordecai. *The Man Who Walked Between the Towers.*   ISBN-13: 9780312368784

In 1974, as the World Trade Center was being completed, a young French aerialist, Philippe Petit, threw a tightrope between the towers and spent almost an hour walking, dancing, and performing tricks along the rope.   Lexile: AD480L   (Grades K–5)   NF

Honor Books

Chodos-Irvine, Margaret. *Ella Sarah Gets Dressed.*   ISBN-13: 9780152164133

Ella Sarah has an interesting sense of style. Her family wants her to dress like them, but she and her friends have a sense of style that is just right.   Lexile: 810L   (Grades Pre-K–2)   F

Page, Robin, and Steve Jenkins. *What Do You Do with a Tail Like This?*

ISBN-13: 9780618256280

This book explores the many things animals can do with their ears, eyes, mouths, noses, feet, and tails.   Lexile: 620L   (Grades Pre-K–4)   NF

Willems, Mo. *Don't Let the Pigeon Drive the Bus!*   ISBN-13: 9780786819881

When a bus driver takes a break, a pigeon takes over. The pigeon chats along the drive, and kids will enjoy answering back and deciding his fate.   Lexile: 120   (Grades Pre-K–2)   F

2003
Award Winner

Rohmann, Eric. *My Friend Rabbit.*   ISBN-13: 9780312367527

This is a story about toys, trouble, and friendship. Mouse lets his best friend Rabbit play with his airplane and gets into some trouble. Rabbit has a solution and sets out to solve the problem, but even bigger problems follow.   Lexile: BRL   (Grades Pre-K–3)   F

Honor Books

DiTerlizzi, Tony, text by Mary Howitt. *The Spider and the Fly.*   ISBN-13: 9780689852893

Classic Hollywood horror movies of the 1920s and 1930s spotlight sweet words to hide not-so-sweet intentions.   Lexile: NPL   (Grades 1–5)   F

McCarty, Peter. *Hondo & Fabian.*   ISBN-13: 9780312367473

A dog named Hondo and his friend Fred are going to the beach for a day of excitement. Fabian the cat is left behind at home to play with the baby.

Lexile: AD180L   (Grades Pre-K–3)   F

Pinkney, Jerry. *Noah's Ark.*   ISBN-13: 9781587172014

This classic retelling of the Bible story describes how for 40 days and 40 nights rain poured from the heavens, enveloping the world, and how God warned Noah about the great flood so he could save life on Earth.   Lexile: 350L   (Grades Pre-K–8)   NF

2002

Award Winner

Wiesner, David. **The Three Pigs.**   ISBN-13: 9780618007011

A mixed-up story about the original three little pigs. The three pigs escape the wolf and meet the cat and the fiddle, the cow that jumped over the moon, and a dragon.

Lexile: NPL   (Grades Pre-K–3)   F

Honor Books

Collier, Bryan, text by Doreen Rappaport. **Martin's Big Words: The Life of Dr. Martin Luther King, Jr.**   ISBN-13: 9781423106357

This biography offers an introduction to one of the world's most influential leaders, Dr. Martin Luther King, Jr.   Lexile: 0410L   (Grades K–6)   NF

Selznick, Brian, text by Barbara Kerley. **The Dinosaurs of Waterhouse Hawkins.**

ISBN-13: 9780439114943

A Victorian artist named Waterhouse Hawkins brought ancient animals to life for all to see by building the first life-sized models of dinosaurs, and he amazed people with his awe-inspiring creations.   Lexile: AD550L   (Grades Pre-K–3)   NF

Simont, Marc. **The Stray Dog.**   ISBN-13: 9780060289331

The story of a family who meets a stray dog while on a picnic. The family says good-bye to the dog and goes home. But a week later, they return for the dog, only to find that the dog-catcher is looking for him, too.   Lexile: 60L   (Grades Pre-K–3)   F

2001

Award Winner

Small, David, text by Judith St. George. **So You Want to Be President?**

ISBN-13: 9780399243172

This book shares a variety of facts about the qualifications and characteristics of U.S. presidents, from George Washington to Barack Obama.   Lexile: 0730L   (Grades Pre-K–8)   NF

Honor Books

Hull, Jim, text by Ernest Lawrence Thayer. **Casey at the Bat.**   ISBN-13: 9780486485102

This story is written as a narrative poem about a celebrated baseball player who strikes out at a critical moment of a game.   Lexile: AD810L   (Grades Pre-K–4)   F

Falconer, Ian. **Olivia.**   ISBN-13: 9780689829536

Olivia is a little pig with a ton of energy. She sings loudly, draws on walls, and engages in many other activities that never seem to tire her out. When it is time for bed, she asks for books to be read when her mother is tired and ready to end the day.

Lexile: AD270L   (Grades Pre-K–1)   F

Lewin, Betsy, text by Doreen Cronin. *Click, Clack, Moo: Cows That Type.*

ISBN-13: 9780689832130

Farmer Brown is surprised when one morning a sound comes in through the fields, "Click, clack, moo." It seems that his cows have begun to type on the old typewriter, demanding heat in the barn.   Lexile: AD160L   (Grades Pre-K–1)   F

2000
Award Winner

Taback, Simms. *Joseph Had a Little Overcoat.*   ISBN-13: 9780670878550

Joseph had an overcoat, but it was full of holes. So when his coat got too old, he made it into a jacket. This story goes on in this fashion and will give readers a chance to guess what he will make next.   Lexile: BRL   (Grades Pre-K–3)   F

Honor Books

Bang, Molly. *When Sophie Gets Angry—Really, Really Angry.*   ISBN-13: 9780439598453

Children will see what Sophie does when she gets angry, offering a platform to talk about anger with children.   Lexile: AD475L   (Grades Pre-K–3)   F

Hyman, Trina Schart, text by John Updike. *A Child's Calendar.*   ISBN-13: 9780823414451

In this collection of poems for all 12 months of the year, each poem celebrates the qualities that make a time of the year unique.   Lexile: NPL   (Grades 1–8)   NF

Pinkney, Jerry, text by Hans Christian Andersen. *The Ugly Duckling.*

ISBN-13: 9780688159320

An awkward little bird holds his head high as he suffers from hecklers, hunters, and the seasons but survives with the outcome of blooming into a graceful swan.

Lexile: AD650L   (Grades Pre-K–3)   F

Wiesner, David. *Sector 7.*   ISBN-13: 9780395746561

Beginning with a school trip to the Empire State Building, a boy makes friends with a little cloud who takes him to the Cloud Dispatch Center for Sector 7, the section that includes New York City. The clouds are bored with their everyday shapes, so the boy starts to sketch some new ones.   Lexile: NPL   (Grades Pre-K–3)   F

Newbery Medal

The Newbery Medal is awarded annually by the American Library Association, acknowledging the most distinguished American children's book published the previous year. The purpose of the Newbery Medal is to encourage original creative work in the field of books for children and to emphasize to the public that contributions to literature for children deserve similar recognition to poetry, plays, and novels. This award allows librarians who work to serve children's reading interests an opportunity to encourage good writing in this field.

When the first Newbery Medal was awarded, committees also cited other books worthy of merit as Newbery "runners-up." In 1971 the runners-up were named Newbery Honor books, including all former runners-up. In the following list, the winner is presented first, followed by the honor titles. Visit http://www.ala.org/alsc/awardsgrants/bookmedia/newberymedal/newberyhonors/newberymedal for awards prior to 2000.

2013

Award Winner

Applegate, Katherine. *The One and Only Ivan.*   ISBN-13: 9780062322876

Inspired by the true story of a captive silverback gorilla known as Ivan, who comes to life through the gorilla's narrative voice. Having spent 27 years behind glass walls in a shopping mall, Ivan is used to humans watching him. Besides thinking of life in a jungle, Ivan watches television, spends times with his friends Stella and Bob, and he paints. But when he meets Ruby, a baby elephant taken from the wild, he is forced to see their home, and his art, through new eyes.   Lexile: 570   (Grades 3–6)   F

Honor Books

Schlitz, Laura Amy. *Splendors & Glooms.*   ISBN-13: 9780763669263

Lizzie Rose, Parsefall, and Clara get caught up with Gaspare Grisini, a master puppeteer and powerful witch, in this dark tale set in Dickensian England, where adventure and suspense are interwoven into good versus evil.   Lexile: 670L   (Grades 4–8)   F

Sheinkin, Steve. *Bomb: The Race to Build—and Steal—the World's Most Dangerous Weapon.*   ISBN-13: 9781596434875

Bomb is a historical, nonfiction drama that explores the complex series of events that led to the creation of the ultimate weapon. This is the story of the atomic bomb.

Lexile: 920L   (Grades 5–10)   NF

Turnage, Sheila. *Three Times Lucky.* ISBN-13: 9780803736702

Sixth-grader Mo LoBeau leads the residents of Tupelo Landing, North Carolina, on a journey of mystery, adventure, and small-town intrigue as she investigates a murder and searches for her long-lost mother. Lexile: 560L (Grades 5–8) F

2012
Award Winner

Gantos, Jack. *Dead End in Norvelt.* ISBN-13: 9781250010230

This novel is about a busy two months for a boy named Jack Gantos, whose plans for vacation are shot down when he is grounded by his parents. But plenty of excitement comes his way once his mom lends him out to help a neighbor who has him typewrite obituaries filled with stories about the people who founded his town. Lexile: 920L (Grades 5–9) F

Honor Books

Lai, Thanhha. *Inside Out & Back Again.* ISBN-13: 9780061962790

When the Vietnam War reaches her home, Hà and her family flee war-torn Vietnam for the American South headed toward hope. Lexile: 800L (Grades 5–9) F

Yelchin, Eugene. *Breaking Stalin's Nose.* ISBN-13: 9781250034106

Ten-year-old Sasha lives with his father and 46 others in a communal apartment. On the eve of his induction into the Young Pioneers, Sasha's world is overturned when his father is arrested by Stalin's guard. Lexile: 670L (Grades 4–6) F

2011
Award Winner

Vanderpool, Clare. *Moon Over Manifest.* ISBN-13: 9780385738835

Abilene is a girl who feels abandoned. Her father sends her to live with an old friend for the summer while he works a railroad job. But she jumps off the train in Manifest, Kansas, to learn about the boy her father once was. Lexile: 800L (Grades 3–8) F

Honor Books

Holm, Jennifer L. *Turtle in Paradise.* ISBN-13: 9780375836886

Turtle is smart and tough, but when Turtle's mom gets a job housekeeping for a lady who doesn't like kids, Turtle says good-bye and leaves for Key West, Florida, to stay with relatives she's never met. Lexile: 610L (Grades 3–5) F

Preus, Margi. *Heart of a Samurai.* ISBN-13: 9781419702006

In 1841, a Japanese fishing boat sinks and the crew is forced to swim to a small island where they are rescued by an American ship. Since Japan's border remained closed to Western nations, the crew sets off for America, learning English on the way.

Lexile: 760L (Grades 5–10) F

Sidman, Joyce. ***Dark Emperor & Other Poems of the Night.***   ISBN-13: 9780547152288

In this book of poems you will meet mice and moths, snails and spiders, and other elements of the night.   Lexile: 1020L   (Grades 3–6)   NF

Williams-Garcia, Rita. ***One Crazy Summer.***   ISBN-13: 9780060760885

This is a distressing but entertaining story of three girls who travel to Oakland, California, in 1968 in search of the mother who abandoned them.   Lexile: 0750L   (Grades 3–8)   F

2010

Award Winner

Stead, Rebecca. ***When You Reach Me.***   ISBN-13: 9780375850868

Someone is sending Miranda anonymous notes, and each one reveals a little bit more about a mystery that changes her life.   Lexile: 750L   (Grades 3–10)   F

Honor Books

Hoose, Philip. ***Claudette Colvin: Twice Toward Justice.***   ISBN-13: 9780312661052

On March 2, 1955, a girl who was tired of the injustices of Jim Crow segregation refused to give her seat to a white woman on a bus in Montgomery, Alabama. Not seen as a hero as Rosa Parks would be nine months later, Claudette Colvin found herself turned away by her classmates and rejected by community leaders.   Lexile: 1000L   (Grades 6–10)   NF

Kelly, Jacqueline. ***The Evolution of Calpurnia Tate.***   ISBN-13: 9780312659301

Callie explores the natural world around her as she develops a relationship with her grandfather, experiences living with six brothers, and learns just what it means to be a girl at the turn of the century.   Lexile: 830L   (Grades 3–10)   F

Lin, Grace. ***Where the Mountain Meets the Moon.***   ISBN-13: 9780316038638

A young girl named Minli lives in a hut with her parents where her father tells her old folktales. Inspired by these stories, Minli sets off on a journey to find the characters in these tales in search of answers about how she can change her family's fortune.

Lexile: 820L   (Grades 3–8)   F

Philbrick, Rodman. ***The Mostly True Adventures of Homer P. Figg.***   ISBN-13: 9780439668217

Twelve-year-old orphan Homer runs away to find his brother, Harold, who has been sold into the Union Army. Homer comes across Civil War–era thieves and other scary characters as he makes his way south to Gettysburg.   Lexile: 950L   (Grades 3–8)   F

2009

Award Winner

Gaiman, Neil. ***The Graveyard Book.***   ISBN-13: 9780060530945

This is the story of Nobody Owens, a boy whose home is a graveyard and who is being raised by a guardian who belongs neither to the mortal world nor the dead.

Lexile: 820L   (Grades 3–8)   F

Honor Books

Appelt, Kathi. *The Underneath.*   ISBN-13: 9781416950592

A cat about to have kittens and a lonely hound dog become an unlikely family. The cat and her babies must hide underneath the porch so the man living inside the house doesn't use them as alligator bait. They are safe in the Underneath as long as they stay there.

Lexile: 830L   (Grades 3–8)   F

Engle, Margarita. *The Surrender Tree: Poems of Cuba's Struggle for Freedom.*

ISBN-13: 9780805086744

In Cuba in 1896, after having fought three wars for independence and still not free, people have been placed in concentration camps with little food and much illness. Rosa is a nurse who doesn't dare go to the camps, so she turns hidden caves into hospitals for those who know how to find her.   Lexile: NPL   (Grades 6–12)   F

Law, Ingrid. *Savvy.*   ISBN-13: 9780142414330

Thirteen years old is the age when Beaumont family members' savvy—their own personal magical power—hits. One brother can cause hurricanes and another creates electricity, so Mibs Beaumont is excited to see what she will get. But before the big day, her Poppa gets in an accident and Mibs needs a savvy that will save him.   Lexile: 1070L   (Grades 3–6)   F

Woodson, Jacqueline. *After Tupac & D Foster.*   ISBN-13: 9780142413999

Neeka and her best friend become aware of things that are happening in the world beyond their block in Queens—like the shooting of Tupac Shakur. After they start searching for their purpose in life, they are left with a sense of how quickly things can change.

Lexile: 750L   (Grades 5–8)   F

2008

Award Winner

Schlitz, Laura Amy. *Good Masters! Sweet Ladies! Voices from a Medieval Village.*

ISBN-13: 9780763650940

This book takes you back to an English village in 1255, where life plays out in dramatic ways, revealing several characters.   Lexile: NP   (Grades 3–8)   NF

Honor Books

Curtis, Christopher Paul. *Elijah of Buxton.*   ISBN-13: 9780439023450

Elijah is the first child born into freedom in Buxton, Canada, a settlement of runaway slaves just beyond the border from Detroit.   Lexile: 1070L   (Grades 3–8)   F

Schmidt, Gary D. *The Wednesday Wars.*   ISBN-13: 9780547237602

This story takes place during the Vietnam era and tells about a teenage boy's experiences over the course of the 1967–1968 school year. He spends Wednesday afternoons with his teacher, Mrs. Baker, while the rest of the class has religious instruction.

Lexile: 990L   (Grades 3–8)   F

Woodson, Jacqueline. *Feathers.*   ISBN-13: 9780142415504

A young girl starts seeing a lot of things in a new light such as her brother Sean's deafness, her mother's fear, the class bully's anger, and her best friend's faith.

Lexile: 760L   (Grades 3–8)   F

2007
Award Winner

Patron, Susan. *The Higher Power of Lucky.*   ISBN-13: 9781416975571

A girl who is afraid of being abandoned by her guardian spends her time eavesdropping on twelve-step meetings and trying to survive a dust storm.   Lexile: 1010L   (Grades 3–8)   F

Honor Books

Holm, Jennifer L. *Penny from Heaven.*   ISBN-13: 9780375836893

This story is about a time in America's history when being Italian meant that you were the enemy. Most of all, it's a story about families and what brings them together and tears them apart.   Lexile: DRA   (Grades 5–8)   F

Larson, Kirby. *Hattie Big Sky.*   ISBN-13: 9780385735957

This story of 16-year-old Hattie takes place in 1917. An orphan who had spent most of her young life going from one relative to another, Hattie receives a letter from an uncle she never knew, and everything changes.   Lexile: 700L   (Grades 6–12)   F

Lord, Cynthia. *Rules.*   ISBN-13: 9780439443838

Twelve-year-old Catherine is in charge of her younger autistic brother. Art is her escape, though she does often hope that her brother will eventually understand how the world works and she won't have to keep explaining things.   Lexile: 780L   (Grades 3–8)   F

2006
Award Winner

Perkins, Lynne Rae. *Criss Cross.*   ISBN-13: 9780060092740

Debbie wishes something good would happen to her, when she meets a boy. She mostly hangs out with her friends Patty, Hector, Lenny, and Phil. Their paths and stories criss cross, and a girl and her wish grow up.   Lexile: 0820L   (Grades 5–12)   F

Honor Books

Armstrong, Alan. *Whittington.*   ISBN-13: 9780375828652

Tom arrives one day at a barn full of rescued animals. This is a story about the healing power of storytelling and how learning to read saves a boy.   Lexile: 0760L   (Grades 3–8)   F

Bartoletti, Susan Campbell. *Hitler Youth: Growing Up in Hitler's Shadow.*

ISBN-13: 9780439353793

This is a chilling tale of a generation of young people who devoted their energy and passion to the Hitler Youth organization and left a mark on world history.

Lexile: 1050L   (Grades 6–12)   NF

Hale, Shannon. *Princess Academy.*   ISBN-13: 9781599900735

Miri is a girl whose family has always lived a simple life. When word comes that the king's priests have chosen her small village as the home of the future princess, Miri finds herself in some conflicting situations.   Lexile: 0890L   (Grades 3–5)   F

Woodson, Jacqueline. *Show Way.*   ISBN-13: 9780399237492

Soonie's great-grandma was just seven years old when she was sold to a big plantation. With only some fabric and needles, she pieced together bright patches with secret meanings and made quilts as maps for slaves to follow to freedom.   Lexile: N/A   (Grades 1–4)   F

2005
Award Winner

Kadohata, Cynthia. *Kira-Kira.*   ISBN-13: 9780689856402

This story is about the close friendship between two Japanese American sisters growing up in Georgia during the late 1950s and early 1960s, and the misery that comes when one sister becomes ill.   Lexile: 740L   (Grades 3–8)   F

Honor Books

Choldenko, Gennifer. *Al Capone Does My Shirts: A Tale from Alcatraz.*

ISBN-13: 9780142403709

Moose Flannagan moves with his family to Alcatraz so his dad can work as a prison guard and his sister, Natalie, can attend a special school.   Lexile: 600L   (Grades 3–8)   F

Freedman, Russell. *The Voice That Challenged a Nation: Marian Anderson and the Struggle for Equal Rights.*   ISBN-13: 9780547480343

This account of the great African American vocalist considers her life and musical career in the context of the history of civil rights in this country.   Lexile: None   (Grades 5–8)   NF

Schmidt, Gary D. *Lizzie Bright and the Buckminster Boy.*   ISBN-13: 9780553494952

No one in town will let Turner Buckminster forget that he's a minister's son, even if he doesn't act like one. But then he meets a girl from a poor nearby island founded by former slaves, and it opens up a whole new world to him.   Lexile: 1000L   (Grades 5–8)   F

2004

Award Winner

DiCamillo, Kate. *The Tale of Despereaux: Being the Story of a Mouse, a Princess, Some Soup, and a Spool of Thread.*   ISBN-13: 9780763625290

The story of Despereaux Tilling, a mouse who loves music, stories, and a princess named Pea.   Lexile: None   (Grades 5–8)   F

Honor Books

Henkes, Kevin. *Olive's Ocean.*   ISBN-13: 9780060535452

Martha Boyle and Olive Barstow are left with eerie connections between them—former classmates who both kept the same secret without knowing it.

Lexile: 0680L   (Grades 5–8)   F

Murphy, Jim. *An American Plague: The True and Terrifying Story of the Yellow Fever Epidemic of 1793.*   ISBN-13: 9780395776087

The nation's capital in North America is devastated by an incurable and unknown disease. This story about the illness known as yellow fever and the toll it took on the city's residents is related to the major social and political events of the day and to 18th-century medical beliefs and practices.   Lexile: 1130L   (Grades 5–8)   NF

2003

Award Winner

Avi. *Crispin: The Cross of Lead.*   ISBN-13: 9780786816583

A young serf fleeing from his past discovers his true identity and a sense of self-worth. On the run, he becomes the servant and then the friend of a juggler. En route to meet with a social reformer, he is captured and imprisoned. This story follows a boy from intense poverty as he evolves into a complex and brave hero, learning that knowledge is the power that leads to true freedom.   Lexile: 0780L   (Grades 5–9)   F

Honor Books

Farmer, Nancy. *The House of the Scorpion.*   ISBN-13: 9780689852237

Matteo Alacran's first cell split and divided inside a petri dish. Then he was placed in the womb of a cow, where he developed from embryo to fetus to baby. He is a boy now, but most consider him a monster—except for El Patron. El Patron loves Matt as he loves himself, because Matt is himself. Unfortunately, escape is the only chance Matt has to survive. But escape is no guarantee of freedom.   Lexile: 660L   (Grades 6–12)   F

Giff, Patricia Reilly. *Pictures of Hollis Woods.*   ISBN-13: 9780440415787

Hollis Woods has been in many foster homes, but when she is sent to Josie, an elderly artist, she wants to stay. However, Josie is growing more forgetful every day, so Hollis fears Social Services will take her away and move Josie into a home. Hollis longs for the only time in her life when she was happy in a foster home with a family who seemed to care about her.

Lexile: 660L   (Grades 3–8)   F

Hiaasen, Carl. *Hoot.*   ISBN-13: 9780440419396

Roy, the new kid in town, stumbles into a mystery and sets out to solve it. Along the way, he meets some interesting characters while becoming involved in another boy's attempt to save a colony of burrowing owls from a proposed construction site.

Lexile: 0760L   (Grades 5–8)   F

Martin, Ann M. *A Corner of the Universe.*   ISBN-13: 9780439388818

Hattie Owen is most welcome in her family's boarding house, but there are secrets in Hattie's family. Hattie learns of her uncle's existence when he shows up in town and the place she thought she knew so well begins to feel different.   Lexile: 0750L   (Grades 3–8)   F

Tolan, Stephanie S. *Surviving the Applewhites.*   ISBN-13: 9780064410441

Jake Semple is rumored to have burned down his old school and got kicked out of every school in his state. Only one place will take him now, and that's a home school run by the Applewhites. There he discovers talents and interests he never knew he had, despite his past indiscretions.   Lexile: 0820L   (Grades 6–10)   F

2002

Award Winner

Park, Linda Sue. *A Single Shard.*   ISBN-13: 9780547534268

In mid- to late 12th-century Korea in Ch'ulp'o, a potter's village, Crane-man raises 10-year-old orphan Tree Ear. The two live under a bridge and survive on trash and fallen grains of rice; they believe stealing and begging make a man no better than a dog. When Tree Ear breaks a piece of pottery by Min, he has to pay his debt in servitude for nine days. The story shows Tree Ear's transformation from apprentice to artist.

Lexile: N/A   (Grades 3–8)   F

Honor Books

Horvath, Polly. *Everything on a Waffle.*   ISBN-13: 9780312380045

Primrose Squarp has a feeling that her parents did not die at sea but cannot convince the other residents of Coal Harbour. She is an orphan without prospective adopters, but the town council is able to locate her Uncle Jack, who takes Primrose into his care.

Lexile: 950L   (Grades 6–8)   F

Nelson, Marilyn. *Carver: A Life in Poems.*   ISBN-13: 9781886910539

This collection of poems provides readers with the life of African American botanist and inventor George Washington Carver.   Lexile: 890L   (Grades 6–9)   NF

2001

Award Winner

Peck, Richard. *A Year Down Yonder.*   ISBN-13: 9780142300701

Mary Alice has always spent summers with her Grandma Dowdel, a woman well-known for shaking up her neighbors—and everyone else. The year Mary Alice turns 15, she moves to Illinois to spend a whole year with Grandma and can't know for certain what life will bring!   Lexile: 0610L   (Grades 5–8)   F

Honor Books

Bauer, Joan. *Hope Was Here.*   ISBN-13: 9780142404249

Hope Yancey, a teenage waitress searches for a sense of belonging. She doesn't mind hard work and has inherited a knack for waiting tables. When Hope moves from Brooklyn to the Welcome Stairways diner in Mulhoney, Wisconsin, she never could have imagined the big changes ahead of her.   Lexile: 0610L   (Grades 6–12)   F

Creech, Sharon. *The Wanderer.*   ISBN-13: 9780061972522

Thirteen-year-old Sophie sets sail for England with her three uncles and two cousins. Sophie and her cousin Cody write in travel logs, and readers hear stories of the past and the daily challenges of surviving at sea.   Lexile: 970L   (Grades 3–6)   F

DiCamillo, Kate. *Because of Winn-Dixie.*   ISBN-13: 9780763644321

A girl named Opal goes into a market and comes out with a dog that she names Winn-Dixie. Because of Winn-Dixie, her preacher father finally tells her things about her mother, and Opal makes a lot of unusual friends in her town. Opal also learns that friendship and forgiveness can sneak up on you.   Lexile: 0610L   (Grades 3–6)   F

Gantos, Jack. *Joey Pigza Loses Control.*   ISBN-13: 9780439338745

Joey Pigza has a mom who loves him, but he has to take Ritalin pills that are supposed to even out his mood swings. Sometimes he makes bad choices and learns the hard way that he shouldn't do certain things. Joey ends up in the school district's special education program, but he is determined not to fall between the cracks.   Lexile: 970L   (Grades 5–8)   F

2000

Award Winner

Curtis, Christopher Paul. *Bud, Not Buddy.*   ISBN-13: 9780553494105

In Flint, Michigan, in 1936, even though times are hard and 10-year-old Bud is motherless, he's got a few things going for him. Although his momma never told him who his father was, she left a clue: posters of Herman E. Calloway and his band, the Dusky Devastators of the Depression. Bud is sure those posters will lead him to his father.

Lexile: 950L   (Grades 3–6)   F

Honor Books

Couloumbis, Audrey. *Getting Near to Baby.* ISBN-13: 9780698118928

After their baby sister dies, Willa Jo and Little Sister's family falls apart. So the two older girls are sent to live with their Aunt Patty and her husband. Since Little Sister refuses to talk, Willa Jo has to try and make things right in their new home, but she can't stop missing her mother. Lexile: 0740L (Grades 5–8) F

dePaola, Tomie. *26 Fairmount Avenue.* ISBN-13: 9780698118645

This funny book is based on Tomie dePaola's stories from the year his family built their new house at 26 Fairmount Avenue. Lexile: 0760Ls (Grades 2–5) F

Holm, Jennifer L. *Our Only May Amelia.* ISBN-13: 9780064408561

It isn't easy being a pioneer in the state of Washington in 1899, but it's even harder when you are the only girl ever born in the new settlement. May Amelia Jackson struggles to behave like a young lady. Lexile: 0900L (Grades 3–6) F

Coretta Scott King Award

The American Library Association established the Coretta Scott King Award in 1969. This award commemorates Dr. Martin Luther King, Jr., and honors his wife, Mrs. Coretta Scott King, for her continued leadership in civil rights and world peace. The award is presented annually to an African American author and an African American illustrator for outstanding contributions published during the previous year. The separate award for illustrator was added in 1979. Visit http://www.ala.org/emiert/cskbookawards /recipients for awards prior to 2000.

2012

Author Award Winner

Nelson, Kadir. *Heart and Soul: The Story of America and African Americans.*

ISBN-13: 9780061730740

The story is told from the viewpoint of an elderly woman who shares her life story while highlighting important historical events, including abolition, the Great Migration, World War II, and the Civil Rights movement. Lexile: 1050L (Grades 2–8) NF

Author Honor Books

Greenfield, Eloise. *The Great Migration: Journey to the North.*   ISBN-13: 9780062184085

In this collection of poems and collage artwork, award winners Eloise Greenfield and Jan Spivey Gilchrist gracefully depict the experiences of families like their own, who found the courage to leave their homes behind and make new lives for themselves elsewhere.

Lexile: N/A   (Grades Pre-K–3)   F

McKissack, Patricia C. *Never Forgotten.*   ISBN-13: 9780375843846

Set in West Africa, here is a lyrical story-in-verse about a young black boy who is kidnapped and sold into slavery. It reminds children that their slave ancestors should never be forgotten and that family is more important than anything else.

Lexile: N/A   (Grades Pre-K–3)   F

Illustrator Award Winner

Evans, Shane W. *Underground: Finding the Light to Freedom.*   ISBN-13: 9781596435384

This story is a portrayal of a band of slaves' nighttime escape. They run, rest, get help from others, and finally celebrate their liberation.   Lexile: N/A   (Grades K–3)   NF

Illustrator Honor Books

Nelson, Kadir. *Heart and Soul: The Story of America and African Americans.*

ISBN-13: 9780061730740

This is the story of the men, women, and children who toiled in the hot sun picking cotton for their masters; it's about the America ripped in two by Jim Crow laws; it's about the brothers and sisters of all colors who rallied against those who would dare bar a child from an education.   Lexile: 1050L   (Grades 2–8)   NF

2011

Author Award Winner

Williams-Garcia, Rita. *One Crazy Summer.*   ISBN-13: 9780060760885

Eleven-year-old Delphine and her two younger sisters travel to Oakland, California, in 1968 to face the emotional challenge of reaching out to a distant mother and to learn about a different side of the Civil Rights movement.   Lexile: 750L   (Grades 3–8)   F

Author Honor Books

Myers, Walter Dean. *Lockdown.*   ISBN-13: 9780061214820

Walter Dean Myers enjoys speaking with kids in schools and juvenile detention facilities about writing and making positive decisions. He says, "I have enormous faith in young people." What's it like in juvie jail? Enter the world of 14-year-old Reese, who's locked up at Progress juvenile detention facility. Can he get a second chance?

Lexile: 0730L   (Grades 7–12)   F

Neri, G. *Yummy: The Last Days of a Southside Shorty.*   ISBN-13: 9781584302674

Yummy killed Shavon in a gang shooting and is on the run. How could a smiling boy who carried a teddy bear and got his nickname from his love of sweets also be an arsonist, an extortionist, and a murderer? All possible answers are explored such as a failed system, a crime-riddled neighborhood, absentee parenting, the allure of gang membership, and a neglected community.   Lexile: GN510L   (Grades 7–12)   F

Rhodes, Jewell Parker. *Ninth Ward.*   ISBN-13: 9780316043083

Twelve-year-old Lanesha lives in a tight-knit community in New Orleans' Ninth Ward. She doesn't have a fancy house like her uptown family or lots of friends like the other kids on her street. But what she does have is Mama Ya-Ya, her fiercely loving caretaker, wise in the ways of the world and able to predict the future. So when Mama Ya-Ya's visions show a powerful hurricane, Katrina, fast approaching, it's up to Lanesha to call upon the hope and strength Mama Ya-Ya has given her to help them both survive the storm. *Ninth Ward* is a deeply emotional story about transformation and a celebration of resilience, friendship, and family as only love can define it.   Lexile: 0470L   (Grades 3–7)   F

Illustrator Award Winner

Collier, Bryan, text by Laban Carrick Hill. *Dave the Potter: Artist, Poet, Slave.*

ISBN-13: 9780316107310

Dave, a slave in 19th-century South Carolina, demonstrated extraordinary talent and skill to achieve creative success creating eloquent poetry on pots despite it being illegal for slaves to read and write.   Lexile: AD1100L   (Grades K–4)   NF

Illustrator Honor Book

Steptoe, Javaka, text by Gary Golio. *Jimi: Sounds Like a Rainbow: A Story of the Young Jimi Hendrix.*   ISBN-13: 9780618852796

Before Jimi Hendrix was a superstar, a rebel, a hero, an innovator, he was a boy who asked himself a question: Could someone paint pictures with sound? This is a story of a talented child who learns to see, hear, and interpret the world around him in his own unique way. It is also a story of a determined kid with a vision, who worked hard to become a devoted and masterful artist.   Lexile: AD900L   (Grades K–4)   NF

2010
Author Award Winner

Nelson, Vaunda Micheaux. *Bad News for Outlaws: The Remarkable Life of Bass Reeves, Deputy U.S. Marshal.*   ISBN-13: 9780822567646

Sitting tall in the saddle, with a wide-brimmed black hat and twin Colt pistols on his belt, Bass Reeves seemed bigger than life. Outlaws feared him. Law-abiding citizens respected him. As a peace officer, he was cunning and fearless. The story of Bass Reeves is the story of a remarkable African American and a remarkable hero of the Old West.

Lexile: 860L   (Grades 3–7)   NF

Author Honor Book

Davis, Tanita S. *Mare's War.*   ISBN-13: 9780375850776

Mare is a World War II veteran and an African American grandmother like no other. She escaped her less-than-perfect life in the deep South to join the Battalion of the Women's Army Corps. Now she is driving her granddaughters—two willful teenagers in their own rite—on a cross-country road trip. The girls are initially skeptical of Mare's flippy wigs and stilletos, but they soon find themselves entranced by the story she has to tell, and readers will be too.   Lexile: 0830L   (Grades 7–12)   F

Illustrator Award Winner

Smith, Charles R., Jr., text by Langston Hughes. *My People.*   ISBN-13: 9781416935407

Langston Hughes's sparing yet eloquent tribute to his people has been cherished for generations. Now acclaimed photographer Charles R. Smith, Jr., interprets this beloved poem in vivid sepia photographs that capture the glory, the beauty, and the soul of being a black American today.   Lexile: N/A   (Grades Pre-K–3)   NF

Illustrator Honor Book

Lewis, E. B., text by Langston Hughes. *The Negro Speaks of Rivers.*

ISBN-13: 9780786818679

Langston Hughes has long been acknowledged as the voice, and his poem, "The Negro Speaks of Rivers," the song, of the Harlem Renaissance. Although he was only 17 when he composed it, Hughes already had the insight to capture in words the strength and courage of black people in America. Artist E. B. Lewis acts as interpreter and visionary, using watercolor to pay tribute to Hughes's timeless poem—a poem that every child deserves to know.

Lexile: N/A   (Grades K–4)   NF

2009

Author Award Winner

Nelson, Kadir. *We Are the Ship: The Story of Negro League Baseball.*

ISBN-13: 9780786808328

The story of Negro League baseball is the story of gifted athletes and determined owners, of racial discrimination and international sportsmanship, of fortunes won and lost, of triumphs and defeats on and off the field. It is a perfect mirror for the social and political history of black America in the first half of the 20th century. This book follows Negro League baseball from its beginnings in the 1920s through its decline after Jackie Robinson crossed over to the majors in 1947.   Lexile: 900L   (Grades 4–7)   NF

Author Honor Books

Smith, Hope Anita. *Keeping the Night Watch.*　　　　ISBN-13: 9780805072020

Through powerful poems, Hope Anita Smith chronicles the nuanced emotions of thirteen-year-old C. J. and his family as they slowly learn how to heal and put the pieces back together.

Lexile: N/A　(Grades 5–8)　F

Thomas, Joyce Carol. *The Blacker the Berry.*　　　　ISBN-13: 9780060253752

This collection of poems, including "Golden Goodness," "Cranberry Red," and "Biscuit Brown," celebrates individuality and Afro-American identity.

Lexile: N/A　(Grades Pre-K–3)　NF

Weatherford, Carole Boston. *Becoming Billie Holiday.*　　　　ISBN-13: 9781590785072

Jazz vocalist Billie Holiday looks back on her early years in this fictional memoir written in verse.　　　　Lexile: N/A　(Grades 7–12)　F

Illustrator Award Winner

Cooper, Floyd, text by Joyce Carol Thomas. *The Blacker the Berry.*　ISBN-13: 9780060253752

This collection of poems, including "Golden Goodness," "Cranberry Red," and "Biscuit Brown," celebrates individuality and Afro-American identity.

Lexile: N/A　(Grades Pre-K–3)　NF

Illustrator Honor Books

Nelson, Kadir. *We Are the Ship: The Story of Negro League Baseball.*

ISBN-13: 9780786808328

The story of Negro League baseball is the story of gifted athletes and determined owners, of racial discrimination and international sportsmanship, of fortunes won and lost, of triumphs and defeats on and off the field. It is a perfect mirror for the social and political history of black America in the first half of the 20th century. This book follows Negro League baseball from its beginnings in the 1920s through its decline after Jackie Robinson crossed over to the majors in 1947.　　　　Lexile: 900L　(Grades 4–7)　NF

Pinkney, Jerry, text by Dianna Hutts Aston. *The Moon Over Star.*　ISBN-13: 9780803731073

In July 1969, the world witnessed an awe-inspiring historical achievement when Neil Armstrong and Buzz Aldrin became the first humans to set foot on the moon. For the young protagonist of this lyrical and hopeful picture book, that landing is something that inspires her to make one giant step toward all of the possibilities that life has to offer.

Lexile: N/A　(Grades K–4)　NF

Qualls, Sean, text by Carole Boston Weatherford. *Before John Was a Jazz Giant: A Song of John Coltrane.*　　　　ISBN-13: 9780805079944

Young John Coltrane was all ears and there was a lot to hear growing up in the South in the 1930s: preachers praying, music on the radio, the bustling of the household. These vivid noises shaped John's own sound as a musician.　Lexile: AD1090L　(Grades K–4)　NF

2008
Author Award Winner

Curtis, Christopher Paul. *Elijah of Buxton.*   ISBN-13: 9780439023450

Eleven-year-old Elijah is the first child born into freedom in Buxton, Canada, a settlement of runaway slaves just over the border from Detroit. He's best known for having made a memorable impression on Frederick Douglass, but that changes when a former slave steals money from Elijah's friend, who has been saving to buy his family out of captivity in the South. Elijah embarks on a dangerous journey to America in pursuit of the thief and discovers firsthand the unimaginable horrors of the life his parents fled, a life from which he'll always be free if he can find the courage to get back home.   Lexile: 1070L   (Grades 3–8)   F

Author Honor Books

Draper, Sharon. *November Blues.*   ISBN-13: 9781416906995

When November Nelson loses her boyfriend, Josh, to a pledge stunt gone horribly wrong, she thinks her life can't possibly get any worse. But Josh left something behind that will change November's life forever, and now she's faced with the biggest decision she could ever imagine.   Lexile: 770L   (Grades 7–8)   F

Smith, Charles R., Jr. *Twelve Rounds to Glory: The Story of Muhammad Ali.*

ISBN-13: 9780763616922

From the moment a fired-up teenager from Kentucky won 1960 Olympic gold to the day in 1996 when a retired legend, hands shaking from Parkinson's, returned to raise the Olympic torch, the boxer known as "The Greatest" waged many a fight. Some were in the ring, against opponents like Sonny Liston and Joe Frazier; others were against societal prejudice and against a war he refused to support because of his Islamic faith.

Lexile: NPL   (Grade 5)   NF

Illustrator Award Winner

Bryan, Ashley. *Let It Shine.*   ISBN-13: 9780689847325

Bryan celebrates three favorite spirituals: "This Little Light of Mine," "Oh, When the Saints Go Marching In," and "He's Got the Whole World in His Hands." The power of these beloved songs simply emanates through his joyous interpretations.

Lexile: NPL   (Grades Pre-K–3)   NF

Illustrator Honor Book

Devard, Nancy, text by N. Joy. *The Secret Olivia Told Me.*   ISBN-13: 9781933491080

Can you keep a secret? Olivia has a secret—a *big* secret. It's a secret that she tells only to Jade, her very best friend. And Jade promises she won't say a word. But the secret is really big and really juicy. What happens when Jade slips and the secret gets out?

Lexile: 350L   (Grades Pre-K–3)   F

Dillon, Leo and Diane. *Jazz on a Saturday Night.*　　　ISBN-13: 9780590478939

In this book you will learn about popular music form of jazz and read a biography of each player pictured—and then hear each instrument play on a specially produced CD.

Lexile: AD580L　(Grades Pre-K–3)　NF

2007
Author Award Winner

Draper, Sharon M. *Copper Sun.*　　　ISBN-13: 9781416953487

Karina has plenty to worry about on the last day of seventh grade: finding three "D"s and a "C" on her report card again, getting laughed at by everyone again, being sent to the principal again. But she's too busy dodging the fists of her stepfather and looking out for her sisters to deal with school. This is the epic story of a young girl torn from an African village, sold into slavery, and stripped of everything she has ever known, except hope.

Lexile: 820L　(Grades 9–12)　F

Author Honor Book

Grimes, Nikki. *The Road to Paris.*　　　ISBN-13: 9780142410820

Paris has just moved in with the Lincoln family, and she isn't thrilled to be in yet another foster home. She has a tough time trusting people, and she misses her brother, who has been sent to a boys' home. Over time, the Lincolns grow on Paris. But no matter how hard she tries to fit in, she can't ignore the feeling that she never will, especially in a town that's mostly white while she is half black. It isn't long before Paris has a big decision to make about where she truly belongs.

Lexile: 0700L　(Grades 3–7)　F

Illustrator Award Winner

Nelson, Kadir, text by Carole Boston Weatherford. *Moses: When Harriet Tubman Led Her People to Freedom.*　　　ISBN-13: 9780786851751

This poetic book is a resounding tribute to Tubman's strength, humility, and devotion.

Lexile: AD660L　(Grades K–5)　NF

Illustrator Honor Books

Andrews, Benny, edited by David Roessel and Arnold Rampersad. *Poetry for Young People: Langston Hughes.*　　　ISBN-13: 9781402718458

This book showcases the work of the extraordinary Langston Hughes. It's edited by two leading poetry experts and features gallery-quality art by Benny Andrews that adds rich dimension to the words.

Lexile: NPL　(Grade 3)　NF

Myers, Christopher, text by Walter Dean Myers. *Jazz.*　　ISBN-13: 9780823421732

Eight jazz classics are arranged for each instrument as stand-alone solos, or all the instruments can play together. Each song includes chord symbols in concert pitch for use by piano or guitar, or the player can use the full backing track from the CD as accompaniment. The CD also includes tuning notes and full-version demonstration tracks of each song to help each musician learn the song.　　Lexile: N/A　(Grades 3–6)　NF

2006
Author Award Winner

Lester, Julius. *Day of Tears: A Novel in Dialogue.*　　ISBN-13: 9781423104094

On March 2 and 3, 1859, the largest auction of slaves in American history took place in Savannah, Georgia. More than 400 slaves were sold. On the first day of the auction, the skies darkened and torrential rain began falling. The rain continued throughout the two days, stopping only when the auction had ended. The simultaneity of the rainstorm with the auction led to these two days being called "the weeping time."

Lexile: N/A　(Grades 4–8)　F

Author Honor Books

Bolden, Tonya. *Maritcha: A Nineteenth-Century American Girl.*　　ISBN-13: 9780810950450

This is based on an actual memoir written by Maritcha Rémond Lyons, who was born and raised in New York City. This story tells what it was like to be a black child born free during the days of slavery. Everyday experiences are interspersed with high-point moments, such as visiting the United States' first world's fair.　　Lexile: 1190L　(Grades K–4)　NF

Grimes, Nikki. *Dark Sons.*　　ISBN-13: 9780310721451

Betrayed, lost, and isolated, the perspectives of two teenage boys—modern-day Sam and biblical Ishmael—unite over millennia to illustrate the power of forgiveness.

Lexile: 0740L　(Grades 10–12)　F

Nelson, Marilyn. *A Wreath for Emmett Till.*　　ISBN-13: 9780547076362

In 1955 people all over the United States knew that Emmett Louis Till was a 14-year-old African American boy lynched for supposedly whistling at a white woman in Mississippi. The brutality of his murder; the open-casket funeral held by his mother, Mamie Till Mobley; and the acquittal of the men tried for the crime drew wide media attention.

Lexile: N/A　(Grades 7+)　NF

Illustrator Award Winner

Collier, Brian, text by Nikki Giovanni. *Rosa.*　　ISBN-13: 9780312376024.

This is a tribute to Rosa Parks, one of the most important figures in the American Civil Rights Movement. Bryan Collier's striking cut-paper images retell the story of this historic event from a wholly unique and original perspective.

Lexile: 900L　(Grades K–6)　NF

Illustrator Honor Book

Christie, R. Gregory, text by Mary Williams. *Brothers in Hope: The Story of the Lost Boys of Sudan.*   ISBN-13: 9781584302322

A young boy unites with thousands of other orphaned boys to walk to safety in a refugee camp in another country, after war destroys their villages in southern Sudan. Based on true events, eight-year-old Garang, orphaned by a civil war in Sudan, finds the inner strength to help lead other boys as they trek hundreds of miles seeking safety in Ethiopia, then Kenya, and finally in the United States.   Lexile: 670L   (Grades 2–4)   NF

2005

Author Award Winner

Morrison, Toni. *Remember: The Journey to School Integration.*   ISBN-13: 9780618397402

This book presents photographs that depict the historical events surrounding school desegregation.   Lexile: 660L   (Grades 4–7)   NF

Author Honor Books

Flake, Sharon G. *Who Am I Without Him?: Short Stories About Girls and the Boys in Their Lives.*   ISBN-13: 9781423132530

Guys and girls get together, get played, and get real. Twelve short stories about guys and girls falling in and out of love and relationships, testing out ways to communicate with one another, and respecting each other and respecting themselves.

Lexile: 650L   (Grades 8-12)   F

Moses, Shelia P. *The Legend of Buddy Bush.*   ISBN-13: 9781416907169

The day Uncle Goodwin "Buddy" Bush came back home from Harlem to Rehobeth Road in Rich Square, North Carolina, Pattie Mae's life changes dramatically. Pattie Mae adores Uncle Buddy though he doesn't believe in the country stuff most people believe in. Buddy's inattention to the protocol of 1947 North Carolina lands him in jail for a crime he didn't commit. This is the story of what happened when a black man is charged with the attempted rape of a white woman and how the African American community faced this situation to show how injustice can sometimes inspire courage and pride.

Lexile: 0760L   (Grades 7–12)   F

Nelson, Marilyn. *Fortune's Bones: The Manumission Requiem.*   ISBN-13: 9781932425123

There is a skeleton on display in the Mattatuck Museum in Waterbury, Connecticut. It has been in the town for more than 200 years. Over time, the bones became the subject of stories and speculation in Waterbury. In 1996 a group of community-based volunteers, working in collaboration with the museum staff, discovered that the bones were those of a slave named Fortune who had been owned by a local doctor. After Fortune's death, the doctor dissected the body, rendered the bones, and assembled the skeleton. A great deal is still not known about Fortune, but it is known that he was baptized, was married, and had four children. He died at about the age of 60, sometime after 1797. Lexile: NPL   (Grades 7–12)   NF

Illustrator Award Winner

Nelson, Kadir, text by Ntozake Shange. *Ellington Was Not a Street.*

ISBN-13: 9780689828843

This reflective tribute to the African American community of old recalls a childhood home and the close-knit group of innovators who often gathered there.

Lexile: NPL (Grades K–6) F

Illustrator Honor Books

Pinkney, Jerry, text by Billie Holiday and Arthur Herzog, Jr. *God Bless the Child.*

ISBN-13: 9780060287979

The song "God Bless the Child" was first performed by legendary jazz vocalist Billie Holiday in 1939 and remains one of her enduring masterpieces. In this picture-book interpretation, renowned illustrator Jerry Pinkney has created images of a family moving from the rural South to the urban North during the Great Migration that reached its peak in the 1930s.

Lexile: NPL (Grades Pre-K–3) NF

Dillon, Diane and Leo, text by Virginia Hamilton. *The People Could Fly: The Picture Book.*

ISBN-13: 9780375845536

This is a fantasy tale of the slaves who possessed the ancient magic words that enabled them to literally fly away to freedom. And it is a moving tale of those who did not have the opportunity to "fly" away and who remained slaves with only their imaginations to set them free as they told and retold this tale.

Lexile: 0480L (Grades 3–12) F

2004

Author Award Winner

Johnson, Angela. *The First Part Last.*

ISBN-13: 9780689849237

Bobby is a typical urban New York City teenager. He is impulsive, eager, and restless. For his 16th birthday he cuts school with his two best buddies, grabs a couple of slices at his favorite pizza joint, catches a flick at a nearby multiplex, and gets some news from his girlfriend, Nia, that changes his life forever: he's going to be a father. Suddenly things like school, house parties, and fun times with friends are replaced by visits to Nia's obstetrician and countless social workers who all say that the only way for Nia and Bobby to lead a normal life is to put their baby up for adoption. Then tragedy strikes Nia, and Bobby finds himself in the role of single, teenage father because his child is all that remains of his lost love. With powerful language and keen insight, Johnson tells the story of a young man's struggle to figure out what "the right thing" is and then to do it.

Lexile: 790L (Grades 7–12) F

Author Honor Books

Draper, Sharon M. *The Battle of Jericho.*

ISBN-13: 9780689842337

A high school junior and his cousin suffer the ramifications of joining what seems to be a "reputable" school club.

Lexile: 0700L (Grades 7–10) F

McKissack, Patricia C. and Fredrick L. *Days of Jubilee: The End of Slavery in the United States.* ISBN-13: 9780590107648

Using slave narratives, letters, diaries, military orders, and other documents, this book describes the pivotal events leading up to and including the long awaited and glorious Days of Jubilee. For two and a half centuries, enslaved African American people sang about, prayed for, and waited on their long anticipated freedom—a day of Jubilee. But freedom didn't come for slaves at the same time. This book chronicles the various stages of U.S. emancipation, beginning with those slaves who were freed for their service during the Revolutionary War, to those who were freed by the 13th Amendment to the Constitution.

Lexile: 1040L   (Grades 5–8)   NF

Woodson, Jacqueline. *Locomotion.* ISBN-13: 9780142415528

In a series of poems, 11-year-old Lonnie writes about his life after the death of his parents, separated from his younger sister, living in a foster home, and finding his poetic voice at school.

Lexile: NP   (Grades 4–7)   F

Illustrator Award Winner

Bryan, Ashley. *Beautiful Blackbird.* ISBN-13: 9780689847318

In a story of the Ila people, the colorful birds of Africa ask Blackbird, whom they think is the most beautiful of birds, to decorate them with some of his "blackening brew."

Lexile: 540L   (Grades Pre-K–3)   F

Illustrator Honor Books

Bootman, Colin, text by Vaunda Michaeux Nelson. *Almost to Freedom.*

ISBN-13: 9781575053424

This is the story of a young girl's dramatic escape from slavery via the Underground Railroad.

Lexile: 530L   (Grades 3–5)   F

Nelson, Kadir, text by Jerdine Nolen. *Thunder Rose.* ISBN-13: 9780152164720

Thunder Rose vows to grow up to be more than just big and strong, thank you very kindly—and boy, does she ever! But when a whirling storm on a riotous rampage threatens, has Rose finally met her match? Unusual from the day she is born, Thunder Rose performs all sorts of amazing feats, including building fences, taming a stampeding herd of steers, capturing a gang of rustlers, and turning aside a tornado.

Lexile: 910LAD   (Grades K–2)   F

2003

Author Award Winner

Grimes, Nikki. *Bronx Masquerade.* ISBN-13: 9780142501894

While studying the Harlem Renaissance, students at a Bronx high school read aloud poems they've written, revealing their innermost thoughts and fears to their formerly clueless classmates.

Lexile: 0670L   (Grades 7–11)   F

Author Honor Books

Grimes, Nikki. *Talkin' About Bessie: The Story of Aviator Elizabeth Coleman.*

ISBN-13: 9780439352437

Elizabeth "Bessie" Coleman was always being told what she could and couldn't do. In an era when Jim Crow laws and segregation were a way of life, it was not easy to survive. Bessie didn't let that stop her. Although she was only 11 when the Wright brothers took their historic flight, she vowed to become the first African American female pilot. Her sturdy faith and determination helped her overcome obstacles of poverty, racism, and gender discrimination. This story is innovatively told through a series of monologues.

Lexile: 970L   (Grades Pre-K–3)   NF

Woods, Brenda. *The Red Rose Box.*   ISBN-13: 9780142501511

In 1953, Leah Hopper dreams of leaving the poverty and segregation of her home in Sulphur, Louisiana, and when Aunt Olivia sends train tickets to Los Angeles as part of her 10th birthday present, Leah gets a first taste of freedom.   Lexile: 0830L   (Grades 3–7)   F

Illustrator Award Winner

Lewis, E. B., text by Nikki Grimes. *Talkin' About Bessie: The Story of Aviator Elizabeth Coleman.*   ISBN-13: 9780439352437

Elizabeth "Bessie" Coleman was always being told what she could and couldn't do. In an era when Jim Crow laws and segregation were a way of life, it was not easy to survive. Bessie didn't let that stop her. Although she was only 11 when the Wright brothers took their historic flight, she vowed to become the first African American female pilot. Her sturdy faith and determination helped her overcome obstacles of poverty, racism, and gender discrimination. This story is innovatively told through a series of monologues.

Lexile: 970L   (Grades Pre-K–3)   NF

Illustrator Honor Book

Dillon, Diane and Leo. *Rap a Tap Tap: Here's Bojangles—Think of That.*

ISBN-13: 9780439560665

Colorful gouache illustrations of inner-city scenes are met with cleverly designed graphics of Bojangles, his tapping feet depicted in shades of gray prompting the illusion of movement.   Lexile: 300L   (Grades Pre-K–3)   NF

2002

Author Award Winner

Taylor, Mildred D. *The Land.*   ISBN-13: 9780142501467

After the Civil War, Paul, the son of a white father and a black mother, finds himself caught between the two worlds of colored folks and white folks as he pursues the dream of owning land of his own.   Lexile: 0760L   (Grades 7–12)   F

Author Honor Books

Flake, Sharon G. *Money Hungry.*   ISBN-13: 9781423103868

This is a haunting story of greed and forgiveness. All 13-year-old Raspberry can think of is making money so that she and her mother never have to worry about living on the streets again.   Lexile: 0650L   (Grades 5–12)   F

Nelson, Marilyn. *Carver: A Life in Poems.*   ISBN-13: 9781886910539

Carver left home in search of an education and eventually earned a master's degree in agriculture. In 1896, he was invited by Booker T. Washington to head the agricultural department at the all-black-staffed Tuskegee Institute. The 44 poems are told from the point of view of revered African American botanist and inventor George Washington Carver.

Lexile: 890L   (Grades 6–9)   NF

Illustrator Award Winner

Pinkney, Jerry, text by Patricia C. McKissack. *Goin' Someplace Special.*

ISBN-13: 9781416927358

In segregated 1950s Nashville, a young African American girl braves a series of indignities and obstacles to get to one of the few integrated places in town: the public library.

Lexile: 0550L   (Grades Pre-K–3)   F

Illustrator Honor Books

Collier, Bryan. *Martin's Big Words.*   ISBN-13: 9781423106357

This picture-book biography is an excellent and accessible introduction for young readers to learn about one of the world's most influential leaders, Dr. Martin Luther King, Jr. Doreen Rappaport weaves the immortal words of Dr. King into a captivating narrative to tell the story of his life.   Lexile: 0410L   (Grades Pre-K–3)   NF

2001

Author Award Winner

Woodson, Jacqueline. *Miracle's Boys.*   ISBN-13: 9780142415535

Twelve-year-old Lafayette's close relationship with his older brother Charlie changes after Charlie is released from a detention home and blames Lafayette for the death of their mother.   Lexile: 660L   (Grades 5–8)   F

Author Honor Book

Pinkney, Andrea Davis, illustrated by Stephen Alcorn. *Let It Shine: Stories of Black Women Freedom Fighters.*   ISBN-13: 9780152010058

Ten freedom fighters let their lights shine on the darkness of discrimination. Rosa Parks refused to give up her seat on a bus and sparked a boycott that changed America. Harriet Tubman helped more than 300 slaves escape the South on the Underground Railroad. Shirley Chisholm became the first black woman elected to the U.S. House of Representatives.

Lexile: 940L   (Grades 3–6)   NF

Illustrator Award Winner

Collier, Bryan. ***Uptown.***   ISBN-13: 9780805073997

Uptown is a rich mix of flavors, colors, sounds, and cultures that come together to create a vibrant community like no other in the world. Seen through the eyes of one little boy who lives there, the details of life in Harlem are as joyous as a game of basketball on a summer's afternoon and as personal as a trip to the barbershop where old-timers reminisce.

Lexile: AD420L   (Grades Pre-K–3)   F

Illustrator Honor Books

Christie, R. Gregory, text by Anne Rockwell. ***Only Passing Through: The Story of Sojourner Truth.***   ISBN-13: 9780440417668

This is a powerful, picture-book biography of one of the abolitionist movement's most compelling voices. Sojourner Truth traveled the country in the latter half of the 19th century, speaking out against slavery.   Lexile: 0790L   (Grades 2–5)   NF

Collier, Bryan, text by Doreen Rappaport. ***Freedom River.***   ISBN-13: 9781423106340

This story describes an incident in the life of John Parker, an ex-slave who became a successful businessman in Ripley, Ohio, and who repeatedly risked his life to help other slaves escape to freedom.   Lexile: N/A   (Grades K–4)   NF

Lewis, E. B., text by Elizabeth Fitzgerald Howard. ***Virgie Goes to School with Us Boys.***

ISBN-13: 9780689877933

All Virgie wants to do is go to school with her brothers, but they keep saying she's too little for the long, seven-mile walk, and that girls don't need school. Virgie doesn't agree, and she doesn't let anything stand in her way.   Lexile: N/A   (Grades Pre-K–3)   F

2000

Author Award Winner

Curtis, Christopher Paul. ***Bud, Not Buddy.***   ISBN-13: 9780553494105

It's 1936, in Flint, Michigan, and when 10-year-old Bud decides to hit the road to find his father, nothing can stop him.   Lexile: 950L   (Grades 3–6)   F

Author Honor Books

English, Karen. ***Francie.***   ISBN-13: 9780312373832

When the 16-year-old boy whom she tutors in reading is accused of attempting to murder a white man, Francie gets herself in serious trouble for her efforts at friendship.

Lexile: 660L   (Grades 4–7)   F

McKissack, Patricia C. and Frederick L. *Black Hands, White Sails: The Story of African-American Whalers.* ISBN-13: 9780590483131

Despite the dangers and challenges of whaling, many African Americans took on the job between 1730 and 1880. A rare look at an important slice of American history describes the contributions of this group to the whaling industry and their role in the abolitionist movement. Lexile: 1130L (Grades 4–7) NF

Myers, Walter Dean. *Monster.* ISBN-13: 9780064407311

This is the incredible story of how one guy's life was turned around by a few events and how he might have to spend the rest of his life behind bars, told as it actually happened. Lexile: 670L (Grades 6–12) F

Illustrator Award Winner

Pinkney, Brian, text by Kim L. Siegelson. *In the Time of the Drums.*

ISBN-13: 9780786804368

Certain to inspire for years to come, this book tells a spellbinding story of strength in slavery times. This is an important addition to classroom and school libraries, especially for use during Black History Month. Lexile: AD570L (Grades 1–4) NF

Illustrator Honor Books

Lewis, E. B., text by Tololwa M. Mollel. *My Rows and Piles of Coins.*

ISBN-13: 9780395751862

Determination and generosity are at the heart of this satisfying tale, set in Tanzania and illustrated with glowing watercolors that capture the warmth of Saruni's family and the excitement of market day. A Tanzanian boy saves his coins to buy a bicycle so he can help his parents carry goods to market, but then he discovers that in spite of all he has saved, he still does not have enough money. Lexile: AD700L (Grades K–4) F

Myers, Christopher. *Black Cat.* ISBN-13: 9780590033756

On an eye-opening journey through urban landscapes, a stray black cat leaps, listens, and dances to the city's pulsating beats while searching for a home. Cool, hip-hop rhythms and innovative, collage artwork combine to create a book layered with meaning about identity, beauty, and home. Lexile: NPL (Grades Pre-K–3) NF

Pura Belpré Award

The Pura Belpré Award is given every year by the Association for Library Service to Children (ALSC) and the National Association to Promote Library and Information Services to Latinos and the Spanish-Speaking (REFORMA). It honors Latino writers and illustrators whose work best portrays, affirms, and celebrates the Latino cultural experience in a work of literature for youth. It is named in honor of Pura Belpré, the first Latina librarian of the New York Public Library. The first awards, given in 1996, were selected from books published 1990–1995. Visit http://www.ala.org/alsc/awardsgrants/book media/belpremedal/belprepast for awards prior to 2000.

2013

Author Award Winner

Sáenz, Benjamin Alire. *Aristotle and Dante Discover the Secrets of the Universe.*

ISBN-13: 9781442408937

This is the story of 15-year-old loner Aristotle Mendoza and his friendship with Dante Quintana, two boys on the edge of manhood. This tale addresses issues of identity, friendship, family and love, sexuality and cultural identity. Lexile: NA (Grades 7–12) F

Author Honor Books

Manzano, Sonia. *The Revolution of Evelyn Serrano.* ISBN-13: 9780545325059

Fourteen-year-old Evelyn Serrano is caught in a mix of events in 1969 Spanish Harlem led by the revolutionary Young Lords. She navigates the tensions between her activist *abuela* and conservative mother, and in turn Evelyn learns to value her own culture and history.

Lexile: 720L (Grades 7–12) F

Illustrator Award Winner

Diaz, David. *Martín de Porres: The Rose in the Desert.* ISBN-13: 9780547612188

This is a story about the first African-heritage saint of the Américas. Martin de Porres was born into extreme poverty, and his mother begged the church fathers to allow him into the priesthood. Martin was accepted as a servant boy, but soon he was performing miracles. Rumors began about the mulatto boy with healing hands. Martin continued to serve in the church, until he was finally received by the Dominican Order as a saint and the rose in the desert. Lexile: 700L (Grades 1–4) F

2012
Author Award Winner

McCall, Guadalupe Garcia. *Under the Mesquite.* ISBN-13: 9781600604294

This story gracefully manages to convey the experience of growing up in a bicultural community in Texas with geographical accuracy and a radiating authentic voice for its main protagonist 14-year-old Lupita, the oldest of eight children, who is dealing with her mother's terminal illness. Overwhelmed by change and loss, she takes refuge in the healing power of words. Lexile: 990L (Grades 7–12) F

Author Honor Books

Engle, Margarita. *Hurricane Dancers: The First Caribbean Pirate Shipwreck.*

ISBN-13: 9780805092400

Engle's beautifully written poetic narrative cuts to the heart of an untold story in Latin American history and describes the enslavement of the native peoples of the Caribbean by the Spanish along with the mixing of Spanish and native blood that now forms the vast majority of Latin America. Lexile: 1170 (Grades 7–12) F

Garza, Xavier. *Maximilian and the Mystery of the Guardian Angel: A Bilingual Lucha Libre Thriller.* ISBN-13: 9781933693989

This story captures the excitement that Max, an 11-year-old Mexican American boy, displays when he discovers that his favorite Lucha Libre wrestler is coming to town and might have a strange connection with his own family! This action-packed bilingual mystery novel uses playful language that reinforces elements of Mexican American culture and overflows with almost unbridled excitement for Lucha wrestling. Lexile: 820L (Grades 3–7) F

Illustrator Award Winner

Tonatiuh, Duncan. *Diego Rivera: His World and Ours.* ISBN-13: 9780810997318

This book introduces one of the most popular artists of the 20th century, Diego Rivera, to young readers. It tells the story of Diego as a young, mischievous boy who demonstrated a clear passion for art and then went on to become one of the most famous painters in the world. Lexile: AD1040L (Grades K–4) NF

Illustrator Honor Books

López, Rafael, text by Samantha R. Vamos. *The Cazuela That the Farm Maiden Stirred.*

ISBN-13: 9781580892421

As a farm girl prepares a *cazuela* (pot) of rice pudding, the animals on the farm eagerly help. Lexile: NPL (Grades Pre-K–1) F

Palacios, Sara, text by Monica Brown. *Marisol McDonald Doesn't Match /*
Marisol McDonald no combina.   ISBN-13: 9780892392353

> Bright and vivacious Marisol, a young Peruvian-Scottish-American girl, loves peanut butter and jelly burritos and speaks both English and Spanish. Unfortunately, her teacher and classmates do not appreciate Marisol's mashing of cultures.   Lexile: AD580L   (Pre-K–3)   F

2011
Author Award Winner

Ryan, Pam Muñoz and Peter Sís. *The Dreamer.*   ISBN-13: 9780439269988

> Combining elements of magical realism with biography, poetry, literary fiction, and sensorial, transporting illustrations, Pam Muñoz Ryan and Peter Sís take readers on a rare journey of the heart and imagination.   Lexile: 760LAD   (Grades 5–9)   F

Author Honor Books

Ancona, George. *¡Olé! Flamenco.*   ISBN-13: 9781600603617

> Flamenco—it's singing, it's dancing, it's guitar playing! It's an exciting, expressive art form that has evolved over hundreds of years. With captivating photographs and engaging text, George Ancona explores the origins, history, techniques, and performance of flamenco. Come along and catch flamenco fever. ¡Olé!   Lexile: 900L   (Grades 2–6)   NF

Engle, Margarita. *The Firefly Letters: A Suffragette's Journey to Cuba.*

ISBN-13: 9780805090826

> The freedom to roam is something that women and girls in Cuba do not have. Yet when Fredrika Bremer visits from Sweden in 1851 to learn about the people of this magical island, she is accompanied by Cecilia, a young slave who longs for her lost home in Africa. Soon Elena, the wealthy daughter of the house, sneaks out to join them. As the three women explore the lush countryside, they form a bond that breaks the barriers of language and culture.   Lexile: N/A   (Grades 5–9)   F

Flores-Galbis, Enrique. *90 Miles to Havana.*   ISBN-13: 9781596431683

> When Julian's parents make the heartbreaking decision to send him and his two brothers away from Cuba to Miami via the Pedro Pan operation, the boys are thrust into a new world where bullies run rampant and it's not always clear how best to protect themselves.

Lexile: 790L   (Grades 4–7)   F

Illustrator Award Winner

Velasquez, Eric. *Grandma's Gift.*   ISBN-13: 9780802735362

> After they prepare their traditional Puerto Rican celebration, Eric and Grandma visit the Metropolitan Museum of Art for a school project, where he sees a painting by Diego Velásquez and realizes for the first time that he could be an artist when he grows up. Grandma witnesses his fascination and presents Eric with the perfect Christmas gift: a sketchbook and colored pencils to use in his first steps toward becoming an artist.

Lexile: N/A   (Grades K–3)   NF

Illustrator Honor Book

Córdova, Amy, text by Carmen Tafolla. *Fiesta Babies.*   ISBN-13: 9781582463193

These Fiesta Babies dance, march on parade, and sing along to mariachi songs in their spirited celebration of fiestas. From piñatas to flower coronas, little ones are introduced to the many colorful aspects of an important and lively Latino cultural tradition.

Lexile: N/A   (Ages up to 3 years)   F

Diaz, David, text by Amy Novesky. *Me, Frida.*   ISBN-13: 9780810989696

The story of how artist Frida Kahlo's experience when she moved to San Francisco from Mexico with her husband, artist Diego Rivera. At first she felt overwhelmed, lost, and lonely. But over time, she began to appreciate the beauty and inspiration that the city offered. Through landscapes, cityscapes, and interiors the story illustrates how this famous artist found her inner strength and made her dreams come true.   Lexile: (Grades Pre-K–3)

Tonatiuh, Duncan. *Dear Primo: A Letter to My Cousin.*   ISBN-13: 9780810938724

Charlie lives in the United States, and his cousin Carlitos lives in Mexico. Through letters, both boys share their experiences growing up, including the sights and sounds of their environment along with the language differences and similarities. Although they seem to live very different lives, they find that they have much more in common as these described experiences are representative of the ancient art of the Mixtecs and other cultures of Mexico.

Lexile: 610   (Grades Pre-K–4)

2010

Author Award Winner

Alvarez, Julia. *Return to Sender.*   ISBN-13: 9780375851230

After Tyler's father is injured in a tractor accident, his family is forced to hire migrant Mexican workers to help save their Vermont farm from foreclosure. Tyler isn't sure what to make of these workers. Are they undocumented? This is a novel full of hope, but no easy answers.

Lexile: 0890L   (Grades 5–7)   F

Author Honor Books

Bernier-Grand, Carmen T. *Diego: Bigger Than Life.*   ISBN-13: 9780761453833

Carmen T. Bernier-Grand's inspiring free verse and David Diaz's vivid paintings capture the defining moments and emotions of Rivera's tumultuous life, including his stormy relationship with artist Frida Kahlo and his passion for his art. Rivera's energy, physique, and love for women, and his work were all "bigger than life." A biography, chronology, glossary, sources, notes, and famous quotations are included.   Lexile: N/A   (Grades 6–9)   NF

Lázaro, Georgina. *Federico García Lorca.*   ISBN-13: 9781933032399

This biography in pictures brings to life the early experiences of Spanish poet Federico García Lorca. Every child can relate to his story such as worrying about fitting in with other children, and readers will be engaged by the colorful and often amusing illustrations showing details from Federico's actual home.   Lexile: N/A   (Grades 4–7)   NF

Illustration Award Winner

⌐, ᴿafael, text by Pat Mora. *Book Fiesta!: Celebrate Children's Day/Book Day / Celebremos El día de los niños/El día de los libros.* ISBN-13: 9780061288777

Take a ride in a long submarine or fly away in a hot air balloon. Whatever you do, just be sure to bring your favorite book. Lexile: N/A (Grades Pre-K–1) F

Illustrator Honor Books

Diaz, David, text by Carmen T. Bernier-Grand. *Diego: Bigger Than Life.*

ISBN-13: 9780761453833

This book presents the defining moments and emotions of Rivera's tumultuous life, including his stormy relationship with artist Frida Kahlo and his passion for his art. Rivera's energy, physique, love for women, and his work were all bigger than life.

Lexile: N/A (Grades 6–9) NF

Morales, Yuyi, text by Tony Johnston. *My Abuelita.* ISBN-13: 9780152163303

Abuelita's hair is the color of salt. Her face is as crinkled as a dried chile. She booms out words as wild as blossoms blooming. She stuffs her *carcacha*, her jalopy, with all the things she needs: a plumed snake, a castle, a skeleton, and more. Her grandson knows he has the most amazing grandmother ever—with a very important job. What does Abuelita do? With her booming voice and wonderful props, Abuelita is a storyteller. Next to being a grandmother, that may be the most important job of all. Lexile: N/A (Grades Pre-K–3) F

Parra, John, text by Pat Mora. *Gracias. Thanks.* ISBN-13: 9781600602580

A young multiracial boy celebrates family, friendship, and fun by telling about some of the everyday things for which he is thankful. Lexile: N/A (Grades Pre-K–2) F

2009

Author Award Winner

Engle, Margarita. *The Surrender Tree: Poems of Cuba's Struggle for Freedom.*

ISBN-13: 9780805086744

It is 1896 and Cuba has fought three wars for independence and still is not free. People have been rounded up in reconcentration camps with too little food and too much illness. Rosa is a nurse, but she dares not go to the camps. So she turns hidden caves into hospitals for those who know how to find her. Lexile: NPL (Grades 6–12) NF

Author Honor Books

González, Lucia. *The Storyteller's Candle / La velita de los cuentos.*

ISBN-13: 9780892392377

In the winter of 1929, cousins Hildamar and Santiago move to New York from Puerto Rico. As Three Kings' Day approaches, Hildamar and Santiago mourn the loss of their home and wonder about their future in this new city. But when a Puerto Rican librarian, Pura Belpré, introduces the public library to immigrants living in El Barrio and hosts the neighborhood's first Three Kings' Day fiesta, the cousins find themselves feeling more welcome in their new city.   Lexile: N/A   (Grade 1)   F

Jiménez, Francisco. *Reaching Out.*   ISBN-13: 9780547250304

This is the story of how Francisco coped with poverty, with his guilt over leaving his family financially strapped, with his self-doubt about succeeding academically, and with separation.   Lexile: 0910L   (Grade 6–11)   F

Morales, Yuyi. *Just in Case: A Trickster Tale and Spanish Alphabet Book.*

ISBN-13: 9781596433298

Morales takes us on a new journey with Señor Calvera, the skeleton from Day of the Dead celebrations.   Lexile: N/A   (Grades Pre-K–3)   F

Illustration Award Winner

Morales, Yuyi. *Just in Case: A Trickster Tale and Spanish Alphabet Book.*

ISBN-13: 9781596433298

Yuyi Morales takes us on a new journey with Señor Calvera, the skeleton from Day of the Dead celebrations.   Lexile: N/A   (Grades Pre-K–3)   F

Illustrator Honor Books

Córdova, Amy, text by Carmen Tafolla. *What Can You Do with a Rebozo?*

ISBN-13: 9781582462202

In a playful celebration of a vibrant culture, a young girl and her family show all the things they do in their daily lives with a rebozo, a traditional Mexican woven shawl. Lively prose and rich illustrations honor a warm and colorful cultural icon. You can do almost anything with a rebozo—and a little imagination!   Lexile: 670L   (Grades Pre-K–3)   F

Delacre, Lula, text by Lucia González. *The Storyteller's Candle / La velita de los cuentos.*

ISBN-13: 9780892392377

In the winter of 1929, cousins Hildamar and Santiago move to New York from Puerto Rico. As Three Kings' Day approaches, Hildamar and Santiago mourn the loss of their home and wonder about their future in this new city. But when a Puerto Rican librarian, Pura Belpré, introduces the immigrants to the public library and hosts the neighborhood's first Three Kings' Day fiesta, the cousins find themselves feeling more welcome in their new city.

Lexile: N/A   (Grade 1)   F

..ly, text by Arthus Dorros. ***Papá and Me.*** ISBN-13: 9780060581565

..oung boy and his papa may speak both Spanish and English, but the most important language they speak is the language of love. Lexile: AD250L (Grades Pre-K–3) F

2008

Author Award Winner

Engle, Margarita. ***The Poet Slave of Cuba: A Biography of Juan Francisco Manzano.***

ISBN-13: 9780312659288

This is a lyrical biography of a Cuban slave who escaped to become a celebrated poet. Powerful, haunting poems and breathtaking illustrations create a portrait of a life in which even the pain of slavery could not extinguish the capacity for hope.

Lexile: NPL (Grades 5–12) NF

Author Honor Books

Bernier-Grand, Carmen T. ***Frida: ¡Viva la vida! Long Live Life!*** ISBN-13: 9780761453369

Frida Kahlo, a native of Mexico, is described here in biographical poems accompanied by her own artwork. Both text and images reveal the anguish and joy of her two marriages to muralist Diego Rivera, her lifelong suffering from a crippling bus accident, and her thirst for life, even as she tasted death. Lexile: N/A (Grades Pre-K–4) NF

Deedy, Carmen Agra. ***Martina the Beautiful Cockroach: A Cuban Folktale.***

ISBN-13: 9781561453993

This retelling of a popular Cuban story shares a secret closely guarded by Cuban grandmothers—at least, by Cuban grandmothers of cockroaches.

Lexile: AD720L (Grades Pre-K–4) F

Montes, Marisa. ***Los Gatos Black on Halloween.*** ISBN-13: 9780805074291

Follow *los monstruos* and *los esqueletos* to the Halloween party. Under October's *luna*, full and bright, the monsters are throwing a ball in the Haunted Hall.

Lexile: N/A (Grades Pre-K–4) F

Illustration Award Winner

Morales, Yuyi, text by Marisa Montes. ***Los Gatos Black on Halloween.***

ISBN-13: 9780805074291

This lively bilingual Halloween poem introduces young readers to a spooky array of Spanish words that will open their *ojos* to the chilling delights of the season. Readers will enjoy October's *luna*, the monsters as the monsters are throwing a ball in the Haunted Hall: *las brujas* on their broomsticks and *los muertos* rising from their coffins to join in the fun. *Los esqueletos* rattle their bones while even more scary creatures plan to join the fun.

Lexile: N/A (Grades Pre-K–4) F

Illustrator Honor Books

Colón, Raul, text by Monica Brown. *My Name Is Gabito: The Life of Gabriel García Márquez / Me llamo Gabito: la vida de Gabriel García Márquez.*   ISBN-13: 9780873589086

Using the imagery from his novels, Monica Brown traces Gabriel García Márquez's life from his childhood in Colombia to today in this creative, nonfiction picture book.

Lexile: AD910L   (Grades Pre-K–4)   NF

Gonzalez, Maya Christina. *My Colors, My World / Mis colores, mi mundo.*

ISBN-13: 9780892392216

Little Maya longs to find brilliant, beautiful, inspiring color in her world . . . but Maya's world, the Mojave Desert, seems to be filled with nothing but sand. With the help of a feathered friend, she searches everywhere to discover color in her world.

Lexile: AD560L   (Grades Pre-K–8)   F

2006

Author Award Winner

Canales, Viola. *The Tequila Worm.*   ISBN-13: 9780375840890

When Sofia is singled out to receive a scholarship to boarding school, she longs to explore life beyond the barrio, even though it means leaving her family to navigate a strange world of rich, privileged kids. It's a different *mundo*, but one where Sofia's traditions take on new meaning and illuminate her path.   Lexile: 0830L   (Grades 7–11)   F

Author Honor Books

Bernier-Grand, Carmen T. *César: ¡Sí, Se Puede! Yes, We Can!*   ISBN-13: 9780761458333

This award-winning, picture-book biography in free-verse celebrates the life of the great labor leader, César Chávez.   Lexile: N/A   (Grades 3–6)   NF

Mora, Pat. *Doña Flor: A Tall Tale About a Giant Woman with a Great Big Heart.*

ISBN-13: 9780375823374

Doña Flor is a giant woman who lives in a puebla with lots of families. She loves her neighbors—she lets the children use her flowers for trumpets, and the families use her leftover tortillas for rafts. So when a huge puma is terrifying the village, of course Flor goes to investigate.   Lexile: AD860L   (Grades Pre-K–3)   F

Ryan, Pam Muñoz and Peter Sís. *Becoming Naomi León.*   ISBN-13: 9780439269971

When young Naomi's absent mother resurfaces to claim her, Naomi runs away to Mexico with her great-grandmother and younger brother in search of her father.

Lexile: 0830L   (Grades 4–7)   F

Illustration Award Winner

Colón, Raul, text by Pat Mora. *Doña Flor: A Tall Tale About a Giant Woman with a Great Big Heart.*   ISBN-13: 9780375823374

Doña Flor is a giant woman who lives in a puebla with lots of families. She loves her neighbors—she lets the children use her flowers for trumpets, and the families use her leftover tortillas for rafts. So when a huge puma is terrifying the village, of course, Flor goes to investigate.   Lexile: AD860   (Grades Pre-K–3)   F

Illustrator Honor Books

Delacre, Lulu. *Arrorró, Mi Niño: Latino Lullabies and Gentle Games.*

ISBN-13: 9781600604416

This award-winning title is written in both Spanish and English. It is designed for use with very young children at playtime or bedtime. The deep love between adults (mostly mothers) and their children is beautifully portrayed.   Lexile: N/A   (Grades Pre-K–1)   F

Diaz, David, text by Carmen T. Bernier-Grand. *César: ¡Sí, Se Puede! Yes, We Can!*

ISBN-13: 9780761458333

An award-winning picture-book biography in free-verse celebrating the life of the great labor leader, César Chávez.   Lexile: N/A   (Grades 3–6)   NF

López, Rafael, text by Monica Brown. *My Name Is Celia / Me Llamo Celia: The Life of Celia Cruz / La Vida de Celia Cruz.*   ISBN-13: 9780873588720

A bilingual story of Celia Cruz's life as she becomes a well-known singer in her homeland of Cuba, then moves to New York City and Miami where she and others create a new type of music called salsa.   Lexile: AD850L   (Grades K–4)   NF

2004
Author Award Winner

Alvarez, Julia. *Before We Were Free.*   ISBN-13: 9780440237846

From renowned author Julia Alvarez comes an unforgettable story about adolescence, perseverance, and one girl's struggle to be free. In the early 1960s in the Dominican Republic, 12-year-old Anita learns that her family is involved in the underground movement to end the bloody rule of the dictator, General Trujillo.   Lexile: 890L   (Grades 7–12)   F

Author Honor Books

Osa, Nancy. *Cuba 15.*   ISBN-13: 9780385732338

All Violet Paz, a Chicago high school student, knows is that she's got to form her own opinions, even if this jolts her family into unwanted confrontations. After all, a *quince* girl is supposed to embrace responsibility—and to Violet that includes understanding the Cuban heritage that binds her to a homeland she's never seen. She reluctantly prepares for her upcoming *quince*, a Spanish nickname for the celebration of an Hispanic girl's 15th birthday.

Lexile: 0750L   (Grade 7)   F

Pérez, Amada Irma. *My Diary from Here to There / Mi diario de aquí hasta allá.*

ISBN-13: 9780892392308

With humor and insight, Pérez recounts the story of her family's immigration to America. Maya Christina Gonzalez's vibrant artwork captures every detail of their journey.

Lexile: N/A   (Grade 1–5)   NF

Illustration Award Winner

Morales, Yuyi. *Just a Minute: A Trickster Tale and Counting Book.*   ISBN-13: 9780811837583

In this version of a traditional trickster tale, Señor Calavera arrives at Grandma Beetle's door, ready to take her to the next life. But after helping her count, in English and Spanish, as she makes her birthday preparations, he changes his mind.

Lexile: 540L   (Grades Pre-K–3)   F

Illustrator Honor Books

Casilla, Robert, text by L. King Pérez. *First Day in Grapes.*   ISBN-13: 9781584300458

Chico's family moves up and down the state of California to pick fruits and vegetables, and every September, Chico has to start at a new school. When Chico starts the third grade after his migrant worker family moves again to begin harvesting California grapes, he finds that self-confidence and math skills help him cope with the first day of school.

Lexile: AD570L   (Grades 1–5)   F

Diaz, David, text by Nancy Andrews-Goebel. *The Pot That Juan Built.*

ISBN-13: 9781600608483

This cumulative rhyme summarizes the life's work of renowned Mexican potter, Juan Quezada. Additional information describes the process he uses to create his pots after the style of the Casas Grandes people.   Lexile: 1000   (Grades 1–4)   NF

Morales, Yuyi, text by Kathleen Krull. *Harvesting Hope: The Story of César Chávez.*

ISBN-13: 9780152014377

A biography of César Chávez, from age 10, when he and his family lived happily on their Arizona ranch, to age 38, when he led a peaceful protest against California migrant workers' miserable working conditions.   Lexile: AD800L   (Grades 1–4)   NF

2002

Author Award Winner

Ryan, Pam Muñoz. *Esperanza Rising.*   ISBN-13: 9780439120425

Esperanza thought she'd always live with her family on their ranch in Mexico—she'd always have fancy dresses, a beautiful home, and servants. But a sudden tragedy forces Esperanza and Mama to flee to California during the Great Depression and to settle in a camp for Mexican farm workers. Esperanza isn't ready for the hard labor, financial struggles, or lack of acceptance she now faces. When their new life is threatened, Esperanza must find a way to rise above her difficult circumstances, as Mama's life and her own depend on it.   Lexile: 750L   (Grades K–4)   F

Author Honor Books

Alarcón, Francisco X. *Iguanas in the Snow / Iguanas en la nieve.* ISBN-13: 9780892391684

This collection invites readers to celebrate winter by the seashore, in the city of San Francisco, and in the ancient redwood forests of the Sierras. Lexile: N/A (Grades K–4) NF

Jiménez, Francisco. *Breaking Through.* ISBN-13: 9780618342488

Without bitterness or sentimentality, Francisco Jimenez finishes telling the story of his youth. Once again, his simple yet powerful words will open readers' hearts and minds. Having come from Mexico to California ten years ago, 14-year-old Francisco is still working in the fields but fighting to improve his life and complete his education.

Lexile: 0750L (Grades 6–12) F

Illustration Award Winner

Guevara, Susan, text by Gary Soto. *Chato and the Party Animals.* ISBN-13: 9780756929213

Chato, the coolest cat in the barrio, loves to party. So when he learns that Novio Boy has never had a birthday party, Chato decides to throw him a surprise *pachanga*. He gets right to work inviting everyone in the neighborhood, cooking up a feast, arranging for music and a piñata, and even ordering a special cake. Chato's sure that he's thought of everything. But when it comes time for the party, he realizes that he forgot the most important thing of all, Novio Boy. Lexile: 0440L (Grades K–4) F

Illustrator Honor Book

Cepeda, Joe, text by Marisa Montes. *Juan Bobo Goes to Work.* ISBN-13: 9780688162337

What can you do with a boy who tries to do things right but leaves only disaster in his wake? Juan Bobo sets out to find work at the farm and the grocery store. His given tasks are simple and the directions are clear but he always finds a way to mess things up.

Lexile: 390L (Grades K–4) F

2000

Author Award Winner

Ada, Alma Flor. *Under the Royal Palms: A Childhood in Cuba.* ISBN-13: 9780689806315

Young readers will be inspired by this collection of stories and reminiscences drawn from a childhood on the island of Cuba. Through those stories we see how the many events and relationships the author experienced helped shape who she is today. We learn of a deep friendship with a beloved dance teacher that helped sustain young Alma Flor through a miserable year in school. Lexile: 1070L (Grades 3–7) NF

Author Honor Books

Alarcón, Francisco X. *From the Bellybutton of the Moon and Other Summer Poems / Del ombligo de la luna y otros poemas de verano.* ISBN-13: 9780892392018

This is a bilingual collection of poems in which the renowned Mexican American poet revisits and celebrates his childhood memories of summers, Mexico, and nature.

Lexile: NPL (Grades 1–5) NF

Herrera, Juan Felipe. *Laughing out Loud, I Fly: Poems in English and Spanish.*

ISBN-13: 9780060276041

Vibrant poems dance across these pages in a dazzling explosion of two languages. Skillfully crafted, beautiful, joyful, fun, the poems are paired with whimsical black-and-white drawings by Karen Barbour. Lexile: NP (Grades 7–12) NF

Illustration Award Winner

Garza, Carmen Lomas. *Magic Windows / Ventanas mágicas.* ISBN-13: 9780892391578

Through the magic windows of her cut-paper art, Garza shows us her family, her life as an artist, and the legends of her Aztec past. Lexile: AD710L (Grades 1–4) NF

Illustrator Honor Books

Ancona, George. *Barrio: José's Neighborhood.* ISBN-13: 9780152010485

A young first-generation American celebrates the festive, intimate spirit of his community. Welcome to Jose's neighborhood. In his barrio, people speak an easy mix of Spanish and English and sometimes even Chinese. Lexile: 0920L (Grades 2–7) F

Carling, Amelia Lau. *Mama & Papa Have a Store.* ISBN-13: 9780803720442

Author and artist Amelia Lau Carling depicts an almost magical kingdom where Chinese, Guatemalan, and native cultures meet in harmony, and where children can play and learn about all the different peoples who bring the city to vibrant life.

Lexile: 810L (Grades Pre-K–3) F

Dávalos, Felipe, text by Joseph Slate. *The Secret Stars.* ISBN-13: 9780761451525

In New Mexico on a rainy, icy Night of the Three Kings, Sila and Pepe worry that the kings will not be able to use the stars to navigate, so their grandmother takes them on a magical journey to see the secret stars all around them. Lexile: N/A (Grades K–3) F

Scott O'Dell Award for Historical Fiction

In 1982, author Scott O'Dell established the Scott O'Dell Award for Historical Fiction. The annual award of $5,000 goes to an author for a commendable book published in the previous year for children or young adults. Scott O'Dell established this award to encourage other writers to focus on historical fiction. Visit http://www.scottodell.com/pages/ScottO'DellAwardforHis toricalFiction.aspx for awards prior to 2000.

Hill, Kirkpatrick, illustrated by LeUyen Pham. (2014). *Bo at Ballard Creek.*

ISBN-13: 9780805093513

Set in 1920's Alaska, two gold miners meet a young orphan girl, Bo, and decide to raise her as their own. With the help of the people living in the nearby Eskimo village, Bo pitches in to help with chores, meets all kinds of people and animals, and experiences all the excitement of growing up after one of Alaska's gold rushes.   Lexile: 840   (Grades 1–4)

Erdrich, Louise. (2013). *Chickadee.*

ISBN-13: 9780060577926

Erdrich has penned a new edition to the Birchbark House series that follows one Ojibwe family through 100 years of living in America. Chicakdee and Makoons are twin brothers who have never been apart. As Chickadee tries to make his way home after the unthinkable happens, his family pulls up stakes and heads out to look for him. This story takes readers on a journey between the boy and his family as they search for each other along the Red River of the North and into the Great Plains.   Lexile: 800   (Grades 3–7)

Gantos, Jack. (2012). *Dead End in Norvelt.*

ISBN-13: 9780374379933

As one obituary leads to another, Jack is launched on a strange adventure involving molten wax, Eleanor Roosevelt, twisted promises, a homemade airplane, Girl Scout cookies, a man on a trike, a dancing plague, voices from the past, Hells Angels, and possibly murder.

Lexile: 920L   (Grades 5–9)   F

Garcia-Williams, Rita. (2011). *One Crazy Summer.*

ISBN-13: 9780060760908

Set during one of the most tumultuous years in recent American history, this book is the heartbreaking, funny tale of three girls in search of the mother who abandoned them.

Lexile: N/A   (Grades 4–7)   F

Phelan, Matt. (2010). *The Storm in the Barn.*

ISBN-13: 9780763652906

This tale of a boy in Dust Bowl America will resonate with readers. In Kansas in the year 1937, 11-year-old Jack Clark faces his share of ordinary challenges: local bullies, his father's failed expectations, a little sister with an eye for trouble. But he also has to deal with the effects of the Dust Bowl, including rising tensions in his small town and the spread of a shadowy illness.   Lexile: GN430L   (Grade 5–7)   F

Anderson, Laurie Halse. (2009). *Chains.*

ISBN-13: 9781416905851

When Isabel meets Curzon, a slave with ties to the Patriots, he encourages her to spy on her owners, who know details of British plans for invasion. She is reluctant at first, but when the unthinkable happens to her sister, Ruth, Isabel realizes her loyalty is available to the bidder who can provide her with freedom.   Lexile: 780L   (Grades 5–7)   F

Curtis, Christopher Paul. (2008). *Elijah of Buxton.*

ISBN-13: 9780439023450

Elijah embarks on a dangerous journey to America in pursuit of the thief who stole his friend's money, and Elijah discovers firsthand the unimaginable horrors of the life his parents fled—a life from which he'll always be free if he can find the courage to get back home.

Lexile: 1070L   (Grades 3–8)   F

Klages, Ellen. (2007). *The Green Glass Sea.* ISBN-13: 9780142411490

A backlist gem gets a brand-new look! It's 1943, and 11-year-old Dewey Kerrigan is en route to New Mexico to live with her mathematician father. Soon she arrives at a town that officially doesn't exist. It is called Los Alamos, and it is abuzz with activity, as scientists and mathematicians from all over America and Europe work on the biggest secret of all—"the gadget." Lexile: 0790L (Grades 4–6) F

Erdrich, Louise. (2006). *The Game of Silence.* ISBN-13: 9780060297893

The chimookomanag, or white people, want Omakayas and her people to leave their island in Lake Superior and move farther west. Omakayas realizes that something so valuable, so important that she never knew she had it in the first place, is in danger: her home and her way of life. Lexile: 900L (Grades 4–7) F

LaFaye, A. (2005). *Worth.* ISBN-13: 9781416916246

After breaking his leg, 11-year-old Nate feels useless because he cannot work on the family farm in 19th-century Nebraska. So when his father brings home an orphan boy to help with the chores, Nate feels even worse. Lexile: 0830L (Grades 4–7) F

Peck, Richard. (2004). *The River Between Us.* ISBN-13: 9780142403105

When Tilly's mother invites two women from a recently landed steamboat to board at her house, the whole world shifts for the Pruitts and for their visitors as well. Within a page-turning tale of mystery, adventure, and the civilian Civil War experience, this is a portrait of the lifelong impact that one person can have on another. Lexile: 0740L (Grades 5–9) F

Pearsall, Shelley. (2003). *Trouble Don't Last.* ISBN-13: 9780440418115

Eleven-year-old Samuel was born as Master Hackler's slave, and working the Kentucky farm is the only life he's ever known until one dark night in 1859, that is. With no warning, cranky old Harrison, a fellow slave, pulls Samuel from his bed and together they run. Lexile: 0720L (Grades 4–8) F

Taylor, Mildred D. (2002). *The Land.* ISBN-13: 9780142501467

After the Civil War, Paul, the son of a white father and a black mother, finds himself caught between the two worlds of colored folks and white folks as he pursues his dream of owning his own land. Lexile: 0760L (Grades 7–12) F

Lisle, Janet Taylor. (2001). *The Art of Keeping Cool.* ISBN-13: 9780689837883

In 1942, Robert and his cousin Elliot uncover long-hidden family secrets while staying in their grandparents' Rhode Island town, where they also become involved with a German artist who is suspected of being a spy. Lexile: 0730L (Grades 5–9) F

Bat-Ami, Miriam. (2000). *Two Suns in the Sky.* ISBN-13: 9780613444255

In 1944, an upstate New York teenager named Christine meets and falls in love with Adam, a Yugoslavian Jew living in a refugee camp, despite their parents' conviction that they do not belong together. Lexile: 550L (Grades 4–8) F

7

Well-Known Authors for Children and Young Adults

In this chapter, you will discover some well-known and highly regarded authors of children's and young adult books. While this list doesn't address all of the many wonderful children's and young adult authors out there today, these authors offer a variety of books across genres that incorporate important themes of age, gender, culture, and other topics. Everyone can relate to these real-life stories of humor, candidness, and a sense of pride in one's background. Many of the books also deal with issues on identity, family, friends, legends, adolescence, and relevant subject areas. Each author is responsible for many, many books, though only a handful are detailed here. With a bit of research on your part, you can discover the extensive lists of books that these authors have produced.

Alma Flor Ada (Grades K–4)

Alma Flor Ada, professor emerita at the University of San Francisco, has devoted her life to social justice, advocating for those who have been marginalized by society, and for critcally conscious pedagogy in teacher practice. Many of her books focus on the celebration of life in all its facets: family, friends, nature, play, activities, discoveries, and joy.

Con Cariño, Amalia.
ISBN-13: 9781442424029, 2012

Amalia finds great comfort in times shared with her grandmother: cooking, listening to stories and music, learning, and looking through her treasured box of family cards. But when another loss racks Amalia's life, nothing makes sense anymore. In her sorrow, will Amalia realize just how special she is, even when the ones she loves are no longer near?

Lexile: 940L   (Grades 3–7)   F

Dancing Home.
ISBN-13: 9781416900887, 2011

A year of discoveries culminates in a performance full of surprises, as two girls find their own way to belong. Mexico may be her parents' home, but it's certainly not Margie's. She has finally convinced the other kids at school she is 100 percent American—just like them. But when her Mexican cousin Lupe visits, the image she's created for herself crumbles. Little by little, the girls' individual steps find the rhythm of one shared dance, and they learn what "home" really means.

Lexile: 960L   (Grades 3–7)   F

Daniel's Mystery Egg.
ISBN-13: 9780152048457, 2003

Daniel finds an egg. What kind of animal will this mystery egg hatch? Imaginations run wild as the kids in Daniel's class guess what sort of surprise the egg has in store.

Lexile: N/A   (Grades K–2)   F

Daniel's Pet.
ISBN-13: 9780152062439, 2008

Daniel loves his new pet. But what will happen when he takes good care of his pet chicken and it hatches a surprise?

Lexile: N/A   (Grades Pre-K–3)   F

Dear Peter Rabbit.
ISBN-13: 9780689812897, 1997

Peter Rabbit has a cold and cannot attend the Three Little Pigs' housewarming party. The festivities could be ruined by the Big Bad Wolf. This story is conveyed through letters exchanged among these beloved characters.

Lexile: 0780L   (Grades K–4)   F

Gathering the Sun: An Alphabet in Spanish and English.
ISBN-13: 9780688170677, 2001

Simple poems in Spanish and English, one for each letter of the Spanish alphabet, describe the wonder of the vegetable and fruit farms. Together, the poems and the rich illustrations celebrate the glory of nature and the hearts of all who dedicate their lives to working the land.

Lexile: 0590L   (Grades K–5)   NF

The Gold Coin.
ISBN-13: 9780689717932, 1994

Determined to steal an old woman's gold coin, a young thief follows her all around the Central America countryside and finds himself involved in a series of unexpected activities that explore love and faith in the human spirit.

Lexile: AD550L   (Grades K–4)   F

I Love Saturdays y Domingos.
ISBN-13: 9780689874093, 2004

As we follow the narrator to the circus and the pier, as she stories from her grandparents' pasts and celebrates her birthday, the depth and joy of both cultures are conveyed in Spanish and English. This affirmation of both heritages will speak to all children who want to know more about their own families and ethnic backgrounds.

Lexile: 0510L   (Grades K–4)   F

Let Me Help! ¡Quiero Ayudar!
ISBN-13: 9780892392322, 2010

This Cinco de Mayo tale is the story of every young reader who has been told he or she is too little or too young to help.   Lexile: AD630L   (Grades Pre-K–3)   F

The Lizard and the Sun / La Lagartija y el Sol.
ISBN-13: 9780440415312, 1999

When the sun disappears from ancient Mexico, a little lizard refuses to give up her quest to bring back light and warmth to everyone.   Lexile: AD580L   (Grades K–4)   F

Mamá Goose: A Latina Nursery Treasure.
ISBN-13: 9780786852406, 2006

A comprehensive bilingual folklore collection full of charm and humor, rich with the diversity of Latino cultures, this one-of-a-kind treasury is the perfect introduction to Latino folklore for English speakers and a treasure of familiar favorites for Spanish speakers.

Lexile: N/A   (Ages up to K)   NF

My Name Is Maria Isabel.
ISBN-13: 9780689802171, 1995

Third-grader Maria Isabel, born in Puerto Rico and now living in the United States, wants badly to fit in at school, and the teacher's writing assignment "My Greatest Wish" gives her that opportunity.   Lexile: 0860L   (Grades 2–5)   F

¡Pio Peep! Traditional Spanish Nursery Rhymes.
ISBN-13: 9780688160197, 2003

A bilingual collection of traditional nursery rhymes that celebrates childhood and Spanish and Latin American heritage.   Lexile: N/A   (Grade Pre–K)   F

Tales Our Abuelitas Told: A Hispanic Folktale Collection.
ISBN-13: 9780689825835, 2006

A mixture of popular tales and literary lore, this anthology celebrates Hispanic culture and its many roots: Indigenous, African, Arab, Hebrew, and Spanish.

Lexile: N/A   (Grades K–5)   F

Ten Little Puppies.
ISBN-13: 9780061470448, 2011

Count along in Spanish and English as each one of the ten adorable puppies disappears from the pages—it's a bilingual bonanza.   Lexile: N/A   (Grades Pre-K–1)   NF

Three Golden Oranges.
ISBN-13: 9781442474963, 2012

A retelling of a well-loved traditional story about Blancaflor, a mythical young woman who appears in various stories throughout the Hispanic world. Acting on the advice of the old woman on the cliff by the sea, three brothers who wish to find brides go in search of three golden oranges.   Lexile: N/A   (Grades K–12)   F

Under the Royal Palms: A Childhood in Cuba.
ISBN-13: 9780689806315, 1998

In this companion volume to Ada's *Where the Flame Trees Bloom*, the author offers young readers another inspiring collection of stories and reminiscences drawn from her childhood on the island of Cuba.   Lexile: 1070L   (Grades 3–7)   NF

The Unicorn of the West.
ISBN-13: 9781416968436, 2007

A young unicorn finds that both friendship on an individual level and peace on a universal level are important. The story is well told and folkloric in its approach as a pattern develops and repeats with each encounter with a different animal.   Lexile: N/A   (Grades Pre-K–3)   F

Where the Flame Trees Bloom.　　　　　ISBN-13: 9781416968405, 2007

Eleven stories from Ada's own childhood in Cuba—true stories about relatives and friends and the hacienda where she grew up for much of her elementary years.

Lexile: 1030L　(Grades 4–7)　NF

With Love, Little Red Hen.　　　　　ISBN-13: 9780689870613, 2004

Hidden Forest has a new resident. Little Red Hen and her seven little chicks have moved into a cottage and plan to grow a bountiful crop of corn in the nearby field. The problem is that none of the Red Hen's neighbors are willing to help with the hard work. "Not I," says the dog, the goose, and the lazy cat. So Goldilocks, who has heard about the new arrivals from her friend Little Red Riding Hood, comes up with a neighborly idea: Why don't all the residents of Hidden Forest chip in and work on the garden? Better yet, why not make it a surprise? Of course, there are a couple of residents who might not be so cooperative.

Lexile: 0610L　(Grades K–4)　F

Yours Truly, Goldilocks.　　　　　ISBN-13: 9780689844522, 2001

In this sequel to *Dear Peter Rabbit*, a few more beloved fairy-tale characters are pen pals. This book presents the correspondence of Goldilocks, the three pigs, Baby Bear, Peter Rabbit, and Little Red Riding Hood as they plan to attend a housewarming party for the pigs and avoid the evil wolves in the forest.　　Lexile: 0810L　(Grades Pre-K–3)　F

Francisco X. Alarcón (Grades K–6)

Alarcón's writing offers perspective on Latino and gay identity, mythology, the Nahuatl language, Mesoamerican history, and American culture. Alarcón's books for children also include bilingual poetry collections.

Angels Ride Bikes: And Other Fall Poems / Los ángeles andan en bicicleta: Y otros poemas de otoño.　　　　　ISBN-13: 9780892391981, 2005

In this bilingual poetry book, Alarcón invites young readers to experience fall in Los Angeles, the City of the Angels, where dreams can come true. In the poet's whimsical imagination, mariachis play like angels, angels ride bikes, and the earth dances the *cha-cha-cha*. Alarcón celebrates the simple joys and trials of everyday life: a visit to the outdoor market, the arrival of the ice cream vendor, the first day of school. He honors his family and pays tribute to his mother, who taught him that with hard work and education he could realize his dreams.　　　　　Lexile: N/A　(Grades 1–4)　NF

Animal Poems of the Iguazú / Animalario del Iguazú.　　　　　ISBN-13: 9780892392254, 2008

In the lush rainforest of the Iguazú National Park, toucans and butterflies flit through the trees while sleek jaguars prowl the jungle floor.　　Lexile: N/A　(Grades 1–6)　NF

From the Bellybutton of the Moon and Other Summer Poems / Del ombligo de la luna y otros poemas de verano.
ISBN-13: 9780892392018, 1998

A bilingual collection of poems in which the renowned Mexican American poet revisits and celebrates his childhood memories of summers, Mexico, and nature.

Lexile: NPL (Grades 1–5) NF

From the Other Side of Night / Des otro lado de la noche.
ISBN-13: 9780816522309, 2002

Alarcón invokes both the mysteries of Mesoamerica and the "otherness" of his gay identity. In 14 lyrical poems open to wide interpretation, he transcends ethnic concerns to address social, sexual, and historical issues of concern to all Americans.

Lexile: N/A (Grades 1–4) NF

Iguanas in the Snow and Other Winter Poems / Iguanas en la nieve y otros poemas de invierno.
ISBN-13: 9780892391684, 2000

This collection invites us to celebrate winter, by the seashore, in the city of San Francisco, and in the ancient redwood forests of the Sierras.

Lexile: N/A (Grades K–4) NF

Laughing Tomatoes and Other Spring Poems / Jitomates risueños y otros poemas de primavera.
ISBN-13: 9780892391394, 1997

A bilingual collection of humorous and serious poems about family, nature, and celebrations by a renowned Mexican American poet.

Lexile: N/A (Grades 1–5) NF

Snake Poems: An Aztec Invocation.
ISBN-13: 9780811801614, 1992

Inspired by one of the few existing treatises on the culture of Nahuatl—the Indian language primarily spoken by the Aztec—*Snake Poems* represents the first time a contemporary writer has returned to the Aztec heritage, empowering himself not only as a translator and commentator but as a medium in the tradition of the poet as a shaman.

Lexile: NPL (Grades 1–4) NF

Eric Carle (Grades Pre-K–3)

The themes of Eric Carle's stories are usually drawn from his knowledge and love of nature, an interest shared by most small children. Besides being beautiful and entertaining, his books offer children the opportunity to learn something about the world around them. Additionally, Eric Carle's art is created in collage technique, using hand-painted papers, which he cuts and layers to form bright and cheerful images to match the text in his books.

10 Little Rubber Ducks.
ISBN-13: 9780061964282, 2010

Ten little rubber ducks overboard! Get swept away on a high seas voyage of discovery with 10 little rubber ducks as they float to every part of the world. They all find adventure, but one duck finds something very special! When a storm strikes a cargo ship, 10 rubber ducks are tossed overboard and swept off in ten different directions.
Lexile: N/A (Grades K–3) F

All in a Day.
ISBN-13: 9780698117723, 1999

Ten outstanding artists illustrate the similarities and differences in children and their activities in eight different parts of the world throughout one day.

Lexile: N/A   (Grades K–5)   NF

Artist to Artist: 23 Major Illustrators Talk to Children About Their Art.
ISBN-13: 9780399246005, 2007

In this anthology, 23 of the most honored and beloved artists in children's literature talk informally to children, sharing secrets about their art and how they began their adventures into illustration.
Lexile: N/A   (Grades K–6)   NF

The Artist Who Painted a Blue Horse.
ISBN-13: 9780399257131, 2011

The artist in this book paints the world as he sees it, just like a child. There's a red crocodile, an orange elephant, a purple fox, and a polka-dotted donkey. More than anything, there's imagination.
Lexile: N/A   (Grades 1–4)   F

Brown Bear, Brown Bear, What Do You See?
ISBN-13: 9780805017441, 1992

Children see a variety of animals, each one a different color, and a teacher looking at them.
Lexile: 0440L   (Grades Pre-K–2)   F

Chip Has Many Brothers.
ISBN-13: 9780399212833, 1985

This story is written by Hans Baumann and is based on Northern European and Native American myths and legends. While Chip's brothers are off hunting, he stays home with his sister Bright Sun and grandmother Nuni. These are the good times when Chip's animal friends Bear, Moose, and Beaver emerge from hiding and visit, safe from the older boys' arrows.
Lexile: N/A   (Grades Pre-K–2)   F

Do You Want to Be My Friend?
ISBN-13: 9780399215988, 1988

"Do you want to be my friend?" asks the little mouse as he hopefully follows a tail, finding at the end of it a rather unfriendly horse. But there's another tail, and another, and a strange, long, green one, too, that follows the mouse on his quest for a friend.

Lexile: 200L   (Grades K–3)   F

Dream Snow.
ISBN-13: 9780399235795, 2000

It's December 24th, and the old farmer settles down for a winter's nap, wondering how Christmas can come when there is no snow! It is in his dream that he imagines a snowstorm coming and covering him and his animals named One, Two, Three, Four, and Five, in a snowy blanket. But when the farmer awakens, he finds that it has really snowed outside, and now he remembers something. Putting on his red suit, he goes outside, puts some gifts under the tree for his animals, and presses a button near a Christmas tree, creating a most surprising musical treat for children everywhere.   Lexile: AD300L   (Grades K–3)   F

The Foolish Tortoise.
ISBN-13: 9780887080029, 1990

Children and adults alike will enjoy this jubilant tale of a tortoise on a journey of self-discovery. A tortoise realizes the need for a shell after several scary encounters.
Lexile: N/A   (Grades Pre-K–3)   F

From Head to Toe.
ISBN-13: 9780694013012, 1999

A delightful story that encourages children to copy a myriad of animal antics as they wiggle, stomp, thump, and bend across each meticulously designed and brilliantly colored page. This book encourages the reader to exercise by following the movements of various animals, which are presented in a question-and-answer format.

Lexile: N/A   (Grades Pre-K–2)   F

The Grouchy Ladybug.
ISBN-13: 9780064434508, 1996

A grouchy ladybug looking for a fight challenges everyone she meets regardless of their size or strength.

Lexile: 560L   (Grades Pre-K–3)   F

A House for Hermit Crab.
ISBN-13: 9780613901871, 2000

Join Hermit Crab as he learns an important lesson about growing up: for every friend and adventure left behind, there are new ones just ahead! A hermit crab who has outgrown his old shell moves into a new one, which he decorates and enhances with the various sea creatures he meets in his travels.

Lexile: 0480L   (Grades K–3)   F

Mister Seahorse.
ISBN-13: 9780399242694, 2004

Astonishingly beautiful collage illustrations introduce the very young to the wonders of aquatic life and some very special daddies. A hide-and-seek feature with acetate overlays adds a colorful surprise. After Mrs. Seahorse lays her eggs on Mr. Seahorse's belly, he drifts through the water, greeting other fish fathers who are taking care of their eggs.

Lexile: AD620L   (Grades K–3)   F

The Mixed-Up Chameleon.
ISBN-13: 9780064431620, 1988

The chameleon's life was not very exciting until the day it discovered it could change not only its color but its shape and size, too. When it saw the wonderful animals in the zoo, it immediately wanted to be like them and ended up like all of them at once with hilarious results.

Lexile: AD450L   (Grades Pre-K–2)   F

My Very First Book of Colors.
ISBN-13: 9780399243868, 2005

What color is a bluebird? Readers will see the color in the top half of a page that matches the picture on the bottom half. From pink flowers to purple grapes, this colorful book is full of fun and surprises.

Lexile: N/A   (Grades K–3)   NF

Pancakes, Pancakes!
ISBN-13: 9780689822469, 1998

The barnyard rooster crows and Jack wakes up—hungry, of course! What does he want for breakfast? A big pancake! But first, Jack's mother needs flour from the mill, an egg from the black hen, milk from the spotted cow, butter churned from fresh cream, and firewood for the stove.

Lexile: 0700L   (Grades Pre-K–3)   F

Papa, Please Get the Moon for Me.
ISBN-13: 9780887080265, 1991

Monica's father fulfills her request for the moon by taking it down after it is small enough to carry, but it continues to change in size.

Lexile: 0310L   (Grades K–3)   F

The Tiny Seed.   ISBN-13: 9780689842443, 2001

Join the tiny seed on an adventure as it becomes a giant flower!

Lexile: N/A   (Grades Pre-K–2)   NF

The Very Busy Spider.   ISBN-13: 9780399215926, 1989

Follow an industrious spider as she carefully spins her web. A cow, a pig, and other farm animals want her to play, but a busy spider needs to finish her work, or there'll be no dinner.

Lexile: 0130L   (Grades Pre-K–3)   F

The Very Clumsy Click Beetle.   ISBN-13: 9780399232015, 1999

A story of perseverance and pride in achievement complete with an ingenious fiber-optic microchip that truly gives voice to the valiant little beetle as it *clicks* its way through the pages.   Lexile: AD210L   (Grades K–3)   F

The Very Hungry Caterpillar.   ISBN-13: 9780399226236, 1984

Carle's classic tale of a voracious caterpillar who eats his way through the days of the week and then changes into a beautiful butterfly.   Lexile: 0460L   (Grades Pre-K–2)   F

The Very Lonely Firefly.   ISBN-13: 9780448458502, 1995

In this classic and heartwarming story, a very lonely firefly finally finds the friends he is seeking after a tireless search for belonging.   Lexile: AD530L   (Grades K–3)   F

The Very Quiet Cricket.   ISBN-13: 9780399218859, 1990

A small cricket hatches one warm day, and the other insects greet him. Though the little guy wants very much to respond, nothing happens when he rubs his wings together. Finally, as night falls, he spies another cricket and attempts to greet her. And this time he chirped the most beautiful sound that she had ever heard.   Lexile: AD430L   (Grades K–3)   F

Walter the Baker.   ISBN-13: 9780689820885, 1998

When the Duke notices that Walter the baker has substituted water for milk in his sweet rolls, he presents Walter with a challenge: create from one piece of dough a roll the sun can shine through three times, or be banished from the Duchy.

Lexile: 0550L   (Grades Pre-K–2)   F

Yangsook Choi (Grades K–4)

Yangsook Choi is a writer for children who feels that she must have a relationship and communication with kids to write for them. Yangsook believes the message needs to be positive with the power to enhance children's lives. She dedicates herself to telling stories of people and conventions of Asian origin.

Behind the Mask.   ISBN-13: 9780374305222, 2006

With vibrant illustrations, Choi joins Korean and American folk traditions in her story about a boy who finds a link to his grandfather, behind the mask.

Lexile: 610L   (Grades Pre-K–3)   F

Good-bye 382 Shin Dang Dong.   ISBN-13: 9780792279853, 2002

When her family moves to America, Jangmi finds it hard to say good-bye to relatives and friends, plus the food, customs, and beautiful things of her home in Korea.

Lexile: 620L   (Grades Pre-K–3)   F

The Name Jar.   ISBN-13: 9780440417996, 2003

After Unhei moves from Korea to the United States, her new classmates help her decide what her name should be.

Lexile: N/A   (Grades K–4)   F

New Cat.   ISBN-13: 9780374355128, 1999

Shortly after coming to America, Mr. Kim, owner of a tofu factory in the Bronx, gets a fluffy silver cat that makes her home in his factory and one night saves it from burning down.

Lexile: N/A   (Grades Pre-K–3)   F

The Sun Girl and the Moon Boy: A Korean Folktale.   ISBN-13: 9780679883869, 1997

This ancient tale reveals how a hungry tiger tries to trick a young boy and girl into thinking that he is their mother. But their sharp wits and a measure of good luck are enough to save the children and reunite them with their mother, high above in the sky.

Lexile: N/A   (Grades K–4)   F

Mem Fox (Grades K–3)

Mem Fox is Australia's most regarded picture-book author. Her first book, *Possum Magic*, is the bestselling children's book ever in Australia. In the United States, *Time for Bed* and *Wilfrid Gordon McDonald Partridge* have each sold more than a million copies. Mem has written 30 picture books for children and five nonfiction books for adults, including the best-selling *Reading Magic*, aimed at parents of very young children.

Harriet, You'll Drive Me Wild!   ISBN-13: 9780152045982, 2003

Harriet doesn't *mean* to be pesky. Sometimes she just is. And her mother doesn't *mean* to lose her temper. Sometimes she just does. But Harriet and her mother know that even when they do things they wish they hadn't, they still love each other very much.

Lexile: 0280L   (Grades Pre-K–7)   F

Hattie the Fox.   ISBN-13: 9780689716119, 1992

Hattie, a big black hen, discovers a fox in the bushes, which creates varying reactions in the other barnyard animals.

Lexile: N/A   (Grades Pre-K–3)   F

Hello Baby!   ISBN-13: 9781416985136, 2009

After meeting a bevy of baby animals, including a clever monkey, a hairy warthog, and a dusty lion cub, the baby in this story discovers the most precious creature of all . . . itself, of course.

Lexile: N/A   (Grade Pre-K)   F

Koala Lou.
ISBN-13: 9780152000769, 1994

A young koala, longing to hear her mother speak lovingly to her as she did before other children came along, plans to win her distracted parent's attention.

Lexile: AD550L   (Grades Pre-K–2)   F

Night Noises.
ISBN-13: 9780152574215, 1992

As elderly Lily Laceby dozes by the fire, her dog, Butch Aggie, becomes alarmed by strange noises outside. Finally awakened by Butch Aggie's growls and barks, Lily finds a lovely surprise waiting for her.

Lexile: 0430L   (Grades Pre-K–2)   F

Possum Magic.
ISBN-13: 9780152632243, 1991

When Grandma Poss's magic turns Hush invisible, the two possums take a culinary tour of Australia to find the food that will make her visible once more.

Lexile: 530L   (Grades Pre-K–2)   F

Shoes from Grandpa.
ISBN-13: 9780531070314, 1992

In a cumulative rhyme, family members describe the clothes they intend to give Jessie to go with her shoes from Grandpa.

Lexile: 540L   (Grades Pre-K–4)   F

Sleepy Bears.
ISBN-13: 9780152020163, 1999

Winter is here, and in winter, bears sleep. But how do you convince six not-so-sleepy bear cubs to go to bed? Mother Bear, of course, has found a way—with a cozy rhyme for each of them.

Lexile: NPL   (Grades Pre-K–1)   F

Ten Little Fingers and Ten Little Toes.
ISBN-13: 9780152060572, 2008

These roly-poly little ones from a variety of backgrounds are adorable, quirky, and true to life, right down to the wrinkles, dimples, and pudges in their completely squishable arms, legs, and tummies.

Lexile: N/A   (Grades Pre-K–1)   F

Time for Bed.
ISBN-13: 9780152881832, 1993

Darkness is falling everywhere, and little ones are becoming sleepy, feeling cozy, and getting ready to be tucked in. It's time for a wide yawn, a big hug, and a snuggle under the covers—sleep tight! As darkness falls parents everywhere try to get their children ready for sleep.

Lexile: NPL   (Grade Pre-K)   F

Tough Boris.
ISBN-13: 9780152018917, 1998

Boris von der Borch is a mean, greedy old pirate, tough as nails, through and through, like all pirates. Or is he? When a young boy sneaks onto Boris's ship, he discovers that Boris and his mates aren't quite what he expected. Although he is a very tough pirate, Boris von der Borch cries when his parrot dies.

Lexile: 190L   (Grades Pre-K–3)   F

Two Little Monkeys.
ISBN-13: 9781416986874, 2012

Can two clever monkeys outwit a hungry creature who's on the prowl for a tasty lunch? And just who is this hungry prowler?

Lexile: N/A   (Grades Pre-K–3)   F

Where Is the Green Sheep?
ISBN-13: 9780152049072, 2004

Complete with sleepy rhymes and bright illustrations, this story is about many different kinds of sheep and one that seems to be missing.   Lexile: AD260L   (Grades Pre-K–3)   F

Whoever You Are.
ISBN-13: 9780152060305, 2006

Every day all over the world, children are laughing and crying, playing and learning, eating and sleeping. They may not look the same. But inside, they are alike.

Lexile: AD280L   (Grades Pre-K–3)   F

Wilfrid Gordon McDonald Partridge.
ISBN-13: 9780916291266, 1989

Wilfred Gordon McDonald Partridge lives next door to a nursing home where several of his good friends reside. Of course, his favorite is Miss Nancy Alison Delacourt Cooper, because she has four names just as he does. The only problem is Miss Nancy, who is 96, has "lost" her memory. Undaunted, Wilfred sets out to "find" Miss Nancy's memory for her.

Lexile: AD760L   (Grade Pre-K)   F

Wombat Divine.
ISBN-13: 9780152020965, 1999

Wombat auditions for the nativity play, but has trouble finding the right part.

Lexile: N/A   (Grades Pre-K–3)   F

Zoo-Looking.
ISBN-13: 9781572550117, 2001

Spend a day at the zoo. While Flora visits the zoo with her father, not only does she look at the animals, but some of them turn to look at her.   Lexile: AD580L   (Pre-K–2)   F

Paul Goble (Grades Pre-K–7)

Paul Goble is an award-winning author and illustrator of children's books. He has illustrated more than 30 books. Goble's fascination with Native Americans of the Great Plains began during his childhood when he came to study their spirituality and culture. His illustrations depict Native American clothing, customs, and surroundings in color and detail. He researches ancient stories and retells them for his young audiences in a manner that is authentic to Native American ways.

Beyond the Ridge.
ISBN-13: 9780689717314, 1993

There is no death; only a change of worlds—according to the customs of the Plains Indian people. Story encompasses Native American rites and rituals surrounding death and dying.

Lexile: AD640L   (Grades Pre-K–3)   F

Buffalo Woman.
ISBN-13: 9780689711091, 1987

A young hunter marries a female buffalo in the form of a beautiful maiden, but when his people reject her he must pass several tests before being allowed to join the buffalo nation.

Lexile: N/A   (Grades K–3)   F

Death of the Iron Horse.
ISBN-13: 9780689716867, 1993

In an act of bravery and defiance against the white men encroaching on their territory in 1867, a group of young Cheyenne braves derail and raid a freight train.

Lexile: AD550L   (Grades K–3)   F

Dream Wolf.
ISBN-13: 9780689815065, 1997

When two Plains Indian children become lost, they are cared for and guided safely home by a friendly wolf.

Lexile: 550L   (Grades Pre-K–4)   F

Gift of the Sacred Dog.
ISBN-13: 9780020432807, 1984

In response to an Indian boy's prayer for help for his hungry people, the Great Spirit sends the gift of the Sacred Dogs—horses—which enable the tribe to hunt for buffalo.

Lexile: 0670L   (Grades K–4)   F

The Girl Who Loved Wild Horses.
ISBN-13: 9780689716966, 1993

Though she is fond of her people, a girl prefers to live among the wild horses where she is truly happy and free.

Lexile: N/A   (Grades K–3)   F

Great Race of the Birds and Animals.
ISBN-13: 9780689714528, 1991

In Sioux and Cheyenne legend, buffalo agreed to give up eating men for dinner, and thanks to the cunning of a single magpie, Man became the guardian of the natural world.

Lexile: 590L   (Grades Pre-K–2)   F

Her Seven Brothers.
ISBN-13: 9780689717307, 1993

This book retells the Cheyenne legend in which a girl and her seven chosen brothers become the Big Dipper.

Lexile: AD520L   (Grades Pre-K–3)   F

The Legend of the White Buffalo Woman.
ISBN-13: 9780792265528, 2002

In this Lakota Indian legend, the White Buffalo Woman presents her people with the Sacred Calf Pipe, which gives them the means to pray to the Great Spirit.

Lexile: 0850L   (Grades 3–7)   F

Lost Children: The Boys Who Were Neglected.
ISBN-13: 9780689819995, 1998

Based on Blackfoot Indian myth, this tale movingly reminds readers that all children are sacred. Six orphaned brothers, neglected by their people and taunted by their peers, abandon Earth for the Above World where they become the constellation known as the Pleiades.

Lexile: 390L   (Grades Pre-K–3)   F

Love Flute.
ISBN-13: 9780780774728, 1997

A gift to a young man from the birds and animals helps him express love when he is too shy to use words.

Lexile: 0630L   (Grades 1–4)   F

The Man Who Dreamed of Elk Dogs & Other Stories from the Tipi.

ISBN-13: 9781937786007, 2012

In this beautifully illustrated book, readers discover the fascinating story of how horses first appeared to the tribes of the American Plains. In his final collection of "stories from the tipi," Goble features a collection of 23 traditional stories from the Blackfoot, Lakota, Assiniboine, Pawnee, and Cheyenne nations.

Lexile: N/A   (Grades 3–7)   F

Mystic Wolf.

ISBN-13: 9780060298135, 2003

Focusing on a poor boy and his grandmother, this adventure begins when the boy discovers an old, limping horse. Though ridiculed by his tribe, the boy cares for the horse and brings it back to health. In turn, the animal helps his friend achieve greatness, only to be betrayed.

Lexile: 580L   (Grades Pre-K–3)   F

Star Boy.

ISBN-13: 9780689714993, 1991

This story relates the Blackfoot Indian legend in which Star Boy gains the Sun's forgiveness and is allowed to return to the Sky World. Star Boy was the son of Morning Star and an earthly bride. He was banished from the Sky World for his mother's disobedience and bore a mysterious scar on his face, the symbol of the Sun's disapproval. As Star Boy grew, he came to love the chief's daughter, and it was she who helped him find the courage to journey to the Sky World and make peace with the Sun. The Sun not only lifted the scar but sent Star Boy back to the world with the sacred knowledge of the Sun Dance, a ceremony of thanks for the Creator's blessing.

Lexile: AD660L   (Grades K–3)   F

The Woman Who Lived with the Wolves & Other Stories from the Tipi.

ISBN-13: 9781935493204, 2010

A collection of 26 traditional stories from different Native American tribes, including the Pawnee, Cheyenne, Blackfoot, and Lakota. These include "The Gift of the Sacred Calf Pipe" and demonstrate the deep spiritual values contained in Native American oral culture.

Lexile: 930L   (Grades K–12)   F

Virginia Hamilton (Grades 3–12)

The late Virginia Hamilton has been awarded the Newbery Medal, three Newbery Honors, the National Book Award, the Boston Globe-Horn Book Award, the Hans Christian Andersen Medal, and many more. Hamilton is known for her engaging, powerful, and witty perspective on African American literature as well as her own experiences as a writer and an American.

Anthony Burns: The Defeat and Triumph of a Fugitive Slave.

ISBN-13: 9780679839972, 1993

This is a biography of the slave who escaped to Boston in 1854, was arrested at the instigation of his owner, and whose trial caused a furor between abolitionists and those determined to enforce the Fugitive Slave Acts.

Lexile: 860L   (Grades 3-6)   NF

Bluish.   ISBN-13: 9780439367868, 2002

Ten-year-old Dreenie feels both intrigued and frightened when she thinks about the girl nicknamed Bluish, whose leukemia makes her pale and causes her to use a wheelchair.

Lexile: 0460L   (Grades 4–9)   F

Cousins.   ISBN-13: 9780590454360, 1992

Concerned that her grandmother may die, Cammy is unprepared for the accidental death of another relative.   Lexile: 550L   (Grades 4–7)   F

Dustland: The Justice Cycle.   ISBN-13: 9780590362177, 2011

Using their psychic abilities, Justice, the Watcher; Dorian, the healer; Thomas, the magician; and Levi, the sufferer, have formed a unit. Together, they mind-travel to a strange future world called Dustland where they can survive anything.

Lexile: N/A   (Grades 6–12)   F

The Gathering: The Justice Trilogy   ISBN-13: 9780152305925, 2011

Knowing they have unfinished business in the future, Justice, Thomas, Levi, and Dorian combine to form their unit and time-travel to Dustland. The unit hopes to guide the beings of Dustland out of the dangerous, barren place to a safer home. This book is the third and final installment of the dystopian fantasy series, the Justice Trilogy.

Lexile: N/A   (Grades 6–12)   F

Her Stories: African American Folktales, Fairy Tales, and True Tales.

ISBN-13: 9780590473705, 1995

In the tradition of Hamilton's *People Could Fly* and *In the Beginning*, a dramatic new collection of 25 compelling tales from the female, African American, storytelling tradition. Each story focuses on the role of women, both real and fantastic, and their particular strengths, joys, and sorrows.   Lexile: 880L   (Grades Pre-K–3)   NF

The House of Dies Drear.   ISBN-13: 9781416914051, 2006

A black family tries to unravel the secrets of their new home, which was once a stop on the Underground Railroad.   Lexile: 0670L   (Grades 6–9)   F

Justice and Her Brothers.   ISBN-13: 9780152416409, 2012

For Justice, the summer begins and Justice starts to notice a strange energy between her identical twin brothers, beyond their normal twin connection. She even discovers that she possesses a mysterious, extraordinary ability.   Lexile: N/A   (Grades 6–12)   F

M. C. Higgins, the Great.   ISBN-13: 9781416914075, 2006

As a slag heap, the result of strip mining, creeps closer to his house in the Ohio hills, 15-year-old M. C. is torn between trying to get his family away and fighting for the home they love.

Lexile: 0620L   (Grades 3–7)   F

The Mystery of Drear House.　　　　　　　　ISBN-13: 9780020434801, 1988

A black family living in the house of long-dead abolitionist Dies Drear must decide what to do with his stupendous treasure, hidden for 100 years in a cavern near their home.

Lexile: N/A　(Grades 4–7)　F

People Could Fly: American Black Folktales.　　ISBN-13: 9780394869254, 2009

Many of the stories in this collection were told among slaves as they dreamt of freedom or remembered their lives in Africa. Hamilton focuses on several themes—animal tales, magical and supernatural tales, and tales of freedom—and following each story is a note explaining its history and meaning.　　　　　　Lexile: 0680L　(Grades 3–12)　NF

Sweet Whispers, Brother Rush.　　　　　　ISBN-13: 9780380651931, 1983

Fourteen-year-old Tree, resentful of her working mother who leaves her in charge of a retarded brother, encounters the ghost of her dead uncle and comes to a deeper understanding of her family's problems.　　　Lexile: 550L　(Grades 7–12)　F

Wee Winnie Witch's Skinny: An Original African Scare Tale.　ISBN-13: 9780590288804, 2004

James Lee and Uncle Big Anthony become victims of Wee Winnie Witch, who takes them on a ride up into the sky, but Mama Granny saves them.　Lexile: 700L　(Grades 2–5)　F

Florence Parry Heide (Grades K–6)

Florence Parry Heide is a bestselling American children's writer. She devoted herself to her children and began her career as a children's author during the 1960s while her own kids were still at home. Her first book, *Maximilian*, was published in 1967. She has since published more than 100 books for children and youth from picture books to adolescent novels and several collections of poetry. Her books are known as stories being told through the eyes of a child.

Always Listen to Your Mother.　　　　　　ISBN-13: 9781423113959, 2010

This is a take on the traditional new neighbor story. Lots of energy and mayhem, and a cool gothic approach to the illustrations make this a great choice for Halloween and all year round.　　　　　　　　　　　Lexile: N/A　(Grades Pre-K–2)　F

The Day of Ahmed's Secret.　　　　　　ISBN-13: 9780785769385, 1995

A young Egyptian boy describes the city of Cairo as he goes about his daily work and waits for the evening to share a special surprise with his family.　Lexile: N/A　(Grades K–4)　F

Dillweed's Revenge: A Deadly Dose of Magic.　ISBN-13: 9780152063948, 2010

Dillweed's parents go on adventures and leave him behind with the butler and the maid who treat him like their slave. Neither the butler or maid or his parents appreciate Dillweed's pet creature named Skorped. When they threaten Skorped's life, Dillweed releases smoky monsters. When it's Dillweed's turn to go on adventures, his happy ending means the end for someone else.　　　　　　Lexile: 200L　(Grades 3–6)　F

The House of Wisdom.
ISBN-13: 9780789425621, 1999

Ishaq, the son of the chief translator to the Caliph of ancient Baghdad, travels the world in search of precious books and manuscripts, and brings them back to the great library known as the House of Wisdom.
Lexile: N/A   (Grades 3–12)   F

Oh, Grow Up! Poems to Help You Survive Parents, Chores, School, and Other Afflictions.
ISBN-13: 9780531087718, 1996

This collection of poems is about surviving daily life presented from a child's point of view.
Lexile: N/A   (Grades Pre-K–3)   NF

The One and Only Marigold.
ISBN-13: 9780375940514, 2009

Marigold is an original character whom all children will laugh over and will love.
Lexile: N/A   (Grades Pre-K–4)   F

Princess Hyacinth: The Surprising Tale of a Girl Who Floated.
ISBN-13: 9780375845017, 2009

Princess Hyacinth has a problem: she floats. And so the king and queen have pebbles sewn into the tops of her socks, and they force her to wear a crown encrusted with the heaviest jewels in the kingdom to keep her earthbound. But one day, Hyacinth comes across a balloon man and decides to take off all her princess clothes, grab a balloon, and float free. Hooray! Alas, when the balloon man lets go of the string—off she goes. Luckily, there is a kite and a boy named Boy to save her.
Lexile: AD600L   (Grades Pre-K–3)   F

A Promise Is a Promise.
ISBN-13: 9780763622855, 2007

A revered author and a Pulitzer Prize–winning cartoonist keep their tongues in their cheeks as they spin a wry tale of promises and pets, befuddled parents, and a triumphant child.
Lexile: N/A   (Grades K–4)   F

Sami and the Time of the Troubles.
ISBN-13: 9780395720851, 1995

A 10-year-old Lebanese boy goes to school, helps his mother with chores, plays with his friends, and lives with his family in a basement shelter when bombings occur and fighting begins on his street.
Lexile: AD600L   (Grades Pre-K–4)   F

Some Things Are Scary.
ISBN-13: 9780763655907, 2011

A list of scary things including roller skating downhill when you haven't learned how to stop, getting hugged by somebody you don't like, and finding out your best friend has a best friend who isn't you are just a few of the scary things that readers will identify in this book.
Lexile: AD110L   (Grades Pre-K–2)   F

Tío Armando.
ISBN-13: 9780688121075, 1998

When Lucita's great-uncle Armando comes to live with them, he teaches her many truths about life.
Lexile: N/A   (Grades 3–5)   F

Karen Hesse (Grades Pre-K–9)

Karen Hesse is an American author of children's literature and literature for young adults, often with historical settings. In addition to the Newbery, she has received honors including the Scott O'Dell Historical Fiction Award, the MacArthur Fellowship "Genius" Award, and the Christopher Award. Hesse was also nominated for a National Jewish Book Award.

Aleutian Sparrow.

ISBN-13: 9781416903277, 2005

An Aleutian Islander recounts her suffering during World War II in American internment camps designed to "protect" the population from the invading Japanese.

Lexile: N/A   (Grades 5–9)   F

Come On, Rain!

ISBN-13: 9780590331258, 1999

A young girl eagerly awaits a coming rainstorm to bring relief from the oppressive summer heat.

Lexile: AD780L   (Grades Pre-K–3)   F

Dear America: A Light in the Storm.

ISBN-13: 9780545415613, 2011

As the Civil War rages on, Amelia slowly learns that she cannot stop the fighting, but by keeping watch in the lighthouse each day, lighting the lamps, cleaning the glass, and rescuing victims of Atlantic storms, she can still make a difference.

Lexile: N/A   (Grades N/A)   F

Just Juice.

ISBN-13: 9780590033831, 1999

Realizing that her father's lack of work has endangered her family, nine-year-old Juice decides that she must return to school and learn to read to help their chances of surviving and keeping their house.

Lexile: 0690L   (Grades 4–7)   F

Lavender.

ISBN-13: 9780312376093, 2010

Hesse incorporates a touch of symbolism with the blanket that the girl is sewing for the infant Lavender—a finished blanket will ensure a full-term, healthy baby. The simple language allows for easy reading, and the full-page pencil illustrations break up the text nicely. Codie is a caring youngster eager to please, even when experiencing some doubts about the arrival of her first cousin.

Lexile: 500L   (Grades 2–5)   F

Letters from Rifka.

ISBN-13: 9780312535612, 2009

In letters to her cousin, a young Jewish girl chronicles her family's flight from Russia in 1919 and her own experiences when she must be left in Belgium for a while when the others immigrate to America.

Lexile: 660L   (Grades 5–9)   F

Music of Dolphins.
ISBN-13: 9780590897983, 1998

After rescuing an adolescent girl from the sea, researchers learn she has been raised by dolphins and attempt to rehabilitate her to the human world.   Lexile: 560L   (Grade 7)   F

Out of the Dust.
ISBN-13: 9780590371254, 1999

Written in free verse, this award-winning story is set in the heart of the Great Depression. It chronicles Oklahoma's staggering dust storms, and the environmental and emotional turmoil they leave in their path.   Lexile: NPL   (Grades 4–7)   F

Phoenix Rising.
ISBN-13: 9780312535629, 2009

Thirteen-year-old Nyle learns about relationships and death when 15-year-old Ezra, who was exposed to radiation leaked from a nearby nuclear plant, comes to stay at her grandmother's Vermont farmhouse.   Lexile: 610L   (Grades 5–9)   F

Sable.
ISBN-13: 9780312376109, 2010

Tate Marshall is delighted when a stray dog turns up in the yard one day, but Sable, named for her dark, silky fur, causes trouble with the neighbors and has to go.

Lexile: 690L   (Grades 2–5)   F

Spuds.
ISBN-13: 9780439879934, 2008

Ma's been working so hard she doesn't have much left over. So her three kids decide to do some work on their own. In the dark of night, they steal into their rich neighbor's potato fields in hopes of collecting the strays that have been left to rot. They dig flat-bellied in the dirt, hiding from passing cars, and drag a sack of spuds through the frost back home. But in the light, the sad truth is revealed: their bag is full of stones! Ma is upset when she sees what they've done and makes them set things right. But in a surprise twist, they learned they have helped the farmer.   Lexile: AD810L   (Grades Pre-K–3)   F

Wish on a Unicorn.
ISBN-13: 9780312376116, 2009

Sixth-grader Maggie feels burdened by her seven-year-old sister Hannie, who is slightly brain-damaged and believes that a toy unicorn has magical powers, until one afternoon a crisis shows her how special Hannie is.   Lexile: 0730L   (Grades 3–7)   F

Witness.
ISBN-13: 9780439272001, 2003

A series of poems express the views of various people in a small Vermont town, including a young black girl and a young Jewish girl, during the early 1920s when the Ku Klux Klan is trying to infiltrate the town.   Lexile: N/A   (Grades 4–7)   F

Francisco Jiménez (Grades K–10)

In 1997, Francisco Jiménez's fictionalized memoir, *The Circuit: Stories from the Life of a Migrant Child*, was published. *The Circuit* parallels the Jiménez family's journey from the time when they first crossed into America through their deportation back to Mexico. A sequel, *Breaking Through*, picks up the autobiographical story and follows the immigrant boy's high school years. His books have received many honors, which include the Americas Award, Booklist Editors' Choice books, and a New York Public Library Book for the Teen Age.

Breaking Through.
ISBN-13: 9780618342488, 2002

Having come from Mexico to California 10 years ago, 14-year-old Francisco is still working in the fields but fighting to improve his life and complete his education.

Lexile: 0750L   (Grades 5–8)   F

The Christmas Gift / El regalo de Navidad.
ISBN-13: 9780547529806, 2008

When his family has to move again a few days before Christmas to find work, Panchito worries that he will not get the ball he has been wanting.   Lexile: N/A   (Grades K–3)   F

The Circuit: Stories from the Life of a Migrant Child.
ISBN-13: 9780395979020, 1999

Seen through the eyes of a boy who longs for an education and the right to call one place home, this is a story of survival, faith, and hope. It is a journey that will open readers' hearts and minds.   Lexile: 0880L   (Grades 6–10)   F

La Mariposa.
ISBN-13: 9780618073177, 2000

Because he can speak only Spanish, Francisco, son of a migrant worker, has trouble when he begins first grade, but his fascination with the caterpillar in the classroom helps him begin to fit in.   Lexile: 0750L   (Grades K–4)   F

Reaching Out.
ISBN-13: 9780547250304, 2009

During his college years, the very family solidarity that allowed Francisco to survive as a child is tested. Not only must he leave his family behind when he goes to Santa Clara University, but while Francisco is there, his father abandons the family and returns to Mexico.

Lexile: 0910L   (Grades 6–11)   F

Gerald McDermott (Grades 2–6)

Gerald McDermott is an award-winning filmmaker, children's book author, illustrator, as well as expert on mythology. His work often combines bright colors and styles with ancient imagery. His picture books encompass folktales and cultures from all around the world. He is best known for his trickster tales that recount the adventures, and misadventures, of well-known folk figures. The main characters do have goals but often have selfish motives. They usually succeed, but sometimes are self-defeating or become victims.

Anansi the Spider: A Tale from the Ashanti.
ISBN-13: 9780805003116, 2009

In trying to determine which of his six sons to reward for saving his life, Anansi the Spider is responsible for placing the moon in the sky.   Lexile: AD290L   (Grades Pre-K–2)   F

Arrow to the Sun: A Pueblo Indian Tale.
ISBN-13: 9780140502114, 1977

This is an adaptation of the Pueblo Indian myth that explains how the spirit of the Lord of the Sun is brought to the world of men. A boy searching for his father is made into an arrow and shot to the sun where he meets the Lord of the Sun and is asked to prove himself by passing through the four chambers of ceremony. The boy's bravery fills him with the power of the sun. The Lord then turns him into an arrow and sends him back to the Pueblos. The boy brings the Sun's spirit to the world of man, and as a result, the people celebrate his return with the Dance of Life.   Lexile: 480L   (Grades Pre-K–3)   F

Coyote: A Trickster Tale from the American Southwest.
ISBN-13: 9780152019587, 1999

Wherever Coyote goes you can be sure he'll find trouble. Now he wants to sing, dance, and fly like the crows, so he begs them to teach him how. The crows agree but soon tire of Coyote's bragging and boasting. They decide to teach the great trickster a lesson, and the experience ends in disaster for him.   Lexile: 0360L   (Grades Pre-K–3)   F

Creation.
ISBN-13: 9780525469056, 1999

In the beginning there was nothing, only darkness. Then came light, water, earth, sun, moon, and stars. Creatures swam in the sea, crawled in the grass, and moved over the land. Man and Woman were created to be the keepers of this beauty.

Lexile: N/A   (Grades K–8)   F

Jabutí the Tortoise: A Trickster Tale from the Amazon.
ISBN-13: 9780152053741, 2005

Jabutí's shell was smooth and shiny, and the songs he played on his flute were sweet. But his music was a reminder, too, of the mischievous pranks Jabutí sometimes played. When a concert takes place in heaven, Vulture offers to fly Jabutí there . . . all the while plotting a trick of his own. All the birds enjoy the songlike flute music of Jabutí, the tortoise, except Vulture who, jealous because he cannot sing, tricks Jabutí into riding on his back to a festival planned by the King of Heaven.   Lexile: 0510L   (Grades Pre-K–3)   F

Monkey: A Trickster Tale from India.
ISBN-13: 9780152165963, 2011

McDermott brings the vibrant colors of India to his telling of this classic trickster tale, which has plenty of cleverness and a sprinkling of mischief.

Lexile: AD630L   (Grades Pre-K–3)   F

Papagayo: The Mischief Maker.
ISBN-13: 9780152594640, 1992

Papagayo, the noisy parrot, helps the night animals save the moon from being eaten up by the moon dog.

Lexile: AD780L   (Grades Pre-K–3)   F

Pig-Boy: A Trickster Tale from Hawai'i.
ISBN-13: 9780152165901, 2009

This is a Hawaiian trickster tale about Pig-Boy. He is hairy. Pig-Boy is dirty. Pig-Boy is hungry. And when trouble comes, he knows just what to do.

Lexile: AD520L   (Grades Pre-K–1)   F

Raven: A Trickster Tale from the Pacific Northwest.
ISBN-13: 9780152024499, 2001

Raven, the trickster, wants to give people the gift of light. But can he find out where Sky Chief keeps it? And if he does, will he be able to escape without being discovered? His dream seems impossible, but if anyone can find a way to bring light to the world, wise and clever Raven can.

Lexile: 0380L   (Grades Pre-K–3)   F

Zomo the Rabbit: A Trickster Tale from West Africa.
ISBN-13: 9780152010102, 1996

Zomo the rabbit, a trickster from West Africa, wants wisdom. But he must accomplish three apparently impossible tasks before Sky God will give him what he wants. Is he clever enough to do as Sky God asks?

Lexile: 370L   (Grades Pre-K–3)   F

Pat Mora (Grades K–5)

Pat Mora is the author of many award-winning children's books, and as a literacy advocate, she is excited about sharing what she calls "bookjoy." Pat founded the family literacy initiative, *El día de los niños / El día de los libros*, Children's Day / Book Day, now housed at the American Library Association.

A Birthday Basket for Tía.
ISBN-13: 9780689813283, 1997

With the help and interference of her cat Chica, Cecilia prepares a surprise gift for her great-aunt's 90th birthday.

Lexile: 0440L   (Grades Pre-K–1)   F

Book Fiesta!: Celebrate Children's Day/Book Day / Celebremos El día de los niños/El día de los libros.
ISBN-13: 9780061288777, 2009

Take a ride in a long submarine or fly away in a hot air balloon. Whatever you do, just be sure to bring your favorite book.

Lexile: N/A   (Grades Pre-K–1)   F

Confetti: Poems for Children / Confeti: Poemas para niños.   ISBN-13: 9781880000854, 2006

Poems celebrating the beauty of the Southwest as experienced by a Mexican American girl who lives there.   Lexile: NP   (Grades Pre-K–5)   NF

The Desert Is My Mother / El desierto es mi madre.   ISBN-13: 9781558851214, 1994

This is a poetic depiction of the desert as the provider of comfort, food, spirit, and life.   Lexile: AD360L   (Grades Pre-K–2)   NF

Dizzy in Your Eyes: Poems About Love.   ISBN-13: 9780375855368, 2012

An original collection of poems, each with a different teen narrator sharing unique thoughts, moments, sadness, or heart's desire: the girl who loves swimming, plunging into the water that creates her own world; the guy who leaves flowers on the windshield of the girl he likes.   Lexile: N/A   (Grades Pre-K–5)   F

Doña Flor: A Tall Tale About a Giant Woman with a Great Big Heart.
ISBN-13: 9780375823374, 2005

Doña Flor is a giant woman who lives in a puebla with lots of families. She loves her neighbors—she lets the children use her flowers for trumpets and the families use her leftover tortillas for rafts. So when a huge puma is terrifying the village, of course Flor goes to investigate.   Lexile: AD860L   (Grades Pre-K–3)   F

Let's Eat! ¡A comer!   ISBN-13: 9780060850388, 2008

This bilingual book centers around the daily life of a loving Hispanic family as they join together for a traditional dinner and find out the true definition of wealth.
Lexile: N/A   (Grades Pre-K–1)   NF

A Library for Juana / Una biblioteca para Juana.   ISBN-13: 9780385908634, 2002

In this biography of a 17th-century Mexican poet, Juana Inés was just a little girl in a village in Mexico. She became learned in many subjects and later became a nun.
Lexile: N/A   (Grades K–3)   F

A Library for Juana: The World of Sor Juana Inés.   ISBN-13: 9780375806438, 2011

Juana Inés was just a little girl in a village in Mexico when she decided that the thing she wanted most in the world was her very own collection of books, just like in her grandfather's library. When she found out that she could learn to read in school, she begged to go. And when she later discovered that only boys could attend university, she dressed like a boy to show her determination to attend. Word of her great intelligence soon spread, and, eventually, Juana Inés was considered one of the best scholars in the Americas—something unheard of for a woman in the 17th century.   Lexile: N/A   (Grades K–3)   NF

Listen to the Desert / Oye al desierto.   ISBN-13: 9780618111442, 2001

This is a bilingual account of some of the animals and sounds commonly found in the Southwestern desert.   Lexile: 0850L   (Grades Pre-K–3)   NF

Love to Mamá: A Tribute to Mothers.   ISBN-13: 9781584302353, 2004

In this beautifully illustrated book, 13 Latino poets write with joy, humor, and love about the powerful and undeniable bond between mothers, grandmothers, and children. These talented poets write passionately and vividly about the tremendous influence their mothers and grandmothers had on them.   Lexile: N/A   (Grades 1–6)   NF

Maria Paints the Hills.   ISBN-13: 9780890134108, 2002

This is a portrayal of a New Mexican way of life.   Lexile: N/A   (Grades Pre-K–2)   F

The Rainbow Tulip.   ISBN-13: 9780142500095, 2003

A Mexican American first-grader experiences the difficulties and pleasures of being different when she wears a tulip costume with all the colors of the rainbow for the school May Day parade.   Lexile: 0310L   (Grades Pre-K–3)   F

Sweet Dreams / Dulces Sueños.   ISBN-13: 9780060850418, 2012

Shh, shh, close your eyes. Outside, the rabbits are sleeping, and the birds, and the squirrels. Inside, Grandma tucks us snugly into bed. The stars and the moon are shining bright.   Lexile: N/A   (Grades Pre-K–1)   F

Tomás and the Library Lady / Tomás y la señora de la biblioteca.

ISBN-13: 9780375803499, 1997

While helping his family in their work as migrant laborers far from their home, Tomás finds an entire world to explore in the books at the local public library.

Lexile: 350L   (Grades K–3)   F

Naomi Shihab Nye (Grades Pre-K–12)

Naomi Shihab Nye describes herself as a "wandering poet." She is the author and editor of more than 30 volumes. She has received a Peter I. B. Lavan Younger Poets Award from the Academy of American Poets, the Isabella Gardner Poetry Award, the Lee Bennett Hopkins Poetry Award, the Paterson Poetry Prize, the Pushcart Prize four times, and numerous honors for her children's literature, including two Jane Addams Children's Book Awards.

19 Varieties of Gazelle: Poems of the Middle East.   ISBN-13: 9780060504045, 2005

"Tell me how to live so many lives at once . . ." Fowzi, who beats everyone at dominoes; Ibtisam, who wanted to be a doctor; Abu Mahmoud, who knows every eggplant and peach in his West Bank garden; mysterious Uncle Mohammed, who moved to the mountain; a girl in a red sweater dangling a book bag; children in velvet dresses who haunt the candy bowl at the party; Baba Kamalyari, age 71; Mr. Dajani and his swans; and Sitti Khadra, who never lost her peace inside.   Lexile: 0910L   (Grades 7–12)   NF

A Maze Me: Poems for Girls.
ISBN-13: 9780060581893, 2005

A sprawling collection of more than 70 poems run the gamut from capturing a moment to probing more abstract ideas, and many seem right for a wider audience than just females.

Lexile: NPL   (Grades 7–8)   NF

Come with Me: Poems for a Journey.
ISBN-13: 9780688159467, 2000

This book challenges readers with a range of poems, linked thematically as an investigation of journeys to inner spaces as well as literal journeys to real and imagined places.

Lexile: 480L   (Grades Pre-K–3)   NF

The Flag of Childhood: Poems from the Middle East.
ISBN-13: 9780689851728, 2002

Eloquent pieces from Palestine, Israel, Egypt, Iraq, and elsewhere help us learn that beneath the veil of stereotypes, our human connections are stronger than our cultural differences.

Lexile: N/A   (Grades 3–7)   NF

Going Going.
ISBN-13: 9780688161859, 2005

In San Antonio, Texas, 16-year-old Florrie leads her friends and a new boyfriend in a campaign that supports small businesses and protests the effects of chain stores.

Lexile: 820L   (Grades 6–10)   F

Habibi.
ISBN-13: 9780689825231, 1999

When 14-year-old Liyanne Abboud, her younger brother, and her parents move from St. Louis to a new home between Jerusalem and the Palestinian village where her father was born, they face many changes and must deal with the tensions between Jews and Palestinians.

Lexile: 850L   (Grades 5–9)   F

Honeybee: Poems and Short Stories.
ISBN-13: 9780060853907, 2008

Honey. Beeswax. Pollinate. Hive. Colony. Work. Dance. Communicate. Industrious. Buzz. Sting. Cooperate. Where would we be without them? Where would we be without one another? In 82 poems and paragraphs, Naomi Shihab Nye alights on the essentials of our time, our loved ones, our dense air, our wars, our memories, our planet and leaves us feeling curiously sweeter and profoundly soothed.

Lexile: NP   (Grades 5–9)   NF

I Feel a Little Jumpy Around You: A Book of Her Poems & His Poems Collected in Pairs.
ISBN-13: 9780689813412, 1999

In this award-winning anthology, the editors grouped almost 200 poems into pairs to demonstrate the different ways in which male and female poets see the same topics.

Lexile: N/A   (Grades 9–12)   NF

I'll Ask You Three Times, Are You OK? Tales of Driving and Being Driven.
ISBN-13: 9780060853921, 2007

As a traveling poet and visiting teacher, Naomi Shihab Nye has spent a considerable amount of time in cars, both driving and being driven. Her observations, stories, encounters, and escapades—and the kernels of truth she gathers from them are laugh-out-loud funny, deeply moving, and unforgettable. Buckle up.

Lexile: N/A   (Grades 8–12)   NF

The Same Sky: A Collection of Poems from Around the World.
ISBN-13: 9780689806308, 1996

In this poetry anthology, 129 poets from 68 different countries celebrate the natural world and its human and animal inhabitants. Lexile: NPL (Grades 7–12) NF

Sitti's Secrets.
ISBN-13: 9780689817069, 1997

A young girl describes a visit to see her grandmother in a Palestinian village on the West Bank. Lexile: AD590L (Grades 1–6) F

There Is No Long Distance Now: Very Short Stories.
ISBN-13: 9780062019653, 2011

In these 40 life-altering, life-affirming, and extremely short stories, Nye proposes that no matter how great the divide between friends, siblings, life and death, classmates, enemies, happiness and misery, war and peace, breakfast and lunch, parent and child, country and city, there is, in fact, no long distance. Lexile: N/A (Grade 8) F

Time You Let Me In: 25 Poets Under 25.
ISBN-13: 9780061896378, 2010

They are inspiring, talented, stunning, remarkable, and wise. They are also fearless, depressed, hilarious, impatient, in love, out of love, pissed off. And they want you to let them in. Lexile: N/A (Grades 7–12) NF

The Tree Is Older Than You Are: A Bilingual Gathering of Poems and Stories from Mexico with Paintings by Mexican Artists.
ISBN-13: 9780689820878, 1998

Sixty-four great Mexican writers and painters are collected here, including Rosario Castellanos, Alberta Blanco, Octavio Paz, and Julio Galan. Lexile: N/A (Grades 2–5) NF

Patricia Polacco (Grades K–7)

Patricia Polacco did not begin writing and illustrating children's books until she was 41 years old. As a child, she spent time with her grandparents who shared stories about the different lands from which they came: the Ukraine, Russia, and Ireland. They influenced her life as a writer and illustrator. In almost every one of Patricia Polacco's books, a very young person interacts with an elderly person. When Polacco's children were older, she began to combine her love of storytelling and drawing into writing and illustrating children's books. With dozens of books to her credit, she continues to work on creating new works for children and all of those who love stories and art.

The Art of Miss Chew.
ISBN-13: 9780399257032, 2012

A substitute teacher tells her she's wasting time on art when she should be studying, but fortunately, this is one battle that Miss Chew and Trisha are up for! This true story shows just how important a teacher can be in a child's life and celebrates the power of art itself. Lexile: N/A (Grades K–3) F

Bully.
ISBN-13: 9780399257049, 2012

Patricia Polacco has taken up the cause against bullies ever since *Thank You, Mr. Falker*, and her passion shines through in this powerful story of a girl who stands up for a friend.

Lexile: N/A   (Grade 2)   F

Bun Bun Button.
ISBN-13: 9780399254727, 2011

This heartwarming story celebrates the special bond between grandparents and grandchildren and is perfect for children who imagine their toys have secret adventures when no one's watching.

Lexile: N/A   (Grade Pre-K)   F

The Butterfly.
ISBN-13: 9780142413067, 2009

During the Nazi occupation of France, Monique's mother hides a Jewish family in her basement and tries to help them escape to freedom.

Lexile: N/A   (Grades 1–3)   F

Chicken Sunday.
ISBN-13: 9780698116153, 1998

To thank Miss Eula for her wonderful Sunday chicken dinners, three children sell decorated eggs to buy her a beautiful Easter hat.

Lexile: 0650L   (Grades K–6)   F

Emma Kate.
ISBN-13: 9780142411964, 2008

That adorable Emma Kate has an imaginary friend. They walk to school together every morning and sit together in class. They sleep over at each other's houses and do their homework side by side. They even have their tonsils out and eat gallons of pink ice cream together. But a hilarious twist will have readers realizing there's more to this imaginary friend than meets the eye.

Lexile: 0520L   (Grade Pre-K)   F

In Our Mothers' House.
ISBN-13: 9780399250767, 2009

How can a family have two moms and no dad? But Marmee and Meema's house is full of love. And they teach their children that different doesn't mean wrong. And no matter how many moms or dads they have, they are everything a family is meant to be.

Lexile: AD750L   (Grades 1–3)   F

Junkyard Wonders.
ISBN-13: 9780399250781, 2010

Based on a real-life event in Polacco's childhood, this ode to teachers will inspire all readers to find their inner genius.

Lexile: 660L   (Grades 1–4)   F

Just in Time, Abraham Lincoln.
ISBN-13: 9780399254710, 2011

Michael and Derek don't expect the adventure of a lifetime visiting a Civil War museum with their grandmother. But the museum keeper invites them to play a game, and before they know it, they're walking through a door straight into a very realistic depiction of 1863. They see the destruction at the battlefield of Antietam and even meet President Lincoln. Soon they start to wonder if it's really a game, after all—and suddenly they're racing across Confederate-occupied land to return to their own time before it's too late.

Lexile: 570L   (Grades 1–4)   F

The Keeping Quilt.
ISBN-13: 9780689844478, 2001

A homemade quilt ties together the lives of four generations of an immigrant Jewish family, remaining a symbol of their enduring love and faith.

Lexile: AD920L (Grades Pre-K–4)   F

The Lemonade Club.
ISBN-13: 9780399245404, 2007

Everyone loves Miss Wichelman's fifth-grade class—especially best friends Traci and Marilyn. That's where they learn that when life hands you lemons, make lemonade!

Lexile: AD740L (Grades K–4)   F

My Rotten Redheaded Older Brother.
ISBN-13: 9780689820366, 1998

After losing running, climbing, throwing, and burping competitions to her obnoxious older brother, a young girl makes a wish on a falling star.

Lexile: AD480L (Grades Pre-K–3)   F

An Orange for Frankie.
ISBN-13: 9780399243028, 2004

Tomorrow is Christmas Eve, and Pa hasn't returned yet from his trip to Lansing. He promised to bring back the oranges for the mantelpiece like every year. This year, heavy snows might mean no oranges or Pa.

Lexile: AD780L (Grades 1–5)   F

Pink and Say.
ISBN-13: 9780399226717, 1994

Drawing from the rich store of Civil War reminiscences handed down in her family, Polacco tells the true story of a remarkable wartime friendship between a young white Union soldier and a young black Union soldier who are captured by Confederate soldiers and sent to Andersonville Prison.

Lexile: 590L (Grades 4–8)   F

Thank You, Mr. Falker.
ISBN-13: 9780399257629, 2012

When Trisha starts school, she can't wait to learn how to read, but the letters just get jumbled up. She hates being different and begins to believe her classmates when they call her a dummy. Then in fifth grade, Mr. Falker changes everything. He sees through her sadness to the gifted artist she really is. And when he discovers that she can't read, he helps her prove to herself that she can and will.

Lexile: N/A (Grades K–4)   F

Thunder Cake.
ISBN-13: 9780698115811, 1997

Grandma finds a way to dispel her grandchild's fear of thunderstorms.

Lexile: 0630L (Grades Pre-K–3)   F

Jack Prelutsky (Grades K–6)

Jack Prelutsky has written more than 50 books of poetry and verse, including the national bestsellers *The Wizard*, *Scranimals*, and *The New Kid on the Block*. He is also the author of *Be Glad Your Nose Is on Your Face*, a collection of his most celebrated verses. He was named the nation's first Children's Poet Laureate by the Poetry Foundation. He has compiled numerous children's anthologies comprising poems of others, and his work is known by children as "silly poems about everyday life." He has also set his poems to music on the audio versions of his anthologies, and he sings and plays guitar on most of them.

For Laughing Out Loud: Poems to Tickle Your Funnybone.
ISBN-13: 9780394821443, 1991

A collection of humorous poems by writers including Ellen Raskin, Karla Kuskin, Ogden Nash, and Arnold Lobel.

Lexile: NPL   (Grades K–3)   NF

The Frogs Wore Red Suspenders.
ISBN-13: 9780060737764, 2005

Twenty-eight rhymes from authors of hilarious verse for children matched with great illustrations in this poetry collection.

Lexile: N/A   (Grades K–4)   NF

Good Sports: Rhymes About Running, Jumping, Throwing, and More.
ISBN-13: 9780375865589, 2011

Kid-friendly verses capture the range of emotions from the thrill of winning to the agony of losing to the sheer joy of participating.

Lexile: N/A   (Grades 3–4)   NF

Hooray for Diffendoofer Day!
ISBN-13: 9780679890089, 1998

The students of Diffendoofer School celebrate their unusual teachers and curriculum, including Miss Fribble who teaches laughing, Miss Bonkers who teaches frogs to dance, and Mr. Katz who builds robotic rats.

Lexile: 0750L   (Grades N/A)   NF

If Not for the Cat.
ISBN-13: 9780060596774, 2004

Seventeen haiku-like poems ask you to think and wonder about 17 favorite residents of the animal kingdom in a new way. Readers will meet a mouse, a skunk, a beaver, a hummingbird, ants, bald eagles, jellyfish, and many others.

Lexile: NPL   (Grades 1–4)   NF

It's Raining Pigs & Noodles: Poems.
ISBN-13: 9780060763909, 2005

This book is a storm of more than 100 hilarious poems and zany drawings.

Lexile: 1090L   (Grades 3–6)   NF

I've Lost My Hippopotamus.
ISBN-13: 9780062014580, 2012

This is a book packed with more than 100 funny poems and silly pictures. Most of the poems are about animals, some are big and some are small, some have unusual interests, and some are just plain unusual.

Lexile: N/A   (Grades K–5)   NF

Pizza, Pigs, and Poetry: How to Write a Poem.
ISBN-13: 9780061434488, 2008

In this book, Prelutsky gives you the inside scoop on writing poetry and shows you how you can turn your own experiences and stories about your family, your pets, and your friends into poems.
Lexile: 870L   (Grades 2–5)   NF

A Pizza the Size of the Sun.
ISBN-13: 9780688132354, 1996

Here is another wondrously rich, varied, clever—and always funny—collection. Meet Miss Misinformation, Swami Gourami, and Gladiola Gloppe (and her Soup Shoppe) and delight in a backward poem, a poem that never ends, and scores of others that will be changed, read, and loved by readers of every age.
Lexile: NPL   (Grades K–6)   NF

The Random House Book of Poetry for Children: A Treasury of 572 Poems for Today's Child.
ISBN-13: 9780394850108, 1983

An upbeat, slender volume of poetry with unusual themes such as food, the city, spooky poems, and word play.
Lexile: NPL   (Grades K–4)   NF

Ride a Purple Pelican.
ISBN-13: 9780688040314, 1986

This is a collection of short nonsense verses and nursery rhymes.
Lexile: N/A   (Grades Pre-K–3)   NF

The Swamps of Sleethe: Poems from Beyond the Solar System.
ISBN-13: 9780375846748, 2009

This book gives an exploration of outer space that is not for the faint of heart. These are poems the older reader will find fun.
Lexile: N/A   (Grades 3–7)   NF

What a Day It Was at School!
ISBN-13: 9780060823375, 2009

School has never been so much fun. When your science homework eats your dog, you spend lunch dodging flying food, and your backpack weighs a thousand pounds, you know you've got a great answer to the question, "What did you do at school today?"
Lexile: N/A   (Grades K–3)   NF

The Wizard.
ISBN-13: 9780062067005, 2010

A mischievous, unpredictable wizard will delight readers in this picture book.
Lexile: N/A   (Grades Pre-K–2)   NF

Luis J. Rodriguez (Grades 3–12)

Luis Rodriguez is an American poet, novelist, journalist, critic, and columnist. His work has won several awards, and he is recognized as a major figure of contemporary Chicano Literature. His best-known work, *Always Running: La Vida Loca: Gang Days in L.A.*, is the recipient of the Carl Sandburg Literary Award, among others, and has been the subject of controversy when included on some reading lists, due to his rank depictions of gang life. Rodriguez has also founded or cofounded numerous organizations, including the Tía Chucha Press, which publishes the work of unknown writers, and the Chicago-based Youth Struggling for Survival, an organization for at-risk youth.

Always Running: La Vida Loca: Gang Days in L.A.   ISBN-13: 9780743276917, 2005

By age twelve, Luis Rodriguez was a veteran of East Los Angeles gang warfare. Lured by a seemingly invincible gang culture, he witnessed countless shootings, beatings, and arrests and then watched with increasing fear as gang life claimed friends and family members. Before long, Rodriguez saw a way out of the barrio through education and the power of words and successfully broke free from years of violence and desperation.

Lexile: N/A   (Grades 9–12)   NF

América Is Her Name.   ISBN-13: 9781880684405, 1998

A Mixteca Indian from Oaxaca, América Soliz suffers from the poverty and hopelessness of her Chicago ghetto, made more endurable by a desire and determination to be a poet.

Lexile: N/A   (Grades 3–8)   NF

It Calls You Back: An Odyssey Through Love, Addiction, Revolutions, and Healing.

ISBN-13: 9781416584179, 2011

When his oldest son is sent to prison for attempted murder, Rodriguez is forced to confront his shortcomings as a father and to acknowledge how and why his own history is repeating itself, right before his eyes.   Lexile: N/A   (Grades 9–12)   NF

It Doesn't Have to Be This Way / No tiene que ser así: A Barrio Story / Una historia del barrio.   ISBN-13: 9780892392032, 2004

Reluctantly a young boy becomes more and more involved in the activities of a local gang, until a tragic event involving his cousin forces him to make a choice about the course of his life.   Lexile: N/A   (Grades 2–8)   NF

Allen Say (Grades K–12)

Allen Say dreamed of becoming a cartoonist from the age of six, and at age 12, he apprenticed himself to Noro Shinpei. For the next four years, he learned to draw and paint under the direction of Noro. Say illustrated his first children's book in 1972. In 1987, while illustrating *The Boy of the Three-Year Nap*, winner of the 1989 Caldecott Honor, he recaptured the joy he had known as a boy working in his master's studio. It was then that Say decided to make a full commitment to writing and illustrating children's books.

The Bicycle Man.
ISBN-13: 9780395506523, 1989

The amazing tricks two American soldiers do on a borrowed bicycle are a fitting finale for the school sports day festivities in a small village in occupied Japan.

Lexile: AD500L   (Grades Pre-K–3)   F

The Boy in the Garden.
ISBN-13: 9780547214108, 2010

There was a story that Mama read to Jiro: Once, in old Japan, a young woodcutter lived alone in a little cottage. One winter day he found a crane struggling in a snare and set it free. When Jiro looks out the window into Mr. Ozu's garden, he sees a crane and remembers that story. Much like the crane, the legend comes to life—and suddenly, Jiro finds himself in a world woven between dream and reality. Which is which?

Lexile: AD480L   (Grades K–4)   F

Drawing from Memory.
ISBN-13: 9780545176866, 2011

This book presents a complex look at the real-life relationship between a mentor and his student as World War II raged.   Lexile: HL560L   (Grades 7–12)   NF

Emma's Rug.
ISBN-13: 9780618335237, 2003

A young artist finds that her creativity comes from within when the rug that she had always relied upon for inspiration is destroyed.   Lexile: 0450L   (Grades K–4)   F

Erika-San.
ISBN-13: 9780618889334, 2009

This is a story about an American girl who seeks adventure in Japan and discovers more than she could have imagined. In her grandmother's house there is one Japanese print of a small house with lighted windows and it pulls her through childhood, across oceans and modern cities, and then into towns she has only dreamed about.

Lexile: AD540L   (Grades K–4)   F

Grandfather's Journey.
ISBN-13: 9780547076805, 2008

A Japanese American man recounts his grandfather's journey to America, which he later also undertakes, and the feelings of being torn by a love for two different countries.

Lexile: 0150L   (Grades K–4)   F

Home of the Brave.
ISBN-13: 9780618212231, 2002

Following a kayaking accident, a man experiences the feelings of children interned during World War II and children on Indian reservations.
Lexile: N/A   (Grades K–4)   F

How My Parents Learned to Eat.
ISBN-13: 9780395442357, 1987

An American sailor courts a young Japanese woman, and each tries, in secret, to learn the other's way of eating.
Lexile: 450L   (Grades 2–4)   F

The Ink-Keeper's Apprentice.
ISBN-13: 9780756968113, 2006

A 14-year-old boy lives on his own in Tokyo and becomes apprenticed to a famous Japanese cartoonist.
Lexile: N/A   (Grades 6–10)   F

Kamishibai Man.
ISBN-13: 9780618479542, 2005

Using two very different yet remarkable styles of art, Allen Say tells a tale within a tale, transporting readers seamlessly to the Japan of his memories.
Lexile: AD690L   (Grades K–4)   F

The Lost Lake.
ISBN-13: 9780395630365, 1992

Luke and his father, who is disgusted by the tourists surrounding the once secluded lake of his childhood, hike deeper into the wilderness to find a "lost lake" of their own. The young boy and his father become closer friends during this camping trip in the mountains.
Lexile: 420L   (Grades K–4)   F

Music for Alice.
ISBN-13: 9780547345970, 2004

This book is based on the true life story of Alice Sumida, who with her husband, Mark, established the largest gladiola bulb farm in the country during the last half of the 20th century.
Lexile: N/A   (Grades K–4)   NF

A River Dream.
ISBN-13: 9780395657492, 1993

A little boy takes a fantasy trip up the river by his house to fly-fish with his uncle. While sick in bed, a young boy opens a box from his uncle and embarks on a fantastical fishing trip.
Lexile: 490L   (Grades K–3)   F

The Sign Painter.
ISBN-13: 9780395979747, 2000

An assignment to paint a large billboard in the desert changes the life of an aspiring artist.
Lexile: 250L   (Grades K–4)   F

Stranger in the Mirror.
ISBN-13: 9780547347325, 1998

When a young Asian American boy wakes up one morning with the face of an old man, he has trouble convincing people that he is still himself.
Lexile: N/A   (Grades K–4)   F

Tea with Milk.
ISBN-13: 9780547237473, 2009

After growing up near San Francisco, a young Japanese woman returns with her parents to their native Japan, but she feels foreign and out of place.
Lexile: N/A   (Grades K–4)   F

Tree of Cranes. ISBN-13: 9780547248301, 2009

As a young Japanese boy recovers from a bad chill, his mother busily folds origami paper into delicate silver cranes and decorates a pine tree in preparation for the boy's very first Christmas. Lexile: N/A (Grades Pre-K–3) F

Under the Cherry Blossom Tree: An Old Japanese Tale. ISBN-13: 9780618556151, 2005

A cherry tree growing from the top of the wicked landlord's head is the beginning of his misfortunes and a better life for the poor villagers. Lexile: N/A (Grades K–4) F

Dr. Seuss (Grades K–4)

Before he became known for cats in hats, Dr. Seuss was once a struggling author eager to sell his first picture book. Dr. Seuss's first children's book, *And to Think That I Saw It on Mulberry Street*, hit the market in 1937. In 1957, Seuss's *The Cat in the Hat* became the prototype for one of Random House's best-selling series, Beginner Books. Winner of the Pulitzer Prize in 1984 and three Academy Awards, Seuss was the author and illustrator of 44 children's books. Long after his death in 1991, Dr. Seuss continues to be the best-selling author of children's books in the world.

The Cat in the Hat. ISBN-13: 9780394800011, 1957

It features a tall, mischievous cat wearing a tall, red-and-white-striped hat and a red bow tie. In this story, one rainy day while two young children are left unattended by their mother, the Cat brings a cheerful form of chaos to their household and performs all sorts of wacky tricks. Lexile: 260L (Grades 1–3) F

Did I Ever Tell You How Lucky You Are? ISBN-13: 9780394827193, 1973

Children will be cheered just contemplating the outrageous array of troubles they're lucky they don't have. Compared to the problems of some of the creatures the old man describes, the boy in the story is really quite lucky. Lexile: AD760L (Grades 1–4) F

Green Eggs and Ham. ISBN-13: 9780394800165, 1960

A character known as Sam I Am pesters a character to taste a dish of green eggs and ham. The character declines, claiming to dislike green eggs and ham. However, Sam I Am will not stop following him around and encouraging him to try the green eggs and ham.
Lexile: 30L (Grades Pre-K–2) F

Hop on Pop. ISBN-13: 9780394800295, 1963

Pairs of rhyming words are introduced and used in simple sentences, such as "Day. Play. We play all day. Night. Fight. We fight all night." Lexile: BRL (Grades Pre-K–1) F

Horton Hears a Who!
ISBN-13: 9780394800783, 1978

Horton, the lovable elephant, tries to protect tiny creatures on a speck of dust. In the Jungle of Nool, Horton encounters a clover inhabited by a society of tiny beings known as the "Whos" of microscopic size. After conversing with the mayor of Whoville, Horton decides to dedicate all of his time to tending to the needs of the Whos and guarding them from the hazards of the much larger world.
Lexile: 490L   (Grades 1–3)   F

The Lorax.
ISBN-13: 9780394823379, 1971

Long before saving the earth became a global concern, Dr. Seuss, speaking through his character the Lorax, warned against mindless progress and the danger it posed to the earth's natural beauty. The Once-ler describes the results of the local pollution problem.
Lexile: 560L   (Grades 1–4)   F

My Book About Me.
ISBN-13: 9780394800936, 1969

This book encourages children to find out about themselves while having fun writing and drawing their own biographies.
Lexile: AD90L   (Grades 1–3)   NF

Oh, the Places You'll Go!
ISBN-13: 9780679805274, 2010

A wonderfully wise and joyous ode to finding one's path through the maze of life.
Lexile: N/A   (Grades Pre-K–12)   F

Oh Say Can You Say?
ISBN-13: 9780394842554, 1979

This is an entertaining collection of 24 nonsensical, silly tongue-twister verses.
Lexile: NPL   (Grades K–4)   F

One Fish, Two Fish, Red Fish, Blue Fish.
ISBN-13: 9780394800134, 1960

This nonsensical romp through a gallery of imaginary creatures introduces beginning readers to a variety of rhyming letter combinations. Meet the Yink, who likes to wink and drink pink ink. Or the Yop, who hops from finger top to finger top. Then there is morose Ned who doesn't like his little bed. The short anecdotal poems have just the right combination of humor and the fantastic to enrapture readers.
Lexile: 180L   (Grades Pre-K–3)   F

The Shape of Me and Other Stuff.
ISBN-13: 9780394826875, 1973

"The shape of you, the shape of me, the shape of everything I see." In this book, readers are introduced to the concept of shapes to babies and toddlers. Rhyme and silhouette drawings introduce the shape of bugs, balloons, peanuts, camels, spider webs, and many other familiar objects.
Lexile: 350L   (Grades Pre-K–1)   F

Sneetches and Other Stories.
ISBN-13: 9780394800899, 1961

These stories touch on moral issues, and while they can be read for sheer pleasure, they are also ideal for sparking conversations about tolerance, the need for compromise, and fear of the unknown.
Lexile: NPL   (Grades 1–4)   F

Shel Silverstein (Grades K–6)

Shel Silverstein is the author and artist of many beloved books of prose and poetry. He was a cartoonist, playwright, poet, performer, recording artist, and Grammy-winning, Oscar-nominated songwriter. Silverstein's editor at Harper & Row encouraged him to write children's poetry, although he said that he never studied the poetry of others and therefore developed his own quirky style, laid-back and conversational.

Different Dances.
ISBN-13: 9780060554309, 1979

A modern ballet where lovers are ground to hamburger, wives are turned into chairs, TV sets eat people, flowers grow from children's heads, God is uncovered—and re-covered—and men are hung by the instrument of their desire.
Lexile: N/A   (Grades 1–6)   F

Don't Bump the Glump! and Other Fantasies.
ISBN-13: 9780061493386, 2008

This book includes a menagerie of imaginary creatures, including the Tongue-Twisted Rubber-Necked Byilliar, the Humplebacked Mo, and the Gorp-Eating Kallikozilliar.
Lexile: N/A   (Grades 4–7)   F

Every Thing On It.
ISBN-13: 9780061998164, 2011

A spider lives inside my head who weaves a strange and wondrous web of silken threads and silver strings to catch all sorts of flying things, like crumbs of thought and bits of smiles, and specks of dried-up tears, and dust of dreams that catch and cling for years and years and years. You will say Hi-ho for the toilet troll, get tongue-tied with Stick-a-Tongue-Out-Sid, play a highly unusual horn, and experience the joys of growing down in this lively book of poems.
Lexile: N/A   (Grades 1–6)   F

Falling Up.
ISBN-13: 9780060248024, 1996

Poor Screamin' Millie is just one of the unforgettable characters in this wondrous book of poems and drawings. You will also meet Allison Beals and her 25 eels; Danny O'Dare, the dancin' bear; the Human Balloon; and Headphone Harold.   Lexile: NPL   (Grades K–2)   NF

A Giraffe and a Half.
ISBN-13: 9780060256555, 1964

Delightfully zany rhymes about a giraffe who accumulates some ridiculous things like glue on his shoe and a bee on his knee only to lose them again, one by one.
Lexile: N/A   (Grades Pre-K–3)   F

The Giving Tree.
ISBN-13: 9780060256654, 1964

Every day the boy would come to the tree to eat her apples, swing from her branches, or slide down her trunk . . . and the tree was happy. But as the boy grew older, he began to want more from the tree, and the tree gave and gave and gave. This is a tender story, touched with sadness, created as a moving parable for readers that offers an affecting interpretation of the gift of giving and a serene acceptance of another's capacity to love in return.

Lexile: 530L   (Grades K–3)   F

Lafcadio, the Lion Who Shot Back.
ISBN-13: 9780060256753, 1963

"You don't have to shoot me," says the young lion. "I will be your rug and I will lie in front of your fireplace and I won't move a muscle and you can sit on me and toast all the marsh-mallows you want. I love marshmallows." But the hunter will not listen to reason, so what is there for a young lion to do? After eating up the hunter, Lafcadio takes the gun home and practices and practices until he becomes the world's greatest sharp-shooter. Now dressed in starched collars and fancy suits, and enjoying all the marshmallows he wants, Lafcadio is pampered and admired wherever he goes. But is a famous, successful, and admired lion a happy lion? Or is he a lion at all?   Lexile: NC1010L   (Grades 1–5)   F

A Light in the Attic.
ISBN-13: 9780061905858, 2009

Here readers will find Backward Bill, Sour Face Ann, the Meehoo with an Exactlywatt, and the Polar Bear in the Frigidaire. Readers will talk with the Broiled Face, and find out what happens when someone steals your knees, you get caught by the Quick-Digesting Gink, a mountain snores, and they've put a brassiere on a camel.   Lexile: NPL   (Grades 3–6)   NF

The Missing Piece.
ISBN-13: 9780060256715, 1976

This fable gently probes the nature of quest and fulfillment. A circle has difficulty finding its missing piece but has a good time looking for it.   Lexile: AD100L   (Grades K–2)   F

The Missing Piece and Big O.
ISBN-13: 9780060256579, 1981

A missing piece, looking for someone to carry it along, finally develops its own momentum.

Lexile: N/A   (Grades 4–12)   F

Runny Babbit: A Billy Sook.
ISBN-13: 9780060256531, 2005

Zany pen-and-ink drawings work in tandem with the poems to maximize the laughs.

Lexile: N/A   (Grades Pre-K–3)   NF

Where the Sidewalk Ends.
ISBN-13: 9780060572341, 2004

This collection of poems and drawings is at once outrageously funny and profound. A boy who turns into a TV set and a girl who eats a whale are only two of the characters in a collection of humorous poetry illustrated with the author's own drawings.

Lexile: NPL   (Grades 1–3)   NF

Who Wants a Cheap Rhinoceros?
ISBN-13: 9780689851131, 2002

This is a loving look at the joys of rhino ownership and may even convince you to be the one to take home this very, very unusual pet. There are lots of things a rhinoceros can do around the house, including eating bad report cards before parents see them, tiptoeing downstairs for a midnight snack, and collecting extra allowance.   Lexile: 0320L   (Grades Pre-K–3)   F

John Steptoe (Grades K–6)

John Steptoe's work first came to national attention in 1969 when his first book, *Stevie*, appeared in its entirety in *Life* magazine, hailed as "a new kind of book for black children." In his 20-year career, Mr. Steptoe illustrated 16 picture books, 12 of which he also wrote. The American Library Association named two of his books Caldecott Honor Books, a prestigious award for children's book illustration: *The Story of Jumping Mouse* (1985) and *Mufaro's Beautiful Daughters* (1988). Mr. Steptoe twice received the Coretta Scott King Award for Illustration—for *Mother Crocodile* (text by Rosa Guy) in 1982 and for *Mufaro's Beautiful Daughters* in 1988.

Baby Says.
ISBN-13: 9780688074241, 1988

Baby wants what babies always want: to get big brother's (or sister's) attention! A baby and big brother figure out how to get along.   Lexile: N/A   (Grades Pre–K)   F

Birthday.
ISBN-13: 9780805053418, 1997

A child whose parents left America to settle in Africa celebrates his eighth birthday with all the people of the community.   Lexile: N/A   (Grades 1–4)   F

Creativity.
ISBN-13: 9780618316779, 2003

Charles, an African American student, learns to appreciate his similarities to and differences from his new friend Hector, who is from Puerto Rico. Charles helps Hector adjust to his new life.   Lexile: 0330L   (Grades 1–5)   F

She Come Bringing Me That Little Baby Girl.
ISBN-13: 9780064432962, 1993

A child's disappointment and jealousy over a new baby sister are dispelled as he becomes aware of the importance of his new role as a big brother.   Lexile: 530L   (Grades Pre-K–2)   F

Stevie.
ISBN-13: 9780064431224, 2003

An African American child resents and then misses a little foster brother. Robert wishes that his houseguest Stevie would go away, but when he does, Robert realizes how much fun they had together.   Lexile: 0330L   (Grades 1–5)   F

The Story of Jumping Mouse.
ISBN-13: 9780688087401, 1989

Based on a Native American legend, this is the tale of a compassionate, courageous mouse who journeys to a far-off land and becomes a magnificent soaring eagle.

Lexile: AD500L   (Grades 1–5)   F

Thank You, Jackie Robinson.   ISBN-13: 9780688152932, 1997

A fatherless white boy who shares with an old black man an enthusiasm for the Brooklyn Dodgers and first baseman, Jackie Robinson, takes a ball autographed by Jackie to his elderly friend's death bed.   Lexile: N/A   (Grades 4–7)   F

Laurence Yep (Grades K–9)

Laurence Yep is the acclaimed author of more than 60 books for young people and a winner of the Laura Ingalls Wilder Award. Laurence Yep writes books that draw from his Chinese American background and speaks to common feelings and experiences of all cultures. Laurence Yep breathes life into historical events through memorable characters who are often cultural outsiders. While his writing is most known for engaging an adolescent audience, Yep is just as good at capturing the imaginations of  younger readers. Dragons, Chinese American immigrants, fantasy, folklore, science fiction, and adventure are just a few of the common threads that are woven throughout Yep's work.

Child of the Owl (Golden Mountain Chronicles: 1965).   ISBN-13: 9780064403368, 1990

A 12-year-old girl who knows little about her Chinese heritage is sent to live with her grandmother in San Francisco's Chinatown.   Lexile: 920L   (Grades 5–9)   F

City of Fire.   ISBN-13: 9780765358790, 2010

When her older sister dies trying to prevent the theft of one of her people's great treasures, 12-year-old Scirye sets out to avenge her and recover the precious item.

Lexile: N/A   (Grades 5–9)   F

Dragon of the Lost Sea (Dragons of the Sea Series #1).   ISBN-13: 9780064402279, 1988

The outlawed princess of the Dragon Clan and her young human companion undergo fearsome trials in their quest for an evil enchantress. Shimmer, a renegade dragon princess, tries to redeem herself by capturing a witch with the help of a human boy.

Lexile: 890L   (Grades 7–9)   F

The Dragon's Child: A Story of Angel Island.   ISBN-13: 9780062018151, 2011

A touching portrait of a father and son and their unforgettable journey from China to the land of the Golden Mountain. It is based on actual conversations between Laurence Yep and his father and on research on his family's immigration history by his niece, Dr. Kathleen Yep.   Lexile: 0640L   (Grades 3–7)   NF

Dragons of Silk.   ISBN-13: 9780060275181, 2011

The story of four girls across a span of 75 years both in China and America, each girl shows the strength and courage of a dragon as she fights and sacrifices for the survival of her family and the pursuit of passion.   Lexile: 830L   (Grades 2–4)   F

Dragonwings.
ISBN-13: 9780064400855, 1995

When Moon Shadow accidentally kills a Manchu, the 15-year-old Chinese boy is sent to America to join his father, an uncle, and other Chinese working to build a tunnel for the transcontinental railroad through the Sierra Nevada mountains in 1867.

Lexile: 0730L   (Grades 5–9)   F

The Earth Dragon Awakes: The San Francisco Earthquake of 1906.
ISBN-13: 9780060008468, 2008

Over the years the earth has moved many times under San Francisco. But it has been 38 years since the last strong earthquake. People have forgotten how bad it can be. But soon they will remember. Based on actual events of the 1906 San Francisco earthquake and told from the alternating perspectives of two young friends, this book chronicles the thrilling story of the destruction of a city and the heroes that emerge in its wake.

Lexile: 0510L   (Grades 3–7)   F

The Lost Garden.
ISBN-13: 9780688137014, 1996

The author describes how he grew up as a Chinese American in San Francisco and how he came to use his writing to celebrate his family and his ethnic heritage.

Lexile: 1110L   (Grades 6–9)   F

The Magic Paintbrush.
ISBN-13: 9780064408523, 2003

A magic paintbrush transports Steve and his elderly caretakers from their drab apartment in Chinatown to a world of adventures.   Lexile: 0440L   (Grades 3–12)   F

The Serpent's Children (Golden Mountain Chronicles: 1849).
ISBN-13: 9780064406451, 1996

In 19th-century China, a young girl struggles to protect her family from the threat of bandits, famine, and an ideological conflict between her father and brother.

Lexile: 770L   (Grades 5–9)   F

The Star Maker.
ISBN-13: 9780060253158, 2010

If only Artie had kept his mouth shut. But his mean cousin Petey was putting him down, so Artie started bragging. Now he has to come up with enough money to buy firecrackers for all his cousins by the Lunar New Year. Luckily, there's one person he can count on, Uncle Chester.   Lexile: 0530L   (Grades 3–7)   F

8

Favorite Young Adult Novels

In 2011, the Association of American Publishers ranked children's and young adult books as the single fastest-growing publishing category. While it's no surprise to see the *Harry Potter* series and the *Hunger Games* trilogy as some of the most popular books read by young adults, this list also highlights some writers with whom readers might not be as familiar. The books we read when we're young can stay with us for a lifetime. This list provides some of the most popular titles being read today as well as some of the titles that are considered "classics."

Young adult literature is important for any secondary classroom because adolescent students can relate to the adolescent characters in the books. Even when the setting or era of a novel is far removed from the reader's own time and place, adolescent experiences, such as the pains of growing up and exploring one's own identity, are universal. They can see themselves going through the experiences in history, since these books are often written from a peer's point-of-view. Through young adult literature set in other times, other cultures, and other places, readers can learn not only about history, but also about the cultural, geographical, and economic concepts that comprise the social studies curriculum (Savage & Savage, 1993).

All of the books discussed in this chapter are fictional, unless otherwise noted.

Alexie, Sherman. *The Absolutely True Diary of a Part-Time Indian.*

ISBN-13: 9780316013697, 2013

This is the story of Junior, growing up on the Spokane Indian Reservation. Determined to take his future into his own hands, Junior leaves his troubled school on the reservation to attend an all-white farm town high school where the only other Indian is the school mascot.

Lexile: 600L   (Grades 6–12)

Anderson, Laurie Halse. *Speak.*

ISBN-13: 9780312674397, 2011

Unable to tell anyone why she busted a party by calling the cops, Melinda becomes a silent observer of the lies and hypocrisies at her high school while she lives in fear of the boy who raped her.

Lexile: 690L   (Grades 6–12)

Anderson, Laurie Halse. *Wintergirls.*

ISBN-13: 9780142415573, 2010

Estranged best friends Lia and Cassie both struggle with anorexia and bulimia. When Cassie dies, Lia must find a way to hold on to hope and eventually to recover.

Lexile: 0730L   (Grades 6–12)

Anderson, M. T. *Feed.*

ISBN-13: 9780763662622, 2012

In the future, most people will have a Feed chip implanted in their heads that connects everyone to an evolved version of the Internet at the cost of even basic privacy. During spring break on the moon, Titus and Violet meet and build a relationship when their Feeds are hacked.

Lexile: N/A   (Grades 6–12)

Asher, Jay. *Thirteen Reasons Why.*

ISBN-13: 9781595141880, 2011

Clay Jensen finds a strange package with his name on it and discovers several cassette tapes recorded by his classmate who committed suicide two weeks earlier. Hannah's voice tells him that there are 13 reasons why she decided to end her life. Clay is one of them. If he listens, he'll find out why.

Lexile: 0550L   (Grades 6–12)

Babbitt, Natalie. *Tuck Everlasting.*

ISBN-13: 9780312369811, 2007

The Tuck family is confronted with an agonizing situation when they discover that a 10-year-old girl and a malicious stranger now share their secret about a spring of magical water that prevents the drinker from ever growing any older.

Lexile: 770L   (Grades 5–10)

Blume, Judy. *Forever.*

ISBN-13: 9781416934004, 2007

This candid account by 18-year-old Katherine explores the intimate details of a first sexual relationship.

Lexile: HL590L   (Grades 6–12)

Bradbury, Ray. *Fahrenheit 451.*

ISBN-13: 9781451673319, 2012

The hero, a book burner, suddenly discovers that books are flesh-and-blood ideas that cry out silently when put to the torch.

Lexile: 890L   (Grades 9–12)

Bradbury, Ray. *Something Wicked This Way Comes.*　ISBN-13: 9780380729401, 1998

When a sinister carnival comes to town just before Halloween, two boys unearth the terrifying and horrible secrets that lurk within Cooger & Dark's Pandemonium Shadow Show—and learn the consequences of wishes, as an evil force is at work in Green Town, Illinois.　Lexile: 820L　(Grades 9-12)

Brooks, Bruce. *The Moves Make the Man.*　ISBN-13: 9780064405645, 1996

Jerome, the only black kid in school, practices his basketball moves alone until Bix enters the scene to teach him the fine points of the game and trouble ensues.

Lexile: 1150L　(Grades 6–9)

Chbosky, Stephen. *The Perks of Being a Wallflower.*　ISBN-13: 9781451696196, 2012

Caught between trying to live his life and trying to run from it, Charlie is navigating through the strange worlds of first love, drugs, *The Rocky Horror Picture Show*, and dealing with the loss of a good friend and his favorite aunt.　Lexile: N/A　(Grades 9–12)

Cisneros, Sandra. *The House on Mango Street.*　ISBN-13: 9780679734772, 1984

For Esperanza, a young girl growing up in the Hispanic quarter of Chicago, life is an endless landscape of concrete and run-down tenements. She tries to rise above the hopelessness and come into her own power.　Lexile: 870L　(Grades 7–12)

Cohn, Rachel, and David Levithan. *Nick & Norah's Infinite Playlist.*

ISBN-13: 9780375846144, 2008

High school student Nick O'Leary, member of a rock band, meets college-bound Norah Silverberg and asks her to be his girlfriend for five minutes to avoid his ex-sweetheart. That fateful five minutes leads to an all-night quest to find their favorite band's secret show.

Lexile: 1020L　(Grades 7–12)

Cormier, Robert. *The Chocolate War.*　ISBN-13: 9780440944591, 1986

High school freshman Jerry Renault discovers the devastating consequences of refusing to join in the school's annual fund-raising drive and angering the school bullies.

Lexile: 0820L　(Grades 6–12)

Cormier, Robert. *Tenderness.*　ISBN-13: 9780385731331, 2004

Runaway Lori has a fixation on 18-year-old Eric, even though she knows he is a serial murderer and will probably kill again.　Lexile: 0960L　(Grades 9–12)

Crutcher, Chris. *Running Loose.*　ISBN-13: 9780060094911, 2003

Louie Banks takes a stand against his coach and playing dirty football; he falls in love, and loses his girlfriend in a fatal accident—all in his senior year of high school.

Lexile: 0870L　(Grades 6–12)

Curtis, Christopher Paul. *Bud, Not Buddy.*   ISBN-13: 9780553494105, 2004

It's 1936 and Bud is on the run from a foster home, riding the rails to find the father he's never met, Herman E. Calloway, and his famous band, the Dusky Devastators of the Depression.   Lexile: 950L   (Grades 3–6)

Curtis, Christopher Paul. *The Watsons Go to Birmingham—1963.*

ISBN-13: 9780440228004, 2000

This novel recounts the trip of a family of four to visit relatives in Alabama, just in time for a terrible historical event.   Lexile: 1000L   (Grades 5–12)

Dessen, Sarah. *Along for the Ride.*   ISBN-13: 9780142415566, 2011

When Auden goes to stay with her father, stepmother, and new baby sister the summer before she starts college, all the trauma of her parents' divorce is revived, even as she is making new friends and learning that there's more to life than schoolwork and perfectionism.

Lexile: 0750   (Grades 6–12)

Dessen, Sarah. *Just Listen.*   ISBN-13: 9780142410974, 2008

Suddenly unpopular 16-year-old Annabel finds an ally in classmate Owen, whose honesty and passion for music help her face what really happened at the end-of-the-year party that changed her life.   Lexile: 0810L   (Grades 9–12)

Dessen, Sarah. *The Truth About Forever.*   ISBN-13: 9780142406250, 2006

When her boyfriend goes away for the summer, Macy, still grieving for her recently deceased father, must make it on her own.   Lexile: 0840L   (Grades 6–12)

Ellis, Deborah. *The Breadwinner.*   ISBN-13: 9780613444880, 2000

Because the Taliban rulers of Kabul, Afghanistan, impose strict limitations on women's freedom and behavior, 11-year-old Parvana must disguise herself as a boy so that her family can survive after her father's arrest.   Lexile: 630L   (Grades 3–7)

Ellis, Deborah. *My Name Is Parvana.*   ISBN-13: 9781554982974, 2011

In this sequel to *The Breadwinner Trilogy*, Parvana is now 15 years old. As she waits for foreign military forces to determine her fate, she remembers the past four years of her life. Reunited with her mother and sisters, she has been living in a village where her mother has finally managed to open a school for girls. But even though the Taliban has been driven from the government, the country is still at war, and many continue to view the education and freedom of girls and women with suspicion and fear.   Lexile: N/A   (Grades 6–9)

Ellis, Deborah. *Parvana's Journey.*   ISBN-13: 9780888995193, 2002

Parvana's father has just died, and her mother, sister, and brother could be anywhere in Kabul. Despite her youth, Parvana sets out alone, masquerading as a boy and forges a family with other children of the war. Volume two of a trilogy.   Lexile: 640L   (Grades 3–7)

Farmer, Nancy. *The House of the Scorpion.*　　　ISBN-13: 9780689852237, 2004

In a future where humans despise clones, Matt enjoys special status as the young clone of El Patron, the 142-year-old leader of a corrupt drug empire nestled between Mexico and the United States. Escape is his only chance to survive but even that may not save him.

Lexile: 660L　(Grades 6–12)

Fleischman, Paul. *Whirligig.*　　　ISBN-13: 9780312629113, 2010

When 16-year-old Brent causes the death of a girl, his sentence is to go to the four corners of the country to build whirligigs in her image and to influence others' lives in ways he never expects.

Lexile: 760L　(Grades 6–12)

Frank, Anne. *Anne Frank: The Diary of a Young Girl.*　　　ISBN-13: 9780553296983, 1993

Discovered in the attic in which she spent the last years of her life, Anne Frank's remarkable diary has since become a world classic—a powerful reminder of the horrors of war and an eloquent testament to the human spirit. In 1942, with Nazis occupying Holland, a 13-year-old Jewish girl and her family fled their home in Amsterdam and went into hiding.

Lexile: 1080L　(Grades 4–12)　NF

García, Cristina. *Dreaming in Cuban.*　　　ISBN-13: 9780345381439, 1993

Set in Havana, Brooklyn, and the Cuban seaside in the 1970s, this novel unravels the lives and fortunes of four women of the colorful Del Pino family.　Lexile: 940L　(Grades 9–12)

Garden, Nancy. *Annie on My Mind.*　　　ISBN-13: 9780374400118, 2007

Liza and Annie meet at New York City's Metropolitan Museum of Art. They fall in love and then find that a public declaration is too threatening to their friends and relatives.

Lexile: 1000L　(Grades 6–12)

Golding, William. *Lord of the Flies.*　　　ISBN-13: 9780399537424, 2011

The classic tale of a group of English school boys who are left stranded on an unpopulated island and must confront not only the defects of their society but also the defects of their own natures. This is a brutal portrait of human nature.　Lexile: 770L　(Grades 9–12)

Goldman, William. *The Princess Bride.*　　　ISBN-13: 9780156035217, 2007

This timeless tale full of high adventure and true love pits country against country, good against evil, and love against hate.　Lexile: 0870L　(Grades 9–12)

Green, John. *The Fault in Our Stars.*　　　ISBN-13: 9780525478812, 2012

Despite the tumor-shrinking medical miracle that has bought her a few years, Hazel has never been anything but terminal, her final chapter inscribed upon diagnosis. But when a gorgeous plot twist named Augustus Waters suddenly appears at Cancer Kid Support Group, Hazel's story is about to be completely rewritten.　Lexile: 850L　(Grades 9–12)

Green, John. *Looking for Alaska.*　　　ISBN-13: 9780142402511, 2006

Miles Halter, a misfit Florida teenager who leaves the safety of home for a boarding school in Alabama and a chance to explore the "Great Perhaps."　Lexile: 0930L　(Grades 7–12)

Green, John. *Paper Towns.* ISBN-13: 9780142414934, 2009

One month before graduating from his Central Florida high school, Quentin "Q" Jacobsen basks in the predictable boringness of his life until the beautiful and exciting Margo Roth Spiegelman, Q's neighbor and classmate, takes him on a midnight adventure and then disappears. Lexile: N/A   (Grades 7–12)

Hesse, Karen. *Out of the Dust.* ISBN-13: 9780590371254, 1999

The moving story in blank verse of a young girl's hard times during the Dust Bowl of the 1930s. Lexile: NPL   (Grades 3–6)

Hinton, S. E. *The Outsiders.* ISBN-13: 9780140385724, 1997

This novel is about gang war between the Socs and the Greasers. Three brothers struggle to stay together after their parents' death, as they search for an identity among the conflicting values of their adolescent society in which they find themselves "outsiders."

Lexile: 750L   (Grades 6–12)

Johnson, Maureen. *13 Little Blue Envelopes.* ISBN-13: 9780060541439, 2006

When 17-year-old Ginny receives a packet of mysterious envelopes from her favorite aunt Peg, she leaves New Jersey to crisscross Europe on a whirlwind tour and scavenger hunt that transforms her life. Lexile: 0770L   (Grades 9–12)

Keyes, Daniel. *Flowers for Algernon.* ISBN-13: 9780156030083, 2004

Mentally handicapped Charlie Gordon participates in an experiment that turns him into a genius—but only temporarily. Lexile: 910L   (Grades 6–12)

Lee, Harper. *To Kill a Mockingbird.* ISBN-13: 9780446310789, 2013

This is an unforgettable novel of a sleepy Southern town and the crisis of conscience that rocked it. Readers consider the roots of human behavior and experience: kindness and cruelty, love and hatred, and humor. Lexile: 870L   (Grades 9–12)

Lewis, C. S. *The Chronicles of Narnia.* ISBN-13: 9780066238500, 2001

Journeys to the end of the world, fantastic creatures, and major battles between good and evil make up this series that began with *The Lion, the Witch and the Wardrobe*, written in 1949, six more books that followed.   Lexiles: *The Lion, the Witch and The Wardrobe*: 940
Prince Caspian: 870
The Voyage of the Dawn Treader: 970
The Silver Chair: 840
The Horse and His Boy: 970
The Magician's Nephew: 790
The Last Battle: 890   (Grades 3–8)

London, Jack. *The Call of the Wild.* ISBN-13: 9780141321059, 2008

This book tells of the adventures of an unusual dog—part St. Bernard, part Scotch shepherd—that is forcibly taken to the Klondike gold fields where he eventually becomes the leader of a wolf pack.

Lexile: 0640L   (Grades 3–6)

Lowry, Lois. *The Giver.* ISBN-13: 9780547995663, 2012

Twelve-year-old Jonas lives in a seemingly ideal world. Not until he is given his life assignment as the Receiver does he begin to understand the dark secrets behind this fragile community. Given his lifetime assignment at the Ceremony of Twelve, Jonas becomes the receiver of memories shared by only one other in his community and discovers the terrible truth about the society in which he lives. Lexile: 760L (Grades 6–12)

Myers, Walter Dean. *Fallen Angels.* ISBN-13: 9780545055765, 2008

Seventeen-year-old Richie Perry's stint in Vietnam brings home to him the agony and futility of war as he learns to kill and watches his comrades die. Lexile: 0650L (Grades 6–9)

Myers, Walter Dean. *Monster.* ISBN-13: 9780064407311, 2001

Is Steve Harmon guilty of being the lookout in a botched robbery during which a store-owner is killed? As he awaits the results of his trial, Steve writes the story as if it were a screenplay for a movie. Lexile: 670L (Grades 6–12)

Oliver, Lauren. *Before I Fall.* ISBN-13: 9780061726804, 2010

Popular, thoughtless Samantha dies in a car crash. But she wakes up the next morning and ends up living out her last day alive seven times in a row until she finally unravels the mystery of her death. Lexile: 860L (Grades 9–12)

Peck, Richard. *Remembering the Good Times.* ISBN-13: 9780440973393, 1986

Tough, beautiful Kate, Buck, and Trav form a friendly trio of mutual support until Trav takes his own life. Lexile: 690L (Grades 6–12)

Perkins, Stephanie. *Anna and the French Kiss.* ISBN-13: 9780525423270, 2010

When Anna's romance-novelist father sends her to an elite American boarding school in Paris for her senior year of high school, she goes reluctantly and meets the amazing Etienne St. Clair. Lexile: N/A (Grades 9–12)

Picoult, Jodi. *My Sister's Keeper.* ISBN-13: 9780743454537, 2005

This story examines what it means to be a good parent, a good sister, and a good person. This story tackles a controversial real-life subject with grace, wisdom, and sensitivity.
Lexile: N/A (Grades 6–12)

Sachar, Louis. *Holes.* ISBN-13: 9780440414803, 2000

There is no lake at Camp Green Lake, but why does the evil-tempered woman who is the warden make Stanley Yelnats and his fellow prisoners dig deep holes every day?
Lexile: 660L (Grades 3–6)

Salinger, J. D. *The Catcher in the Rye.* ISBN-13: 9780316769488, 1991

This is the coming-of-age story about one young man's experiences with life, love, and sex.
Lexile: 790L (Grades 9–12)

Smith, Dodie. *I Capture the Castle.*   ISBN-13: 9780312201654, 1999

Seventeen-year-old Cassandra Mortmain lives with her older sister, father, and stepmother in a crumbling English castle. A well-to-do American family buys the castle, becoming the Mortmains' landlords. Cassandra uses a diary to record the months that follow.

Lexile: 0920L   (Grades 6–12)

Soto, Gary. *Buried Onions.*   ISBN-13: 9780152062651, 2006

Eddie, a homeboy in Fresno, is trying to make a life for himself in a violent world.

Lexile: 0850L   (Grades 6–12)

Sparks, B. *Go Ask Alice.*   ISBN-13: 9780689817854, 1998

This is the purportedly anonymous diary of a girl destroyed by drugs.

Lexile: 1010   (Grades 6–12)   NF

Spinelli, Jerry. *Maniac Magee.*   ISBN-13: 9780316809061, 1999

Young Jeffrey Magee comes out of nowhere to become a legend as he brings the warring racial factions of the town of Two Mills together.   Lexile: 820L   (Grades 3–6)

Spinelli, Jerry. *Stargirl.*   ISBN-13: 9780440416777, 2004

This is the story about the perils of popularity, the courage of nonconformity, and the thrill of first love.   Lexile: 590L   (Grades 6–12)

Stevenson, R. L. *Treasure Island.*   ISBN-13: 9781593082475, 2005

While going through the possessions of a deceased guest who owed them money, an innkeeper and her son find a treasure map that leads them across the Spanish Main to a notorious pirate's treasure.   Lexile: N/A   (Grades 6–12)

Taylor, Laini. *Daughter of Smoke and Bone.*   ISBN-13: 9780316134026, 2011

Seventeen-year-old Karou, a lovely, enigmatic art student living in Prague, has a necklace of wish-granting beads and a sketchbook of hideous, frightening monsters who form the only family she has ever known.   Lexile: 850L   (Grades 9–12)

Taylor, Mildred D. *Roll of Thunder, Hear My Cry.*   ISBN-13: 9780140384512, 2002

An African American family stands strong against the harsh racial climate of 1930s Mississippi.   Lexile: 920L   (Grades 3–6)

Udall, Brady. *Miracle Life of Edgar Mint.*   ISBN-13: 9780375719189, 2002

In this story, what persists is Edgar's innate goodness, his belief in the redeeming power of language, and his determination to find and forgive the man who almost killed him.

Lexile: N/A   (Grades 6–12)

Vizzini, Ned. *It's Kind of a Funny Story.*   ISBN-13: 9781467630474, 2012

A new student at Manhattan's prestigious Executive Pre-Professional High School, Craig Gilner discovers that he has become an average kid among a group of brilliant students. This causes anxiety and a battle with clinical depression, during which he encounters fellow patients battling their own problems.   Lexile: N/A   (Grades 6–12)

Voigt, Cynthia. *Homecoming.*　　　　　　　　ISBN-13: 9781442428782, 2012

After their unstable mother abandons them in the middle of a trip, 13-year-old Dicey leads her brothers and sister on a long walk to find a home with their feisty grandmother.

Lexile: 630 L　(Grades 6–12)

Voigt, Cynthia. *When She Hollers.*　　　　　　ISBN-13: 9780590467155, 1996

One morning Tish challenges her molesting stepfather with a knife and must face the dread of what he will do to retaliate that night.　　　　Lexile: 740L　(Grades 4–12)

Zusak, Marcus. *The Book Thief.*　　　　　　　ISBN-13: 9780375842207, 2007

Liesel scratches out a meager existence for herself by stealing when she encounters something she can't resist—books. With the help of her accordion-playing foster father, she learns to read and shares her stolen books with her neighbors during bombing raids, as well as with the Jewish man hidden in her basement before he is marched to Dachau.

Lexile: 730L　(Grades 6–12)

Reference

Savage, M. K., & Savage, T. V. (1993). "Children's Literature in Middle School Social Studies." *The Social Studies,* 84, 32–36.

9

Multicultural Literature
for Children and Young Adults

Books chosen for this section include multicultural books that stem from an authentic portrayal of various cultural elements. For some, authentic books include only those written by a member of an ethnic group about that ethnic group, its cultural traditions, and its people. Others feel that books about race cultures and other cultural elements are authentic when written by "insiders," meaning those who write literature about the culture they immediately identify with or an author writing about her or his own culture. In other cases, authenticity can include authors who have lived within the culture they are writing about all or most of their lives, regardless of their race, with a growing awareness of a society of other cultures.

In creating culturally conscious curriculum and practice, you might consider literature in which the author is sensitive to aspects of the culture that he or she is writing about. Even in culturally conscious books, finding differences in books written by members and non-members of that cultural group can occur. Additionally, if the illustrator does not have an accurate picture of the culture he or she is depicting, the result is an inauthentic portrayal of that culture and this can cause much controversy and confusion on the part of the reader. After reading books to include in the classroom or school library, it's up to teachers to decide whether or not the authenticity includes the accuracy and validity of the text as well as of the illustrations.

Hazel Rochman (1993) in her book *Against Borders* offers a meaningful explanation of the purpose of multicultural literature:

> A good book can help to break down barriers. Books can make a difference in dispelling prejudice and building community: not with role models and literal recipes, not with noble messages about the human family, but with enthralling stories that make us imagine the lives of others. A good story lets you know people as individuals in all their particularity and conflict; and once you see someone as a person—flawed, complex, striving—then you've reached beyond stereotype. Stories, writing them, telling them, sharing them, transforming them, enrich us and connect us and help us know each other. (p. 19)

Multicultural literature can highlight and help make the reality of our pluralistic society relevant and accessible. The books selected for classrooms and school libraries need to not only reflect the diversity of the students in the classroom, school, and community, but also the diversity we live with. In books that you select, be sure that your student population is accurately represented and that negative images and inaccurate stereotyping of people and cultures in children's books are absent. This can be harmful to students whose ethnicity is being portrayed. More important, students should be able to see themselves and their lives reflected in the books they read. Students should have access to texts that they see themselves in, where their experiences are represented and valued, and that represent a diversity of characters, settings, and stories reflective of our broader society.

In addition to being selective about the general quality of texts, finding books that are culturally relevant to the lives of students in the classroom is an important factor in building a library. Including texts with characters similar in age to students in the classroom who share experiences they have had can be critical for fostering connections. Cultural and linguistic familiarity may be an especially important factor for literacy acquisition for English language learners (Vardell, Hardaway, & Young, 2006).

Evaluating Literary Quality

Being selective about choosing authentic multicultural books is important. Several researchers and reviewers of children's multicultural literature have laid out criteria they believe to be important in selecting books for the multicultural classroom. The following is an evaluation checklist for use with multicultural children's books. This checklist stems from the works of Day (1994), Sims Bishop (1992), and Slapin, Seale, and Gonzales (1992). The checklist was created to help evaluate books for high literary quality, stereotypes, negative images of cultural groups, and historical accuracy (Higgins, 2010):

- **Stereotyping:** There are no negative or inaccurate stereotypes of the ethnic group being portrayed.
- **Loaded words:** There are no derogatory overtones to the words used to describe the characters and culture, such as *savage, primitive, lazy,* or *backward.*
- **Lifestyles:** The lifestyles of the characters are genuine and complex, not oversimplified, generalized, or watered down, though not overt and confusing, either.
- **Dialogue:** The characters use speech that accurately represents their oral tradition.
- **Standards of success:** The characters are strong and independent, not helpless or in need of the assistance of a white authority figure.
- **Roles of females, elders, and family:** These are portrayed accurately within their culture.
- **Possible effects on a child's self-image:** These could embarrass or offend a child whose culture is being portrayed if not done so in a respectful way. A good rule of thumb: would you be willing to share this book with a mixed-race group of children?
- **Author's and/or illustrator's background:** The author and/or illustrator must have the qualifications needed to represent the cultural group accurately and respectfully and is most likely a member of the cultural group being portrayed in the story.
- **Illustrations:** The illustrations do not generalize about or include stereotypes of a cultural group and its people. The characters are depicted as genuine individuals. Characters of the same ethnic group do not all look alike, but show a variety of physical attributes.
- **Relationships between characters from different cultures:** Minority characters are leaders within their community and solve their own problems. Whites do not possess the power while cultural minorities play a supporting or subservient role.
- **Heroines and heroes:** Heroines and heroes are accurately defined according to the concepts of and struggles for justice appropriate to their cultural group.
- **Copyright date:** During the mid- and late 1960s most books on minority themes were written by white authors and reflected a white, middle-class, mainstream point of view. More recently (beginning in the 1970s) books began to reflect a pluralistic society. The copyright date of a book may be *one* clue as to the possible biases to be found within it (Day, 1994).
- **Historical facts:** These must be correct without being overbearing to the story. There should be no clear distortions or omissions of history.
- **Dialogue, thoughts, actions, and motivations:** These aspects of the characters must be true to the time period of the story. The stories should not shield readers from potentially disturbing events of our history.
- **Setting, characters, plot, mood, word choice, and themes:** These aspects of the story need to be interesting to keep the attention of readers.

The books listed in this chapter are organized by multicultural topics of high interest to children and young adults.

Family

Adoff, Arnold. *Black Is Brown Is Tan.*

ISBN-13: 9780064436441, 1973

A story poem about a family delighting in each other and in the good things of the earth. This book describes a family with a brown-skinned mother, white-skinned father, two children, and their various relatives.

Lexile: N/A   (Grades Pre-K–3)   NF

Brown, Laurie Krasny, and Marc Brown. *Dinosaurs Divorce: A Guide for Changing Families.*   ISBN-13: 9780316109963, 1986

This is the perfect resource to help young children and their families deal with the confusion, misconceptions, and anxieties that come up when divorce occurs.   Lexile: AD530L   (Grades Pre-K–3)   NF

Bunting, Eve. *Jin Woo.*

ISBN: 9780395938720, 2001

David likes his family the way it has always been, just him and Mom and Dad. He never wanted to be a big brother. Now Jin Woo, his new baby brother, is getting all the attention and David feels as if no one cares about him anymore.   Lexile: 390L   (Grades Pre-K–3)   F

Bunting, Eve. *The Wednesday Surprise.*

ISBN: 9780395547762, 1989

On Wednesday nights when Grandma stays with Anna, everyone thinks she is teaching Anna to read.   Lexile: 540L   (Grades Pre-K–3)   F

Clark, Emma Chichester. *No More Kissing!*   ISBN-13: 9780440417613, 2004

A catch-and-kiss story filled with delightful rhyming action and fun words that toddlers will love to repeat again and again.   Lexile: N/A   (Grades Pre-K–3)   F

Curtis, Jamie Lee. *Tell Me Again About the Night I Was Born.*

ISBN-13: 9780064435819, 1996

A child asks her parents to tell her again about the night of her birth, a tale she knows by heart.   Lexile: 1080L   (Grades Pre-K–3)   F

Dorros, Arthur. *Radio Man: A Story in English and Spanish.*   ISBN-13: 9780064434829, 1993

As he travels with his family of migrant farm workers, Diego uses his radio for companionship and to connect him to all the different places he has lived.

Lexile: AD560L   (Grades 1–5)   F

Flournoy, Valerie. *The Patchwork Quilt.*   ISBN-13: 9780590897532, 1985

Using scraps cut from the family's old clothing, Tanya helps her grandmother and mother make a beautiful quilt that tells the story of her family's life.

Lexile: AD520L   (Grades K–4)   F

Fox, Mem. *Wilfrid Gordon McDonald Partridge.*   ISBN-13: 9780916291266, 1989

Wilfred Gordon McDonald Partridge lives next door to a nursing home in which several of his good friends reside. Miss Nancy Alison Delacourt Cooper is his favorite, because she has four names like him. He tries to discover the meaning of "memory" so he can help her.

Lexile: AD760L   (Grades Pre-K–3)   F

Friedman, Ina R. *How My Parents Learned to Eat.*   ISBN-13: 9780395442357, 1987

An American sailor courts a young Japanese woman, and each tries, in secret, to learn the other's way of eating.   Lexile: 450L   (Grades K–4)   F

Greenfield, Eloise. *Grandmama's Jo.*   ISBN-13: 9780698117549, 1980

When Rhondy can't seem to cheer Grandmama up with a song, a dance, or a gift from the backyard, she tries the one thing she's sure will work. This is a story that shows the loving relationship between a grandma and a child.   Lexile: N/A   (Grades Pre-K–3)   F

Hallinan, P. K. *We're Very Good Friends, My Brother and I.*   ISBN-13: 9780824953874, 1973

This is the story of a close relationship between siblings as a boy explains why he is glad to have a brother to play with, to feel sad and happy with, or just to be with.

Lexile: N/A   (Grades Pre-K–3)   F

Jones, Rebecca C. *Great Aunt Martha.*   ISBN-13: 9780525452577, 1995

Great-Aunt Martha is coming to visit but not to the delight of the children until they discover Great-Aunt Martha dancing with her cane and ordering pizza for all.

Lexile: 510L   (Grades Pre-K–3)   F

McKissack, Patricia C. *Ma Dear's Aprons.*   ISBN-13: 9780689832628, 2000

A young boy always knows what day of the week it is, because his mother has a different apron for every day except Sunday.   Lexile: 0800L   (Grades Pre-K–3)   F

Miles, Miska. *Aaron's Door.*   ISBN-13: 9780316570176, 1977

Unable to adjust to the idea of being adopted and having a new mother and father, Aaron locks his door against the world.   Lexile: N/A   (Grades 2–5)   F

Pellegrini, Nina. *Families Are Different.*   ISBN-13: 9780823408870, 1991

The book is the story of a family composed of Caucasian parents and their two adopted Korean daughters and their dog. While focused on adoption, it is more a story about love.

Lexile: 540L   (Grades K–2)   F

Sharmat, Marjorie Weinman. *Sometimes Mama and Papa Fight.*

ISBN-13: 9780060256111, 1980

Kevin and his sister realize that fights, even between parents, can be a natural part of life in a family.   Lexile: N/A   (Grades K–3)   F

Similarities and Differences

Beaumont, Karen. *I Like Myself.* ISBN-13: 9780439799058, 2004

In this rhyming story, a little girl expresses confidence and joy in her uniqueness, no matter what she looks like.

Lexile: N/A (Grades K–3) F

Bottner, Barbara. *Two Messy Friends.*

ISBN-13: 9780590632850, 1998

Grace and her best friend are very different. Grace is neat and quiet, while her friend is messy and loud, but when they have sleepovers, each of them becomes more like the other.

Lexile: 290L (Grades K–3) F

Bunting, Eve. *One Green Apple.* ISBN-13: 9780547350110, 2006

This is a story where readers will get to walk in the shoes of a young Muslim immigrant. It's hard being the new kid in school, especially when you're from another country and don't know the language. On a field trip to an apple orchard, Farah connects with the other students and begins to feel that she belongs. Lexile: 450L (Grades K–3) F

Bunting, Eve. *Smoky Night.* ISBN-13: 9780152018849, 1999

When the Los Angeles riots break out in the streets, Daniel and his mother are forced to leave their apartment for the safety of a shelter and learn the values of getting along with others no matter what their background or nationality. Lexile: 360L (Grades K–4) F

Cheltenham Elementary. *We Are All Alike . . . We Are All Different.*

ISBN-13: 9780590491730, 1991

This book celebrates the multitude of differences in our society. Written by children for children, this book reinforces multicultural and anti-bias learning and appreciation.

Lexile: 70L (Grades 1–5) NF

De Luise, Dom. *Charlie the Caterpillar.* ISBN-13: 9780671796075, 1990

Charlie, a caterpillar, is rejected by various groups of animals because he is ugly, until he turns into a beautiful butterfly and is able to befriend a similarly unhappy caterpillar.

Lexile: AD280L (Grades K–3) F

Dorros, Arthur. *This Is My House.* ISBN-13: 9780590453035, 1992

This picture book is an overview of houses worldwide and teaches how to say the phrase, "This is my house," in the language of each country. Lexile: 550L (Grades K–3) F

Fox, Mem. *Whoever You Are.* ISBN-13: 9780152060305, 2006

This is a celebration of the world's diverse cultures and how both similarities and differences join people together, such as pain, joy, and love. Lexile: AD480L (Grades Pre-K–5) F

Gantos, Jack, illustrated by Nicole Rubel. *Back to School for Rotten Ralph.*

ISBN-13: 9780064437059, 1998

Afraid of being left alone, Rotten Ralph, a nasty cat, follows Sarah to school and tries to prevent her from making new friends.   Lexile: 280L   (Grades Pre-K–3)   F

Gliori, Debi. *When I'm Big.*   ISBN-13: 9781564022417, 1992

Toasting marshmallows, swimming with whales, and riding a motorbike are just some of the things a young boy, who does not want to go to bed, would do if he were big.

Lexile: N/A   (Grades Pre-K–3)   F

Heide, Florence Parry, and Judith Heide Gilliland. *The Day of Ahmed's Secret.*

ISBN-13: 9780688140236, 1990

Ahmed describes the city of Cairo as he goes about his daily work of delivering bottles of propane gas and waits for the evening to share a special surprise with his family.

Lexile: AD810L 460L   (Grades 1–4)   F

Henkes, Kevin. *Chrysanthemum.*   ISBN-13: 9780688147327, 1991

Chrysanthemum loves her name, until she starts going to school and the other children make fun of it.   Lexile: 460L   (Grades Pre-K–3)   F

Kraus, Robert. *Leo the Late Bloomer.*   ISBN-13: 9780064433488, 1971

Leo isn't reading, writing, drawing, or even speaking, and his father is concerned. But Leo's mother knows her son will do all those things when he blooms.

Lexile: 0120L   (Grades Pre-K–1)   F

Lester, Helen. *Hooway for Wodney Wat.*   ISBN-13: 9780618216123, 1999

Poor Rodney Rat can't pronounce his *R*'s and the other rodents tease him for it, but it is Rodney's speech impediment that drives away the class bully.

Lexile: AD360L   (Grades K–2)   F

Lester, Helen. *Tacky the Penguin.*   ISBN-13: 9780590994514, 1988

Tacky is an odd bird who doesn't fit in with his sleek and graceful companions, but his odd behavior comes in handy when hunters come with maps and traps.

Lexile: AD810L   (Grades K–2)   F

Lovell, Patty. *Stand Tall, Molly Lou Mellon.*   ISBN-13: 9780439434522, 2001

Even when the class bully at her new school makes fun of her, Molly remembers what her grandmother told her and she feels good about herself.

Lexile: AD560L   (Grades Pre-K–2)   F

Madrigal, Antonio Hernandez. *Erandi's Braids.*   ISBN-13: 9780698118850, 1999

The yellow dress Erandi wants for her birthday will look beautiful with her long, thick braids. But Mama's fishing net is full of holes, and there isn't enough money to buy both a new net and a birthday dress, so Erandi surprises her mother by offering to sell her long, beautiful hair to raise enough money to buy a new fishing net.

Lexile: AD500L   (Grades Pre-K–2)   F

Polacco, Patricia. ***The Butterfly.***   ISBN-13: 9780142413067, 2009

During the Nazi occupation of France, Monique's mother hides a Jewish family in her basement.   Lexile: 430L   (Grades K–3)   F

Polacco, Patricia. ***The Lemonade Club.***   ISBN-13: 9780399245404, 2007

Traci and Marilyn learn that when life hands you lemons, you make lemonade—especially when Traci finds out that Marilyn has leukemia and a tough road of chemotherapy.

Lexile: AD740L   (Grades Pre-K–4)   F

Rathmann, Peggy. ***Ruby the Copycat.***   ISBN-13: 9780590437486, 1991

Ruby insists on copying her classmate Angela until her teacher helps her discover her own uniqueness.   Lexile: 500L   (Grades Pre-K–3)   F

Reitano, John. ***What if the Zebras Lost Their Stripes***?   ISBN-13: 9780439210324, 1998

If the zebras lost their stripes and became different from one another, some white and some black, would they be friends?   Lexile: NP   (Grades Pre-K–2)   F

Rohmer, Harriet. ***Uncle Nacho's Hat / El Sombrero del Tío Nacho.***

ISBN-13: 9780892391127, 1989

A bilingual folktale from Nicaragua about a man who can't figure out how to make changes in his life until his niece shows him how.   Lexile: 410L   (Grades 1–4)   F

Simon, Norma. ***Why Am I Different***?   ISBN-13: 9780807590768, 1979

This story portrays everyday situations in which children see themselves as "different" in family life, preferences, and aptitudes, while feeling that being different is good.

Lexile: N/A   (Grades K–3)   NF

Smith Jr., Charles R. ***I Am America.***   ISBN-13: 9780439431798, 2003

In poem form, this book represents children of diverse ethnic and racial backgrounds.

Lexile: N/A   (Grades K–3)   NF

Soto, Gary. ***Chato's Kitchen.***   ISBN-13: 9780698116009, 1997

To get the *ratoncitos*, little mice, who have moved into the *barrio* to come to his house, Chato the cat prepares all kinds of good food and invites them over.

Lexile: 740L   (Grades Pre-K–4)   F

Steel, Danielle. ***Martha's Best Friend.***   ISBN-13: 9780385298018, 1989

Martha and Max deal with some of childhood's biggest challenges: the impending arrival of a sibling, divorce and the subsequent remarriage of a parent, the anxieties of moving to a new school, and more.   Lexile: N/A   (Grades Pre-K–2)   F

Taylor, Bonnie Highsmith. ***The Best Sign.***   ISBN-13: 9780789129000, 1999

Adam is determined to be just like the other boys at camp even though he's deaf.

Lexile: 390L   (Grades K–3)   F

Wells, Rosemary. *Yoko.*   ISBN-13: 9780439104722, 1998

When Yoko's mom packs sushi for lunch, her classmates don't think it looks quite so yummy until one of them tries it for himself.   Lexile: AD350L   (Grades K–3)   F

Wilson-Max, Ken. *Halala Means Welcome! A Book of Zulu Words.*

ISBN-13: 9780439253826, 1998

Michael goes to visit his friend Chindi. As they play, they introduce each other to some basic Zulu words, sounds, and culture.   Lexile: N/A   (Grades Pre-K–2)   F

Woodson, Jacqueline. *The Other Side.*   ISBN-13: 9780399231162, 2001

Clover's mom says it isn't safe to cross the fence that segregates their African American side of town from the white side where Anna lives. But the two girls strike up a friendship by sitting on top of the fence together.   Lexile: AD300L   (Grades K–5)   F

Immigration, Migration, and Language

Aliki. *Marianthe's Story: Painted Words and Spoken Memories.*

ISBN-13: 9780688156626, 1998

Marianthe's paintings help her become less of an outsider as she struggles to adjust to a new language and a new school by illustrating the history of her family, and eventually she begins to decipher the meaning of words.   Lexile: 550L   (Grades 3–8)   F

Ancona, George. *Barrio: José's Neighborhood.*

ISBN-13: 9780152010485, 1998

This is a story about an eight-year-old boy's life in a barrio in San Francisco, including the school, recreation, holidays, and family life.   Lexile: 0920L   (Grades 2–7)   F

Bunting, Eve. *A Day's Work.*   ISBN-13: 9780395845189, 1997

Francisco, a young Mexican American boy, helps his grandfather find work as a gardener, even though the old man cannot speak English and doesn't know anything about gardening.

Lexile: 0350L   (Grades K–3)   F

Bunting, Eve. *Dreaming of America: An Ellis Island Story.*   ISBN-13: 9780816765218, 2000

On January 1, 1892, her 15th birthday, Annie Moore of Cork, Ireland, became the first immigrant to enter the United States through Ellis Island. This story is about her voyage across the Atlantic on the S.S. *Nevada* with her two younger brothers to join their parents in New York after a three-year separation.   Lexile: 320L   (Grades 3–6)   F

Bunting, Eve. *How Many Days to America? A Thanksgiving Story.*

ISBN-13: 9780395547779, 1990

After the police come, a family is forced to flee their Caribbean island and set sail for America in a small fishing boat. These refugees embark on a dangerous boat trip to America where they eventually celebrate Thanksgiving.   Lexile: 460L   (Grades 2–5)   F

Bunting, Eve. *The Wall.*   ISBN-13: 9780395629772, 1992

A boy and his father travel from far away to visit the Vietnam War Memorial in Washington, D.C., and find the name of the boy's grandfather, who was killed in the conflict.

Lexile: 270L   (Grades 1–4)   F

Freedman, Russell. *Immigrant Kids.*   ISBN-13: 9780590465656, 1980

This book offers a glimpse of what it meant to be a young newcomer to America as it chronicles the life of immigrant children at home, school, work, and play during the late 1800s and early 1900s.   Lexile: 1050L   (Grades 3–6)   NF

Hosozawa-Nagano, Elaine. *Chopsticks from America.*   ISBN-13: 9781879965119, 1994

This book follows two Japanese American children in their adjustment to a new home in a Tokyo suburb.   Lexile: N/A   (Grades 5–8)   F

Iijima, Geneva Cobb. *The Way We Do It in Japan.*   ISBN-13: 9780807578223, 2002

Gregory and his family are moving to Japan for his dad's job. After the long flight, they arrive at their new apartment. Gregory is surprised to find lots of things that are different.

Lexile: N/A (Grades 2–5)   F

Jiménez, Francisco. *La Mariposa.*   ISBN-13: 9780618073177, 2000

Because he can speak only Spanish, Francisco has trouble when he begins first grade. But his fascination and study about the classroom caterpillar helps him begin to fit in, especially when his illustration of a butterfly wins him a first-place prize.

Lexile: 0750L   (Grades Pre-K–3)   F

Lachtman, Ofelia Dumas. *Pepita Talks Twice / Pepita habla dos veces.*

ISBN-13: 9781558850774, 1995

This is a story about a young girl who learns the value of being bilingual. This little girl who can converse in Spanish and English, decides not to "speak twice" until unanticipated problems cause her to think twice about her decision.   Lexile: N/A   (Grades Pre-K–2)   F

Lawrence, Jacob. *The Great Migration: An American Story.*   ISBN-13: 9780064434287, 1993

This book tells of the journey of African Americans who left their homes in the South around World War I and traveled in search of better lives in the northern industrial cities.

Lexile: 830L   (Grades 3–8)   NF

Levine, Ellen. *I Hate English.*   ISBN-13: 9780590423045, 1995

With the help of her teacher, a young girl named Mei Mei learns that she can have the best of two worlds by learning to communicate in two languages.   Lexile: 390L   (Grades K–3)   F

Levinson, Riki. *Watch the Stars Come Out.*   ISBN-13: 9780140555066, 1985

A little girl hears how her great-grandmother sailed across the sea with her older brother to join their immigrant parents in America.   Lexile: 460L   (Grades Pre-K–2)   F

Miller, Elizabeth. *Just Like Home / Como en Mi Tierra.*   ISBN-13: 9780807540688, 1999

In both English and Spanish, a young girl shares the story of how she and her family arrived in the United States. She describes her experiences as being "just like home" or "not like home."   Lexile: 198L   (Grades 1–4)   F

Namioka, Lensey. *Yang the Youngest and His Terrible Ear.*   ISBN-13: 9780440409175, 1994

After just arriving in Seattle from China, Yingtao is faced with giving a violin performance to attract new students for his father, when he would rather be playing baseball and making new friends.   Lexile: 700L   (Grades 3–6)   F

Pérez, Amada Irma. *My Diary from Here and There / Mi diario de aquí hasta allá.*

          ISBN-13: 9780892392308, 2002

As Amanda and her family make the journey from Mexico to Los Angeles, she records her fears, hopes, and dreams for their new life in her diary.   Lexile: 720   (Grades 1–5)   F

Pérez, L. King. *First Day in Grapes.*   ISBN-13: 9781584300458, 2002

When Chico starts the third grade after his migrant worker family moves to begin harvesting California grapes, he finds confidence as his math skills help him cope with the first day in a school.   Lexile: AD570L   (Grades 1–5)   F

Rael, Elsa Okon. *What Zeesie Saw on Delancey Street.*   ISBN-13: 9780689835353, 1996

A young Jewish girl living on Manhattan's Lower East Side attends her first party where she learns about the traditions of generosity, courage, and community among Jewish immigrants.   Lexile: 490L   (Grades K–3)   F

Recorvits, Helen. *My Name Is Yoon.*   ISBN-13: 9780374351144, 2003

Disliking her name as written in English, Yoon refers to herself as "cat," "bird," and "cupcake" as a way to feel more comfortable in her new school and new country.

          Lexile: 320L   (Grades Pre-K–3)   F

Say, Allen. *Grandfather's Journey.*   ISBN-13: 9780547076805, 2008

A Japanese American man recounts his grandfather's journey to America and the feelings of being torn by a love for two different countries.   Lexile: 0150L (Grades K–4)   F

Say, Allen. *Tea with Milk.*   ISBN-13: 9780547237473, 2009

May is sure that she will never feel at home in this country. When expected to marry, May sets out to find her own way in the big city. This is a path to discovering where home really is.   Lexile: AD450L   (Grades K–4)   F

Surat, Michele Maria. *Angel Child, Dragon Child.*   ISBN-13: 9780590422710, 1989

Ut, an immigrant child from Vietnam, tries to adjust to a new life in America.

          Lexile: 420L   (Grades Pre-K–4)   F

Whitman, Sylvia. *Immigrant Children.*　　　ISBN-13: 9781575053950, 2000

This book describes the massive waves of immigration hitting the United States' shores in the late-19th and early-20th centuries.　　　Lexile: N/A　(Grades 2–6)　NF

Williams, Sherley Anne. *Working Cotton.*　　　ISBN-13: 9780152014827, 1992

A young black girl relates the daily events of her family's migrant life in the cotton fields of central California.　　　Lexile: 600L　(Grades 2–6)　F

Traditions

Barasch, Lynne. *The Reluctant Flower Girl.*

ISBN-13: 9780060288099, 2001

Afraid of losing her best friend, a little girl does everything she can to stop her big sister's wedding.　　Lexile: 330L　(Grades Pre-K–3)　F

Bulion, Leslie. *Fatuma's New Cloth.*　　　ISBN-13: 9781931659055, 2002

In East Africa, a young girl learns that one cannot always judge by appearances as she and her mother visit a market in search of kanga cloth and meet merchants who all claim they have the secret to good chai (tea).　　　Lexile: N/A　(Grades 2–6)　F

Chavarria-Chairez, Becky. *Magda's Piñata Magic / Magda y la piñata mágica.*　　　ISBN-13: 9781558853201, 2001

It is up to the irrepressible Magda to save the day for her little brother. When an uncle brings home a special piñata for Gabriel's birthday party, but he doesn't want anyone to smash it to get the candy it contains, Magda comes up with a way to save the piñata while still allowing it to scatter candy to all the children at the party.

Lexile: N/A　(Grades Pre-K–2)　F

Chavarria-Chairez, Becky. *Magda's Tortillas / Las tortillas de Magda.*

ISBN-13: 9781558852877, 2002

The story of little Magda, who on her seventh birthday learns the art of tortilla-making from her grandmother.　　　Lexile: AD510L　(Grades Pre-K–2)　F

Cheng, Andrea. *Grandfather Counts.*　　　ISBN-13: 9781584301585, 2003

Gong Gong (Grandfather) is coming from China to live with Helen's family. Helen is excited, but anxious about how she and her siblings, who only know English, will communicate with Gong Gong, who speaks only Chinese.　　　Lexile: 0410L　(Grades Pre-K–2)　F

Chinn, Karen. *Sam and the Lucky Money.*　　　ISBN-13: 9781880000533, 1997

Sam must decide how to spend the lucky money he's received for Chinese New Year.

Lexile: AD660L　(Grades Pre-K–2)　F

Daly, Niki. *What's Cooking, Jamela?*　　　ISBN-13: 9780711217058, 2001

Jamela is responsible for fattening up the chicken intended for Christmas dinner, but instead she gives it a name and makes it her friend.　　　Lexile: N/A　(Grades Pre-K–2)　F

Fine, Edith Hope. *Under the Lemon Moon.*   ISBN-13: 9781584300519, 2010

One night Rosalinda is awakened by a noise in the family's garden. She is astonished to see a man creeping away with a sack of fruit from her beloved lemon tree. Rosalinda seeks out La Anciana for advice. The wise old woman offers an inventive way to help the tree and the man driven to steal her lemons.   Lexile: 0520L   (Grades Pre-K–3)   F

Gray, Nigel. *A Country Far Away.*   ISBN-13: 9780531070246, 1988

This book shows how children are alike the world over, while at the same time it celebrates the rich and interesting diversity of their lives.   Lexile: N/A   (Grades Pre-K–4)   F

Heide, Florence Parry and Judith Heide Gilliland. *The Day of Ahmed's Secret.*

ISBN-13: 9780688140236, 1995

As Ahmed delivers bottles of propane gas through the city of Cairo, he treasures a special secret he can't wait to share with his family.   Lexile: AD810L   (Grades 2–5)   F

Hru, Dakari. *Joshua's Masai Mask.*   ISBN-13: 9781880000328, 1993

Fearing that his classmates will make fun of his playing the kalimba in the school talent show, Joshua uses a magical Masai mask to transform himself into different people he thinks are more interesting, before he realizes that his own identity is one of value.

Lexile: 580L   (Grades 2–4)   F

Kleven, Elisa. *Hooray, a Piñata!*   ISBN-13: 9780140567649, 1996

Clara picks an adorable dog piñata for her birthday party. She names him Lucky, and he becomes her constant companion. Clara has so much fun with Lucky, she doesn't want to let everybody break him. But if she keeps Lucky as a pet, she won't have a piñata at her party. Happily, Clara's friend, Samson, comes to the rescue with a wonderful solution.

Lexile: 260L   (Grades Pre-K–3)   F

Lachtman, Ofelia Dumas. *Big Enough / Bastante grande.*   ISBN-13: 9781558852211, 1998

When a treasured piñata is threatened, little Lupita discovers that she is big enough to help her mother.   Lexile: 481L   (Grades Pre-K–2)   F

Schotter, Roni. *Passover Magic.*   ISBN-13: 9780761458425, 1995

A young girl and her relatives celebrate Passover with the traditional seder, a dinner with special foods and special meaning.   Lexile: N/A   (Grades Pre-K–2)   F

Soto, Gary. *The Old Man and His Door.*   ISBN-13: 9780698116542, 1996

Who would bring the door, *la puerta*, to a picnic instead of the pig, *el puerco*? That would be an old man who's great at gardening but lousy at listening to his wife.

Lexile: 0700L   (Grades Pre–K-3)   F

Soto, Gary. *Snapshots from the Wedding.*   ISBN-13: 9780698117525, 1997

Maya, the flower girl, describes a Mexican American wedding through snapshots of the day's events, beginning with the procession to the altar and ending with her sleeping after the dance.   Lexile: NPL   (Grades Pre-K–3)   F

Soto, Gary. *Too Many Tamales.* ISBN-13: 9780698114128, 1993

Maria tries on her mother's wedding ring while helping make tamales for a Christmas family get-together. Panic ensues when hours later, she realizes the ring is missing.

Lexile: 670L (Grades Pre-K–4) F

Uegaki, Chieri. *Suki's Kimono.* ISBN-13: 9781553377528, 2005

Suki's favorite possession is her blue cotton kimono, a gift from her grandmother's visit last summer. Suki takes it to school, and when it's her turn to share with her classmates, she tells them about the street festival she attended with her obachan and the circle dance that they took part in.

Lexile: 690L (Grades Pre-K–3) F

Multicultural Fairy Tales

Ada, Alma Flor. *Yours Truly, Goldilocks.*

ISBN-13: 9780689844522, 2001

Everyone who's anyone will be at the Three Little Pigs' housewarming party, including Goldilocks, Baby Bear, Peter Rabbit, and Little Red Riding Hood.

Lexile: 810L (Grades Pre-K–3) F

Climo, Shirley. *The Egyptian Cinderella.* ISBN-13: 9780064432795, 1989

In this version of Cinderella set in Egypt in the sixth century BC, Rhodopes, a slave girl, eventually comes to be chosen by the Pharaoh to be his queen.

Lexile: AD620L (Grades Pre-K–3) F

Climo, Shirley. *The Irish Cinderlad.* ISBN-13: 9780064435772, 1996

Becan, a poor boy belittled by his stepmother and stepsisters, rescues a princess in distress after meeting a magical bull.

Lexile: 730L (Grades K–4) F

Climo, Shirley. *The Persian Cinderella.* ISBN-13: 9780064438537, 1999

Magic enables Settareh to outsmart two jealous stepsisters and win the heart of a prince. Settareh, neglected and abused by her stepmother and stepsisters, finds her life transformed with the help of a little blue jug.

Lexile: 760L (Grades K–3) F

Coburn, Jewell R. *Angkat the Cambodian Cinderella.* ISBN-13: 9781885008091, 1998

A Cambodian version of Cinderella in which a poor girl marries a prince, is killed by her jealous stepfamily, and then, through her virtue, returns to become queen.

Lexile: 660L (Grades 1–3) F

De La Paz, Myrna J. *Abadeha: The Philippine Cinderella.* ISBN-13: 9780962925504, 1991

This is the story of a beautiful daughter, wicked stepmother and stepsisters, absent father, and the Spirit of the Forest who magically rescues the heroine.

Lexile: N/A (Grades K–5) F

Demi. ***The Emperor's New Clothes.***   ISBN-13: 9780689830686, 2000

Two rascals sell a vain Chinese emperor an invisible suit of clothes.

Lexile: 780L   (Grades K–5)   F

dePaola, Tomie. ***Adelita: A Mexican Cinderella Story.***   ISBN-13: 9780142401873, 2002

After the death of her mother and father, Adelita is mistreated by her stepmother and step-sisters until she finds her own true love at a grand fiesta.

Lexile: AD660L   (Grades K–3)   F

Huck, Charlotte. ***Princess Furball.***   ISBN-13: 9780688078386, 1989

A princess in a coat of a thousand furs hides her identity from a king who falls in love with her.

Lexile: 920L   (Grades K–3)   F

Johnston, Tony. ***Bigfoot Cinderrrrrella.***   ISBN-13: 9780399230219, 1998

The Cinderella story set in an old-growth forest with Bigfoot characters that finds a Bigfoot prince searching for a Bigfoot princess.

Lexile: 0570L   (Grades Pre-K–3)   F

Kimmel, Eric A. ***The Four Gallant Sisters.***   ISBN-13: 9780805019018, 1992

A reformulated Brothers Grimm tale where four orphaned yet powerful and good-hearted sisters disguise themselves as men, learn a trade, join a household of a king, conquer a dragon, and later have to decide if they want to continue convincing the king that they are men.

Lexile: 640L   (Grades Pre-K–3)   F

Kimmel, Eric A. ***The Three Princes: A Tale from the Middle East.***

ISBN-13: 9780736227766, 1994

In this retelling of a Middle Eastern folktale, a princess sends three prince suitors to find a "wonderous object" to prove himself worthy of her hand. This story of mystery and wonder is set in an exotic Arabian landscape.

Lexile: AD770L   (Grades K–4)   F

Louie, Ai-Ling. ***Yeh-Shen: A Cinderella Story from China.***

ISBN-13: 9780698113886, 1982

A Chinese version of the classic Cinderella story, where a girl overcomes family challenges and evil stepsisters to become the bride of a prince.

Lexile: 840L   (Grades K–4)   F

Lowell, Susan. ***Dusty Locks and the Three Bears.***   ISBN-13: 9780805075342, 2001

A Western retelling of the traditional Goldilocks story in which a little girl, Dusty Locks, finds a bear family and makes herself at home.

Lexile: 490L   (Grades Pre-K–3)   F

Martin, Rafe. ***The Rough-Face Girl.***   ISBN-13: 9780698116269, 1992

In this Algonquin Indian version of the Cinderella story, the Rough-Face Girl, scarred from working by the fire, and her two beautiful but heartless sisters compete for the affections of the Invisible Being.

Lexile: 0540L   (Grades K–4)   F

Minters, Frances. *Cinder-elly.* ISBN-13: 9781563347238, 1994

In this rhyming-urban-rap fairy tale with pictures that capture the hipness and movement of New York City, today's Cinderella wants to find her Prince Charming on the basketball court, but she may need the help of a trash can, a copy machine, or even a glass slipper.

Lexile: NPL (Grades K–4) F

Minters, Frances. *Sleepless Beauty.* ISBN-13: 9780439270045, 1996

This is a modern twist on the classic Sleeping Beauty with a rhyming twist on an age-old story. Lexile: 490L (Grades Pre-K–3) F

Osborne, Mary Pope. *Kate and the Beanstalk.* ISBN-13: 9781416908180, 2000

In this magical retelling of a favorite tale, a girl uses her quick wit to outsmart a giant and regain her mother's fortune. Lexile: 440L (Grades Pre-K–3) F

Salinas, Bobbi. *The Three Pigs / Los tres cerdos: Nacho, Tito, and Miguel.*

ISBN-13: 9780934925051, 1998

A spicy, Southwestern retelling of the familiar tale of the three little pigs, told in a Spanglish/English text. Lexile: N/A (Grades Pre-K–3) F

San Souci, Robert. *Cendrillon: A Caribbean Cinderella.* ISBN-13: 9780689848889, 1988

As a Caribbean fairy godmother sets the record straight, her spirited telling provides a fresh twist on a well-known tale. A poor washerwoman, she longs to help Cendrillon but doesn't see how until the girl falls in love with a rich man's son. Then she uses her magic wand to create a carriage, horses, a coachman, and a gown so Cendrillon can attend her true love's birthday celebration. Lexile: 540L (Grades K–4) F

Steptoe, John. *Mufaro's Beautiful Daughters: An African Tale.*

ISBN-13: 9780618062232, 1987

A memorable, modern fable where Mufaro's daughters, one bad tempered and one kind, are presented before the king who must chose a wife. Lexile: 720L (Grades Pre-K–3) F

Stewig, John Warren. *Princess Florecita and the Iron Shoes.* ISBN-13: 9780679847755, 1995

In this Spanish fairytale, with the help of three ancianas (old women), Princess Florecita, the spirited heroine, travels for six months in her quest to win the heart of her prince.

Lexile: N/A (Grades Pre-K–3) F

Young, Ed. *Lon Po Po: A Red-Riding Hood Story from China.*

ISBN-13: 9780590440691, 1989

A hungry wolf disguised as three sisters' grandmother gives the girls a scare.

Lexile: 670L (Grades Pre-K–3) F

Gender Roles

Allard, Harry. *It's So Nice to Have a Wolf Around the House.*

ISBN-13: 9780440413530, 1977

Devine tries to hide the fact that he is a wolf with a shady past by becoming the companion to a kind old man and his pets.

Lexile: N/A   (Grades Pre-K–3)   F

Allard, Harry. *Miss Nelson Has a Field Day.*

ISBN-13: 9780395486542, 1985

The kids in Room 207 take advantage of their teacher's good nature until she disappears and they are faced with a substitute.

Lexile: 390L   (Grades K–4)   F

Beck, Martine. *The Wedding of Brown Bear and White Bear.*

ISBN-13: 9780316086523, 1989

This is the sweet tale of Brown Bear admiring pink-frocked White Bear while she is skating, writing her love letters, and eventually asking her, "Would you like to look at the moon and the stars with me always and forever?"

Lexile: N/A   (Grades Pre-K–3)   F

Berry, Christine. *Mama Went Walking.*   ISBN-13: 9780805012613, 1990

In this parent-comforting-frightened-child-themed adventure, Sarah saves her Mama from lions in the Jaba-Jaba Jungle, from a flash flood in the Ropacactus Canyon, from snakes in the Rattlesnake River, and from sleeping bears who are snoring too loudly in the Blacken-batty Caves.   Lexile: N/A   (Grades Pre-K–3)   F

Browne, Anthony. *My Dad.*   ISBN-13: 9780374351014, 2000

An endearing homage to dads everywhere, with the message of, "I love my dad, and he loves me." A boy describes the many accomplishments of his father: his enormous talent for singing; his near-professional wrestling skills; his extreme bravery in the face of danger (he's not even afraid of the Big Bad Wolf!); and his ability to eat like a horse, jump over the moon, swim like a fish, and be as warm as toast.   Lexile: BRL   (Grades K–3)   F

Browne, Anthony. *The Tunnel.*   ISBN-13: 9781406313291, 1989

Brown's sibling rivalry metaphors can be experienced on many levels as this fantasy explores Rose and her brother Jack's strengthened bond through overcoming obstacles.

Lexile: 570L   (Grades K–4)   F

Carlstrom, Nancy White. *Wild Wild Sunflower Child Anna.*   ISBN-13: 9780590443463, 1987

An African American girl spends a day outdoors and enjoys the sun, sky, grass, flowers, berries, frogs, ants, and beetles.   Lexile: NP   (Grades Pre-K–3)   F

Corey, Shana. *You Forgot Your Skirt, Amelia Bloomer.*   ISBN-13: 9780439078191, 2000

This is an inspiring story of the nonconformity of feminist pioneer Amelia Bloomer.

Lexile: AD350L   (Grades K–3)   NF

Curtis, Jamie Lee. *Tell Me Again About the Night I Was Born.*

ISBN-13: 9780064435819, 1996

In asking her parents to tell her again about the night of her birth, a young girl (who is adopted) shows that it is a cherished tale she knows by heart.

Lexile: 1080L   (Grades Pre-K–3)   F

Geeslin, Campbell. *How Nanita Learns to Make Flan.*   ISBN-13: 9780689815461, 1999

The cobbler in a tiny Mexican town is so busy he cannot make shoes for his daughter. So she makes her own shoes, which take her far away to a rich man's home where she must clean and cook all day.   Lexile: N/A   (Grades Pre-K–3)   F

Hilton, Nette. *A Proper Little Lady.*   ISBN-13: 9780207170089, 1989

Annabella Jones decides that she will make herself into a proper little lady. Although she fails, she will succeed in finding her way into readers' hearts. Both text and pictures make her a thoroughly winning girl.   Lexile: N/A   (Grades Pre-K–3)   F

Hoban, Russell. *Best Friends for Frances.*   ISBN-13: 9780060838034, 1969

Frances doesn't think her little sister, Gloria, can be her friend. But when Frances's friend Albert has a no-girls baseball game, Frances shows him what girls can do. Frances even discovers that sisters can be friends.   Lexile: AD640L   (Grades Pre-K–3)   F

Moore, Eva. *The Day of the Bad Haircut.*   ISBN-13: 9780590697705, 1996

This is a good story for teaching first, how to read through cause-and-effect scenarios and second, learning how to read "self-to-text" connections that ask, "What connections do you have with the girl who gets her hair cut?" and "Have they ever been embarrassed by a haircut?"   Lexile: 220L   (Grades Pre-K–3)   F

Munsch, Robert. *The Paper Bag Princess.*   ISBN-13: 9780920236161, 1980

This is a delightful, modern classic of a feisty princess and her hapless prince that showcases the value of a high self-esteem.   Lexile: AD470L   (Grades Pre-K–3)   F

Nolen, Jerdine. *In My Momma's Kitchen.*   ISBN-13: 9780064437868, 1999

A celebration of African American families and mommas everywhere, as a young girl's momma and her aunts all gather yearly to make the biggest pot of soup in town.

Lexile: 0530L   (Grades K–4)   F

Pfanner, Louise. *Louise Builds a House.*   ISBN-13: 9780590636872, 1987

This lighthearted and whimsical tale follows all stages of building a house, from windows to roof, the reader imagines what it would be like to design and build his or her own house.

Lexile: N/A   (Grades Pre-K–3)   F

Zolotow, Charlotte. *William's Doll.*   ISBN-13: 9780064430678, 1972

Playing against traditional gender roles, William wants a doll. Even though he is called a "creep" and a "sissy," he still wants a doll. One day someone really understands William's wish and makes it easy for others to understand, too.   Lexile: 840L   (Grades Pre-K–3)   F

Alternative Families

Brown, Laurie Krasny, and Marc Brown. ***Dinosaurs Divorce: A Guide for Changing Families.***   ISBN-13: 9780316109963, 1986

This book looks at the emotional (sadness, anger) and physical (separation from loved ones, what to call your new father's ex-wife's children) problems of divorce. It discusses aspects of divorce such as its causes and effects, living with a single parent, spending holidays in two separate households, and adjusting to a stepparent.   Lexile: 0530L   (Grades Pre-K–3)   NF

Caines, Jeannette. ***Just Us Women.***

ISBN-13: 9780064430562, 1982

A young girl and her favorite aunt share the excitement of planning a very special car trip for just the two of them.

Lexile: 0610L   (Grades K–4)   F

Combs, Bobbie. ***123: A Family Counting Book.***   ISBN-13: 9780967446806, 2001

This colorful book shows children how to count to 20 by following families with different lifestyles.   Lexile: N/A   (GradesPre-K–5)   F

Combs, Bobbie. ***ABC: A Family Alphabet Book.***   ISBN-13: 9780967446813, 2001

It's family fun from A to Z in this alphabet book that shows kids and their parents laughing, playing, and enjoying family life.   Lexile: N/A   (Grades Pre-K–3)   F

DeHaan, Linda, and Stern Nijland. ***King & King.***   ISBN-13: 9781582460611, 2002

When the queen insists that the prince get married and take over as king, the search for a suitable mate does not turn out as expected.   Lexile: N/A   (Grades 4–12)   F

DeHaan, Linda, and Stern Nijland. ***King & King & Family.***   ISBN-13: 9781582461137, 2004

Join newlyweds King Lee and King Bertie on their journey into wanting a family of their own and adoption.   Lexile: N/A   (Grades 4–12)   F

Elwin, Rosamund, and Michele Pause. ***Asha's Mums.***   ISBN-13: 9780889611436, 1990

Asha, an African Canadian girl whose lesbian mums become an issue for the teacher and the curiosity of classmates, responds with clarity and assuredness that having two mums is no big deal—they are a family.   Lexile: N/A   (Grades 1–5)   F

Katz, Karen. ***Over the Moon: An Adoption Tale.***   ISBN-13: 9780805067071, 1997

A loving couple's prayers are answered in this magical, reassuring story of one adoptive family's beginnings.   Lexile: N/A   (Grades Pre-K–3)   F

Koehler, Phoebe. ***The Day We Met You.***   ISBN-13: 9780689809644, 1997

This book chronicles a loving couple's preparations made for the day their adoptive baby came home, "The minute we saw you we knew that we loved you."

Lexile: AD380L   (Grades Pre-K–3)   F

Krakow, Kari. *The Harvey Milk Story.*   ISBN-13: 9780967446837, 2002

This is a picture-book biography of the first openly gay elected official in the United States.
     Lexile: N/A   (Grades K–4)   NF

Lindenbaum, Pija, and Gabrielle Charbonnet. *Else-Marie and Her Seven Little Daddies.*

     ISBN-13: 9780805017526, 1991

This off-the-wall Swedish-imported story celebrates Else-Marie and her seven tiny, identical daddies who, apart from their size, behave like daddies everywhere. Although terror strikes one morning when Else-Marie's mother announces that her daddies will pick Else-Marie up at school, they end up being a big hit.   Lexile: N/A   (Grades Pre-K–3)   F

Loewen, Iris. *My Mom Is So Unusual.*   ISBN-13: 9780919143371, 1996

This is the story of a special single-parent family where the roles are often reversed. The little girl at times takes care of her mother, such as when the daughter sleeps with her mom because her mom is afraid of the dark.   Lexile: N/A   (Grades Pre-K–3)   F

Newman, Lesléa. *Felicia's Favorite Story.*   ISBN-13: 9780967446851, 2002

This story is set in a loving family with two women as parents. Their little girl asks for her favorite bedtime story—the tale of how she became part of the family. As Felicia asks questions and fills in the blanks, her mothers playfully relate the tale of their decision to share their love by bringing her into their lives.   Lexile: N/A   (Grades Pre-K–3)   F

Newman, Lesléa. *Heather Has Two Mommies.*   ISBN 13: 9781555835439, 1990

Heather has two lesbian mothers. At first she feels bad because she has two mothers and no father, but then she learns that there are lots of different kinds of families and the most important thing is that all the people love each other.   Lexile: N/A   (Grades 5–12)   F

Newman, Lesléa. *Saturday Is Pattyday.*   ISBN-13: 9780934678513, 1993

When Frankie's two moms get divorced, he is very unhappy. This is a reassuring look at what happens when a child is caught in the middle. Although Frankie is hurt and confused when his two mommies separate, he is comforted by knowing that Patty will still be part of his life.   Lexile: N/A   (Grades K–4)   F

Okimoto, Jean Davies, and Elaine M. Aoki. *The White Swan Express: A Story About Adoption.*   ISBN-13: 9780618164530, 2002

This tender and humorous story of people who travel to China to be united with their daughters describes the adoption process step by step and the anxiety, suspense, and delight of becoming a family.   Lexile: N/A   (Grades K–4)   F

Ransom, Jeanie Franz. *I Don't Want to Talk About It.*   ISBN-13: 9781557987037, 2000

A child's parents tell her they decided to divorce, and the last thing she wants to do is talk about it. Instead, she wants to roar as loud as a lion, turn into a fish and hide her tears in the sea, or become a bird and fly away. This story emphasizes that divorce does not change parents' love and commitment regarding their children.   Lexile: N/A   (Grades Pre-K–3)   F

Resier, Lynn. *The Surprise Family.* ISBN-13: 9780688154769, 1994

A baby chicken accepts a young boy as her mother and later becomes a surrogate mother for some ducklings that she has hatched. Lexile: 370L (Grades Pre-K–3) F

Rogasky, Barbara. *Winter Poems.* ISBN-13: 9780590428729, 1994

A selection of 25 poems as wide-ranging as William Shakespeare's "When icicles hang by the wall," and excerpts of longer poems by William Wordsworth, Thomas Hardy, Richard Wright, Sara Teasdale, and Robert Frost. Lexile: N/A (Grades 1–5) NF

Say, Allen. *Allison.* ISBN-13: 9780618495375, 1997

When Allison realizes that she looks more like her favorite doll than like her parents, and her parents explain that she is adopted, she comes to terms with this unwelcomed discovery through the help of a stray cat. Lexile: 430L (Grades K–4) F

Updike, John. *A Child's Calendar.* ISBN-13: 9780823417667, 2002

This collection of 12 poems describes the activities in a child's life and the changes in the weather as the year moves from January to December. Lexile: NPL (Grades K–6) NF

Vigna, Judith. *My Two Uncles.* ISBN-13: 9780807555071, 1995

Plans for Elly's grandparents' 50th wedding anniversary party are upset when Grampy refuses to invite Uncle Phil and his friend, Ned, who are gay. Lexile: N/A (Grades 3–7) F

Willhoite, Michael. *Daddy's Roommate.* ISBN-13: 9781555831189, 1990

This book for and about the children of lesbian and gay parents lends to consciousness-raising concerning gay issues. The new arrival at Daddy's house is male. Frank and Daddy are seen pursuing their daily routine (eating, shaving, sleeping—even fighting), and on weekends the three interact easily on their various outings. Lexile: N/A (Grades Pre-K–3) F

Discrimination

Adler, David A. *Child of the Warsaw Ghetto.* ISBN-13: 9780823411603, 1995

This is the sad story of a child living in the Warsaw Ghetto who manages to survive not only the ghetto but also the Dachau concentration camp. Liberated by American soldiers, his story is a memorial to the one and a half million children who did not survive.

Lexile: N/A (Grades 3–7) NF

Adler, David A. *Hiding from the Nazis.* ISBN-13: 9780823416660, 1997

This is the true story of Lore Baer who as a four-year-old Jewish child was placed with a Christian family in the Dutch farm country to avoid persecution by the Nazis.

Lexile: 620L (Grades 3–7) NF

Adler, David A. *A Picture Book of Rosa Parks.* ISBN-13: 9780823411771, 1993

This is a biographical account of the longtime and committed civil-rights activist, whose role in initiating the Montgomery bus boycott ignited discussions about school desegregation, the Ku Klux Klan, and *Brown v. Board of Education.*

Lexile: AD880L (Grades K–4) NF

Bunting, Eve. *Smoky Night.* ISBN-13: 9780152018849, 1999

When the Los Angeles riots break out in the streets of their neighborhood, a young boy and his mother learn the values of getting along with others no matter their background or nationality.

Lexile: 360L   (Grades K–4)   F

Coleman, Evelyn. *White Socks Only.*

ISBN-13: 9780807589564, 1996

Grandma tells the story about her first trip into town during the days when segregation still existed in Mississippi. In the segregated South, a young girl thinks that she can drink from a fountain marked "Whites Only" because she is wearing her white socks.

Lexile: N/A   (Grades K–4)   F

Coles, Robert. *The Story of Ruby Bridges.*   ISBN-13: 9780439472265, 2010

In 1960, six-year-old Ruby Bridges and her family have recently moved from Mississippi to New Orleans in search of a better life. When a judge orders Ruby to attend first grade at William Frantz Elementary, an all-white school, Ruby must face angry mobs of parents who refuse to send their children to school with her.   Lexile: AD730L   (Grades K–4)   NF

Golenbock, Peter, and illustrated by Paul Bacon. *Teammates.*

ISBN-13: 9780152842864, 2010

A moving story of how Jackie Robinson became the first black player on a major league baseball team and the racial prejudice he experienced.   Lexile: 930L   (Grades K–3)   NF

Gray, Libba Moore. *Dear Willie Rudd.*   ISBN-13: 9780689831058, 2000

Fifty years have passed since Miss Elizabeth was a girl, but she still remembers Willie Rudd, the black female housekeeper who helped raise her. In a heartfelt letter, Miss Elizabeth has the chance to tell Willie Rudd something she never told her while she was alive—that she loved her.   Lexile: AD580L   (Grades K–4)   F

Greenfield, Eloise. *Paul Robeson.*   ISBN-13: 9781600602627, 1975

This picture-book biography is of a brilliant but troubled man: the legendary activist, singer, and actor who worked for civil rights and confronted racism and many personal issues.

Lexile: 810L   (Grades 3–7)   NF

Hudson, Wade. *Five Bold Freedom Fighters.*   ISBN-13: 9780590480260, 2001

This is an easy-to-read collection of brief biographies of five black freedom fighters: Richard Allen, Harriet Tubman, Mary Church Terrell, Medgar Evers, and Fannie Lou Hamer.

Lexile: 810L   (Grades K–4)   NF

Krull, Kathleen, translated by F. Isabel Campoy and Alma Flor Ada. *Cosechando esperanza: La historia de César Chávez / Harvesting Hope: The Story of César Chávez.*

ISBN-13: 9780152051693, 2004

The author follows the Chávez family through the Depression and into the hard life as migrant farm laborers. Reflecting on the discrimination and disenfranchisement that plagued his family and fellow Mexican Americans, César decides to work for change.

Lexile: 880L   (Grades K–4)   NF

Lorbiecki, Marybeth. *Sister Anne's Hands.*   ISBN-13: 9780140565348, 2000

It's the early 1960s, and a young girl has never seen a person with dark skin—until she meets Sister Anne. When a classmate directs a racist remark toward Sister Anne, the teacher's wise way of turning the incident into a powerful learning experience has a profound impact on Anna.   Lexile: 580L   (Grades Pre-K–4)   F

McKissack, Patricia C. *Goin' Someplace Special.*   ISBN-13: 9781416927358, 2008

In segregated 1950s Nashville, a young African American girl braves a series of indignities and obstacles to get to one of the few integrated places in town: the public library.

Lexile: 0550L   (Grades Pre-K–4)   F

McKissack, Patricia C., and Frederick L. McKissack. *Mary Church Terrell: Leader for Equality.*   ISBN-13: 9780766016972, 2002

This inspiring biography chronicles the life and accomplishments of this African American civil rights activist.   Lexile: N/A   (Grades K–4)   NF

Mochizuki, Ken. *Baseball Saved Us.*   ISBN-13: 9781880000199, 1995

When a Japanese American boy and his family are interned in a camp during World War II, they decide to combat their depression by building a baseball field. During a game the boy channels his humiliation—both from being a prisoner and from being a bad player—to anger, giving him the strength to hit a game-winning home run.

Lexile: AD550L   (Grades 1–4)   F

Noguchi, Rick, and Deneen Jenks. *Flowers from Mariko.*   ISBN-13: 9781584300328, 2001

Mariko's family has been freed from a Japanese American internment camp, but the transition hasn't been easy. This book tells of a family striving to reestablish their lives through hope, perseverance, and love.   Lexile: N/A   (Grades K–4)   F

Paek, Min. *Aekyung's Dream.*   ISBN-13: 9780892390427, 1988

A shy Korean girl experiencing great difficulty in adjusting to America, overcomes her tears and fears, learns English, and gains her classmates' respect through her painting skills.

Lexile: 480L   (Grades K–4)   F

Pak, Soyung. *Sumi's First Day of School Ever.*   ISBN-13: 9780670035229, 2003

This is a book about a young Korean girl on her first day of school. She has a considerate teacher and even a new friend who helps Sumi discover that school might not be so lonely.

Lexile: N/A   (Grades Pre-K–3)   F

Pérez, L. King. *First Day in Grapes.* ISBN-13: 9781584300458, 2002

When Chico starts the third grade after his migrant worker family moves to begin harvesting California grapes, he finds that self-confidence and math skills help him cope with the first day in a new school. Lexile: AD570L (Grades 1–5) F

Ringgold, Faith. *Aunt Harriet's Underground Railroad in the Sky.*

ISBN-13: 9780517885437, 1992

With Harriet Tubman as her guide, Cassie retraces the steps escaping slaves took on the Underground Railroad to reunite with her younger brother.

Lexile: AD760L (Grades K–4) F

Ringgold, Faith. *If a Bus Could Talk: The Story of Rosa Parks.*

ISBN-13: 9780689856761, 2003

Marcie learns why Rosa Parks is the mother of the Civil Rights movement. At the end of Marcie's magical ride, she meets Rosa Parks herself at a birthday party with several distinguished guests. Lexile: 0790L (Grades K–4) F

Uchida, Yoshiko. *The Bracelet.* ISBN-13: 9780698113909, 1996

The year is 1942 and America is at war with Japan. All Japanese Americans are being sent to live in internment camps for the duration of the war, including seven-year-old Emi and her family. Emi's friend, Laurie, gives her a gold heart bracelet to remember their friendship. But Emi loses the bracelet and worries how she will remember her friend.

Lexile: 970L (Grades K–5) F

Uchida, Yoshiko. *Journey to Topaz.* ISBN-13: 9781890771911, 1971

This is the moving story of one girl's struggle to remain brave during the Japanese internment of World War II. In a bleak and dusty prison camp, 11-year-old Yuki and her family experience both true friendship and heart-wrenching tragedy. Lexile: N/A (Grades K–4) F

Wells, Rosemary. *Streets of Gold.* ISBN-13: 9780803721494, 1991

Based on a memoir written in the early 20th century, this picture book tells the story of a young girl and her life in Russia, her travels to America, and her subsequent life in the United States. Lexile: AD770L (Grades K–5) NF

Wiles, Deborah. *Freedom Summer.* ISBN-13: 9780689878299, 2001

Set in 1964, Joe and John Henry like shooting marbles, they both want to be firemen, and they both love to swim; however, there's one important way they're different: Joe is white and John Henry is black. Laws and attitudes are changing in the South, but it takes more than a new law to change people's hearts. Lexile: 0460L (Grades Pre-K–3) F

Woodson, Jacqueline. *The Other Side.* ISBN-13: 9780399231162, 2001

Two girls, one white and one black, gradually get to know each other as they sit on the fence that divides their town. Lexile: AD300L (Grades K–5) F

Yin. *Coolies.*   ISBN-13: 9780142500552, 2003

This story reveals the harsh truth about life for the Chinese railroad workers in 1865, while celebrating their perseverance and bravery. A young boy hears the story of his great-great-great-grandfather and his brother who came to the United States to make a better life for themselves and to help build the transcontinental railroad.   Lexile: 660L   (Grades K–4)   F

Homelessness

Bunting, Eve. *December.* ISBN-13: 9780152024222, 2000

Simon and his mom live in a cardboard box, but they have a scrap of a Christmas tree and some decorations they found, including Simon's toy soldier and an angel on the wall, named December, torn from an old calendar. On Christmas Eve, an old woman begs them to share their box, and they let her in, where Simon offers her one of the two cookies he is saving for Christmas day. The next Christmas Eve finds Simon and his mother in a real apartment.   Lexile: 0510L   (Grades Pre-K–3)   F

Bunting, Eve. *Fly Away Home.*   ISBN-13: 9780395664155, 1998

A small child narrates the facts of his homeless existence sleeping, sitting up, washing in the restroom, and, above all, avoiding being noticed.   Lexile: 0450L   (Grades Pre-K–3)   F

Carlson, Nancy Savage. *The Family Under the Bridge.*   ISBN-13: 9780064402507, 1989

Old Armand, enjoyed his solitary, carefree life in Paris until he found that three homeless children and their working mother had claimed his shelter under the bridge.

Lexile: 0680L   (Grades 3–8)   F

Creel, Ann Howard. *A Ceiling of Stars.*   ISBN-13: 9781562477530, 1999

In figuring out how to cope when life gets tough, 12-year-old Vivien must face her sudden homelessness alone in a big city when her mother abandons her. Vivien tells her story through a series of hopeful letters and journal entries.   Lexile: N/A   (Grades 4–8)   F

Evans, Douglas. *So What Do You Do?*   ISBN-13: 9781886910201, 1997

Charlie isn't sure why he follows the filthy, shambling street person into the public library—until he realizes with a shock that it's Joe Adams, his all-time favorite teacher.

Lexile: N/A   (Grades 4–12)   F

Guthrie, Donna. *A Rose for Abby.*   ISBN-13: 9780687060801, 1997

Abby, whose father preaches in a large urban church, sees a homeless old woman searching the trash cans nearby and is inspired to do something for the neighborhood's many street people.   Lexile: AD370L   (Grades Pre-K–3)   F

Holtwijk, Ineke. *Asphalt Angels.*   ISBN-13: 9781886910249, 1995

When 13-year-old Alex is kicked out of the house by his abusive stepfather after his mother's death, he decides to make his home on the streets of Rio de Janeiro, where he must survive confrontations with corrupt police officers, pedophiles, and fellow homeless persons.

Lexile: 490L   (Grades 7–12)   F

Lobel, Anita. *No Pretty Pictures: A Child of War.*   ISBN-13: 9780061565892, 2008

Since coming to the United States as a teenager, Anita has spent her life making pictures. She has never gone back. She has never looked back.   Lexile: 0750L   (Grades 3–8)   F

London, Jonathan. *Where's Home?*   ISBN-13: 9780140375138, 1997

Adrian tells how he and his Vietnam vet dad have lost everything, and now they've hitch-hiked west to San Francisco. They meet all kinds of down-and-out people while making friends along the way.   Lexile: N/A   (Grades 5–7)   F

Martin, Chia. *Rosie: The Shopping Cart Lady.*   ISBN-13: 9780934252515, 1996

This book paints the picture of Rosie through a child's eyes and shows the magic power of simple love.   Lexile: N/A   (Grades 3–6)   F

McGovern, Ann. *Lady in the Box.*   ISBN-13: 9781890515157, 1999

When Lizzie and Ben discover a homeless lady living in their neighborhood, they must reconcile their desire to help her with their mother's admonition not to talk to strangers.

Lexile: AD370L   (Grades K–5)   F

Polacco, Patricia. *I Can Hear the Sun: A Modern Myth.*   ISBN-13: 9780698118577, 1999

Stephanie Michelle, who cares for animals and listens to the sun, believes Fondo, the homeless child, when he tells her that the geese have invited him to fly away with them.

Lexile: 0530L   (Grades Pre-K–3)   F

Powell, E. Sandy. *Chance to Grow.*   ISBN-13: 9780876145807, 1992

Joe, his sister, Gracey, and their mother are evicted from their apartment and left homeless. They work together and find a hopeful ending as the family obtains a one-room flat in exchange for doing housework.   Lexile: N/A   (Grades Pre-K–3)   F

Special Needs

Abbott, Deborah, and Henry Kisor. *One TV Blasting and a Pig Outdoors.*   ISBN-13: 9780807560754, 1994

Conan describes life with his father who lost his hearing at the age of three.   Lexile: N/A   (Grades 3–8)   F

Alexander, Sally Hobart. *Mom's Best Friend.*

ISBN-13: 9780027003932, 1992

This book describes how a blind mother adjusts to getting a new guide dog.   Lexile: N/A   (Grades 3–8)   NF

Bang, Molly. *Tiger's Fall.*   ISBN-13: 9780805066890, 2001

After 11-year-old Lupe is partially paralyzed in an accident in her Mexican village, other people with disabilities help her realize that her life can have real purpose.

Lexile: N/A   (Grades 3–8)   F

Blatchford, Claire H. *Going with the Flow.*   ISBN-13: 9781575052847, 1998

When Mark changes schools in mid-year, he is angry, lonely, and embarrassed by his deafness, but he soon begins to adjust. The book includes information about deafness and illustrations of sign language.   Lexile: N/A   (Grades 2–5)   F

Brimner, Larry Dane. *The Sidewalk Patrol.*   ISBN-13: 9780516273877, 2002

Gabby and her friends take time to move some bicycles so that their blind neighbor can walk on the sidewalk.   Lexile: N/A   (Grades 1–3)   F

Carlson, Nancy. *Arnie and the New Kid.*   ISBN-13: 9780440845768, 1992

When an accident requires Arnie to use crutches, he begins to understand the limits and possibilities of his new classmate, who has a wheelchair.   Lexile: N/A   (Grades 1–3)   F

Carter, Carol S. *Seeing Things My Way.*   ISBN-13: 9780807572962, 1998

A second-grader describes how she and other students learn to use a variety of equipment and methods to cope with their visual impairments.   Lexile: N/A   (Grades 1–3)   F

Christopher, Matt. *Wheel Wizards.*   ISBN-13: 9780316094580, 2009

Angry and unhappy because he is now in a wheelchair and apparently no longer able to play basketball, 12-year-old Seth is amazed to discover wheelchair basketball and finds that his life is not over after all.   Lexile: N/A   (Grades 4–8)   F

Cohen, Miriam. *See You Tomorrow, Charles.*   ISBN-13: 9780440411512, 1997

The first graders learn to accept the new boy, who is blind, as just like themselves.

Lexile: 390L   (Grades 1–3)   F

Daly, Niki. *Once Upon a Time.*   ISBN-13: 9780374356330, 2003

Sarie struggles when she reads aloud in class in her South African school, but then she and her friend Auntie Anna find a book about Cinderella in Auntie's old car and begin to read together.   Lexile: N/A   (Grades Pre-K–3)   F

Davis, Patricia Anne. *Brian's Bird.*   ISBN-13: 9780807508817, 2000

Eight-year-old Brian, who is blind, learns how to take care of his new parakeet and comes to realize that his older brother, while sometimes careless, is not so bad after all.

Lexile: N/A   (Grades Pre-K–3)   F

Ely, Lesley. *Looking After Lewis.*   ISBN-13: 9780807547465, 2004

When a new boy with autism joins their classroom, the children try to understand his world and to include him in theirs.   Lexile: N/A   (Grades Pre-K–3)   F

Fleming, Virginia. *Be Good to Eddie Lee.*　　　　ISBN-13: 9780399219931, 1993

Although Christy considered him a pest, when Eddie Lee, a boy with Down syndrome, follows her into the woods, he shares several special discoveries with her.

Lexile: N/A　(Grades Pre-K–3)　F

Gantos, Jack. *Joey Pigza Swallowed the Key.*　　　ISBN-13: 9780312623555, 2001

To the constant disappointment of his mother and his teachers, Joey has trouble paying attention or controlling his mood swings when his prescription meds wear off and he starts getting worked up and acting wired.　　　Lexile: 970L　(Grades 5–9)　F

Gehret, Jeanne. *The Don't-Give-Up Kid and Learning Differences.*

ISBN-13: 9781884281105, 1996

As Alex becomes aware of his different learning style, he realizes his hero Thomas Edison had similar problems. Together they try new solutions until they succeed at their dream to create things that no one ever thought of before.　　Lexile: N/A　(Grades 1–5)　F

Gifaldi, David. *Ben, King of the River.*　　　　　ISBN-13: 9780807506356, 2001

Chad experiences a range of emotions when he goes camping with his parents and his five-year-old mentally disabled brother Ben, who has many developmental problems.

Lexile: N/A　(Grades K–3)　F

Greenberg, Judith E. *What Is the Sign for Friend?*　　ISBN-13: 9780531049396, 1988

Text and photographs depict the life of Shane, a deaf child who goes to regular school and enjoys normal activities with the help of sign language and a hearing aid.

Lexile: N/A　(Grades K–6)　F

Gregory, Nan. *How Smudge Came.*　　　　　　ISBN-13: 9780802775221, 1997

Cindy, who lives in a group home and works all day at Hospice House, fights to keep the small stray dog she finds on the street.　　Lexile: 280L　(Grades K–3)　F

Harrar, George. *Parents Wanted.*　　　　　　ISBN-13: 9781571316332, 2001

Twelve-year-old Andrew, who has ADD, is adopted by new parents after years of living in foster homes, and he desperately hopes that he will not mess up the situation.

Lexile: N/A　(Grades 3–8)　F

Harshman, Marc. *The Storm.*　　　　　　　ISBN-13: 9780525651505, 1995

Although confined to a wheelchair, Jonathan faces the terror of a tornado all by himself and saves the lives of the horses on the family farm.　Lexile: AD860L　(Grades K–3)　F

Lears, Laurie. *Ian's Walk: A Story About Autism.*　ISBN-13: 9780807534816, 1998

A young girl realizes how much she cares about her autistic brother when he gets lost at the park.　　　　　　　　　　Lexile: 0430L　(Grades K–3)　F

Lears, Laurie. *Nathan's Wish: A Story About Cerebral Palsy.*　ISBN-13: 9780807571019, 2005

A boy with cerebral palsy helps out at a raptor rehabilitation center and is inspired himself when an owl that cannot fly finds another purpose in life.　Lexile: N/A　(Grades 1–4)　F

Lears, Laurie. *Waiting for Mr. Goose.*   ISBN-13: 9780807586280, 1999

Stephen, who has trouble sitting still and paying attention, surprises himself when he summons up the patience to catch and help an injured goose.   Lexile: N/A   (Grades K–3)   F

Matlin, Marlee. *Deaf Child Crossing.*   ISBN-13: 9780689866968, 2004

Despite the fact that Megan is deaf and Cindy can hear, the two girls become friends when Cindy moves into Megan's neighborhood. But when they go away to camp, their friendship is put to the test.   Lexile: N/A   (Grades 3–6)   F

Millman, Isaac. *Moses Goes to a Concert.*   ISBN-13: 9780374453664, 2002

Moses and his schoolmates who are deaf attend a concert where the orchestra's percussionist is also deaf.   Lexile: 0670L   (Grades K–3)   F

Moore-Malinos, Jennifer. *It's Called Dyslexia.*   ISBN-13: 9780764137945, 2007

The little girl in this story is unhappy and she no longer enjoys school. When learning to read and write, she tries to remember which way the letters go, but she often gets them all mixed up. After she discovers that dyslexia is the reason for her trouble, she begins to understand that with extra practice and help from others, she will begin to read and write correctly.   Lexile: N/A   (Grades 1–3)   F

Niner, Holly L. *I Can't Stop! A Story About Tourette's Syndrome.*

ISBN-13: 9780807536209, 2005

A boy is diagnosed with Tourette's syndrome and learns about constructive ways he can manage his condition.   Lexile: N/A   (Grades 2–5)   F

Paterson, Katherine. *Marvin One Too Many.*   ISBN-13: 9780064442794, 2003

Marvin cannot read, but he eventually learns how with some help from his father.

Lexile: N/A   (Grades 2–5)   F

Peterson, Jeanne Whitehouse. *I Have a Sister: My Sister Is Deaf.*

ISBN-13: 9780064430593, 1984

A young girl describes how her deaf sister experiences everyday things.

Lexile: 520L   (Grades K–4)   F

Polacco, Patricia. *Thank You, Mr. Falker.*   ISBN-13: 9780399257629, 2012

At first, Trisha loves school, but her difficulty learning to read makes her feel dumb, until she reaches the fifth grade and a new teacher helps her understand and overcome her problem.   Lexile: N/A   (Grades K–4)   F

Powell, Jillian. *Jordan Has a Hearing Loss.*   ISBN-13: 9780791081792, 2004

This story follows a day in the life of Jordan, who uses sign language, reads lips, and wakes up each day with a vibrating alarm clock.   Lexile: N/A   (Grades 2–4)   NF

Powell, Jillian. *Luke Has Down's Syndrome.*   ISBN-13: 9780791081839, 2004

Luke shares a first-person account of what it's like to have Down syndrome.

Lexile: N/A   (Grades 2–4)   NF

Pulver, Robin. *Way to Go, Alex!*   ISBN-13: 9780807515839, 1999

Carly learns a lot about Alex, her mentally disabled older brother, as he trains for and competes in the Special Olympics.   Lexile: N/A   (Grades 2–4)   F

Rau, Dana Meachen. *The Secret Code.*   ISBN-13: 9780516263625, 1998

Oscar, who is blind, teaches Lucy how to read his braille book.

Lexile: 0330L   (Grades 2–4)   F

Robb, Diane Burton. *The Alphabet War: A Story About Dyslexia.*

ISBN-13: 9780807503027, 2004

Learning to read is a great struggle for Adam, but with expert help, hard work, and belief in himself, he wins "The Alphabet War." This book includes information about dyslexia.

Lexile: N/A   (Grades 2–5)   F

Senisi, Ellen B. *All Kinds of Friends, Even Green!*   ISBN-13: 9781890627355, 2002

In a school assignment, seven-year-old Moses, who has spina bifida and uses a wheelchair, reflects that his neighbor's disabled iguana resembles him because they both have figured out how to get where they want to be in different ways than those around them.

Lexile: N/A   (Grades 2–5)   F

Senisi, Ellen B. *Just Kids: Visiting a Class for Children with Special Needs.*

ISBN-13: 9780525456469, 1998

Second-grader Cindy is assigned to spend part of each day in the class for students with special needs, where she finds out that even though some kids may learn differently or have different abilities, they are all "just kids."   Lexile: 690L   (Grades 2–5)   F

Shriver, Maria. *What's Wrong with Timmy?*   ISBN-13: 9780316233378, 2001

Making friends with a mentally handicapped boy helps Kate learn that the two of them have a lot in common.   Lexile: 570L   (Grades 1–6)   F

Smith, Mark. *Pay Attention, Slosh!*   ISBN-13: 9780807563786, 1997

Eight-year-old Josh hates being unable to concentrate or control himself, but with the help of his parents, his teacher, and a doctor, he learns to deal with his condition, known as ADHD or attention-deficit hyperactivity disorder.   Lexile: N/A   (Grades 2–4)   F

Spinelli, Jerry. *Loser.*   ISBN-13: 9780060540746, 2003

Other kids have their own word to describe him, but Zinkoff is too busy to hear it. He doesn't know he's not like everyone else. And one winter night, Zinkoff's differences show that any name can someday become "hero."   Lexile: 0650L   (Grades 3–8)   F

Stuve-Bodeen, Stephanie. *We'll Paint the Octopus.*   ISBN-13: 9781890627065, 1998

Emma and her father discuss what they will do when the new baby arrives, but they adjust their expectations when he is born with Down syndrome.

Lexile: N/A   (Grades Pre-K–3)   F

Thompson, Mary. *Andy and His Yellow Frisbee.*　　　ISBN-13: 9780933149830, 1996

The new girl at school tries to befriend Andy, a boy with autism who spends every recess by himself, spinning a yellow Frisbee under the watchful eye of his older sister.

Lexile: N/A　(Grades 2–4)　F

Woloson, Eliza. *My Friend Isabelle.*　　　ISBN-13: 9781890627508, 2003

A young boy named Charlie describes the activities he shares with his friend Isabelle, a girl with Down syndrome.　　　Lexile: N/A　(Grades K–4)　F

Yolen, Jane. *The Seeing Stick.*　　　ISBN-13: 9780762420483, 2009

This folktale relates the story of how an old man teaches the emperor's blind daughter to see with the use of a mysterious seeing stick.　　　Lexile: N/A　(Grades Pre-K–2)　F

Zimmett, Debbie. *Eddie, Enough!*　　　ISBN-13: 9781890627256, 2001

Third-grader Eddie Minetti is always getting in trouble at school until his ADHD is diagnosed and treated.　　　Lexile: N/A　(Grades Pre-K–2)　F

References

Day, F. A. (1994). *Multicultural Voices in Contemporary Literature.* Portsmouth, NH: Heinemann.

Higgins, J. (2010). *Multicultural Children's Literature: Creating and Applying an Evaluation Tool in Response to the Needs of Urban Educators.* School of Education at Johns Hopkins University. http://education.jhu.edu/newhorizons/strategies/topics/literacy /articles/multicultural_childrens_literature_/index.html

Rochman, H. (1993). *Against Borders: Promoting Books for a Multicultural World.* Chicago, IL: American Library Association. ISBN-13: 9780838906019

Sims Bishop, R. (1992). "Multicultural Literature for Children: Making Informed Choices." In Harris, V. J. (Ed.), *Teaching Multicultural Literature in Grades K–8.* Norwood, MA: Christopher-Gordon Publishers, Inc.

Slapin, B., Seale, D., & Gonzales, R. (1992). "How to Tell the Difference: A Checklist." In Slapin, B., & Seale, D. (Ed.), *Through Indian Eyes: The Native Experience in Books for Children.* Philadelphia, PA: New Society Publishers.

Vardell, S. M., Hardaway, N. L., & Young, T. A. (2006). "Matching Books and Readers: Selecting Literature for English Language Learners." *The Reading Teacher*, 59, 734–748.

10

Literature for Children and Young Adults That Highlights Character Traits

Today, a variety of character education programs take place in schools. Some are commercial, some are nonprofit, and some are designed by states or specifically by districts and schools. These programs typically include a list of principles, pillars, values, or virtues that provide the basis of themed activities. It is commonly claimed that the values included in any particular list are universally recognized. But when taking background, culture, religion, gender, age, and other variables into account, it is difficult to agree on what constitutes core values. Nonetheless, a handful of general character traits are often considered—for example, honesty, stewardship, kindness, generosity, courage, freedom, justice, equality, and respect.

Character education can refer to teaching that imparts positive character qualities such as moral, civic-minded, good, well-mannered, non-bullying, healthy, critical, successful, traditional, cooperative, and social members of society. Concepts that now and in the past have fallen under this designation include social and emotional learning, moral reasoning, cognitive development, life-skills education, health education, violence prevention, critical thinking, ethical reasoning, and conflict resolution and mediation.

No matter what your state, district, or school requires in terms of teaching character education, including books in the daily curriculum related to such topics as an authentic and organic way to open conversations in the classroom, regardless of age or grade level. Reading books aloud on character traits and having critical discussions to follow allows students to hear from one another and experience how their classmates respond to said topics.

The following lists are organized by character trait and provide corresponding literature that can serve your classroom library, school library, read-alouds, silent reading, and more. Incorporating group strategies, reading strategies, and English language development (ELD) strategies when sharing these books with your students allows for full focus on the topics of these books and offers a good starting place for planning strong curriculum in this area.

Citizenship

Craig, Joe. *Top 10 Tips for Ethical Living and Good Citizenship.*

ISBN-13: 9781448868643, 2012

This book has several ideas that young people can do to be good citizens. Lexile: N/A (Grades 6–12) NF

DiSalvo-Ryan, DyAnne. *City Green.*

ISBN-13: 9780688127862, 1994

In the middle of a city block is a vacant lot, and Marcy decides it is time to turn it into a community garden.

Lexile: AD480L (Grades 2–3) F

Fleischman, Paul. *Seedfolks.* ISBN-13: 9780064472074, 1999

In a vacant lot surrounded by a diverse community of people, a young girl clears a space to plant bean seeds. Over time, community members plant their own cultural seeds, and eventually the community is sharing vegetables and finding that they share many things in common. Lexile: 710L (Grades 4–8) F

Glassman, Bruce. *Citizenship.* ISBN-13: 9781601085023, 2008

This book explains the importance of citizenship in both history and contemporary society, for instance, the Boston Tea Party and today's voter turnout. It shows how citizenship is important in students' own lives, explaining what steps they can take to develop it.

Lexile: N/A (Grades 3–6) NF

Harper, Leslie. *What Is Citizenship?* ISBN-13: 9781448874354, 2012

This book includes a description and discussion related to good citizenship.

Lexile: N/A (Grades 3–6) NF

Munson, Derek. *Enemy Pie.* ISBN-13: 9780811827782, 2000

It was the perfect summer until Jeremy Ross moved into the house down the street and became the neighborhood enemy. Luckily Dad had a surefire way to get rid of enemies: Enemy Pie. But part of the secret recipe is doing the right thing even when you don't want to—by spending an entire day playing with the enemy. Lexile: N/A (Grades K–3) F

Naylor, Phyllis Reynolds. *King of the Playground.* ISBN-13: 9780689718021, 1994

Kevin loves the playground, but not when Sammy is there. Sammy thinks he is King of the Playground. If he catches Kevin playing there, Sammy says, he will do mean things to him. Kevin gets his courage up and goes to the playground even though Sammy says he can't come in. Lexile: 310L (Grades K–3) F

Raatma, Lucia. *Citizenship.* ISBN-13: 9781602793248, 2009

This book includes simple activities that encourage students to look, think, make a guess, ask questions, and create materials that relate to good citizenship.
Lexile: 910L (Grades 3–6) NF

Skog, Jason. *Citizenship.* ISBN-13: 9781429613316, 2008

This book looks at the rights and responsibilities of U.S. citizens, starting with an exploration of "people power," and gives readers a brief explanation of voting rights.
Lexile: GN750L (Grades 3–6) NF

Small, Mary. *Being a Good Citizen.* ISBN-13: 9781404810501, 2005

This book has many examples of ideas that children can do to be good citizens. The values taught in this book will show children the importance of being a good citizen and the importance of being a good person. Lexile: NC650L (Grades K–3) NF

Courage

Bains, Rae. *Harriet Tubman: The Road to Freedom.*
ISBN-13: 9780893757618, 1996

This is a biography of a slave whose flight to freedom became the first step of her becoming a "conductor" on the Underground Railroad. Lexile: 680L (Grades 3–8) NF

Bridges, Ruby. *Through My Eyes: Ruby Bridges.*
ISBN-13: 9780590189231, 1999

In November 1960, all of America watched as a tiny six-year-old black girl, surrounded by federal marshalls, walked through a mob of screaming segregationists and into her school. An icon of the civil rights movement, Ruby Bridges chronicles each dramatic step of this pivotal event in history. Lexile: 860l (Grades 3–6) NF

Bunting, Eve. *Girls: A to Z.*   ISBN-13: 9781620910283, 2013

The world is full of great things to be and do. Meet Aliki, Belinda, Chris, and 23 more girls who are imagining what they will be when they grow up—from astronaut to zookeeper.

Lexile: N/A   (Grades K–2)   NF

Catt, Michael. *Courageous Teens.*   ISBN-13: 9781433679063, 2012

This is a book of stories of people in the Bible who displayed great courage when it would have been easier to play it safe.   Lexile: N/A   (Grades 7–12)   NF

Cushman, Karen. *Catherine, Called Birdy.*   ISBN-13: 9780547722184, 2012

Can a sharp-tongued, high-spirited, clever young maiden with a mind of her own actually lose the battle against an ill-mannered, piglike lord and an unimaginative, greedy toad of a father? Not if Catherine has anything to say about it!   Lexile: N/A   (Grades 4–8)   F

DiCamillo, Kate. *Because of Winn-Dixie.*   ISBN-13: 9780763644321, 2009

Ten-year-old India Opal Buloni describes her first summer in the town of Naomi, Florida, and all the good things that happen to her because of her big ugly dog, Winn-Dixie.

Lexile: 610L   (Grades 3–6)   F

Fosberry, Jennifer. *My Name Is Not Isabella: Just How Big Can a Little Girl Dream?*

ISBN-13: 9781402243950, 2010

Join Isabella on an adventure of discovery—and find out how imagining to be these extraordinary women teaches her the importance of being her extraordinary self.

Lexile: AD640L   (Grades K–3)   F

Frank, Anne. *The Diary of a Young Girl.*   ISBN-13: 9780553296983, 1993

Anne Frank is an inspirational story of the hardships of World War II from the perspective of a 13-year old Jewish girl in hiding during the Holocaust. In her diary, Anne shares her thoughts, feelings, and insights about the many issues and conflicts in an attic where her own family and another family hid for two years.   Lexile: 1080L   (Grades 4–8)   NF

Greive, Bradley Trevor. *A Teaspoon of Courage for Kids: A Little Book of Encouragement for Whenever You Need It.*   ISBN-13: 9780740769498, 2007

This book is meant for those young, timid children who could use a little courage to face tough and intimidating times.   Lexile: N/A   (Grades K–4)   NF

Littell, Alan. *Courage.*   ISBN-13: 9780312384364, 2008

In this ocean adventure the story involves a cargo ship in distress during a storm 150 miles off the coast of Ireland in the winter of 1950, and a second ship that sends part of its crew on a rescue mission. The protagonist, John Driscoll, overcomes his fear of the water to follow the path of a life at sea.   Lexile: N/A   (Grades 7–12)   F

McCain, Becky Ray. *Nobody Knew What to Do: A Story About Bullying.*

ISBN-13: 9780807557112, 2001

This story tells how one child found the courage to tell a teacher about Ray, who was being picked on and bullied by other kids in school.   Lexile: N/A   (Grades 1–4)   F

Opdyke, Irene Gut. *In My Hands: Memories of a Holocaust Rescuer.*

ISBN-13: 9780553494112, 2004

This memoir recounts the experiences of the author who, as a young Polish girl, hid and saved Jews during the Holocaust. Lexile: 0890L (Grades 9–12) NF

Pinkney, Andrea Davis. *Let It Shine: Stories of Black Women Freedom Fighters.*

ISBN-13: 9780547906041, 2013

Harriet Tubman escaped slavery, but she returned often to the South to lead slaves to freedom. Rosa Parks refused to give up her seat on a bus and sparked a protest that changed America. These two, along with Sojourner Truth, Mary McLeod Bethune, Biddy Mason, Ida B. Wells-Barnett, Ella Josephine Baker, Dorothy Irene Height, Fannie Lou Harner, and Shirley Chisholm are 10 of the many who let their light shine brightly on the darkness of discrimination. Lexile: N/A (Grades 3–6) NF

Pinkney, Andrea Davis. *With the Might of Angels (Dear America Series).*

ISBN-13: 9780545297059, 2011

In the fall of 1955, 12-year-old Dawn Rae Johnson's life turns upside down. After the Supreme Court ruling in *Brown v. Board of Education*, Dawnie learns she will be attending a previously all-white school. She's the only one of her friends to go to this new school and to leave the comfort of all that is familiar to face great uncertainty in the school year ahead. However, not everyone supports integration, and much of the town is outraged at the decision. Dawnie must endure the harsh realities of racism firsthand, while continuing to work hard to get a good education and prove she deserves the opportunity.

Lexile: 740L (Grades 3–6) NF

Talbott, Hudson. *O'Sullivan Stew.* ISBN-13: 9780698118898, 2001

Someone has stolen the witch of Crookhaven's horse, and there will be no peace in the village until it is returned. So bold, brassy Kate O'Sullivan takes matters into her own hands. But instead of saving the day, she manages to land herself and her family in trouble with the king. So Kate sets out to save their hides. Lexile: N/A (Grades K–3) F

Turnage, Sheila. *Three Times Lucky.* ISBN-13: 9780803736702, 2012

Sixth-grader Miss Moses LoBeau lives in the small town of Tupelo Landing, North Carolina. She washed ashore in a hurricane 11 years ago. Mo hopes someday to find her mother, but she's found a home with the Colonel and Miss Lana. She will protect those she loves with every bit of her strong will and tough attitude. So when a lawman comes to town asking about a murder, Mo and her best friend, Dale Earnhardt Johnson III, set out to uncover the truth in hopes of saving the only family Mo has ever known.

Lexile: 560L (Grades 5–8) F

Waber, Bernard. *Courage.* ISBN-13: 9780618238552, 2002

There are many kinds of courage. This thoughtful picture book explores different types of courage. Lexile: N/A (Grades K–3) F

Fairness

Bausum, Ann. *With Courage and Cloth: Winning the Fight for a Woman's Right to Vote.*

ISBN-13: 9780792276470, 2004

The book starts with basic history on the struggle for women's rights, other groups' battles for the vote, and background on the 19th-century women's suffrage movement before focusing on the 20th-century efforts to enfranchise women. It details and illustrates the political lobbying and public protests organized by women's groups and the backlash against these efforts, including intimidation, imprisonment, hunger strikes, and forced feeding of prisoners.   Lexile: 1080L   (Grades 5–12)   NF

Blumenthal, Karen. *Let Me Play: The Story of Title IX: The Law That Changed the Future of Girls in America.*   ISBN-13: 9780689859571, 2005

This is a powerful tale of courage and persistence—the stories of the people who believed that girls could do anything and were willing to fight to prove it.

Lexile: 1140L   (Grades 3–6)   NF

Finn, Carrie. *Kids Talk About Fairness.*   ISBN-13: 9781404823167, 2006

This book teaches the concept of fairness in relation to giving and receiving gifts, girls in sports, and navigating fairness issues in relation to children with disabilities. It also delves into tough questions kids pose about the social world in which they live.

Lexile: 590L   (Grades 2–5)   NF

Hoose, Philip. *Claudette Colvin: Twice Toward Justice.*   ISBN-13: 9780312661052, 2010

On March 2, 1955, an impassioned teenager, fed up with the daily injustices of Jim Crow segregation, refused to give her seat to a white woman on a segregated bus in Montgomery, Alabama. Instead of being celebrated as Rosa Parks would be just nine months later, 15-year-old Claudette Colvin found herself shunned by her classmates and dismissed by community leaders.   Lexile: 1000L   (Grades 6–10)   NF

Loewen, Nancy. *No Fair! Kids Talk About Fairness.*   ISBN-13: 9781404803664, 2005

Life isn't always fair, or is it? Hear what Tina Truly has to say about fairness.

Lexile: 640L   (Grades 3–6)   NF

McDermott, Gerald. *The Fox and the Stork.*   ISBN-13: 9780152048372, 2003

The story of a fox who thinks he is so clever—until Stork outfoxes him and teaches him about friendship.   Lexile: 250L   (Grades K–8)   F

Ludwig, Trudy. *Trouble Talk.*   ISBN-13: 9781582462400, 2008

Maya's friend Bailey loves to talk about everything and everyone. At first, Maya thinks Bailey is funny. But when Bailey's talk leads to harmful rumors and hurt feelings, Maya begins to think twice about their friendship.   Lexile: N/A   (Grades 1–4)   F

Matsuno, Masuko. *A Pair of Red Clogs.*   ISBN-13: 9781930900202, 2002

Mako, a little Japanese girl, delights in her new shoes—clogs painted with red lacquer that shone beautifully. This is the story of what happened after she cracked the new clogs playing the weather-telling game and so longed for a bright, shiny new pair to replace them that she almost did a dishonest thing.   Lexile: N/A   (Grades Pre-K–3)   F

McKissack, Patricia C. *The Honest-to-Goodness Truth.*   ISBN-13: 9780689826689, 2000

After promising never to lie, Libby learns that it's not always necessary to blurt out the whole truth either.   Lexile: 450L   (Grades Pre–K–3)   F

Naylor, Phyllis Reynolds. *Shiloh.*   ISBN-13: 9780689835827, 2000

Marty, 11, finds an abused beagle pup and wants to keep it instead of returning it to the abusive owner. His parents convince him that returning the dog is the right thing to do, but soon after he returns Shiloh, the dog runs back to Marty, who decides to keep the dog and hide him in the woods. Marty must lie to cover up his efforts to save the dog.

Lexile: 0890L   (Grades 3–8)   F

Nettleton, Pamela Hill. *Is That True? Kids Talk About Honesty.*

ISBN-13: 9781404806191, 2004

A 13-year-old gives computer-generated written responses to younger children who request advice on everything from cheating to protective lies.   Lexile: 660L   (Grades K–6)   NF

Recorvits, Helen. *Yoon and the Jade Bracelet.*   ISBN-13: 9780374386894, 2008

It is Yoon's birthday and all she wants is a jump rope so she can play with the other girls in the school yard. Instead, Yoon's mother gives her a Korean storybook about a silly girl who is tricked by a tiger. Yoon also receives a jade bracelet that once belonged to her grandmother. The next day at school, a girl offers to teach Yoon how to jump rope, but for a price: she wants to borrow the jade bracelet. When Yoon tries to get her bracelet back, the girl swears it belongs to her.   Lexile: N/A   (Grades Pre-K–3)   F

Sharmat, Marjorie Weinman. *The Big Fat Enormous Lie.*   ISBN-13: 9780140547375, 1993

A boy's little lie comes alive in the form of a monster that grows and grows, until he finds the only way to make it go away—by telling the truth to his parents and taking the consequences for lying in the first place.   Lexile: 290L   (Grades K–2)   F

Smothers, Ethel Footman. *The Hard-Times Jar.*   ISBN-13: 9780374328528, 2003

Emma, the daughter of poor migrant workers, longs to own a real book, and when she turns eight and must attend school for the first time, she is amazed to discover a whole library in her classroom.   Lexile: AD520L   (Grades K–2)   F

Kindness and Caring

Bang, Molly. *The Paper Crane.*   ISBN-13: 9780688073336, 1987

A restaurant owner and his son lose their customers when a new highway comes to their street. One night a poor man comes to them and they serve him a meal. Before leaving, this kind man gives them a paper crane, which will become a living, dancing bird when they clap their hands. This crane brings crowds to the restaurant and prosperity.

Lexile: 790L   (Grades 2–8)   F

Fine, Edith Hope. *Under the Lemon Moon.*   ISBN-13: 9781584300519, 2010

One night Rosalinda wakes to a noise in the family's garden. She sees a man creeping away with a sack of fruit from her lemon tree. Rosalinda seeks out La Anciana for advice. The wise old woman offers a way to help the tree and the man driven to steal Rosalinda's lemons.

Lexile: 0520L   (Grades Pre-K–3)   F

Glavich, Mary Kathleen. *Blessed Teresa of Calcutta: Missionary of Charity.*

ISBN-13: 9780819811608, 2003

In this book, read about the kind contributions Mother Theresa made during her lifetime.

Lexile: N/A   (Grades 4–8)   NF

Grimm, Jacob. *The Elves and the Shoemaker.*   ISBN-13: 9780811834773, 2003

A poor shoemaker and his wife become rich when elves make beautiful shoes for them to sell. They return the favor by making clothes for the elves. The theme is about kindness and giving.   Lexile: AD840L   (Grades 2–5)   F

Nolan, Jerdine. *Raising Dragons.*   ISBN-13: 9780152165369, 2002

A farmer's young daughter shares numerous adventures with the dragon that she raises from infancy.   Lexile: 0670L   (Grades 1–4)   F

Polacco, Patricia. *Chicken Sunday.*   ISBN-13: 9780698116153, 1998

A young Russian American girl and her African American brothers buy their grandma a beautiful Easter hat to thank Miss Eula for her wonderful Sunday chicken dinners. To raise the money, they sell decorated eggs to buy her gift.   Lexile: 650L   (Grades K–6)   F

Polacco, Patricia. *Thank You, Mr. Falker.* ISBN-13: 9780399257629, 2012

When Trisha starts school, she can't wait to learn how to read, but the letters just get jumbled up. She hates being different and begins to believe her classmates when they call her a dummy. Then in fifth grade, Mr. Falker changes everything. When he discovers that she can't read, he helps her prove to herself that she can. Lexile: N/A (Grades K–4) F

Rania, Queen of Jordan Al Abdullah. *The Sandwich Shop.* ISBN-13: 9781423124849, 2010

The smallest things can pull us apart—until we learn that friendship is far more powerful than difference. In a glorious three-page gatefold at the end of the book, Salma, Lily, and all their classmates come together in the true spirit of tolerance and acceptance. Lexile: AD630L (Grades Pre-K–1) F

Silverstein, Shel. *The Giving Tree.* ISBN-13: 9780060256654, 1964

This story reminds us about the gift of giving and the capacity to love, told throughout the life of a boy who grows to adulthood and a tree that selflessly gives him her resources throughout the years. Lexile: 530L (Grades K–3) F

Snihura, Ulana. *I Miss Franklin P. Shuckles.* ISBN-13: 9781550375169, 1998

A story about an unlikely friendship and how easy it is to lose a friendship if you are not kind and how hard it is to get it back even if you change your ways. Lexile: 300L (Grades 2–4) F

Wallace, Nancy Elizabeth. *The Kindness Quilt.* ISBN-13: 9780761453130, 2006

Minna does a lot of thinking about her assignment: do something kind, make a picture about it, and share it with classmates. She finally comes up with an idea that can be shared with the whole school. Lexile: N/A (Grades 2–6) F

Whittell, Giles. *The Story of Three Whales.* ISBN-13: 9780744513677, 1989

In 1988, the three gray whales who waited too long to begin their southern migration became trapped in the Arctic ice. But they were saved by the hard work of the people who tried to help them. Lexile: N/A (Grades 3–8) NF

Williams-Garcia, Rita. *One Crazy Summer.* ISBN-13: 9780060760908, 2011

Set during 1968, one of the most tumultuous years in recent American history, this is the heartfelt, funny story of three girls who travel cross-country in search of the mother who abandoned them. Lexile: N/A (Grades 3–8) F

Woodson, Jacqueline. *Coming on Home Soon.* ISBN-13: 9780399237485, 2004

Ada Ruth's mama must go away to Chicago to work, leaving Ada Ruth and Grandma behind. It's wartime, and women are needed to fill the men's jobs. As winter sets in, Ada Ruth and her grandma keep up their daily routine, missing Mama all the time. They find strength in each other, and a stray kitten arrives one day to keep them company, but nothing can fill the hole Mama left. Every day they wait, watching for the letter that says Mama will be coming home soon. Lexile: 550L (Grades K–5) F

Wortche, Allison. *Rosie Sprout's Time to Shine.*   ISBN-13: 9780375867217, 2011

This empathetic story captures every child's desire to be noticed and praised, as well as the subtle competitions that go on in a classroom. It's a book to swell every shy child's heart.

Lexile: N/A   (Grades K–3)   F

Loyalty and Friendship

Anzaldua, Gloria. *Friends from the Other Side / Amigos del otro lado.*   ISBN-13: 9780892391301, 1995

Having crossed the Rio Grande into Texas with his mother in search of a new life, Joaquin receives help and friendship from Prietita, a brave young Mexican American girl.   Lexile: N/A   (Grades 2–8)   F

Boyne, John. *The Boy in the Striped Pajamas.*   ISBN-13: 9780385751537, 2007

An eight-year-old boy named Bruno returns home from school to discover that his belongings are being packed. His father has received a promotion, and the family must move from their home to a new house far away, where there is no one to play with and nothing to do. A tall fence running alongside stretches as far as the eye can see and cuts him off from the strange people he can see in the distance. While exploring his new environment, he meets another boy whose life and circumstances are very different to his own, and their meeting results in a friendship that has devastating consequences.   Lexile: 1080L   (Grades 7–12)   F

Cook, Julia. *Making Friends Is an Art!*   ISBN-13: 9781934490303, 2012

This book teaches kids of all ages (and adults too!) how to practice the art of friendship and getting along with others.   Lexile: N/A   (Grades K–3)   F

Davis, Sampson, George Jenkins, and Ramech Hunt. *We Beat the Street: How a Friendship Pact Led to Success.*   ISBN-13: 9780142406274, 2006

Growing up on the rough streets of Newark, New Jersey, three friends could have followed their childhood friends into drug dealing, gangs, and prison. But a presentation at their school made them aware of the opportunities available to them in the medical and dental professions, so they made a pact among themselves that they would become doctors. It took a lot of determination, and despite all the hardships along the way, the three succeeded.

Lexile: 860L   (Grades 4–8)   NF

Munson, Derek. *Enemy Pie.*   ISBN-13: 9780811827782, 2000

What should have been a perfect summer for one young boy is ruined when Jeremy Ross moves in and becomes number one on the narrator's enemy list. Luckily, his father has a secret recipe for a pie that is guaranteed to help get rid of enemies.

Lexile: AD330L   (Grades K–3)   F

O'Neill, Alexis. *Recess Queen.* ISBN-13: 9780439206372, 2002

A schoolyard bully is enlightened by the new kid in class in this lively story about the power of kindness and friendship. Lexile: AD450L (Grades Pre-K–3) F

Pfister, Marcus. *Rainbow Fish.* ISBN-13: 9781558580091, 1999

The most beautiful fish in the entire ocean discovers the real value of personal beauty and friendship. Lexile: AD410L (Grades K–2) F

Steptoe, John. *Stevie.* ISBN-13: 9780064431224, 1986

Robert wishes that his houseguest Stevie would go away, but when he does, Robert realizes how much fun they had together. Lexile: 580L (Grades K–3) F

Taylor, Mildred D. *Friendship.* ISBN-13: 9780140389647, 1998

In Mississippi in 1933, Cassie Logan and her brothers witness Mr. Tom Bee, an elderly black man, daring to call the white storekeeper by his first name, and any child knows that some things just aren't done. Lexile: 750L (Grades 2–6) F

Uchida, Yoshiko. *The Bracelet.* ISBN-13: 9780698113909, 1996

Emi, a Japanese American in the second grade, is sent with her family to an internment camp during World War II, but the loss of the bracelet her best friend has given her proves that she does not need a physical reminder of that friendship.

Lexile: AD710L (Grades K–5) F

Woodson, Jacqueline. *The Other Side.* ISBN-13: 9780399231162, 2001

Two girls, one white and one black, gradually get to know each other as they sit on the fence that divides their town. Lexile: AD300L (Grades K–5) F

Perseverance

Bach, Richard. *Jonathon Livingston Seagull.*

ISBN-13: 9780743278904, 2006

Jonathan Livingston Seagull is no ordinary bird. He believes it is every gull's right to fly, to reach the ultimate freedom of challenge and discovery. He finds his greatest reward in teaching younger gulls the joy of flight and the power of dreams. Lexile: N/A (Grades 6–8) F

Bridges, Shirin. *Ruby's Wish.* ISBN-13: 9780811834902, 2002

In China, at a time when few girls are taught to read or write, Ruby dreams of going to the university with her brothers and male cousins.

Lexile: 600L (Grades K–3) F

Coffelt, Nancy. *Fred Stays with Me!*   ISBN-13: 9780316077910, 2011

Told from the point of view of a young child whose parents are divorced, this story follows a girl and her dog, Fred, from one parent's house to the other's, giving her a sense of continuity and stability.   Lexile: 0430L   (Grades Pre-K–3)   F

Curtis, Jamie Lee. *Is There Really a Human Race?*   ISBN-13: 9780060753467, 2006

There are so many great messages in this book. The little boy's questions capture many common childhood anxieties about what the future holds and whether or not the child is up to the challenges ahead of him. Woven throughout the book are his mother's reassuring responses.   Lexile: N/A   (Grades Pre-K–3)   NF

de Beer, Hans. *Leonardo's Dream.*   ISBN-13: 9780735819269, 2004

Leonardo spends his days dreaming of flying, but penguins can't fly. Day after day he hops and flaps, hops and flaps, all to no avail. Leonardo learns, with some help from a friendly albatross, that perseverance pays off in this uplifting story.   Lexile: N/A   (Grades K–4)   F

Fox, Mem. *Koala Lou.*   ISBN-13: 9780152000769, 1994

When Koala Lou's mother becomes so busy that she forgets to tell her firstborn how much she loves her, Koala Lou enters the Bush Olympics, intending to win an event and her mother's love all at one time.   Lexile: AD550L   (Grades Pre-K–2)   F

Gerstein, Mordecai. *The Man Who Walked Between the Towers.*

        ISBN-13: 9780312368784, 2007

In 1974, as the World Trade Center was being completed, a young French aerialist, Philippe Petit, threw a tight rope between the towers and spent almost an hour walking, dancing, and performing tricks a quarter of a mile in the sky.   Lexile: AD480L   (Grades K–5)   NF

Gibson, William. *The Miracle Worker.*   ISBN-13: 9781416590842, 2008

Helen Keller, blind, deaf, and mute since infancy, is in danger of being sent to an institution because of her inability to communicate. But her parents seek help from the Perkins Institute, which sends Annie Sullivan to tutor Helen. Annie suspects that within Helen lies the potential for more, and through persistence and perseverance Annie helps Helen learn to communicate.   Lexile: NP   (Grades 5–8)   NF

Giovanni, Nikki. *Rosa.*   ISBN-13: 9780312376024, 2007

This picture book is a tribute to Rosa Parks and her refusal to give up her seat on a Montgomery, Alabama, city bus.   Lexile: 900L   (Grades K–6)   NF

Jordan, Deloris, and Roslyn Jordan. *Salt in His Shoes: Michael Jordan in Pursuit of a Dream.*   ISBN-13: 9780689834196, 2003

Young Michael Jordan, who is smaller than the other players, learns that determination and hard work are more important than size when playing the game of basketball.

    Lexile: 0460L   (Grades Pre-K–3)   NF

Krull, Kathleen. *Wilma Unlimited: How Wilma Rudolph Became the World's Fastest Woman.*   ISBN-13: 9780152020989, 2000

This is the biography of the African American woman who overcame crippling polio as a child to become the first woman to win three gold medals in track in a single Olympics.

Lexile: 0730L   (Grades Pre-K–4)   NF

Laden, Nina. *Roberto the Insect Architect.*   ISBN-13: 9780811824651, 2000

No one will hire Roberto the architect because he also happens to be a termite. So he sets off to the city to find success on his own.   Lexile: 400L   (Grades 1–4)   F

Lichtenheld, Tom. *Cloudette.*   ISBN-13: 9780805087765, 2011

Sometimes being small can have its advantages. If you're a little cloud like Cloudette, people call you cute nicknames, and you can always find a good spot to watch the fireworks. But what about when you want to do something big, such as help a giant garden grow or make a brook babble?   Lexile: AD660L   (Grades Pre-K–2)   F

Park, Barbara. *Junie B. Jones, First Grader: One Man Band.*   ISBN-13: 9780375825361, 2004

Since Junie B. cannot play in the school kickball tournament because of a sore toe, she perseveres and brings her other talents to the halftime show.   Lexile: 250L   (Grades K–2)   F

Say, Allen. *Tree of Cranes.*   ISBN-13: 9780547248301, 2009

As a young Japanese boy recovers from a cold, his mother diligently folds origami paper into beautiful silver cranes in preparation for the boy's very first Christmas.

Lexile: 470L   (Grades K–4)   F

Senisi, Ellen B. *All Kinds of Friends, Even Green!*   ISBN-13: 9781890627355, 2002

In a school assignment, seven-year-old Moses, who has spina bifida and uses a wheelchair, struggles with whom he should choose to write about. In considering this, he reflects on his neighbor's disabled iguana whom he relates to because they both have figured out how to get where they want to be in different ways than those around them.

Lexile: N/A   (Grades K–5)   F

Seuss, Dr. *Green Eggs and Ham.*   ISBN-13: 9780394800165, 1960

Sam-I-am won't give up! He keeps trying to get the grumpy grown-up in the story to taste green eggs and ham.   Lexile: 30L   (Grades K–2)   F

Seuss, Dr. *Oh, the Places You'll Go!*   ISBN-13: 9780679805274, 1990

All journeys face threats, whether from indecision, loneliness, or from too much waiting. This pajama-clad hero is up to the challenge, evoking both the good times and the bad.

Lexile: AD600L   (Grades Pre-K–12)   F

Respect

Fox, Mem. *Wilfrid Gordon McDonald Partridge.*

ISBN-13: 9780916291266, 1989

Wilfred Gordon McDonald Partridge lives next door to a nursing home where several of his friends reside. His favorite is Miss Nancy Alison Delacourt Cooper because she has four names just as he does. The only problem is Miss Nancy, who is 96, has "lost" her memory, but Wilfred sets out to "find" Miss Nancy's memory for her.   Lexile: N/A   (Grades Pre-K–3)   F

Glassman, Bruce. *Respect.*   ISBN-13: 9781601085078, 2008

This book about respect supports the Character Counts curriculum.

Lexile: N/A   (Grades 3–6)   NF

Kunjufu, Jawanza. *Culture of Respect.*   ISBN-13: 9781934155066, 2007

This book emphasizes the value of space that supports mutual respect among teachers and classmates and the immediate and long-term benefits to students who practice these behaviors. While this book focuses on the specific needs of African American schoolchildren, this helpful resource is a useful tool for all teachers who wish to foster a sense of courtesy in their students, for a calmer, more focused classroom.   Lexile: N/A   (Grades K–2)   NF

Macavinta, Courtney. *Respect: A Girl's Guide to Getting Respect & Dealing When Your Line Is Crossed.*   ISBN-13: 9781575421773, 2005

This book helps teen girls get respect and hold on to it at home, at school, with their friends, and in the world. Girls learn that respect is connected to everything and every girl deserves respect.   Lexile: N/A   (Grades 6–12)   NF

Medina, Sarah. *Respect Others, Respect Yourself.*   ISBN-13: 9781432927233, 2009

This book includes valuable tips, real-life case studies, and quizzes to help young people succeed in the adult world. It asks readers if they are respectful of others and the community they live in. It's about the basic principles of respect.   Lexile: 910L   (Grades 5–10)   NF

Nelson, Robin. *Respecting Others.*   ISBN-13: 9780822513230, 2003

An introduction to respecting yourself, friends, parents, teachers, people you don't know, and the earth, with specific examples of how to show respect at home and at school.

Lexile: N/A   (Grades 1–3)   NF

Raatma, Lucia. *Respect.*   ISBN-13: 9781602793200, 2009

Multicultural faces appear in the photographs in this book on respect.

Lexile: 0440L   (Grades 1–3)   NF

Riehecky, Janet. **Respect.**   ISBN-13: 9780736836821, 2005

Treating people with respect means treating them as if they are important, because everyone is important. In this book, examples of ways to show respect help young readers understand the concept. The lesson is related to friendships, family relationships, and cultures. Historical examples are also offered.   Lexile: N/A   (Grades 1–3)   NF

Responsibility

Avi. **Secret School.**   ISBN-13: 9780152046996, 2003

In 1925, a 14-year-old girl secretly takes over as teacher when her one-room schoolhouse in rural Colorado is closed. When the teacher must depart unexpectedly, the head of the school board decides to close the school and end the academic year right then, a month and a half before the summer break. Fourteen-year-old Ida Bidson protests, because without exit exams, she cannot move on to high school in the fall. She takes over and swears the students to secrecy. It's no easy task, and she takes on great responsibility with her farm chores and with her own studies. When the county examiner discovers the secret, he agrees to keep it only if all the students take a final exam.   Lexile: 540L   (Grades 5–8)   F

Brinckloe, Julie. **Fireflies.**   ISBN-13: 9780689710551, 1986

A young boy is proud of having caught a jar full of fireflies, which seems to him like owning a piece of moonlight. But as the light begins to dim he realizes he must set the insects free or they will die.   Lexile: AD630L   (Grades K–3)   F

Loewen, Nancy. **Do I Have To? Kids Talk About Responsibility.**

ISBN-13: 9781404800304, 2002

This book uses an advice-column format to define responsibility as a character value and demonstrates how it can be used in daily situations.   Lexile: 730L   (Grades K–4)   NF

Nelson, Robin. **Respecting Others.**   ISBN-13: 9780822513230, 2003

This book is an introduction to respecting yourself, friends, parents, teachers, people you don't know, and the earth—with specific examples of how to show respect at home and at school.   Lexile: N/A   (Grades 1–3)   NF

Raatma, Lucia. **Responsibility.**   ISBN-13: 9780736091561, 2001

This book explains the character trait of responsibility and how readers can practice it at home, in school, in the community, and with each other.   Lexile: 440L   (Grades K–3)   NF

Roberts, Cynthia. **Responsibility.**   ISBN-13: 9781592966769, 2007

This book has real-life examples of young people taking responsibility for chores and tasks.

Lexile: N/A   (Grades 3–6)   NF

Seuss, Dr. *The Lorax.*   ISBN-13: 9780394823379, 1971

Long before saving the earth became a global concern, Dr. Seuss, speaking through his character the Lorax, warned against mindless progress and the danger it posed to the earth's natural beauty. In this classic story, the Once-ler describes how his greedy actions destroyed a beautiful and thriving environment through the subtle messages about the negative effects of deforestation, habitat destruction, and air and water pollution.

Lexile: 560L   (Grades K–6)   F

Small, Mary. *Being Responsible: A Book About Responsibility.*

ISBN-13: 9781404817883, 2005

This book presents real-life examples of young people taking responsibility of chores and tasks.   Lexile: 510L   (Grades K–3)   NF

Self-Control

Burch, Regina. *Think Before You Act: Learning About Self-Discipline and Self-Control.*

ISBN-13: 9781574718331, 2002

Help put an end to bullying and violence by focusing on and teaching positive peer interaction. Soon your students will be singing their way toward building a more caring classroom community.   Lexile: N/A   (Grades K–2)   NF

Cook, Julia. *A Bad Case of Tattle Tongue.*   ISBN-13: 9781931636865, 2006

This title offers a creative way to address the tattling-related issues that often cause more trouble at home, on the playground, in the grocery store, or anywhere else. It will help children understand the differences between unnecessary tattling and the necessity of warning others about important matters.   Lexile: N/A   (Grades K–2)   F

Cook, Julia. *I Just Don't Like the Sound of No! My Story About Accepting No for an Answer and Disagreeing the Right Way!*   ISBN-13: 9781934490259, 2011

This book has tips on how to teach and encourage kids to use the skills of accepting "No" for an answer and disagreeing appropriately.   Lexile: N/A   (Grades K–2)   F

Cook, Julia. *It's Hard to Be a Verb!*   ISBN-13: 9781931636841, 2008

Louis is a verb! He has a lot of trouble focusing, and he is always doing something, but the problem is usually it is the wrong something. This is a must-have book for all who struggle with paying attention.   Lexile: N/A   (Grades K–8)   F

Cook, Julia. *My Mouth Is a Volcano.*   ISBN-13: 9781931636858, 2008

This story provides parents, teachers, and counselors with an entertaining way to teach children the value of respecting others by listening and waiting for their turn to speak.

Lexile: N/A   (Grades K–2)   F

Cook, Julia. *Personal Space Camp.* ISBN-13: 9781931636872, 2008

This book addresses the complex issue of respect for another person's physical boundaries.

Lexile: N/A (Grades K–2) F

Cook, Julia. *Soda Pop Head.* ISBN-13: 9781931636773, 2011

Soda Pop Head will help children control their anger while helping them manage stress.

Lexile: N/A (Grades K–8) F

Cook, Julia. *Sorry, I Forgot to Ask! My Story About Asking Permission and Making an Apology.* ISBN-13: 9781934490280, 2011

RJ feels a lot happier when he says he's sorry to his teacher, the bus driver, and Grandma, and he learns that asking for permission will mean fewer trips to the time-out chair.

Lexile: TK (Grades Pre-K–2) F

Cook, Julia. *Wilma Jean the Worry Machine.* ISBN-13: 9781937870010, 2011

Everyone feels fear, worry, and apprehension from time to time, but when these feelings prevent a person from doing what he or she wants or needs to do, anxiety becomes a disability. This book addresses the problem of anxiety and offers creative strategies to use that can lessen the severity of anxiety. The goal of the book is to give children the tools needed to feel more in control of their anxiety. For those worries that are not in anyone's control, a worry hat is introduced. Lexile: N/A (Grades K–5) NF

Cook, Julia. *The Worst Day of My Life Ever!* ISBN-13: 9781934490204, 2011

RJ has a rough day. He wakes up with gum stuck in his hair, misses recess because he's late to school, earns a zero on his math homework, and messes up Mom's kitchen. With his mother's help, RJ learns that his problems happen because he doesn't listen or pay attention to directions. Lexile: N/A (Grades K–6) F

Hay, Louise. *I Think, I Am! Teaching Kids the Power of Affirmations.*

ISBN-13: 9781401922085, 2008

Kids read about the difference between negative thoughts and positive affirmations. It's all about how to make the change from negative thoughts and words to those that are positive.

Lexile: N/A (Grades K–3) NF

Huebner, Dawn. *What to Do When Your Temper Flares: A Kid's Guide to Overcoming Problems with Anger.* ISBN-13: 9781433801341, 2007

Teachers and parents seem to be faced more and more with young people unable to control their anger or handle emotions appropriately. This workbook is a guide for students, with the aid of an adult, to understand their feelings, their effect on others, and how to handle them appropriately. Lexile: N/A (Grades 5–8) NF

Humphrey, Sandra McLeod. *More If You Had to Choose, What Would You Do?*

ISBN-13: 9781591020776, 2003

This book presents a number of scenarios involving ethical dilemmas and asks the reader to decide what to do. Lexile: N/A (Grades K–3) NF

Lester, Helen. *Listen Buddy.*

ISBN-13: 9780395854020, 1997

Buddy has huge ears, but listening is not his strongest feature. He misinterprets his parent's requests, causing much confusion such as when his father asks for a pen, Buddy brings him a hen, and instead of the slice of bread his mother wants, Buddy brings her a slice of a bed. Taking his first hop alone, Buddy forgets whether he is supposed to take a left or a right when the road forks. He selects the wrong route and ends up at the cave of the Scruffy Varmint, where he continues to make similar mistakes. After the varmint decides that he'd rather eat stew made from bunny rabbit, Buddy hears him loud and clear. This tale will help nudge kids whose direction-following skills need some honing.

Lexile: 520L (Grades K–2) F

Miller, Connie Colwell. *Self-Discipline.*

ISBN-13: 9780736861380, 2006

Practicing to become good at anything, whether it is playing a musical instrument, ice-skating, or getting an "A" in a school subject requires hard work and discipline. It is tempting to do only what is fun or what others are doing; it takes extra effort to say "No" when you need to finish a chore, do homework, or fulfill a commitment before you can join your friends. Lexile: N/A (Grades K–2) NF

Mulcahy, William. *Zach Gets Frustrated.*

ISBN-13: 9781575423906, 2012

Zach, his brothers Alex and Scott, and his parents are a typical family. The boys struggle with getting along, frustrations, social issues, and other everyday problems.

Lexile: AD580L (Grades K–3) NF

Sportsmanship and Teamwork

Binkow, Howard. *Howard B. Wigglebottom Learns About Sportsmanship.*

ISBN-13: 9780982616567, 2011

Howard has a hard time losing in any game he plays. He goes so far as to cheat and hurt his friends in the process of winning. Howard will do whatever it takes to win a game, so he will continue being the best. Lexile: 0580L (Grades K–3) F

Cook, Julia. *Teamwork Isn't My Thing, and I Don't Like to Share!*
ISBN-13: 9781934490358, 2012

With the help of his coach, RJ learns that working as a team and sharing are skills needed not just on the soccer field, but in school and at home, too.   Lexile: N/A   (Grades K–3)   F

Derolf, Shane. *The Crayon Box That Talked.*
ISBN-13: 9780679886112, 1997

Quarrelsome talking crayons learn to appreciate one another when the narrator draws with them, thus showing them how each helps create a bigger picture.

Lexile: 590L   (Grades K–3)   F

Golenbock, Peter. *Teammates.*
ISBN-13: 9780152842864, 2010

This is the moving story of how Jackie Robinson became the first black player on a major league baseball team and how on a fateful day in Cincinnati, PeeWee Reese took a stand and declared Jackie his teammate.   Lexile: 930L   (Grades K–3)   NF

Kauchak, Therese. *Good Sports: Winning, Losing, and Everything in Between.*
ISBN-13: 9780613253567, 1999

Sound advice and encouragement about getting in shape, eating right, training, playing under adverse conditions, and boys and girls as teammates and competitors will be found in this title.   Lexile: N/A   (Grades 2–4)   NF

Ludwig, Trudy. *Better Than You.*
ISBN-13: 9781582463803, 2011

Jake's bragging is really starting to get to his neighbor Tyler. Tyler can't show Jake a basketball move, a school assignment, or a new toy without Jake saying he can do better. With the help of his uncle Kevin, Tyler begins to understand that Jake's bragging has nothing to do with Tyler's own abilities and that puffing yourself up leaves little room for friends.

Lexile: AD640L   (Grades K–3)   F

Moss, Peggy. *One of Us.*
ISBN-13: 9780884483229, 2010

This is a simple but powerful story about diversity, friendships, acceptance of others despite apparent differences, and the importance of being oneself.   Lexile: N/A   (Grades K–3)   F

Raatma, Lucia. *Sportsmanship.*
ISBN-13: 9780736846820, 2000

This simple book defines the title word, provides examples of the trait, and tells how to practice it at home, in school, and in the community.   Lexile: N/A   (Grades 2–4)   NF

Williams, Laura E. *The Can Man.*
ISBN-13: 9781600602665, 2010

Tim is friendly with Mr. Peters, a homeless man who collects cans in his neighborhood. Tim decides this is a good way to earn money to buy a skateboard. Tim tells Mr. Peters about his goal for the cans and learns that Mr. Peters is hoping to buy a coat before winter settles in. Tim gives his bag of coins to the homeless man so he can buy a new coat.

Lexile: 630L   (Grades 1–5)   F

Tolerance

Abdel-Fattah, Randa. *Does My Head Look Big In This?* ISBN-13: 9780439922333, 2008

Sixteen-year-old Amal makes the decision to start wearing the hijab, the Muslim head scarf, full-time and everyone has a reaction—her parents, her teachers, her friends, people on the street. But she stands by her decision to embrace her faith and all that it is, even if it does make her a little different from everyone else. Lexile: 0850L (Grades 6–12) F

Brown, Monica. *Marisol McDonald Doesn't Match / Marisol McDonald no combina.*
ISBN-13: 9780892392353, 2011

Marisol McDonald has flaming red hair and nut-brown skin. Polka dots and stripes are her favorite combination. She prefers peanut butter and jelly burritos in her lunch box. And for Marisol McDonald, these mismatched things make perfect sense together.

Lexile: AD580 (Grades Pre-K–3) F

Bunting, Eve. *One Green Apple.* ISBN-13: 9780547350110, 2006

Farah feels alone, even when surrounded by her classmates. She listens and nods but doesn't speak. It's hard being the new kid in school, especially when you're from another country and don't know the language. On a field trip to an apple orchard, Farah discovers there are lots of things she and her classmates have in common. As she helps the class make apple cider, Farah connects with the other students and begins to feel that she belongs.

Lexile: N/A (Grades K–3) F

Estes, Eleanor. *The Hundred Dresses.* ISBN-13: 9780152052607, 2004

Wanda Petronski is a Polish girl in a Connecticut school who is ridiculed by her classmates for wearing the same faded blue dress every day. Wanda claims she has one hundred dresses at home, but everyone knows she doesn't and bullies her mercilessly.

Lexile: 870L (Grades 2–5) F

Glaser, Linda. *Hannah's Way.* ISBN-13: 9780761351382, 2012

Hannah is eager to fit into her new school. It's the Depression, and her family has relocated from Minneapolis to rural Minnesota. She is the only Jewish girl in her class, and her family is the only Jewish family in the community. Lexile: N/A (Grades K–3) F

Kerr, Judith. *When Hitler Stole Pink Rabbit.* ISBN-13: 9780142414088, 2009

This book recounts the adventures of a nine-year-old Jewish girl and her family in the early 1930s as they travel from Germany to England. Lexile: N/A (Grades 3–6) F

LeGuin, Ursula K. *Voices.* ISBN-13: 9780152062422, 2008

Ansul was once a peaceful town filled with libraries, schools, and temples. But that was long ago and to 17-year-old Memer, the house is the only place where she feels truly safe.

Lexile: 0890L (Grades 6–12) F

Lorbiecki, Marybeth. *Sister Anne's Hands.*   ISBN-13: 9780140565348, 2000

It's the early 1960s, and Anna has never seen a person with dark skin—until she meets Sister Anne. At first she is afraid of her new teacher, but she quickly discovers how wonderful Sister Anne is. Then one of Anna's classmates directs a racist remark toward Sister Anne. The teacher's wise way of turning the incident into a powerful learning experience has a profound impact on Anna.   Lexile: 0580L   (Grades Pre-K–4)   F

Polacco, Patricia. *Junkyard Wonders.*   ISBN-13: 9780399250781, 2010

Trisha finds out her class at the new school is known as "The Junkyard." But then she meets her teacher, Mrs. Peterson, and her classmates, each with his or her own unique talent. And it is here in the Junkyard that Trisha learns the true meaning of genius, and that this group of misfits are in fact wonders—all of them.   Lexile: 660L   (Grades 1–4)   F

Ramsey, Calvin Alexander. *Ruth and the Green Book.*   ISBN-13: 9780761352556, 2010

Ruth was so excited to take a trip in her family's new car! In the early 1950s, few African Americans could afford to buy cars, so this would be an adventure. But she soon found out that black travelers weren't treated very well in some towns. Many hotels and gas stations refused service to black people. Daddy was upset about something called Jim Crow laws. . . . Finally, a friendly attendant at a gas station showed Ruth's family *The Green Book*. It listed all of the places that would welcome black travelers.   Lexile: 810L   (Grades 3–6)   F

Recorvits, Helen. *My Name Is Yoon.*   ISBN-13: 9780374351144, 2003

Yoon's name means "Shining Wisdom," and when she writes it in Korean, it looks happy, like dancing figures. But her father tells her that she must learn to write it in English. In English, all the lines and circles stand alone, which is just how Yoon feels in the United States. Yoon isn't sure that she wants to be YOON. At her new school, she tries out different names.   Lexile: 320L   (Grades Pre-K–3)   F

Silverman, Erica. *The Story of Emma Lazarus: Liberty's Voice.*   ISBN-13: 9780525478591, 2011

Emma Lazarus overcame the barriers of her day to become one of the leading poets of the 19th century. She used her celebrity to help the poor and impoverished immigrants of Eastern Europe. When the Liberty Enlightening the World, or the Statue of Liberty, came to the United States as a gift from France, it was Emma's poem "The New Colossus" that became forever connected with this American icon. Emma's words have served as a rallying call to generations of immigrants.   Lexile: AD810L   (Grades 2–4)   NF

Stratton, Allan. *Chanda's Secrets.*   ISBN-13: 9781550378344, 2004

This is an unforgettable novel about family, loyalty, and survival in sub-Saharan Africa. This is the powerful story of one girl's struggle for survival amid the African HIV/AIDS pandemic, a story of harsh realities and hard-won hopefulness.

     Lexile: 590L   (Grades 9–12)   F

Wojtowicz, Jen. ***The Boy Who Grew Flowers.***   ISBN-13: 9781846867491, 2012

Rink is a very unusual boy who grows beautiful flowers all over his body whenever the moon is full. In town and at school, Rink and his family are treated as outcasts although no one knows his strange botanical secret. But one day a new girl arrives at school, and Rink discovers she has some unique qualities of her own.   Lexile: N/A   (Grades 1–4)   F

Woodson, Jacqueline. ***The Other Side.***   ISBN-13: 9780399231162, 2001

Two girls, one white and one black, gradually get to know each other as they sit on the fence that divides their town.   Lexile: AD300   (Grades K–5)   F

11

Literature for Children and Young Adults That Explores Race and Culture

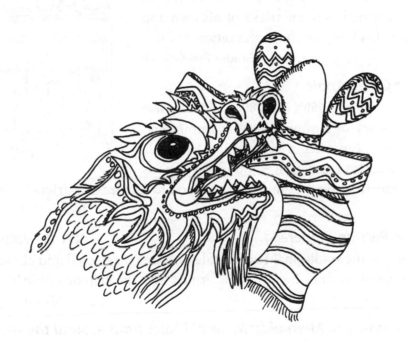

Naming and appreciating difference is a key factor for discussion about race with young people. Children make these observations early in their lives, and offering them a safe and organized space to have these conversations gives children permission to talk about what they see and to ask questions without fear of ridicule and protest by other people. Teachers can help children develop positive racial associations of both themselves and people different from them.

Book titles portraying positive interactions across race cultures help reduce prejudice and lack of understanding. These books show cross-racial interactions and friendships, which can strengthen children's developing appreciation of and sense of connection to people who look, talk, and act differently from them.

Stories of similarities and differences are a significant part of race-related topics. When presenting books and dialoguing about race relations in a broad context through ongoing conversation, these stories can be powerful and meaningful in the development of empathy, tolerance, and equity. They offer readers insight into history, geography, and political concerns. The titles in this chapter offer a wide variety of age-appropriate books that offer opportunities for discussions not only about race cultures, but also about the past and current times.

Middle Eastern Literature

Balouch, Kristen. ***The King and the Three Thieves.***

ISBN-13: 9780670880591, 2000

In this fresh retelling of an intriguing Persian folktale, King Abbas appears to get caught up in the schemes of three thieves, but he has a few tricks of his own and ultimately saves his kingdom from starvation.

Lexile: N/A   (Grades Pre-K–3)   F

Bunting, Eve. ***One Green Apple.***

ISBN-13: 9780547350110, 2006

In this timely story of a young Muslim immigrant, Farah feels alone. But after a field trip to an apple orchard, she discovers many things sound the same as they did at home, from dogs crunching their food to the ripple of friendly laughter.

Lexile: 450L   (Grades K–3)   F

Climo, Shirley. ***The Persian Cinderella.***   ISBN-13: 9780064438537, 1999

In this retelling of the traditional Persian tale, Settareh, neglected and abused by her stepmother and stepsisters, finds her life transformed with the help of a little blue jug.

Lexile: AD760L   (Grades K–3)   F

Climo, Shirley. ***A Treasury of Mermaids: Mermaid Tales from Around the World.***

ISBN-13: 9780060238766, 1997

Gathered from diverse cultures (from a Japanese *ningyo* and a Swiss *nix* to an Irish *merrow* and an Alaskan *nuquot*), the stories in this collection tell of mortals who strive to capture mermaids—and mermen—as well as those who seek to rescue them from peril; mortals who entice mermaids to live on dry land; and those who dare follow mermaids under the waves.

Lexile: N/A   (Grades 3–7)   F

Climo, Shirley. ***A Treasury of Princesses: Princess Tales from Around the World.***

ISBN-13: 9780060245320, 1996

A discussion of princess lore precedes each retelling of seldom-heard princess tales, featuring such heroines as White Jade, Gulnara, and Vasilisa the Frog Princess.

Lexile: N/A   (Grades 1–5)   F

D'Adamo, Francesco. *Iqbal.* ISBN-13: 9781416903291, 2001

This moving, fictionalized account of the life of Iqbal Masih, a Pakistani boy who brings hope to child workers in a carpet factory, is told through the voice of Fatima, a young Pakistani girl whose life is changed by Iqbal's courage. Lexile: 730L (Grades 3–7) F

Ellis, Deborah. *The Breadwinner.* ISBN-13: 9780888999597, 2009

Because the Taliban rulers of Kabul, Afghanistan, impose strict limitations on women's freedom and behavior, 11-year-old Parvana must disguise herself as a boy so that her family can survive after her father's arrest. Lexile: 630L (Grades 3–7) F

Ellis, Deborah. *My Name Is Parvana.* ISBN-13: 9781554982974, 2011

In this long-awaited sequel to *The Breadwinner Trilogy*, Parvana is now 15 years old. As she waits for foreign military forces to determine her fate, she remembers the past four years of her life. Reunited with her mother and sisters, she has been living in a village where her mother has finally managed to open a school for girls. But even though the Taliban has been driven from the government, the country is still at war, and many continue to view the education and freedom of girls and women with suspicion and fear.

Lexile: N/A (Grades 6–9) F

Ellis, Deborah. *Parvana's Journey.* ISBN-13: 9780888995193, 2002

Parvana's father has just died, and her mother, sister, and brother could be anywhere in Kabul. Despite her youth, Parvana sets out alone, masquerading as a boy and forges a family with other children of the war. Lexile: 640L (Grades 3–7) F

English, Karen. *Nadia's Hands.* ISBN-13: 9781590787847, 1999

Nadia is to be the flower girl at Auntie Laila's wedding. The downside is that in the tradition of her Pakistani family, she must have her hands decorated with *mehndi*, or henna designs. As she gives in reluctantly, Nadia learns *sabr*, or patience, and comes to terms with her heritage. Lexile: N/A (Grades K–4) F

Heide, Florence Parry. *Sami and the Time of the Troubles.* ISBN-13: 9780395720851, 1995

A 10-year-old Lebanese boy goes to school, helps his mother with chores, plays with his friends, and lives with his family in a basement shelter when bombings occur and fighting begins on his street. Lexile: AD600L (Grades Pre-K–4) F

Hickox, Rebecca. *The Golden Sandal: A Middle Eastern Cinderella Story.*

ISBN-13: 9780823415137, 1998

This Iraqi Cinderella tale is great for teaching the origin of this genre, as well as teaching about other countries. It is a delightful story just for sharing, but can also be used in instruction during multicultural units. Lexile: AD870L (Grades K–4) F

Kahn, Rukhsana. *The Roses in My Carpet.* ISBN-13: 9781550050691, 1998

When a young boy and his mother and sister come to a refugee camp to escape the war in Afghanistan, he finds some comfort in the beauty of the carpets he is learning to weave.

Lexile: N/A (Grades K–4) F

Kahn, Rukhsana. *Silly Chicken.*   ISBN-13: 9780670059126, 2005

In Pakistan, Rani believes that her mother loves their pet chicken Bibi more than Rani cares for her, until the day a fluffy chick appears and steals Rani's own affections.

Lexile: N/A   (Grades Pre-K–3)   F

Lattimore, Deborah Nourse. *Arabian Nights: Three Tales.*   ISBN-13: 9780064421362, 1995

In these three tales, young Aladdin engages in a battle of wits with an evil sorcerer, the Queen of the Serpents waits in her cave, and the reader journeys across a boundless desert to find the Lost City of Brass and the horrible fate that befell its inhabitants.

Lexile: N/A   (Grades 2–4)   F

Nafisi, Azar. *Reading Lolita in Tehran: A Memoir in Books.*   ISBN-13: 9780812971064, 2004

Every Thursday morning for two years in the Islamic Republic of Iran, Azar Nafisi, a bold and inspired teacher, secretly gathered seven of her most committed female students to read forbidden Western classics.   Lexile: N/A   (Grades 6–12)   NF

Nye, Naomi Shihab. *19 Varieties of Gazelle: Poems of the Middle East.*

ISBN-13: 9780060504045, 2005

This volume collects in one place for the first time all of Naomi Shihab Nye's poems about the Middle East, about peace, and about being an Arab American in the United States.

Lexile: 910L   (Grades 7–12)   NF

Nye, Naomi Shihab. *Come with Me: Poems for a Journey.*   ISBN-13: 9780688159467, 2000

A collection of 16 poems that takes you on a journey and includes "Secrets," "When You Come to a Corner," "Mad," and "Come with Me."   Lexile: 480L   (Grades Pre-K–3)   NF

Nye, Naomi Shihab. *Sitti's Secrets.*   ISBN-13: 9780689817069, 1997

When Sitti, an American girl, goes to visit her grandmother in her small Palestinian village on the West Bank, they don't need words to understand each other's heart.

Lexile: AD590L   (Grades 1–6)   F

Nye, Naomi Shihab. *The Space Between Our Footsteps.*   ISBN-13: 9780689812330, 1998

Honored anthologist Naomi Shihab Nye brings together the work of more than 120 poets and artists from 19 countries in the Middle East and North America.

Lexile: NPL   (Grades Pre-K–3)   NF

Shah, Idries. *The Clever Boy and the Terrible, Dangerous Animal.*

ISBN-13: 9781883536510, 2000

This is a Sufi teaching tale of a boy who visits another village and helps the townspeople deal with their fear of something that they have mistaken for a terrible, dangerous animal.

Lexile: N/A   (Grades Pre-K–3)   F

Shah, Idries. *The Silly Chicken.*   ISBN-13: 9781883536190, 2000

Set in the Middle East, Shah's retelling of a Sufi story sends a gentle message to readers: just because someone says it's so, does not make it so.   Lexile: N/A   (Grades Pre-K–3)   F

Jewish Literature

Adler, David A. *A Picture Book of Jewish Holidays.*

ISBN-13: 9780823407569, 1981

Beginning with the Jewish calendar, which is based on the moon, and comparing it to the Julian calendar, readers understand why the dates of Jewish holidays can vary so much each year. That said, the book begins with the Sabbath and Rosh Hashanah and ends with Tishah b'Av. It also mentions six other holidays and includes a glossary.   Lexile: N/A   (Grades Pre-K–3)   NF

Chaikin, Miriam. *Alexandra's Scroll: The Story of the First Hanukkah.*

ISBN-13: 9780805063844, 2002

The events leading up to the first Hanukkah come to vivid life through the eyes of a Jewish girl growing up in Jerusalem circa 165 BCE.   Lexile: N/A   (Grades 4–8)   F

Chaikin, Miriam. *Hanukkah.*   ISBN-13: 9780823409051, 1990

The first part of this book discusses the acts of King Antiochus, the uprising of the Jews under Mattathias, and the miracle of the holy oil. The next part shows families celebrating Hanukkah today.   Lexile: N/A   (Grades 6–12)   NF

Davis, Aubrey. *Bagels from Benny.*   ISBN-13: 9781553377498, 2003

When Grandpa explains to Benny that God should be thanked for the wonderful bagels, he decides to leave God a bagful of bagels in the synagogue at the end of each week. This book explores the values of caring and sharing, building a strong sense of community, and finding joy in giving thanks, through the loving relationship between Grandpa and Benny.

Lexile: AD330L   (Grades Pre-K–3)   F

Emerman, Ellen. *Is It Shabbos Yet?*   ISBN-13: 9781929628025, 2001

Malkie just can't wait for Shabbos. This book helps children relate to Shabbos preparations with descriptions of all the household tasks that enliven the end of the week.

Lexile: N/A   (Grades Pre-K–3)   F

Gershator, Phillis. *Wise and Not-So-Wise: Ten Tales from the Rabbis.*

ISBN-13: 9780827607552, 2004

Stories of flying rabbis, miraculous loaves of bread, wise women, muscle-bound angels, and goats that carry bears on their heads make up this collection of stories to teach moral lessons in a humorous way.   Lexile: N/A   (Grades K–4)   F

Gerstein, Mordecai. *The White Ram: A Story of Abraham and Issac.*

ISBN-13: 9780823418978, 2006

This book is inspired by Jewish legends called Midrashim, and it imagines the viewpoint of the white ram that plays a key role in the Bible story of Abraham and Isaac leading up to Rosh Hashanah or New Year's Day.   Lexile: AD700L   (Grades Pre-K–3)   F

Gold, Sharlya, and Mishael Caspi. *The Answered Prayer: And Other Yemenite Folktales.*

ISBN-13: 9780827607729, 1990

Yemenite Jews were the victims of harsh laws and persecution, yet out of their troubled lives came tales of joy as well as of sorrow. When the Jews left Yemen for Israel, the stories came with them, reflecting their culture, their heritage, and their struggle to survive. This collection of 12 Yemen folktales, originally published in 1990, is sure to entertain new readers and introduce them to the rich lore of this ancient culture.   Lexile: N/A   (Grades 3–7)   NF

Gold-Vukson, Marji E. *Grandpa and Me on Tu B'Shevat.*   ISBN-13: 9781580131223, 2004

B'Shevat, a minor Jewish holiday, is celebrated in January or February and commemorates the environmental need to plant new trees. A little boy and his grandfather plant a seedling and watch it develop into an apple tree as they grow older, passing on to succeeding generations the tradition of caring for the tree and enjoying its fruit.

Lexile: N/A   (Grades Pre-K–3)   F

Hesse, Karen. *The Cats in Krasinski Square.*   ISBN-13: 9780439435406, 2004

Two Jewish sisters, escapees of the infamous Warsaw ghetto, devise a plan to thwart an attempt by the Gestapo to intercept food bound for starving people behind the dark Wall.

Lexile: AD990L   (Grades 2–5)   F

Hoyt-Goldsmith, Diane. *Celebrating Passover.*   ISBN-13: 9780823414208, 2000

The straightforward Micah is a Cincinnati Reds fan and enjoys spring for two reasons—baseball and Passover. This depiction of ordinary American children celebrating a culturally specific holiday sends a positive message.   Lexile: 720L   (Grades 3–7)   NF

Kimmel, Eric. *Hershel and the Hanukkah Goblins.*   ISBN-13: 9780823411313, 1990

In this humorous, entertaining, and slightly scary story, Hershel successfully uses his wits to oust the eight creatures haunting the old synagogue and who are preventing the villagers from celebrating Hanukkah.   Lexile: 400L   (Grades K–4)   F

Kimmel, Eric A. *When Mindy Saved Hanukkah.*   ISBN-13: 9780439769907, 1998

Little Mindy Klein lives with her tiny family behind the walls of the Eldridge Street Synagogue. When Mindy's father sprains his ankle right before Hanukkah, he is unable to bring home a candle for the menorah. So Mindy decides to set out and find the candle herself. She manages to save Hanukkah just in time . . . and learns the true meaning behind the Festival of Lights.   Lexile: 470L   (Grades K–4)   F

Lehman-Wilzig, Tami. *Keeping the Promise: A Torah's Journey.*

ISBN-13: 9781580131186, 2003

The Torah—the sacred scriptures of the Jews—has traveled the world in the hands of its faithful adherents, and in this book it also travels into space, as one of the personal items taken aboard the space shuttle *Columbia* by Israel's first astronaut, Ilan Ramon.

Lexile: N/A   (Grades K–4)   NF

Lowry, Lois. *Number the Stars.* ISBN-13: 9780547577098, 2011

In 1943, during the German occupation of Denmark, 10-year-old Annemarie learns how to be brave and courageous when she helps shelter her Jewish friend from the Nazis.

Lexile: 670L   (Grades 5–8)   F

Manushkin, Fran. *Latkes and Applesauce.* ISBN-13: 9780590422659, 1990

Despite a blizzard and scarcity of food, the beloved Menashe family enjoys a joyous holiday celebration. The book includes notes on Hanukkah, a bibliography, a recipe for making latkes, and rules for playing dreidel. Lexile: AD650L   (Grades Pre-K–3)   F

Musleah, Rahel. *Apples and Pomegranates: A Family Seder for Rosh Hashanah.*

ISBN-13: 9781580131230, 2004

On Rosh Hashanah, the Jewish New Year, it is traditional to dip apples in honey in hopes of a sweet New Year. Jews around the world share other foods as well—such as pomegranates, pumpkins, beets, and dates—foods that grow abundantly and symbolize prosperity.

Lexile: N/A   (Grades 3–8)   NF

Nerlove, Miriam. *Flowers on the Wall.* ISBN-13: 9780689506147, 1996

Rachel, a young Jewish girl living in 1938 Nazi-occupied Warsaw, struggles to survive with her family and maintains hope by painting colorful flowers on her dingy apartment walls.

Lexile: N/A   (Grades K–4)   F

Oberman, Sheldon. *The Always Prayer Shawl.* ISBN-13: 9780140561579, 1994

This moving story invokes the power of Jewish tradition. Adam is a Jewish boy growing up in czarist Russia, where his grandfather, also named Adam, teaches him the importance of Jewish beliefs and customs, stressing that "some things change and some things don't."

Lexile: 460L   (Grades K–4)   F

Oberman, Sheldon. *Solomon and the Ant and Other Jewish Folktales.*

ISBN-13: 9781590783078, 2006

This book introduces the reader to the origins of the 43 folktales, some of which will be new to readers, others of which will be familiar. Examples include a quartet of Chelm tales and "The Smell of Money," in which wise Solomon allows a greedy baker to hear the jingle of money in exchange for the aroma of his bread, enjoyed by a passerby.

Lexile: N/A   (Grades 4–12)   F

Polacco, Patricia. *The Keeping Quilt.* ISBN-13: 9780689844478, 2001

When Patricia's Great-Gramma Anna came to America as a child, the only things she brought along from Russia were her dress and the babushka she liked to throw up into. Anna's mother made a quilt that would be passed down through their family for almost a century. From one generation to the next, the quilt was used as a Sabbath tablecloth, a wedding canopy, and a blanket to welcome each new child into the world.

Lexile: 990L   (Grades Pre-K–4)   F

Polacco, Patricia. *Mrs. Katz and Tush.*   ISBN-13: 9780440409366, 1992

A long-lasting friendship develops between Larnel, a young African American, and Mrs. Katz, a lonely Jewish widow, when Larnel presents Mrs. Katz with a scrawny kitten without a tail.   Lexile: 530L   (Grades Pre-K–3)   F

Ringgold, Faith. *Bonjour, Lonnie.*   ISBN-13: 9780786820627, 1996

An African American Jewish boy, with red hair and green eyes, traces his ancestry through time travel and with the help of the "Love Bird of Paris."   Lexile: 710L   (Grades 3–7)   F

Rosenbaum, Andria Warmflash. *A Grandma Like Yours. A Grandpa Like Yours.*

ISBN-13: 9781580131681, 2006

Although this book is geared toward a Jewish audience, the warm and loving portrayal of the special relationship between grandparents and their beloved grandchildren shines through on every page, making this a lovely choice for Grandparents Day in any community.
Lexile: N/A   (Grades Pre-K–3)   F

Rouss, Sylvia. *Sammy Spider's First Sukkot.*   ISBN-13: 9781580131421, 2004

Your favorite spider learns about building a sukkah, an outdoor house, for the holiday of Sukkot. We follow the clever arachnid as we learn about the holiday when the ancient Israelites gathered in their harvest while dwelling in temporary huts in the field.

Lexile: N/A   (Grades K–4)   F

Shulman, Lisa. *The Matzo Ball Boy.*   ISBN-13: 9780142407691, 2005

Before long, a yenta and her children, a rabbi, and a fox are all on a mad chase to catch the matzo ball boy!   Lexile: 690L   (Grades Pre-K–3)   F

Silverman, Erica. *When the Chickens Went on Strike.*   ISBN-13: 9780142402795, 2003

This amusing and telling Rosh Hashanah story about wise chickens and foolish villagers will be enjoyed by anyone who has ever wanted to be a better person.

Lexile: N/A   (Grades K–4)   F

Tarbescu, Edith. *Annushka's Voyage.*   ISBN-13: 9780395643662, 1998

Set at the turn of the century, the Sabbath candlesticks given to them by their grandmother when they leave Russia help two sisters make it safely to join their father in New York.

Lexile: 400L   (Grades K–4)   F

Wing, Natasha. *Jalapeño Bagels.*   ISBN-13: 9780689805301, 1996

Jalapeño bagels are the delicious coming together of two cultures as the son of a Jewish baker and his Mexican wife decides what to bring to school for International Day.

Lexile: AD460L   (Grades K–4)   F

Wood, Angela. *Jewish Synagogue.*   ISBN-13: 9780713653434, 2000

As part of the "Places of Worship" series, this book explains the Jewish house of worship, the Ark, the Torah scrolls, and teachings about God.

Lexile: N/A   (Grades K–4)   NF

Zemach, Margot. *It Could Always Be Worse.* ISBN-13: 9780374436360, 1976

A poor, unfortunate man follows the Rabbi's unlikely advice, and his life goes from bad to worse, with increasingly uproarious results. In his little hut, silly calamity follows foolish catastrophe, all memorably depicted in full-color illustrations that are both funnier and lovelier than any other this distinguished artist has done in the past.

Lexile: AD650L   (Grades Pre-K–3)   F

Zucker, Jonny. *Apples and Honey: A Rosh Hashanah Story.* ISBN-13: 9780711220164, 2002

This delightful picture book depicts a typical Jewish family as they celebrate one of the year's most important holidays, Rosh Hashanah. The traditional warmth of the Jewish holidays are reflected in cheerful and attractive little stories that speak not only to Jewish children but also to boys and girls of all faiths. Lexile: N/A   (Grades Pre-K–3)   F

Latin American Literature

Ada, Alma Flor. *Gathering the Sun: An Alphabet in Spanish and English.* ISBN-13: 9780688170677, 2001

Simple poems and glorious paintings, one for each letter of the Spanish alphabet, offer a deeply moving portrait of migrant Chicano farmworker families at work and play.   Lexile: AD590L   (Grades K–5)   NF

Bunting, Eve. *A Day's Work.*

ISBN-13: 9780395845189, 1997

Francisco, a young Mexican American boy, helps his grandfather find work as a gardener, even though the old man cannot speak English and knows nothing about gardening.   Lexile: 0350L   (Grades K–3)   F

Bunting, Eve. *Going Home.* ISBN-13: 9780064435093, 1998

Christmas is coming and Carlos and his family are going south across the border to Mexico, though it doesn't seem like home to Carlos anymore, even though he and his sisters were born there.   Lexile: 0480L   (Grades K–4)   F

Cisneros, Sandra. *Hairs / Pelitos.* ISBN-13: 9780679890072, 1997

A Latina girl describes the unique hair of all of the people in her family.

Lexile: AD190L   (Grades Pre-K–3)   F

Cowley, Joy. *Big Moon Tortilla.* ISBN-13: 9781590780374, 2004

Marta Enos is having a bad day. It begins when the wind blows her homework out the window, and the dogs chew it to pieces. Her grandmother consoles her with a tortilla as "big and pale as a rising full moon," along with ancient words of advice.

Lexile: N/A   (Grades K–4)   F

dePaola, Tomie. *The Night of Las Posadas.* ISBN-13: 9780698119017, 1999

At the annual celebration of Las Posadas in old Santa Fe, the husband and wife slated to play Mary and Joseph are delayed by car trouble, but a mysterious couple appears who seem perfect for the part. Lexile: AD410L (Grades K–4) F

Garay, Luis. *The Kite.* ISBN-13: 9780887765032, 2002

Young Francisco and his mother are very poor. Francisco rises at dawn to deliver newspapers in the marketplace. One day he sees a kite hanging in one of the crowded stalls, and he knows he has found his heart's desire. He longs for the beautiful kite that could fly free in the blue sky far above the squalid city in which he lives. It seems that he will have to put off his dream because his mother is expecting a baby, and every penny he earns will soon be needed. Lexile: N/A (Grades 2–4) F

Garza, Carmen Lomas. *Family Pictures / Cuadros de familia.* ISBN-13: 9780892392070, 1990

The day-to-day experiences of Garza are told through 14 vignettes of art and a descriptive narrative, each focusing on a different aspect of traditional Mexican American culture such as celebrating birthdays, making tamales, finding a hammerhead shark on the beach, picking cactus, going to a fair in Mexico, and confiding to her sister her dreams of becoming an artist. Lexile: N/A (Grades K–4) NF

Guy, Ginger Foglesong. *¡Fiesta!* ISBN-13: 9780688143312, 2003

This bilingual text describes a children's party and provides practice counting in English and Spanish. Lexile: BR (Grades Pre-K–3) F

Herrera, Juan Felipe. *Calling the Doves / El canto de las palomas.*

ISBN-13: 9780892391660, 1995

The author recalls his childhood in the mountains and valleys of California with his farmworker parents who inspired him with poetry and song.

Lexile: AD910L (Grades K–4) NF

Hobbs, Will. *Crossing the Wire.* ISBN-13: 9780060741402, 2007

Victor leaves Mexico after the death of his father and begins his journey across the Arizona desert. He meets up with a friend, and they experience many adventures and challenges from coyotes, drug smuggling, starvation, and train hopping.

Lexile: 0670L (Grades 7–12) F

Johnston, Tony. *Uncle Rain Cloud.* ISBN-13: 9780881063721, 2003

Uncle Tom looks after Carlos until his parents get home. He tells his nephew stories of the Aztec gods, but troubles him with his bad temper. Their relationship is sometimes difficult, until the day that they discover that they both struggle with English and they make a pact. Carlos will help his uncle with English—the source of his grouchiness—and Uncle Tom will teach him more stories, but in Spanish. Lexile: 0370L (Grades K–4) F

Lawery, Linda. *Cinco de mayo.* ISBN-13: 9781575057644, 2005

This book tells of how this holiday commemorates the Battle of Puebla. On May 5, 1862, the Mexican army of 3,000 soldiers met the French army of 6,000 soldiers at Puebla, a town east of Mexico City where the Mexicans fought to protect their families and their way of life.

Lexile: N/A   (Grades 1–4)   NF

Medina, Jane. *My Name Is Jorge: On Both Sides of the River.* ISBN-13: 9781563978425, 1999

This is a book of poems in Spanish and then in English, written from the standpoint of Jorge. They vividly depict his experiences and feelings about coming from Mexico to the United States by crossing a river. Sure to provoke thought and conversation, especially among recent immigrants who will identify with the many slights both inadvertent and intentional, this collection of the many small moments that make people feel either accepted or rejected in a new culture.   Lexile: AD340L   (Grades 3–7)   NF

Mora, Pat. *Listen to the Desert / Oye al desierto.* ISBN-13: 9780618111442, 1994

A gentle text and innovative artwork depict a pivotal summer in a boy's life when he and his family leave their Texas home for farmwork in Iowa.   Lexile: AD360L   (Grades K–4)   F

Mora, Pat. *The Rainbow Tulip.* ISBN-13: 9780142500095, 2003

A Mexican American first-grader experiences the difficulties and pleasures of being different when she wears a tulip costume with all the colors of the rainbow for the school May Day parade.   Lexile: 0310L   (Grades Pre-K–3)   F

Mora, Pat. *Tomás and the Library Lady.* ISBN-13: 9780375803499, 1997

While helping his family in their work as migrant laborers far from their home, Tomás finds an entire world to explore in the books at the local public library.

Lexile: 440L   (Grades K–4)   F

Pérez, L. King. *First Day in Grapes.* ISBN-13: 9781584300458, 2002

When Chico starts the third grade in a new school after his migrant-worker family moves to begin harvesting California grapes, he finds that self-confidence and math skills help him cope with the first day of school.   Lexile: AD570L   (Grades 1–5)   F

Politi, Leo. *Pedro: The Angel of Olvera Street.* ISBN-13: 9780892369904, 1946

Pedro tells of Los Angeles's original Latino settlement on Olvera Street and the community Christmas traditions of the Posada, a procession that reenacts Mary and Joseph's pilgrimage to Bethlehem, and of the *piñata*, a papier-mâché vessel filled with toys that children break open at the Posada's end.   Lexile: AD360L   (Grades K–4)   F

Ryan, Pam Muñoz. *Esperanza Rising* ISBN-13: 9780439120425, 2002

This is the story of a young Mexican girl who must leave her life on a great farm to come to California and become a migrant worker.   Lexile: 740L   (Grades 3–6)   F

Soto, Gary. *Big Bushy Mustache.* ISBN-13: 9780679880301, 1998

To look more like his father, Ricky borrows a mustache from a school costume, but when he loses it on the way home, his father comes up with a replacement.

Lexile: AD320L   (Grades K–4)   F

Soto, Gary. *Chato and the Party Animals.*   ISBN-13: 9780756929213, 2004

Chato decides to throw a *pachanga* for his friend Novio Boy, who has never had a birthday party. But when it is time to party, Novio Boy cannot be found.

Lexile: 0440L   (Grades K–4)   F

Soto, Gary. *Chato's Kitchen.*   ISBN-13: 9780698116009, 1997

To get the *ratoncitos*, little mice, who have moved into the barrio to come to his house, Chato the cat prepares all kinds of good food: fajitas, frijoles, salsa, enchiladas, and more.

Lexile: 0740L   (Grades Pre-K–4)   F

Soto, Gary. *Too Many Tamales.*   ISBN-13: 9780698114128, 1993

Maria tries on her mother's wedding ring while helping make tamales for a Christmas family get-together. Panic ensues when hours later, Maria realizes the ring is missing.

Lexile: 670L   (Grades Pre-K–4)   F

Stevens, Jeanne. *Carlos and the Squash Plant / Carlos y la planta de calabaza.*

ISBN-13: 9780873586252, 1993

Having ignored his mother's warnings about what will happen if he doesn't bathe after working on his family's New Mexican farm, Carlos awakens one morning to find a squash growing out of his ear.   Lexile: AD320L   (Grades K–4)   F

Trottier, Maxine. *Migrant.*   ISBN-13: 9780888999757, 2011

Anna is the child of Mennonites from Mexico, who have come north to harvest fruit and vegetables.   Lexile: AD880L   (Grades Pre-K–2)   F

Urrutia, Maria Cristina, and Rebeca Orozco. *Cinco de Mayo: Yesterday and Today.*

ISBN-13: 9780888994844, 2002

This book is a basic introduction to Cinco de Mayo and explains the history of the holiday and why it continues to resonate.   Lexile: N/A   (Grades Pre-K–2)   NF

Wing, Natasha. *Jalapeño Bagels.*   ISBN-13: 9780689805301, 1996

For International Day at school, Pablo wants to bring something that reflects the cultures of both his parents. Jalapeno bagels are the delicious coming together of two cultures as the son of a Jewish baker and his Mexican wife.   Lexile: AD460L   (Grades K–4)   F

African American Literature

Adler, A. David. *A Picture Book of Martin Luther King, Jr.*

ISBN-13: 9780823408474, 1989

This is a brief, illustrated biography of the Baptist minister and civil rights leader whose philosophy and practice of nonviolent civil disobedience helped American blacks win many battles for equal rights.   Lexile: AD680L   (Grades K–4)   NF

Allen, Debbie. *Dancing in the Wings.* ISBN-13: 9780142501412, 2000

This story is loosely based on actress and choreographer Debbie Allen's own experiences as a young dancer. "Sassy" tries out for a summer dance festival in Washington, D.C., despite the other girls' taunts that she is much too tall. Lexile: 540L (Grades K–4) F

Chocolate, Deborah M. Newton. *My First Kwanzaa Book.* ISBN-13: 9780439129268, 1992

During the last week of December, Kwanzaa is a time of celebration in the African American community, and families across the nation gather for this colorful holiday highlighting their heritage. Lexile: AD910L (Grades K–4) NF

Coleman, Evelyn. *White Socks Only.* ISBN-13: 9780807589564, 1996

In the segregated South, a young girl thinks that she can drink from a fountain marked "Whites Only" because she is wearing her white socks. Lexile: N/A (Grades K–4) F

Cowen-Fletcher, Jane. *It Takes a Village.* ISBN-13: 9780590465731, 1994

On market day in a small village in Benin, Yemi tries to watch her little brother Kokou and finds that the entire village is watching out for him, too. Lexile: 390L (Grades Pre-K–3) F

Crews, Donald. *Shortcut.* ISBN-13: 9780688135768, 1992

Children taking a shortcut by walking along a railroad track find excitement and danger when a train approaches. Lexile: AD210L (Grades Pre-K–3) F

Daly, Niki. *The Boy on the Beach.* ISBN-13: 9780689821752, 1999

Reluctant to let the surf crash over him, Joe runs down the beach and has an adventure with an old boat. Lexile: AD450L (Grades Pre-K–3) F

Daly, Niki. *Jamela's Dress.* ISBN-13: 9780374336677, 1999

Jamela gets in trouble when she takes the expensive material intended for a new dress for Mama, parades it in the street, and allows it to become dirty and torn.

Lexile: AD420L (Grades Pre-K–3) F

Diakité, Penda. *I Lost My Tooth in Africa.* ISBN-13: 9780439662260, 2006

A young girl, Amina, is visiting relatives in Mali with her family. She is hopeful that her tooth will fall out in Mali before she gets back to Oregon. Her father had told her that in Mali, when a child loses a tooth, they get a chicken from the African tooth fairy.

Lexile: N/A (Grades Pre-K–3) F

Duncan, Alice Faye. *Honey Baby Sugar Child.* ISBN-13: 9780689846786, 2005

A mother expresses her everlasting love for her child in this warm, poetic picture book.

Lexile: N/A (Grades Pre-K–3) F

Ford, Juwanda G. *K is for Kwanzaa. A Kwanzaa Alphabet Book.*

ISBN-13: 9780590922005, 1997

This unique and beautifully illustrated book celebrates the joyful African American holiday Kwanzaa by introducing related words from *A* to *Z*, including *Africa*, *bendera*, *dashiki*, and *yams*. Lexile: N/A (Grades K–4) NF

Greenfield, Eloise. *Honey, I Love.*   ISBN-13: 9780060091231, 1978

Each of these 16 "love poems" is spoken straight from the heart of a child. Riding on a train, listening to music, playing with a friend . . . each poem elicits a new appreciation of the rich content of everyday life.   Lexile: NP   (Grades K–3)   NF

Hesse, Karen. *Come On, Rain!*   ISBN-13: 9780590331258, 1999

A young girl eagerly awaits a coming rainstorm to bring relief from the oppressive summer heat.   Lexile: AD780L   (Grades Pre-K–3)   F

Hoffman, Mary. *Amazing Grace.*   ISBN-13: 9780803710405, 1991

Grace loves stories, whether they're from books, movies, or the kind her grandmother tells. So when she gets a chance to play a part in *Peter Pan*, she knows exactly who she wants to be.   Lexile: 680L   (Grades Pre-K–3)   F

Hoffman, Mary. *Boundless Grace.*   ISBN-13: 9780140556674, 2000

When Grace gets the opportunity to go to Africa and visit with her father and his new family, she feels a little strange.   Lexile: 680L   (Grades Pre-K–3)   F

Hooks, Bell. *Happy to Be Nappy.*   ISBN-13: 9780786807567, 1999

This book is a joyous look at all types and styles of hair, and the girls who wear them.   Lexile: AD40L   (Grades Pre-K–3)   F

Hooks, Bell. *Homemade Love.*   ISBN-13: 9780786806430, 2002

A girl who is Girlpie to her mama and Honey Bun Chocolate Dewdrop to her daddy savors the warmth and love of her family.   Lexile: N/A   (Grades K–4)   F

Hopkinson Deborah. *Sweet Clara and the Freedom Quilt.*   ISBN-13: 9780679874720, 1993

A young slave stitches a quilt with a map pattern, which guides her to freedom in the North.   Lexile: AD680L   (Grades Pre-K–3)   F

Hopkinson, Deborah. *Under the Quilt of Night.*   ISBN-13: 9780689877001, 2002

A young girl flees from the farm where she was a slave and uses the Underground Railroad to escape to freedom in the North.   Lexile: AD580L   (Grades 1–3)   F

Hudson, Wade. *Pass It On: African-American Poetry for Children.*

ISBN-13: 9780590457705, 1993

A potpourri of poems by Gwendolyn Brooks, Eloise Greenfield, Nikki Giovanni, and Langston Hughes are interspersed with works by lesser-known writers. Although some selections focus on experiences unique to African Americans, many of them deal with the common experiences of children of all races—eating chocolate, jumping in a puddle, taking a bath.   Lexile: NP   (Grades Pre-K–4)   NF

Keats, Ezra Jack. *Peter's Chair.*   ISBN-13: 9780140564419, 1967

When Peter discovers his blue furniture is being painted pink for a new baby sister, he rescues the last unpainted item, a chair, and runs away.   Lexile: 390L   (Grades Pre-K–4)   F

Keats, Ezra Jack. *Whistle for Willie.*   ISBN-13: 9780140502022, 1964

This is the story of Peter, who longs to learn to whistle so he can call for his dog.

Lexile: AD410L   (Grades Pre-K–4)   F

Machado, Ana Maria. *Nina Bonita.*   ISBN-13: 9780916291631, 1996

Enchanted by Nina Bonita's black skin, a white rabbit determines to find a way to have children as beautiful and black as she is.   Lexile: N/A   (Grades Pre-K–4)   F

McDonough, Yona Zeldis. *Who Was Louis Armstrong?*   ISBN-13: 9780448433684, 2004

This is the story of Louis Armstrong's passion and genius that pushed jazz into new realms with his amazing, improvisational trumpet playing.   Lexile: 780L.   (Grades 3–8)   NF

McKissack, Patricia C. *A Million Fish . . . More or Less.*   ISBN-13: 9780679880868, 1992

A boy learns that the truth is often stretched on the Bayou Clapateaux and gets the chance to tell his own version of a bayou tale when he goes fishing.

Lexile: 0690L   (Grades Pre-K–3)   F

Mendez, Phil. *The Black Snowman.*   ISBN-13: 9780439769938, 1989

Through the powers of a magical kente, a black snowman comes to life and helps young Jacob discover the beauty of his black heritage as well as his own self-worth.

Lexile: 550L   (Grades Pre-K–3)   F

Miller, William. *The Piano.*   ISBN-13: 9781584302421, 2004

This story takes place in the deep South of the early 1900s and is about an African American girl who learns to play the piano from her white employer. In return, she shows the elderly woman the power of friendship and caring.   Lexile: 0440   (Grades K–4)   F

Monjo, F. N. *The Drinking Gourd: A Story of the Underground Railroad.*

ISBN-13: 9780064440424, 1970

Tommy Fuller is surprised to find a family of runaway slaves hiding in his barn, which is a stop on the Underground Railroad.   Lexile: 370L   (Grades 1–4)   F

Pinkney, Andrea Davis. *Duke Ellington: The Piano Prince and His Orchestra.*

ISBN-13: 9780786814206, 1998

This is a brief recounting of the career of this jazz musician and composer who, along with his orchestra, created music that was beyond category.   Lexile: 0800L   (Grades K–4)   NF

Polacco, Patricia. *Chicken Sunday.*   ISBN-13: 9780698116153, 1998

After being initiated into a neighbor's family by a solemn backyard ceremony, a young Russian American girl and her African American brothers determine to buy their Gramma Eula a beautiful Easter hat.   Lexile: 650L   (Grades K–6)   F

Rappaport, Doreen. *Martin's Big Words: The Life of Dr. Martin Luther King, Jr.*

ISBN-13: 9781423106357, 2001

This is a portrait of a man whose dream changed America and the world forever.

Lexile: AD410L   (Grades K–6)   NF

Ringgold, Faith. *Tar Beach.*   ISBN-13: 9780517885444, 1991

A young girl dreams of flying above her Harlem home, claiming all she sees for herself and her family.   Lexile: AD790L   (Grades K–4)   F

Smalls, Irene. *Don't Say Ain't.*   ISBN-13: 9781570913822, 2004

In this tale set in 1957 Harlem, a girl learns to reconcile the ideas of her new integrated school with her home life.   Lexile: N/A   (Grades K–6)   F

Steptoe, Javaka. *The Jones Family Express.*   ISBN-13: 9781584302629, 2003

Steven tries to find just the right present for Aunt Carolyn in time for the annual block party.   Lexile: N/A   (Grades K–4)   F

Steptoe, John. *Creativity.*   ISBN-13: 9780618316779, 2003

Charles helps Hector, a student who has just moved from Puerto Rico, adjust to his new life.   Lexile: 330L   (Grades K–5)   F

Steptoe, John. *Daddy Is a Monster . . . Sometimes.*   ISBN-13: 9780397318933, 1980

Bweela and Javaka relate the incidents that make Daddy a monster in their eyes.   Lexile: N/A   (Grades K–4)   F

Steptoe, John. *Mufaro's Beautiful Daughters: An African Tale.*

ISBN-13: 9780618032232, 1987

Mufaro's two beautiful daughters, one bad-tempered, one kind and sweet, go before the king, who is choosing a wife.   Lexile: AD720L   (Grades K–4)   F

Udry, Janice May. *What Mary Jo Shared.*   ISBN-13: 9780590437578, 1966

In this now classic story about a black family, shy Mary Jo shares her father at show-and-tell.   Lexile: AD530L   (Grades Pre-K–3)   F

Weatherford, Carole Boston. *Becoming Billie Holiday.*   ISBN-13: 9781590785072, 2008

In 1915, Sadie Fagan gave birth to a daughter she named Eleanora. The world, however, would know her as Billie Holiday, possibly the greatest jazz singer of all time. Eleanora's journey into legend took her through pain, poverty, and run-ins with the law. By the time she was 15, she knew she possessed something that could possibly change her life—a voice. Eleanora could sing. Her remarkable voice led her to a place in the spotlight with some of the era's hottest big bands.   Lexile: N/A   (Grades 7–12)   NF

Wiles, Deborah. *Freedom Summer.*   ISBN-13: 9780689878299, 2005

Set in Mississippi during the summer of 1964, this book is about two boys—one white and the other African American—and the aftermath of the passage of the Civil Rights Act.   Lexile: 0460L   (Grades Pre-K–3)   F

Williams, Karen Lynn. *My Name Is Sangoel.*　　　ISBN-13: 9780802853073, 2009

Sangoel is a refugee, leaving behind his homeland of Sudan, where his father died in the war. He only has his name, a Dinka name handed down proudly from his father and grandfather before him. Now living in the United States, everything seems very strange and unlike home. Sangoel quietly endures the fact that no one can pronounce his name. Lonely and homesick, he finally comes up with a solution to this problem, and in the process he at last begins to feel at home.　　　Lexile: AD440L　(Grades 2–6)　F

Woodson, Jacqueline. *I Hadn't Meant to Tell You This.*　　　ISBN-13: 9780142417041, 2010

Marie, the only black girl in the eighth grade willing to befriend her white classmate Lena, discovers that Lena's father is doing horrible things to her in private.

　　　Lexile: N/A　(Grades 6–10)　F

Woodson, Jacqueline. *The Other Side.*　　　ISBN-13: 9780399231162, 2001

Two girls, one white and one black, gradually get to know each other as they sit on the fence that divides their town.　　　Lexile: AD300L　(Grades K–5)　F

Wyeth, Sharon Dennis. *Always My Dad.*　　　ISBN-13: 9780679889342, 1995

Although she does not get to see her father very often, a girl enjoys the time she and her brothers spend with him one summer while they are visiting their grandparents' farm.

　　　Lexile: N/A　(Grades K–4)　F

Zelver, Patricia. *The Wonderful Towers of Watts.*　　　ISBN-13: 9781590782552, 1994

When Sam Rodia, an Italian immigrant was about 47 years old, he began collecting broken bits of colored tiles, empty bottles, faucet handles, horseshoes, seashells, old shoes, and other found objects. As he listened to grand opera, he took 33 years to transform his California backyard into the Wonderful Towers of Watts.　　　Lexile: AD860L　(Grades K–4)　NF

Asian American Literature

Ashley, Bernard. *Cleversticks.*

ISBN-13: 9780517883327, 1995

Wishing he had something to be clever at like each of the other children in his class, Ling Sung unexpectedly and happily discovers that others admire his prowess with chopsticks.

Lexile: AD370L　(Grades Pre-K–2)　F

Bunting, Eve. *The Wall.*　　　ISBN-13: 9780395629772, 1992

A boy travels to the Vietnam Veterans Memorial with his father to seek out his grandfather's name.　　　Lexile: AD270L　(Grades 1–4)　F

Cheng, Andrea. *Grandfather Counts.* ISBN-13: 9781584301585, 2003

A moving intergenerational story, this book highlights the universality of the love shared between grandparent and grandchild, a love that helps cross the boundaries of language and culture. Lexile: 0410L (Grades K–2) F

Choi, Yangsook. *The Name Jar.* ISBN-13: 9780440417996, 2003

After Unhei moves from Korea to the United States, her new classmates help her decide what her name should be. Lexile: N/A (Grades K–4) F

Coerr, Eleanor. *Sadako and the Thousand Paper Cranes.* ISBN-13: 9780698118027, 1977

Hospitalized with the dreaded atom bomb disease, leukemia, a child in Hiroshima races against time to fold one thousand paper cranes to verify the legend that by doing so a sick person will become healthy. Lexile: 0630L (Grades K–4) NF

Demi. *Liang and the Magic Paintbrush.* ISBN-13: 9780805008012, 1988

When a poor boy in China receives a magical paintbrush, everything he paints turns to life. But the wicked emperor wants to capture the boy when he hears the news. The story will excite readers as the ruler gets his just reward when the boy creates a masterpiece that spells the emperor's doom. Lexile: AD480L (Grades Pre-K–3) F

Friedman, Ina R. *How My Parents Learned to Eat.* ISBN-13: 9780395442357, 1987

An American sailor courts a young Japanese woman, and each tries, in secret, to learn the other's way of eating. Lexile: 450L (Grades K–4) F

Levine, Ellen. *I Hate English.* ISBN-13: 9780590423045, 1995

When her family moves to New York from Hong Kong, Mei Mei finds it difficult to adjust to school and learn the alien sounds of English. Lexile: 390L (Grades K–3) F

Lewis, Rose. *I Love You Like Crazy Cakes.* ISBN-13: 9780316525381, 2000

A woman describes how she went to China to adopt a special baby girl. The story is based on the author's own experiences. Lexile: AD550L (Grades Pre-K–3) F

Loo, Sanne Te. *Ping-Li's Kite.* ISBN-13: 9781886910751, 2001

Even though he knows he might anger the emperor of the sky, Ping-Li is tempted to fly his kite before he paints it. Lexile: N/A (Grades Pre-K–3) F

Look, Lenore. *Uncle Peter's Amazing Chinese Wedding.* ISBN-13: 9780689844584, 2006

Jenny describes her uncle Peter's traditional Chinese wedding, but she is upset because the wedding means that less attention is going to her. In the process of being upset, however, she goes into great detail about the traditions that go along with a Chinese wedding. Lexile: AD860L (Grades K–7) F

Mochizuki, Ken. *Baseball Saved Us.*   ISBN-13: 9781880000199, 1995

When a Japanese American boy and his family are interned in a camp during World War II, they decide to combat their depression by building a baseball field. During a game the boy channels his humiliation—both from being a prisoner and from being a bad player—to anger, giving him the strength to hit a game-winning home run.

Lexile: AD550L   (Grades 1–4) F

Rattigan, Jama Kim. *Dumpling Soup.*   ISBN-13: 9780316730471, 1998

A young, Asian American girl living in Hawaii tries to make dumplings for her family's New Year's celebration.   Lexile: 500L   (Grades K–3) F

Say, Allen. *Allison.*   ISBN-13: 9780618495375, 1997

When Allison realizes that she looks more like her favorite doll than like her parents, she comes to terms with this unwelcomed discovery through the help of a stray cat.

Lexile: 430L   (Grades K–4) F

Say, Allen. *The Bicycle Man.*   ISBN-13: 9780395506523, 1989

The amazing tricks two American soldiers do on a borrowed bicycle are a fitting finale for the school sports-day festivities in a small village in occupied Japan.

Lexile: N/A   (Grades Pre-K–3) F

Say, Allen. *Grandfather's Journey.*   ISBN-13: 9780547076805, 2008

A Japanese American man recounts his grandfather's journey to America, which he later also undertakes, and the feelings of being torn by a love for two different countries.

Lexile: 0150L   (Grades K–4) NF

Say, Allen. *Music for Alice.*   ISBN-13: 9780547345970, 2004

A Japanese American farmer recounts her agricultural successes and setbacks and her enduring love of dance. It is based on the true-life story of Alice Sumida, who with her husband, Mark, established the largest gladiola bulb farm in the country during the last half of the 20th century.   Lexile: N/A   (Grades K–4) NF

Say, Allen. *Tea with Milk.*   ISBN-13: 9780547237473, 2009

After growing up near San Francisco, a young Japanese woman returns with her parents to their native Japan, but she feels foreign and out of place.   Lexile: N/A   (Grades K–4) F

Say, Allen. *Under the Cherry Blossom Tree: An Old Japanese Tale.*   ISBN-13: 9780618556151, 2005

A cherry tree growing from the top of the wicked landlord's head is the beginning of his misfortunes and a better life for the poor villagers.   Lexile: N/A   (Grades K–4) F

Snyder, Dianne. *The Boy of the Three-Year Nap.*   ISBN-13: 9780395669570, 1993

A poor Japanese woman maneuvers events to change the lazy habits of her son.

Lexile: AD610L   (Grades K–4) F

Surat, Michele Maria. *Angel Child, Dragon Child.*   ISBN-13: 9780590422710, 1989

Ut, an immigrant child from Vietnam, tries to adjust to a new life in America.

Lexile: 420L   (Grades Pre-K–4)   F

Tseng, Grace. *White Tiger, Blue Serpent.*   ISBN-13: 9780688125165, 1999

In this stirring retelling of a favorite Chinese folktale, we learn a young Chinese boy's mother has her brocade stolen by a greedy goddess. The boy faces many perils to get it back for his mother.   Lexile: N/A   (Grades K–4)   F

Uchida, Yoshiko. *The Bracelet.*   ISBN-13: 9780698113909, 1996

Emi, a Japanese American in the second grade, is sent with her family to an internment camp during World War II. But the loss of the bracelet her best friend has given her proves that she does not need a physical reminder of that friendship.

Lexile: AD710L   (Grades K–5)   F

Waboose, Jan Bourdeau. *Morning on the Lake.*   ISBN-13: 9781550745887, 1997

Under the patient and gentle guidance of his grandfather, a boy gradually comes to respect the ways of nature and to understand his own place in the world.

Lexile: 0510   (Grades K–4)   F

Zhang, Song Nan. *The Ballad of Mulan.*   ISBN-13: 9781572270572, 1998

Mulan is the mythic woman warrior who 15 centuries ago disguised herself as a man to take her ailing father's place in battle. Mulan joins the Imperial Army and after years of successful military service, she is offered a reward for her dedication. All she wants is to return home to live quietly.   Lexile: N/A   (Grades K–4)   F

Native American Literature

Ata, Te, and Lynn Moroney. *Baby Rattlesnake.*

ISBN-13: 9780892392162, 1989

Willful Baby Rattlesnake throws tantrums to get his rattle before he's ready, but he misuses it and learns a lesson.

Lexile: 0550L   (Grades Pre-K–3)   F

Baylor, Byrd. *When Clay Sings.*   ISBN-13: 9780689711060, 1972

The daily life and customs of prehistoric southwest Indian tribes are retraced from the designs on the remains of their pottery.   Lexile: AD880L   (Grades Pre-K–3)   NF

Begaye, Lisa Shook. *Building a Bridge.*   ISBN-13: 9780873587273, 1999

Anna, an Anglo, and Juanita, a Navajo, are both reservation children and find the first day of school exciting and scary. This book explores how the two girls find mutual understanding.   Lexile: N/A   (Grades K–4)   F

Boyden, Linda. **The Blue Roses.**   ISBN-13: 9781600606557, 2002

A Native American girl gardens with her grandfather, who helps raise her. She learns about life and loss when he dies and then speaks to her from a dream where he is surrounded by blue roses.   Lexile: N/A   (Grades K–4)   F

Bruchac, Joseph. **The Boy Called Slow.**   ISBN-13: 9780698116160, 1998

Anxious to be given a name as strong and brave as that of his father, a proud Lakota Sioux grows into manhood, acting with careful deliberation, determination, and bravery, which eventually earns him his proud new name: Sitting Bull.

Lexile: AD690L   (Grades Pre-K–3)   F

Bruchac, Joseph. **Crazy Horse's Vision.**   ISBN-13: 9781584302827, 2010

This story is based on the life of the dedicated young Lakota boy who grew up to be one of the bravest defenders of his people.   Lexile: 420L   (Grades K–4)   F

Bruchac, Joseph. **The First Strawberries: A Cherokee Story.**   ISBN-13: 9780140564099, 1998

A quarrel between the first man and the first woman is reconciled when the Sun causes strawberries to grow out of the earth.   Lexile: AD320L   (Grades K–3)   F

Bruchac, Joseph. **Gluskabe and the Four Wishes.**   ISBN-13: 9780525651642, 1995

After making an arduous journey to visit Gluskabe, the Great Spirit's helper, four men are each granted a wish. Gluskabe gives each man a pouch, saying that it contains his heart's desire, but warns them not to open the pouches until they return home.

Lexile: N/A   (Grades Pre-K–4)   F

Cherry, Lynne. **A River Ran Wild.**   ISBN-13: 9780152163723, 1992

This is an environmental history of the Nashua River, from its discovery by Indians through the polluting years of the Industrial Revolution to the ambitious cleanup that revitalized it.

Lexile: 670L   (Grades K–4)   NF

Cohen, Caron Lee. **The Mud Pony.**   ISBN-13: 9780812478051, 1988

A poor boy becomes a powerful leader when Mother Earth turns his mud pony into a real one, but after the pony turns back to mud, the boy must find his own strength.

Lexile: AD610L   (Grades Pre-K–3)   F

dePaola, Tomie. **The Legend of the Indian Paintbrush.**   ISBN-13: 9780698113602, 2000

Little Gopher follows his destiny, as revealed in a dream-vision, of becoming an artist for his people and eventually is able to bring the colors of the sunset down to earth.

Lexile: AD840L   (Grades Pre-K–3)   F

Dixon, Ann **The Sleeping Lady.**   ISBN-13: 9780882404950, 1994

Gazing across Cook Inlet from Anchorage at Mount Susitna, people have imagined that the sprawling peak is a slumbering woman, inspiring this ageless tale about a time of peace and the consequences of war.   Lexile: N/A   (Grades 3–7)   F

Dominic, Gloria. *Coyote and the Grasshoppers—A Pomo Legend.*

ISBN-13: 9780865934276, 1996

By listening to the Great Spirit and eating huge quantities of grasshoppers, Coyote is able to save the Pomo from drought and starvation.   Lexile: N/A   (Grades K–4)   F

Dominic, Gloria. *Red Hawk and the Sky Sisters—A Shawnee Legend.*

ISBN-13: 9780816745142, 1996

This book relates the story of the skilled hunter Red Hawk who captures and marries the youngest daughter of Bright Star, only to have her return to the sky with their son.

Lexile: N/A   (Grades 3–7)   F

Dwyer, Mindy. *Coyote in Love: The Story of Crater Lake.*   ISBN-13: 9780882404851, 1997

This is a retelling of a Native American legend about Coyote's love for a beautiful blue star, which resulted in the creation of Crater Lake, Oregon.   Lexile: 640L   (Grades Pre-K–7)   F

Esbensen, Barbara Juster. *The Star Maiden: An Ojibway Tale.*

ISBN-13: 9780316249553, 1988

This old Ojibway tale is about a time when fish swam in clear streams, wigwams and birch-bark canoes lined lake shores, and "the earth was rich with everything the people needed."

Lexile: 430L   (Grades Pre-K–3)   F

Goble, Paul. *The Gift of the Sacred Dog.*   ISBN-13: 9780020432807, 1984

In response to an Indian boy's prayer for help for his hungry people, the Great Spirit sends the gift of the Sacred Dogs (horses), which enable the tribe to hunt for buffalo.

Lexile: 670L   (Grades K–4)   F

Goble, Paul. *Her Seven Brothers.*   ISBN-13: 9780689717307, 1993

This book retells the Cheyenne legend in which a girl and her seven chosen brothers become the Big Dipper.   Lexile: AD520L   (Grades Pre-K–3)   F

Goble, Paul and Dorothy. *Lone Bull's Horse Raid.*   ISBN-13: 9780333147542, 1973

Two young Sioux join a raiding party to capture horses from some neighboring Crows.

Lexile: N/A   (Grades Pre-K–3)   F

Grossman, Virginia, and Sylvia Long. *Ten Little Rabbits.*   ISBN-13: 9780811810579, 1991

This spirited book celebrates Native American traditions as it teaches young children to count from 1 to 10 through Pueblo corn dances or Navajo weaving. The simple, rhyming text is enhanced by a brief afterword on Native American customs.

Lexile: N/A   (Grades 3–7)   NF

Harjo, Joy. *The Good Luck Cat.*   ISBN-13: 9780152321970, 2000

Because her good luck cat Woogie has already used up eight of his nine lives in narrow escapes from disaster, a Native American girl worries when he disappears.

Lexile: AD540L   (Grades Pre-K–3)   F

Jeffers, Susan. *Brother Eagle, Sister Sky.*   ISBN-13: 9780142301326, 2002

American Indian Chief Seattle's lesson to respect the earth and every creature on it has endured the test of time and is imbued with passion born of love of the land and the environment.   Lexile: 0740L   (Grades 3–7)   NF

Joosse, Barbara M. *Mama, Do You Love Me?*   ISBN-13: 9780877017592, 2010

A child living in the Arctic learns that a mother's love is unconditional and everlasting.   Lexile: 0420L   (Grades Pre-K–6)   F

Martin, Rafe. *The Rough-Face Girl.*   ISBN-13: 9780698116269, 1998

In this Algonquin Indian version of the Cinderella story, the Rough-Face Girl and her two beautiful but heartless sisters compete for the affections of the Invisible Being.   Lexile: 0540L   (Grades K–4)   F

McDermott, Gerald. *Arrow to the Sun: A Pueblo Indian Tale.*   ISBN-13: 9780140502114, 1977

This is the adaptation of the Pueblo Indian myth that explains how the spirit of the Lord of the Sun is brought to the world of men and how a boy searching for his father is made into an arrow and shot to the sun.   Lexile: 480L   (Grades Pre-K–3)   F

Miles, Miska. *Annie and the Old One.*   ISBN-13: 9780316571203, 1971

Annie is a young Navajo girl who refuses to believe that her grandmother, the Old One, will die. Sadly, Annie learns that she cannot change the course of life.

Lexile: 700L   (Grades K–4)   F

Mitchell, Marianne. *Maya Moon.*   ISBN-13: 9781568017945, 1995

In this retold folktale from Mexico, pesky turtles keep climbing into Maya's bed so she can't rest. But she solves this problem, explaining why the moon changes shape.

Lexile: N/A   (Grades K–4)   F

Osofsky, Audrey. *Dreamcatcher.*   ISBN-13: 9780531085882, 1992

While a sister uses a dreamcatcher to catch bad dreams and hold them until the sun destroys their power, an Ojibwa baby sleeps peacefully in a cradle nearby.

Lexile: N/A   (Grades Pre-K–3)   F

Sleator, William. *The Angry Moon.*   ISBN-13: 9780316797375, 1970

An Indian girl insults the moon and is held prisoner by him until her friend reaches the sky country to rescue her.   Lexile: N/A   (Grades Pre-K–3)   F

Taylor, Harriet Peck. *Brother Wolf: A Seneca Tale.*   ISBN-13: 9780374309978, 1996

This dignified retelling of a tale from Seneca lore is filled with mischief and fun and "explains" two of nature's mysteries—how the wolf came to be seen as wily and wise, and how the birds became resplendent with color.   Lexile: N/A   (Grades Pre-K–3)   F

Taylor, Harriet Peck. *Coyote and the Laughing Butterflies.*   ISBN-13: 9780027888461, 1995

Based on a Tewa Native American legend, Coyote is tricked by some butterflies who laugh so hard about their joke that they cannot fly straight.   Lexile: N/A   (Grades Pre-K–3)   F

Van Camp, Richard. *A Man Called Raven.*   ISBN-13: 9780892391448, 1997

A mysterious man tells two Indian brothers why they must not hurt the ravens that annoy them as the ravens spread garbage all over the street.   Lexile: N/A   (Grades K–4)   F

Van Laan, Nancy. *Buffalo Dance: A Blackfoot Legend.*   ISBN-13: 9780316897280, 1993

A retelling of a complex legend posits a mythical origin for the sacred buffalo dance of the Blackfoot people. Powerful themes of sacrifice and rebirth dominate the legend.

Lexile: N/A   (Grades K–4)   F

Wood, Nancy. *The Girl Who Loved Coyotes: Stories of the Southwest.*

ISBN-13: 9780688139827, 1995

This collection of 12 Southwestern folktales features the infamous trickster Coyote. Many of the tales have an aura that includes the spirit of the land, the mysticism of its ancestors, and the geography of the Southwest. They describe the native peoples that lived there and the development of their folktales.   Lexile: N/A   (Grades Pre-K–3)   F

Yolen, Jane. *Encounter.*   ISBN-13: 9780152013899, 1996

A Taino Indian boy on the island of San Salvador recounts the landing of Columbus and his men in 1492.   Lexile: 0760L   (Grades 2–6)   F

12

Teaching History Through Literature

Literature and literary materials should play an important part in social studies instruction because they convey so well the affective dimension of human experience. The realism achieved through vivid portrayals in works of literature stirs the imagination of the young reader and helps develop a feeling for and an identification with the topic being studied.

—Jarolimek, 1990, p. 207

Knowing that the Common Core Standards are asking teachers to become savvier at linking subjects across the curriculum, this is the perfect time to think about including children's and young adult literature in the history curriculum. Literature written on a variety of reading levels can be integrated into the curriculum as a complement to traditional textbooks. It can make the study of history, geography, and the other social sciences more interesting, relevant, and meaningful to students. With the English Language Arts (ELA) Common Core requirements, skills such as increasing vocabulary, including content-specific terms, will benefit students in all subject areas, especially history, where vocabulary can be most difficult for learners.

Since literature goes beyond facts, can be more up-to-date than textbooks, and may be more appealing to readers, it serves as a useful mode of delivery instruction in history. Historical fiction and nonfiction allows readers to experience other times, places, people, and cultures with empathy and can be a powerful means for thoughtful analysis and critical thinking. This type of literature leads to interesting discussions of historical eras and increased understanding of the major figures who shaped history. Students will also get to explore the culture of the times and places they are studying about. Reading and discussing literature allows for meaningful student involvement and higher interest in discovering the past and its connection to our lives today.

These books lend themselves to opportunities for discussion during and after chapters whether the book is being delivered as a shared reading, independent reading, or guided reading. Some general questions that can be used to guide whole group or small group dialogue might include:

- Describe a typical day for the main character (include details related to the time period/era).
- In what ways is the setting in this book different from your neighborhood, city, state, or country?
- Create a list of qualities that one of the characters has in your story that differ from your own (keep in mind the details related to the time period or era).
- Describe the conflict or problem that the main character faces. If you lived back then and were his or her friend, in what ways would you help that character?
- Describe the strain between the main character and other characters in the book (keep in mind the details related to the time period or era).
- Describe significant events and relate them to your own personal experiences (keep in mind the details related to the time period or era).
- If you were living back in that historical time period, what would you want to change?
- What do you find most appealing about the historical time period in this book that you would like to experience?

In this chapter, you will find a list of books starting with Native Americans in early America and going through the Vietnam War. History has clearly continued since the Vietnam War, and titles reflective of other historical eras can be found throughout this book in the chapters on race cultures, awards, young adult literature, and more.

Native Americans in Early America

Bruchac, Joseph. *A Boy Called Slow.*   ISBN-13: 9780698116160, 1998
> This is a biography of Sitting Bull, a Lakota Sioux who grew up with the name Slow. Determined to be a great warrior, he tried his hardest in hunting, wrestling, and riding, so he was ready by age 14 to go on his first raid with the warriors. On the raid he ran ahead of the older warriors to attack the Crows, who ran away; so his father renamed him Sitting Bill.
>
> Lexile: AD690L   (Grades Pre-K–3)   NF

Bruchac, Joseph. *Crazy Horse's Vision.*   ISBN-13: 9781584302827, 2010

This is a retelling of the story of Crazy Horse, who as a boy saw U.S. soldiers attack his people and through a vision quest saw that he would lead his people against their attacks.

Lexile: N/A   (Grades K–4)   NF

Bruchac, Joseph. *Geronimo.*   ISBN-13: 9780439353601, 2006

Geronimo's fictional grandson, Little Foot, tells this story from his perspective and points out where history books were wrong about his grandfather. The story follows the Apaches from their Arizona home to Florida via train, shows them having to send their children to the Carlisle Indian School, and presents the hardships endured by those who followed Geronimo.

Lexile: 900L   (Grades 3–6)   F

dePaola, Tomie. *The Legend of the Bluebonnet.*   ISBN-13: 9780698113596, 1996

This is a retelling of a popular Comanche legend that explains how the bluebonnet (Texas's state flower) came to be. A young orphan Indian girl named She-Who-Is-Alone offers her most cherished possession to the Great Spirits in return for an end to the long drought that has plagued her people, and in return for her selfless act, bluebonnet flowers appear on the landscape.

Lexile: AD740L   (Grades K–3)   F

dePaola, Tomie. *The Legend of the Indian Paintbrush.*   ISBN-13: 9780698113602, 2000

This story retells an old Texas folktale about how the "Indian paintbrush" flower came to be. One night in a dream, a young Native American boy named Little Gopher is told where to find brushes filled with vibrant colors. The next day he locates them and paints the beautifully colored flowers.

Lexile: AD840L   (Grades Pre-K–3)   F

Dorris, Michael. *Sees Behind Trees.*   ISBN-13: 9780786813575, 1999

A Native American boy with a special gift to "see" beyond his poor eyesight journeys with an old warrior to a land of mystery and beauty.

Lexile: 0840L   (Grades 3–6)   F

Erdrich, Louise. *The Birchbark House.*   ISBN-13: 9780786814541, 2002

This is a story of an Ojibwa family living on an island in Lake Superior in 1847.

Lexile: N/A   (Grades 3–6)   F

Freedman, Russell. *The Life and Death of Crazy Horse.*   ISBN-13: 9780823412198, 2002

This is the story about Crazy Horse's life, placing it within the larger dynamics of the period (gold rush, railroads, white settlers' desire for land, etc.)   Lexile: 0970L   (Grades 3–6)   NF

Hightower, Jamake. *Anpao: An American Indian Odyssey.*   ISBN-13: 9780064404372, 1992

A brave named Anpao wants to marry KoKoMikeis, but she is unwilling, claiming she belongs to the Sun only. So Anpao embarks a journey to the house of the Sun, to ask permission to marry KoKoMikeis. But first he has to go back to the beginning of the world and accomplish a series of tasks to discover his genuine self and show the Sun why he should have KoKoMikeis for a wife.

Lexile: 880L   (Grades 3–6)   F

Hudson, Jan. *Sweetgrass.*   ISBN-13: 9780698117631, 1999

Sweetgrass wants to be married like other Blackfoot girls her age, but her father thinks she is too young. Over the subsequent year, she proves her wisdom, bravery, and maturity through selfless acts to help members of her family and community, and finally her father begins to see her as a woman.   Lexile: 0640L   (Grades 3–6)   F

O'Dell, Scott, and Elizabeth Hall. *Thunder Rolling in the Mountains.*

ISBN-13: 9780547406282, 2010

Sound of Running Feet, daughter of Chief Joseph of the Nez Perce Indians, narrates the betrayal of her people and the bloody, tearful trail they were made to follow from their home in Oregon to Montana.   Lexile: N/A   (Grades 5–8)   F

Osborne, Mary Pope. *Standing in the Light: The Diary of Catherine Carey Logan.*

ISBN-13: 9780545266871, 2011

A young Quaker girl named Caty keeps a journal of being captured from her 18th-century Pennsylvania home by Lenape Indians, her gradual understanding and appreciation of their culture and beliefs, and the struggles she has readjusting to Quaker life once she has been returned.   Lexile: N/A   (Grades 3–6)   F

Patent, Dorothy Hinshaw. *The Buffalo and the Indians: A Shared Destiny.*

ISBN-13: 9780618485703, 2006

This is the story of the buffalo herds that roamed the plains and prairies for nearly 10,000 years before slaughter by European settlers almost drove them to extinction. This book discusses the role of the buffalo in the spirituality and survival of Native American cultures, and how in modern times, the buffalo herds are being restored.

Lexile: 1120L   (Grades 3–6)   NF

Discovery of America and Christopher Columbus's Voyages

Conrad, Pam. *Pedro's Journal: A Voyage with Christopher Columbus.*

ISBN-13: 9781878093172, 1991

Pedro is a ship's boy on Columbus's first voyage to the Americas. His journal brings to life the emotions and hardships that the crew endured. He describes life aboard the great ship, including his duties, the duties of other sailors, and his interactions with Columbus, thus providing a window into who the man was and what motivated him on his great voyages.   Lexile: 1030L   (Grades 3–6)   F

Freedman, Russell. *Who Was First? Discovering the Americas.*   ISBN-13: 9780618663910, 2007

This book discusses the many theories on who really discovered America (Vikings, Europeans, Chinese, etc.).   Lexile: 1030L   (Grades 3–6)   NF

Fritz, Jean. *Where Do You Think You're Going, Christopher Columbus?*

ISBN-13: 9780698115804, 1997

This book covers Columbus's life and voyages, presenting him as very human and full of vanities and flaws.

Lexile: 0890L   (Grades 2–6)   NF

Hart, Avery. *Who Really Discovered America?*

ISBN-13: 9781885593467, 2003

The book presents 10 theories about the discovery of the Americas and does not make any final pronouncement on the question, instead encouraging readers to decide for themselves which theory sounds most true.

Lexile: 830L   (Grades 5–7)   NF

Yolen, Jane. *Encounter.*

ISBN-13: 9780152013899, 1996

A Taino Indian boy on the island of San Salvador recounts the landing of Columbus and his men in 1492.

Lexile: 0760L   (Grades 2–6)   F

European Arrival and Life in Colonial America

Bruchac, Joseph. *Squanto's Journey: The Story of the First Thanksgiving.*

ISBN-13: 9780152060442, 2007

This is Squanto's story in a first-person narrative packed with historical detail.

Lexile: 6448L   (Grades 1–3)   F

Carbone, Elisa. *Blood on the River: James Town 1607.*   ISBN-13: 9780142409329, 2007

This book describes the New World and the early years of the Jamestown settlement through the eyes of an 11-year-old orphan named Samuel. Descriptions of the dreadful first winter; key figures like Pocahontas, John Smith, and Powhatan; as well as details about daily life (food, chores, etc.) bring this period to life.

Lexile: 0820L   (Grades 5–8)   F

Goodman, Susan E. *Pilgrims of Plymouth.*   ISBN-13: 9780792266754, 2001

This book provides a photo-essay and brief text about life in the Plymouth colony, from chores to games to family life and more. The format highlights comparisons between then and now.

Lexile: N/A   (Grades 3–6)   NF

Harness, Cheryl. *Our Colonial Year.*   ISBN-13: 9780689834790, 2005

A journey through the months and the colonies—with each month showing children engaged in colonial chores and games in a different colony.

Lexile: N/A   (Grades Pre-K–2)   NF

Kay, Verla. *Homespun Sarah.*   ISBN-13: 9780399234170, 2003

This title shows what daily life was like on a colonial-era farm, including a long list of chores.

Lexile: N/A   (Grades 1–4)   NF

Kay, Verla. *Tattered Sails.*   ISBN-13: 9780399233456, 2001

This is the story about one family's 1653 journey to the New World and portrays the family in London, on board the ship, and then upon arrival in the New World.

Lexile: N/A   (Grades Pre-K–6)   F

Lange, Karen. *1607: A New Look at Jamestown.*
ISBN-13: 9781426300127, 2007

This book uses photographs of costumed interpreters and reconstructed buildings to show how residents of Jamestown lived and what their interactions with the natives were really like. Lexile: N/A (Grades 3–6) NF

Rees, Celia. *Witch Child.*
ISBN-13: 9780763642280, 2009

Mary's grandmother was executed as a witch in England. Now in America, Mary is being accused because of her knowledge of healing remedies, which she learned from her grandmother. Lexile: N/A (Grades 7–12) F

Rinaldi, Ann. *A Break with Charity: A Story About the Salem Witch Trials.*
ISBN-13: 9780152046828, 2003

Susanna provides an eyewitness account of the drama and fear that pervaded Puritan Salem during the Witch Trials. When one of the girls who "cried out" confides in Susanna that they made everything up, Susanna cannot tell the truth for fear that they will turn their accusations on her family. Lexile: 0730L (Grades 6–12) F

Schanzer, Rosalyn. *John Smith Escapes Again!*
ISBN-13: 9780792259305, 2006

This book shares details of John Smith's adventures, from sailing on a pirate ship to fighting in a war for Spain to almost drowning more than once. Lexile: AD980L (Grades 3–6) NF

Yolen, Jane. *The Salem Witch Trials: An Unsolved Mystery from History.*
ISBN-13: 9780689846205, 2004

A girl and her father investigate the Salem Witch Trials, gathering and presenting information about the case and then offering possible scenarios. Lexile: N/A (Grades 2–6) F

American Revolution and Independence

Blair, Margaret Whitman. *Liberty or Death: The Surprising Story of Runaway Slaves Who Sided with the British During the American Revolution.*
ISBN-13: 9781426305900, 2010

While the colonies were fighting for their own freedom from the oppression of the British government, slaves decided to fight for their own freedom. Lord Dunmore had issued a proclamation that all slaves who would fight for the British shall be granted freedom. Readers will find out why the slaves would choose to fight for the British and exactly what the cost of liberty and freedom is.
Lexile: 1160L (Grades 5–8) NF

Calkhoven, Laurie. ***Boys of Wartime: Daniel at the Siege of Boston, 1776.***

ISBN-13: 9780142417508, 2011

Daniel's hometown of Boston is under invasion by the British forces. Readers will live their lives through the eyes of Daniel as he supports the Sons of Liberty. His adventure will take him through some treacherous moments as he helps famous figures such as Samuel Adams and George Washington. Set across the historical backdrop of the beginning of the American Revolution, readers will learn about actual key events in the war that impacted the everyday citizens in colonial America.   Lexile: 0710L   (Grades 3–6)   F

Catrow, David. ***We the Kids: The Preamble to the Constitution of the United States.***

ISBN-13: 9780142402764, 2005

The words of the Preamble are the text in this fun picture book that helps kids understand that the Constitution shows us ways to have happiness, safety, and comfort.

Lexile: N/A   (Grades K–8)   NF

Cheney, Lynne. ***We the People: The Story of Our Constitution.***

ISBN-13: 9781442444225, 2012

The Revolutionary War was over, but there were still so many problems that citizens wondered if the country would survive. This title sets the scene and then describes the convention, including the key issues and arguments.   Lexile: 1120L   (Grades 3–6)   NF

Fink, Sam. ***The Declaration of Independence: The Words That Made America.***

ISBN-13: 9780439703154, 2007

This is a verbatim copy of the Declaration of Independence. Find out why our Founding Fathers determined this was a necessary article and the reasons behind their declaration.

Lexile: N/A   (Grades 4–8)   NF

Forbes, Esther. ***Johnny Tremain.***   ISBN-13: 9780547614328, 2011

This is a novel that defines events leading up to the Revolutionary War as seen through the eyes of a boy. The boy is motivated to fight for the liberty of America and turns his tools into a rifle. At 14 he is motivated to fight, but he injures his hand. He becomes a horse boy, which allows him to meet important people. Johnny then becomes involved in critical events that shape the American Revolution.   Lexile: 0840L   (Grades 4–8)   F

Freedman, Russell. ***Give Me Liberty! The Story of the Declaration of Independence.***

ISBN-13: 9780823417537, 2002

This book presents the drama, tension, and events that led up to the drafting of this document, as well as key people and events, and the role and impact on larger groups such as women and slaves.   Lexile: 1070L   (Grades 4–8)   NF

Fritz, Jean. ***Shh! We're Writing the Constitution.***   ISBN-13: 9780698116245, 1997

This account of the 1787 Constitutional Convention shows how the Constitution came into being. Interspersed in the facts are fun tidbits that really bring the people and events to life.

Lexile: N/A   (Grades 2–6)   NF

Maestro, Betsy, and Giulio Maestro. *A More Perfect Union: The Story of Our Constitution.*

ISBN-13: 9780688101923, 1990

This is a very basic book about the background of the Constitution, from the initial decision to hold a convention to the final adoption of the Bill of Rights.

Lexile: AD850L   (Grades 2–6)   NF

Murphy, Jim. *The Crossing: How George Washington Saved the American Revolution.*

ISBN-13: 9780439691864, 2010

This book expands the importance of George Washington far beyond the painting of his crossing of the Delaware River. Readers will read the humble beginnings of the commanding general of the continental army alongside his early failures and eventually rise.

Lexile: N/A   (Grades 2–5)   NF

Osornio, Catherine. *The Declaration of Independence from A to Z.*

ISBN-13: 9781589806764, 2010

Using an alphabet book format, this title touches on a range of events leading up to the Declaration of Independence as well as the subsequent impacts of the document.

Lexile: N/A   (Grades 2–5)   NF

St. George, Jean. *The Journey of the One and Only Declaration of Independence.*

ISBN-13: 9780399237386, 2005

This title provides a fun and interesting look at the packed history of the Declaration of Independence, including all that this document has "lived" through.

Lexile: AD890L   (Grades 3–6)   NF

Travis, Cathy. *Constitution Translated for Kids / La Constitución traducida para niños.*

ISBN-13: 9780981453422, 2009

This is a straightforward book on the Constitution with a sentence-by-sentence, article-by-article discussion that has the original wording on the left and a more readable, easy-to-understand translation on the right. There is also a section on how the Constitution evolved, the branches of the government, and the different amendments.

Lexile: N/A   (Grades 3–6)   NF

Civil War

Avi. *Iron Thunder: The Battle Between the Monitor & the Merrimac.*

ISBN-13: 9780606124782, 2009

Thirteen-year-old Tom works on the construction of the Union ironclad the *Monitor*, where he meets the inventor and has a run-in with Confederate spies. He then sails aboard the *Monitor* in its historic battle against the Confederate *Merrimac*, providing a well-written "eyewitness" account.

Lexile: 0620L   (Grades 4–8)   F

Bartoletti, Susan. *No Man's Land: A Young Soldier's Story.*   ISBN-13: 9780590383738, 2000

Thrasher is only 14 when he joins the Confederate Army, largely to prove his manliness to his father. His company arrives too late for their first big battle and are disappointed, feeling they have missed all the action.   Lexile: N/A   (Grades 4–8)   F

Beatty, Patrica. *Charley Skedaddle.*   ISBN-13: 9780816713172, 1988

This is the story of a young boy who runs off and joins the army, totally unprepared for the true horrors of war. Charley is a smart kid from New York who joins the Union army, excited for battle, but then runs off in terror after shooting a Confederate soldier. He is taken in by an old woman, and while there he slowly begins to see the war in a whole new light.   Lexile: 870L   (Grades 5–8)   F

Beatty, Patricia. *Turn Homeward, Hannalee.*   ISBN-13: 9780688166762, 1999

Twelve-year-old Hannalee works in a Georgia cloth factory making material for the uniforms of Confederate soldiers. When the area is conquered, all the workers are shipped up North to work in a Yankee mill, and thus Hannalee is separated from her family.

Lexile: 0830L   (Grades 3–8)   F

Fleischman, Paul. *Bull Run.*   ISBN-13: 9780064405881, 1995

This book tells the Civil War stories of 16 different people—men, women, black, white, soldiers, civilians, North, South—providing a very human face to this crucial first battle of the war.   Lexile: 0810L   (Grades 3–6)   NF

King, Wilma. *Children of the Emancipation.*   ISBN-13: 9780822547488, 2001

This is a moving and educational photo essay about the lives of young slaves, both before and after the Emancipation Proclamation.   Lexile: N/A   (Grades 3–6)   NF

Matas, Carol. *The War Within: A Novel of the Civil War.*   ISBN-13: 9780689843587, 2002

Thirteen-year-old Hannah Greene lives a comfortable life in Mississippi until the Civil War breaks out and General Grant issues an order requiring all Jews to evacuate the areas under his control. This book takes the form of a journal, with Hannah recording her changing opinions about the war, about slavery, and about being Jewish.

Lexile: N/A   (Grades 5–8)   F

McKissack, Patricia C., and Frederick L. McKissack. *Days of Jubilee: The End of Slavery in the United States.*   ISBN-13: 9780590107648, 2003

This book chronicles the process of ending slavery, an event that didn't happen on one particular day. From the Revolutionary War onward, slaves had their own "days of Jubilee"—their own Emancipation Days. This book includes many slave narratives and historic photographs   Lexile: 1040L   (Grades 5–8)   NF

Noble, Trinka Hakes. *The Last Brother: A Civil War Tale.*   ISBN-13: 9781585362530, 2006

Eleven-year-old Gabe is a Union Army bugle boy, in the same regiment as his "last brother" (the other two having already died in the war). They are fighting a fierce battle at Gettysburg, and Gabe is desperate to save his last brother from danger. Papp's illustrations are attractive and dramatic, adding detail about the battle and the emotions of the soldiers.

Lexile: N/A   (Grades 3–6)   F

Paulsen, Gary. *Soldier's Heart.*   ISBN-13: 9780440228387, 2000

This is the story of a 15-year-old Minnesota farm boy who lied about his age to join the Union Army. Like many young men, he is at first excited and eager to fight the "Southern crackers," but when he participates in the Battle of Bull Run, he quickly learns about the true, terrible realities of war.   Lexile: 1000L   (Grades 7–12)   F

Peck, Richard. *The River Between Us.*   ISBN-13: 9780142403105, 2005

On the eve of Civil War, Tilly and her family are struggling to get by, especially with their father gone. Then when a strange couple arrives one night, Tilly's mother agrees to take them in as boarders.   Lexile: 0740L   (Grades 5–9)   F

Polacco, Patricia. *Pink and Say.*   ISBN-13: 9781930332546, 2003

Pinkus Aylee, an African American Union soldier, finds Say, a white Union soldier about Pink's age, lying on the ground, badly wounded. Pink carries Say to his mother, who nurses him back to health. During that time, a friendship is kindled. Sadly, the boys are captured and taken to a prison where Pink meets a tragic end.   Lexile: 600L   (Grades 4–8)   F

Rappaport, Doreen. *Free at Last! Stories and Songs of Emancipation.*

ISBN-13: 9780763631475, 2006

Riveting personal stories share the experiences of African Americans from the Emancipation Proclamation to the 1954 end to "Separate but Equal" laws. Poetry, memoirs, songs, letters, and court testimonies are all used.   Lexile: 0910L   (Grades 3–8)   NF

Rinaldi, Ann. *Come Juneteenth.*   ISBN-13: 9780152059477, 2007

Texas slave owners kept news of the proclamation a secret from their slaves until they were forced to reveal it on June 19, 1865, known as Juneteenth to ex-slaves. It has been celebrated ever since. This story follows Sis Goose, a mulatto slave who, despite a close relationship with her owners, is not told of her freedom until it is too late.   Lexile: N/A   (Grades 5–8)   F

Rinaldi, Ann. *Girl in Blue.*   ISBN-13: 9780439676465, 2005

Fleeing an abusive father and an arranged marriage, 15-year-old Sarah runs joins the Union army posing as a boy. Her true identity is eventually discovered and she is transferred to Pinkerton's spy network, where she gets the assignment to pose as a servant in the home of a Southern sympathizer.   Lexile: 0680L   (Grades 4–9)   F

Sherman, Pat. *Ben and the Emancipation Proclamation.*   ISBN-13: 9780802853196, 2010

Ben's father taught him to read and write, even though that was illegal for slaves. Then one night after being put in jail, he read a smuggled newspaper and discovered Lincoln had signed the Emancipation Proclamation.   Lexile: 670L   (Grades 3–6)   F

Tanaka, Shelley. *A Day That Changed America: Gettysburg.*   ISBN-13: 9780786819225, 2003

This title is a good, solid introduction to the bloodiest battle ever fought on American soil and to the powerful presidential address in dedication of the men who died there.

Lexile: N/A   (Grades 4–6)   NF

Westward Expansion, Pioneer and Frontier Life

Adler, David. *A Picture Book of Lewis and Clark.*   ISBN-13: 9780823417957, 2003

This is a biography of Lewis and Clark, providing just enough information about these men for young readers.   Lexile: AD800L   (Grades K–3)   NF

Avi. *I Witness: Hard Gold: The Colorado Gold Rush of 1859.*   ISBN-13: 9781423105190, 2008

Early Whitcomb wants to help save the family farm, so when he hears about the gold rush, he thinks he's found the answer.   Lexile: 740L   (Grades 4–8)   F

Benoit, Peter. *The California Gold Rush.*   ISBN-13: 9780531281536, 2012

This book offers the history and stunning images, with an in-depth look at the ideas, people, and events around the gold rush.   Lexile: N/A   (Grades 4–8)   NF

Blos, Joan, W. *Letters from the Corrugated Castle: A Novel of Gold Rush California 1850–1852.*   ISBN-13: 9780689870781, 2008

This book is set in 1850 in San Francisco, the rapidly growing city that is the heart of the California gold rush. Shortly after their arrival, 13-year-old Eldora and the people that she calls "Aunt" and "Uncle" receive a letter from an unknown woman who believes she is Eldora's mother. Every day seems to bring something different and new to consider.

Lexile: 1000L   (Grades 4–8)   F

Blumberg, Rhoda. *Full Steam Ahead: The Race to Build a Transcontinental Railroad.*

ISBN-13: 9780792227151, 1996

This is an account of the construction of the railroad, describing the workers, the construction process, and the bravery and heroism involved. It also includes a discussion of con men, the lawless Wild West towns, and the Indian raids.   Lexile: 1130L   (Grades 4–6)   NF

Bunting, Eve. *Train to Somewhere.*   ISBN-13: 9780618040315, 2000

This is the story of a young girl's experience on the orphan train and then with her new adoptive family.   Lexile: 0440L   (Grades 2–5)   F

Cushman, Karen. *The Ballad of Lucy Whipple.*   ISBN-13: 9780547722153, 2012

Young Lucy and her family have left their comfortable life in the East to relocate in a rough mining community in California. Lucy is not happy about the move and saves every penny for a trip back East.   Lexile: 1030L   (Grades 3–6)   F

Cushman. Karen. **Rodzina.** ISBN-13: 9788493388300, 2005

It's 1881, and 12-year-old Rodzina is on an orphan train heading West. She can't imagine that someone will adopt her; more likely she will become a slave to some stranger. If only she could find the family she desperately wants. Lexile: N/A (Grades 4–8) F

Ernst, Kathleen. **Whistler in the Dark.** ISBN-13: 9781607544326, 2009

Emma and her mother have just moved to a Colorado gold-rush town so her mother can start a newspaper. They are not warmly welcomed, however, and it becomes clear that someone doesn't want them there and doesn't want the newspaper to prosper.

Lexile: 680L (Grades 3–6) F

Eubank, Patricia Reeder. **Seaman's Journal: On the Trail with Lewis and Clark.**

ISBN-13: 9780824954420, 2002

Meriwether Lewis brought his Newfoundland dog, Seaman, along on the three-year expedition. This engaging picture book tells the story of that expedition through the dog's point of view, sharing encounters with Native Americans, dealing with wild buffalo, and more.

Lexile: 690L (Grades K–3) F

Fleischman, Sid. **By the Great Horn Spoon!** ISBN-13: 9780316286121, 1988

When Jack's aunt loses her much-loved mansion and is desperate for money to pay her creditors, Jack and the butler go West to strike it rich and help her. This tale of love and adventure is set during the gold rush, with travel by sea and land, many different mishaps en route, and a cast of memorable characters. Lexile: 730L (Grades 4–7) F

Fraser, Mary Ann. **Ten Mile Day and the Building of the Transcontinental Railroad.**

ISBN-13: 9780805047035, 1996

Due to a $10,000 wager, Central Pacific track-laying crews laid a record 10 miles of track in one day—a record that has never been duplicated. Lexile: 890L (Grades 3–6) NF

Harness, Cheryl. **They're Off! The Story of the Pony Express.** ISBN-13: 9780689851216, 2002

This is a history of the Pony Express from the historical events that led to its creation to what eventually caused its demise. Lexile: 0820L (Grades K–4) NF

Hopkinson, Deborah. **Apples to Oregon.** ISBN-13: 9780689847691, 2004

This story is about a family who sets out along the Oregon Trail and brings their Papa's beloved fruit trees along. Lexile: 0840L (Grades K–4) F

Kay, Verla. **Covered Wagons, Bumpy Trails.** ISBN-13: 9780399229282, 2000

Mother, Father, and Baby John head west on the pioneer trail to California. Bouncing rhyming verses and charming panoramic illustrations capture the journey and the range of emotions along the way. Lexile: N/A (Grades K–3) F

Kay, Verla. *Gold Fever.* ISBN-13: 9780142501832, 2003

Jasper, a young farmer, watches a stream of '49ers pass by and soon decides to join them. Readers accompany him on the long route to the west and see how he faces all manner of hardships. Soon Jasper decides it's not worth it, and he heads home with a new appreciation for his life as a farmer. Lexile: N/A (Grades 2–4) F

Kay, Verla. *Iron Horses.* ISBN-13: 9780399231193, 1999

The dramatic railroad construction race is brought to life in this book with rhyming, chanting words, which deliver information and the feeling of railroad sound and movement.

Lexile: NPL (Grades K–3) F

Kay, Verla. *Orphan Train.* ISBN-13: 9780399236136, 2003

This book relays the orphan train experience of three siblings whose parents have died of typhoid fever. Lexile: N/A (Grades 1–4) F

Kay, Verla. *Whatever Happened to the Pony Express?* ISBN-13: 9780399244834, 2010

The story uses letters exchanged between siblings to present details about mail-delivery systems in the mid-19th century. Lexile: AD460L (Grades 2–4) F

Moody, Ralph. *Riders of the Pony Express.* ISBN-13: 9780803283053, 2004

The Pony Express became an important element in the frontier history of our country, and this book provides an interesting window into the lives of the Pony Express riders.

Lexile: N/A (Grades 7–12) NF

Moss, Marissa. *Rachel's Journal: The Story of a Pioneer Girl.* ISBN-13: 9780152021689, 2001

Ten-year-old Rachel and her family are traveling on the Oregon Trail to California. En route, she keeps this journal about life on the trail. Lexile: N/A (Grades 3–6) F

O'Dell, Scott. *Streams to the River, River to the Sea.* ISBN-13: 9780547053165, 2008

This is the Lewis and Clark journey as seen through the eyes of Sacagawea, the Shoshone interpreter who accompanied the men. Lexile: 740L (Grades 6–8) F

Rivera, Sheila. *American Moments: The California Gold Rush.*

ISBN-13: 9781591972815, 2004

The book discusses the early history of California, focusing especially on the gold rush period including the discovery of gold, the arrival of prospectors hoping to strike it rich, and the effects on the people and environment of the region. The book also discusses other aspects of California's history and includes a timeline of the period, facts on the topic, and a website that may help answer any questions about the gold rush.

Lexile: N/A (Grades 4–8) NF

Rohrbough, Malcom J. *Days of Gold: The California Gold Rush and the American Nation.*

ISBN-13: 9780520206229, 1998

Through extensive research in diaries, letters, and other archival sources, this book uncovers the personal dilemmas and confusion that the gold rush brought. It depicts the complexity of human motivation behind the event and the effects of the gold rush as it spread outward in ever-widening circles to touch the lives of families and communities everywhere in the United States.　　　　　Lexile: N/A　(Grades 4–12)　NF

Roop, Connie and Peter. *The Diary of David R. Leeper—Rushing for Gold (In My Own Words).*

ISBN-13: 9780761410119, 2000

A young prospector describes his experiences traveling overland to the California gold fields and the five years he spent digging for gold.　　Lexile: N/A　(Grades 4–8)　F

Saffer, Barbara. *The California Gold Rush.*　　　　ISBN-13: 9781590840603, 2002

The book describes the discovery of gold in California, the rush to California to look for gold, establishment of mining towns, the outbreak of criminal activity, and other aspects of this volatile period in California history.　　　Lexile: N/A　(Grades 4–8)　NF

Schanzer, Rosalyn. *Gold Fever! Tales of the California Gold Rush.*

ISBN-13: 9781426300400, 2007

Beginning with the discovery of gold at Sutter's Mill, the story of the California gold rush is described in detail, including what the miners ate and wore, how they lived and played, and how they struggled to survive, and more.　　Lexile: N/A　(Grades 2–6)　NF

Schanzer, Rosalyn. *How We Crossed West: The Adventures of Lewis & Clark.*

ISBN-13: 9781426313288, 2012

The 40 volumes of the diaries of Lewis and Clark were condensed into this one book that focuses on the excitement and adventures of the expedition. Information from letters, notebooks, and the many journals was used to describe this trek.

Lexile: AD890L　(Grades 2–6)　NF

Steiner, Barbara. *Mystery at Chilkoot Pass.*　　　ISBN-13: 9781607544340, 2009

Twelve-year-old Hetty, her father, and her uncle are off to make their fortunes in the Klondike gold rush of 1897. Just as the group is passing through the most arduous part of the journey, the Chilkoot Pass, Hetty and others discover that their treasured family mementos are starting to disappear.　　　　　Lexile: 700L　(Grades 4–8)　F

Waldorf, Mary. *The Gold Rush Kid.*　　　　　ISBN-13: 9780547562971, 2008

This story of grit, luck, and survival of the Klondike gold rush of the 1890s is told with humor and suspense in this action-packed account about 12-year old Billy.

Lexile: N/A　(Grades 3–6)　F

Warren, Andrea. *Orphan Train Rider: One Boy's True Story.*　ISBN-13: 9780395913628, 1998

This is an account of one boy's experience from his abandonment to riding the train west in 1926 to his final arrival in Texas.　　　　Lexile: 0960L　(Grades 4–8)　F

White, Stewart Edward. *The Forty-Niners: The California Gold Rush.*

ISBN-13: 9781470103613, 2012

This chronicle of the California gold rush gives a historical view of those early days of the mid-19th century and the many challenges of the formation of a new frontier: incoming population, law and order issues, greed and power, political differences, successes and failures. Lexile: N/A   (Grades 3–6)   NF

Yin. *Coolies.*   ISBN-13: 9780142500552, 2003

This is the story of two immigrant brothers from China who worked on the crew to build the First Continental Railroad.   Lexile: AD660L   (Grades K–4)   F

Immigration and Early 20th Century

Adler, David A. *The Babe & I.*   ISBN-13: 9780152050269, 2004

In this story set during the Great Depression, a boy finds out his dad is unemployed, so he becomes a newsboy at Yankee Stadium to help his family. He uses baseball news to sell a lot of papers, and one day even Babe Ruth buys a paper from him.

Lexile: 0330L   (Grades K–3)   F

Ayres, Katherine. *Macaroni Boy.*   ISBN-13: 9780440418849, 2004

It's the height of the Depression and when he's not in school, Mike works as a rat catcher. When he starts to notice dead rats in the street and hears of a mysterious sickness that has killed local hoboes, he decides to find out if there's a connection.

Lexile: 0700L   (Grades 4–8)   F

Bartoletti, Susan. *Growing Up in Coal Country.*   ISBN-13: 9780395979143, 1999

The voices of men, women, and children fill the pages of this photo-essay about coal-mining immigrants in northeastern Pennsylvania 100 years ago.

Lexile: 1110L   (Grades 5–8)   NF

Bausum, Ann. *With Courage and Cloth: Winning the Fight for a Woman's Right to Vote.*

ISBN-13: 9780792276470, 2004

Various groups of the suffragette movement took different paths toward voting rights. This book shows the groups did not always get along, but in the end they were all fighting for the same cause.   Lexile: 1080L   (Grades 5–12)   NF

Cooper, Michael L. *Dust to Eat: Drought and Depression in the 1930s.*

ISBN-13: 9780618154494, 2004

This book pulls together letters and interviews with people who lived through the Dust Bowl.   Lexile: 1120L   (Grades 4–7)   NF

Corey, Shana. *You Forgot Your Skirt, Amelia Bloomer.*   ISBN-13: 9780439078191, 2000

This book tells the story of Amelia Bloomer, a women's magazine editor who publically applauded the baggy, knee-length pants the suffragettes were wearing, and before long people were calling them bloomers.   Lexile: AD350L   (Grades K–3)   NF

Curtis, Christopher Paul. *Bud, Not Buddy.*   ISBN-13: 9780553494105, 2004

Ten-year old Buddy is an orphan who has lived in a string of foster homes in Depression-era Michigan. But he is sure that jazz musician Herman Calloway is his father, so he sets off to find him. And when he does, he finds a family of sorts, although it's not the one he imagined.   Lexile: 950L   (Grades 3–6)   F

Durbin, William. *The Journal of C.J. Jackson: A Dust Bowl Migrant.*

ISBN-13: 9780439153065, 2002

After living in the Dust Bowl for years, C.J.'s family has decided to abandon their farm and head west to find work in California. In his journal he writes about the discrimination, disappointment, and hardship that his family and the others endure.

Lexile: 1000L   (Grades 4–7)   F

Fritz, Jean. *You Want Women to Vote, Lizzie Stanton?*   ISBN-13: 9780698117648, 1999

Readers learn about Stanton's accomplishments and the suffragette movement, with interesting anecdotes woven in.   Lexile: 870L   (Grades 3–6)   NF

Hesse, Karen. *Out of the Dust.*   ISBN-13: 9780590371254, 1999

This Newbery Award–winning book tells the story of Billie Jo and her family as they face death, poverty, and the pervasive drought and windstorms that have ravaged their Oklahoma farm. Readers really get a feel for what life was like in the Dust Bowl states and how residents helped each other and held onto a hope.   Lexile: N/A   (Grades 3–6)   F

Holm, Jennifer. *Turtle in Paradise.*   ISBN-13: 9780375836909, 2011

In a book full of small details about life during the Great Depression, readers meet Turtle. Turtle's mom has a new job so Turtle is sent to live with relatives in Key West, Florida. It's a different environment, but soon Turtle adapts and even embarks on a treasure hunt to land her family on "Easy Street."   Lexile: 0610L   (Grades 3–5)   F

Hopkinson, Deborah. *Sky Boys: How They Built the Empire State Building.*

ISBN-13: 9780375865411, 2012

A young boy describes the building of the Empire State Building, which was built in record time by hundreds of men during the Great Depression. To the boy, it's more than just a tall building—it's a symbol of hope during the Depression.   Lexile: N/A   (Grades 3–8)   NF

Hopkinson, Deborah. *Up Before Daybreak: Cotton and People in America.*

ISBN-13: 9780439639019, 2006

This is the story of the lives of the men, women, and children who spent much of their lives working in the cotton industry in America.   Lexile: 1060L   (Grades 4–8)   NF

Janke, Katelan. *Survival in the Storm: The Dust Bowl Diary of Grace Edwards.*

ISBN-13: 9780439215992, 2002

Grace uses her journal to tell about a year in the town of Dalhart, Texas, during the Dust Bowl year of 1935. She conveys the hardships endured at home and at school, but also incorporates glimpses into the tiny joys that kept people going.

Lexile: 990L   (Grades 4–8)   F

Lied, Kate. *Potato: A Tale from the Great Depression.*   ISBN-13: 9780792269465, 2002

After Dorothy's father loses his job, the family borrows a car and heads to Idaho to earn money, digging potatoes for two weeks. They live in tents, pick during the day, pick at night for themselves, and go home loaded with potatoes.   Lexile: N/A   (Grades K–2)   F

Mackall, Dandi Daley. *Rudy Rides the Rails: A Depression Era Story.*

ISBN-13: 9781585362868, 2007

In this book set during the Great Depression, teenaged Rudy "rides the rails," looking for work. He meets other travelers and generous people and slowly begins to doubt his father's advice to "look out for you and yours, and nobody else."   Lexile: N/A   (Grades 3–6)   F

Moss, Marissa. *Rose's Journal: The Story of a Girl in the Great Depression.*

ISBN-13: 9780152046057, 2003

Rose writes "good riddance" to 1934 in her journal, but it's the middle of the Depression and 1935 isn't any better. She writes about events on the farm in Kansas and throughout the nation and about her family's struggle to keep their land.   Lexile: 820L   (Grades 3–5)   F

Paterson, Katherine. *Bread and Roses, Too.*   ISBN-13: 9780547076515, 2008

The workers are striking at the Bread and Roses mill in Lawrence, Massachusetts, and it's looking to get violent. Worried for their safety, the children are offered an opportunity to go live in Vermont until the strike is settled. Some, like Rosa, miss their family and do not want to go. Others, like young Jake, are ready for the adventure.

Lexile: 0470L   (Grades 3–8)   F

Paterson, Katherine. *Lyddie.*   ISBN-13: 9780140373899, 1995

Ten-year-old Lyddie and her younger brother are hired out as servants after their father abandons their failing farm. Lyddie runs away to find a better job and is hired at a cloth factory that has terrible working conditions. She's enslaved by her dismal job, can't go home, and just wants to better her life by going to college.   Lexile: 0860L   (Grades 4–8)   F

Phelan, Matt. *The Storm in the Barn.*   ISBN-13: 9780763652906, 2009

In this book set during the Dust Bowl, 11-year-old Jack has a lot to deal with, including bullies at school and dust storms that have ruined the family's harvest. Jack becomes part of a tall tale and is forced to face the dreaded Storm King who has been holding back the rains.

Lexile: GN430L   (Grades 5–7)   F

Stanley, Jerry. *Children of the Dust Bowl: The True Story of the School at Weedpatch Camp.*   ISBN-13: 9780517880944, 1993

This portrait of the Oakies follows their journey west, their continuing struggles in California, and daily life for the residents of Weedpatch Camp (a government farm labor camp), where residents created their own "emergency" school.   Lexile: 1120   (Grades 6–12)   NF

Stewart, Sarah. *The Gardener.*   ISBN-13: 9780374325176, 1997

It's the Depression, and Lydia is living with her uncle in the city. She misses her family and life on the farm, and she writes home often about how she is helping in her uncle's bakery and how the flowers she has planted are growing.   Lexile: AD570L   (Grades K–2)   F

Stone, Tanya Lee. *Elizabeth Leads the Way: Elizabeth Cady Stanton and the Right to Vote.*   ISBN-13: 9780312602369, 2010

Elizabeth Cady Stanton stood up and fought for what she believed in. From an early age, she knew that women were not given rights equal to men. But rather than accept her lesser status, Elizabeth went to college and later gathered other like-minded women to challenge the right to vote.   Lexile: AD700L   (Grades 1–6)   NF

Vanderpool, Clare. *Moon Over Manifest.*   ISBN-13: 9780375858291, 2011

This is the story about life during the Great Depression, when a young girl is sent to live with family friends in her father's hometown, while he's working at a new job. Disappointed at first, she meets some new friends and together they begin a spy mystery right in their town. Soon her father's hometown doesn't seem so boring.   Lexile: N/A   (Grades 5–8)   F

White, Linda Arms. *I Could Do That! Esther Morris Gets Women the Vote.*

ISBN-13: 9780374335274, 2005

Esther Morris was the first female judge and the first woman to hold political office. She was influential in getting women the right to vote in Wyoming . . . all while raising a family. Through it all, Esther had the same determined mantra: "I could do that!"

Lexile: AD780L   (Grades 2–4)   NF

World Wars I and II

Avi. *Don't You Know There's a War On?*   ISBN-13: 9780380815449, 2003

This story is about two boys living in Brooklyn during World War II. Both boys have fathers serving abroad and both boys have a crush on their young fifth-grade teacher, Miss Gossim. When one of them overhears the principal's plan to fire Miss Gossim, they decide they must do something to save her.   Lexile: 0500L   (Grades 4–6)   F

Ayer, Eleanor. *Parallel Journeys.*   ISBN-13: 9780689832369, 2000

Readers learn the stories of two young people living under Nazi rule during World War II. Alfons is a normal, loving boy until he joins the Hitler Youth and is manipulated and changed. During this same time, Jewish Helen attempts to flee Nazi persecution of Jews but is caught and struggles to survive.   Lexile: N/A   (Grades 7–12)   F

Bartoletti, Susan. *The Boy Who Dared.*   ISBN-13: 9780439680134, 2008

Helmuth Hubener is impressed with the outward show of the Hitler Youth, but his Mormon-based Christian beliefs make him question the ways Jews are being treated, the media control, and the invasion of other countries. He risks his life to start a newsletter to inform others about what is really happening and is eventually caught.

Lexile: 760L   (Grades 6–10)   F

Bartoletti, Susan. *Hitler Youth: Growing Up in Hitler's Shadow.*

ISBN-13: 9780439353793, 2005

This is the story of 12 young members of the Hitler Youth, whose innocence, enthusiasm, and patriotic devotion were taken advantage of for evil means. Each one discusses their reasons for joining, how Hitler used them, and what it was like.

Lexile: 1050L   (Grades 6–12)   NF

Bitten-Jackson, Livia. *I Have Lived a Thousand Years: Growing Up in the Holocaust.*

ISBN-13: 9780689823954, 1999

This holocaust memoir is about a 13-year-old Jewish girl's experiences and focuses on hope. She and her mother help each other survive and keep their humanity, and the words of comfort shared amongst the Jews even in the middle of horrible situations are very touching.   Lexile: 702L   (Grades 8–12)   NF

Borden, Louise. *Across the Blue Pacific: A World War II Story.*   ISBN-13: 9780618339228, 2006

This is a fictional memoir of a childhood on the American homefront.

Lexile: AD840L   (Grades 3–5)   F

Borden, Louise. *The Little Ships: A Heroic Rescue at Dunkirk in World War II.*

ISBN-13: 9780689808272, 1997

This is the story of the evacuation of Dunkirk, where the British army was rescued by small civilian boats. In this fictional account, a young girl accompanying her father on a rescue boat narrates the events.   Lexile: AD690L   (Grades 3–6)   F

Boyne, John. *The Boy in the Striped Pajamas.*   ISBN-13: 9780385751537, 2007

When Bruno returns home from school one day, he discovers that his belongings are being packed in crates. His father has received a promotion, and the family must move from their home to a new house far away, where there is no one to play with and nothing to do. While exploring his new environment, he meets another boy whose life and circumstances are very different to his own, and their meeting results in a friendship that has devastating consequences.   Lexile: 1080L   (Grades 7–12)   F

Breslin, Theresa. *Remembrance.* ISBN-13: 9780307433688, 2007

Five teens in rural Scotland experience the traumas of World War I as they take part in different activities to support the war effort, including on the battlefield. Many social changes within civilian society take place, too, especially for women.

Lexile: N/A   (Grades 7–12)   F

Bunting, Eve. *So Far from the Sea.* ISBN-13: 9780547237527, 2009

Before moving out of California, Laura and her family make a final visit to the grave of her grandfather at the Manzanar Relocation Camp where her father and his parents were interned during World War II. While there, they discuss the experience of the internees and the impact on her grandfather to be "so far from the sea" that he so loved.

Lexile: 590L   (Grades 2–5)   F

Chotjewitz, David. *Daniel Half Human.* ISBN-13: 9780689857485, 2006

Two friends want to join the Hitler Youth, but Daniel is horrified to find out that his mother is Jewish. He wants to keep it a secret and still join. His friend, Armin, is loyal to Daniel, but he is also under Nazi pressure to abandon him as a friend. He joins and tries to warn Daniel of a coming danger. Lexile: 740L   (Grades 7–12)   F

Colman, Penny. *Rosie the Riveter: Women Working on the Home Front in World War II.*

ISBN-13: 9780517885673, 1998

The need for supplies and the shortage of workers led to a female-dominated workforce during World War II. Resistance to taking on men's jobs had to be overcome—by both men and women—and these experiences led the way to future reforms for women.

Lexile: 1060L   (Grades 6–9)   NF

Cooper, Michael L. *Remembering Manzanar: Life in a Japanese Relocation Camp.*

ISBN-13: 9780618067787, 2002

This title describes and provides photographs of the Manzanar Internment Camp and the living conditions and daily lives of the Japanese Americans who were interned there.

Lexile: N/A   (Grades 5–8)   NF

Drez, Ronald J. *Remember D-Day: The Plan, the Invasion, Survivor Stories.*

ISBN-13: 9780792269656, 2004

This book looks at the World War II turning point, the D-Day invasion of Normandy. The strategy, intelligence, and deceptions that led up to D-Day are explained, as well as what happened during the invasion and what helped the Allies win.

Lexile: N/A   (Grades 6–9)   NF

Foreman, Michael. *War Game.* ISBN-13: 9781857937138, 1995

This is based on a true story of four soldiers who are finding war to be much less exciting than they imagined. During a short-lived Christmas day cease-fire, the English and German troops play a game of soccer, raising spirits and hope, which are then dashed again by the realities of war. Lexile: N/A   (Grades 3–6)   NF

Freedman, Russell. ***The War to End All Wars: World War I.***   ISBN-13: 9780544021716, 2013

People hoped World War I would be the only war of its kind, but the seeds of a second world war were sown during the first. The beginnings, meaning, and legacy of the world's first war are told.   Lexile: N/A   (Grades 6–9)   NF

Giblin, James Cross. ***The Life and Death of Adolf Hitler.***   ISBN-13: 9780395903711, 2002

Beginning with his modest upbringing in Austria, his life is followed in this most complete biography of the man available for this age group. His growing abilities as a public speaker and his gradual rise in power, as well as the conditions that made for his ascent, are clearly explained.   Lexile: 1100L   (Grades 7–12)   NF

Giff, Patricia Reilly. ***Lily's Crossing.***   ISBN-13: 9780440414537, 2008

Lily's father is called overseas to fight in World War II, so Lily moves in with her grandmother. While there, she befriends Albert, a Hungarian refugee boy, who shares his secret sadness with her—that his little sister was left behind in Europe and that he wants to cross the ocean to find her.   Lexile: N/A   (Grades 3–5)   F

Gleitzman, Morris. ***Once.***   ISBN-13: 9780312653040, 2013

Felix has been safe at the Catholic orphanage, but when the Nazis finally arrive, he is forced to flee in search of his Jewish family. He desperately hopes they are still alive, but the more atrocities he sees, the more he realizes his alternate reality—a reality where everything will be fine—is less and less likely.   Lexile: 0640L   (Grades 6–9)   F

Hesse, Karen. ***Aleutian Sparrow.***   ISBN-13: 9781416903277, 2005

In 1942, after a Japanese attack on their Aleutian Island homes, the native peoples of the island were forcibly moved to deplorable relocation centers in Alaska's southwest, supposedly for their protection.   Lexile: N/A   (Grades 5–9)   F

Hesse, Karen. ***The Cats in Krasinski Square.***   ISBN-13: 9780439435406, 2004

Set in Poland during World War II, this story, based on a little-known true story of Jewish resistance, features stray cats and a little Jewish girl who outfoxes the Nazis to deliver food to starving residents in the Warsaw Ghetto.   Lexile: N/A   (Grades 2–5)   NF

Johnson, Angela. ***Wind Flyers.***   ISBN-13: 9780689848797, 2007

An African American boy tells about his great-great-uncle's heroic acts as a Tuskegee airman in World War II.   Lexile: N/A   (Grades 2–4)   F

Judge, Lita. ***One Thousand Tracings: Healing the Wounds of World War II.***

ISBN-13: 9781423100089, 2007

At the end of World War II, residents of war-ravaged European countries were in desperate need of basic food, clothing, and other supplies, so Americans organized to help.

Lexile: N/A   (Grades 1–6)   NF

Kadohata, Cynthia. *Weedflower.* ISBN-13: 9781416975663, 2009

During World War II, Sumiko and her Japanese American family are sent to an internment camp in the Arizona desert where they live in dusty military barracks on an Indian reservation. Her friendship with a young Mohave boy depicts the joys and problems of an interracial friendship and foreshadows the futures of these populations afterward.

Lexile: 750L   (Grades 5–8)   F

Kuhn, Betsy. *Angels of Mercy: The Army Nurses of World War II.*

ISBN-13: 9780689820441, 1999

Almost 60,000 American women served as nurses in World War II. For this book, several were interviewed and their stories are told here. Air raids, terrible living conditions, being taken prisoner, deaths, and more are chronicled.   Lexile: 970L   (Grades 6–12)   NF

Lawrence, Iain. *Lord of the Nutcracker Men.* ISBN-13: 9780440418122, 2003

Johnny, age 10, loves to play war with the soldiers his father made for him. Soon people he knows are sent away to the war, including his father, whose letters home are upbeat at first, but then speak of the horrors of the war. A confused young Johnny starts to believe his toy soldier battles are influencing the real war.   Lexile: N/A   (Grades 5–8)   F

Lee, Milly. *Nim and the War Effort.* ISBN-13: 9780374455064, 2002

Nim and her classmates are gathering old newspapers to help the war effort, and Nim desperately wants to gather more than her rival. Set in San Francisco, this book touches on life for young children during World War II, the merits of honesty and hard work, and the Chinese American culture.   Lexile: 0510L   (Grades 2–4)   F

Lee-Tai, Amy. *A Place Where Sunflowers Grow.* ISBN-13: 9780892392155, 2006

It's World War II, and Mari and her family have been taken to the Topaz Internment Camp with thousands of other Japanese Americans. She's frightened and confused until an art class provides a way for her to express her feelings and a new friendship, and the budding desert sunflowers bring new hope.   Lexile: 790L   (Grades 1–4)   F

Lisle, Janet Taylor. *The Art of Keeping Cool.* ISBN-13: 9780689837883, 2002

Robert's family is living with his grandparents, while his dad is fighting Nazis. Their whole coastal Rhode Island village is afraid—afraid of Nazi submarines offshore, afraid that the German artist living outside of town is a spy, afraid of everything.

Lexile: 0730L   (Grades 5–9)   F

Lisle, Janet Taylor. *Sirens and Spies.* ISBN-13: 9780689844577, 2002

No one agrees on the truth about the mysterious violin teacher, Renee Fitch, until she herself tells the definitive story of her life and brings together all the differing views people have of her.   Lexile: 0640L   (Grades 5–8)   F

Lowry, Lois. *Crow Call.* ISBN-13: 9780545030359, 2009

When Liz's father came back from World War II, it took some time for the two to reconnect and get to know each other again. Liz was quite shy around her father until a day out hunting crows helped them to bond.   Lexile: N/A   (Grades K–4)   F

Lowry, Lois. *Number the Stars.*   ISBN-13: 9780547577098, 2011

This book is told through the experiences of one girl, Annemarie Johansen, and her family, who help Annemarie's best friend's family escape death. Word had gotten out that the Nazis were going to send Denmark's Jews to death camps, so 7,000 Jews were snuck out of the country within hours.   Lexile: AD750L   (Grades 5–8)   F

Mazer, Harry. *A Boy No More.*   ISBN-13: 9781416914044, 2006

Adam's father is killed in the attack on Pearl Harbor. Adam, his mother, and sister are evacuated from Hawaii to California, where he must deal with his feelings about the war, Japanese internment camps, his father, and his own identity.   Lexile: N/A   (Grades 6–8)   F

Mazer, Harry. *A Boy at War: A Novel of Pearl Harbor.*   ISBN-13: 9780689841606, 2002

When they sneak off to go fishing on December 7, 1941, Adam and his friends could not fathom what was about to happen. Having drifted close to the fleet at Pearl Harbor, they watch in shock as the Japanese planes approach and then attack the fleet and harbor.

Lexile: 530L   (Grades 5–9)   F

Mochizuki, Ken. *Baseball Saved Us.*   ISBN-13: 9781880000199, 1995

Set in a Japanese internment camp during World War II, this is the story of a young boy and his father, who build a baseball diamond to pull the camp together.

Lexile: AD550L   (Grades 1–4)   F

Morpurgo, Michael. *Private Peaceful.*   ISBN-13: 9780439636537, 2006

Thomas Peaceful lies about his age so he can fight in World War I. As he stands watch one night, he remembers his life up to that moment—a simple life as a poor farm boy in a happy family, with an older brother he looks up to.   Lexile: 0860L   (Grades 7–12)   F

Murphy, Jim. *Truce: The Day the Soldiers Stopped Fighting.*   ISBN-13: 9780545130493, 2009

On December 25 during World War I, troops defied orders and ceased fighting in honor of Christmas, even celebrating the holiday with their enemies.   Lexile: N/A   (Grades 5–8)   NF

Opdyke, Irene Gut. *In My Hands: Memories of a Holocaust Rescuer.*

ISBN-13: 9780553494112, 2004

This memoir tells of the experiences of Irene Gutowna, a 17-year-old Polish nursing student who found every opportunity she could to help the Jews living in Nazi-occupied countries, first leaving food for those in the ghetto, then protecting and hiding Jews who worked with her.   Lexile: 890L   (Grades 9–12)   NF

Polacco, Patricia. *The Butterfly.*   ISBN-13: 9780142413067, 2009

This tells the story of a girl named Monique who first sees Nazi cruelty when one of them crushes a butterfly she has been looking at. When she later discovers that a Jewish family is hiding in her family's basement with the help of her parents, she understands the family is in great danger. This is a well-told story about the terror of Nazi Germany and the courageous and selfless acts of Nazi resisters.   Lexile: 430L   (Grades K–3)   F

Poole, Josephine. *Anne Frank.* ISBN-13: 9780099409762, 2007

A sense of foreboding is in this picture book biography told from Anne's point of view.

Lexile: N/A (Grades 3–8) NF

Rostkowski, Margaret. *After the Dancing Days.* ISBN-13: 9780064402484, 1988

At the end of World War I, Annie sees many wounded soldiers being wheeled off a train, headed to the hospital where her father works. She becomes friends with two soldiers in the hospital and begins to wonder about the war, about her uncle's death, and about the future of her new soldier friends. Lexile: 650L (Grades 6–9) F

Roy, Jennifer. *Yellow Star.* ISBN-13: 9780761452775, 2006

Sylvia was four years old when her family was sent to the Lodz ghetto in wartime Poland, and six years later she was one of only 12 children who survived it. This story is told in vignettes, as each recalls a particular memory in Sylvia's life.

Lexile: 710L (Grades 5–9) NF

Russo, Marisabina. *Always Remember Me: How One Family Survived World War II.*

ISBN-13: 9780689869204, 2005

Rachel's grandmother shares the family album with Rachel, discussing their first life in Germany and their second life after the war. Lexile: 720L (Grades 2–5) NF

Rylant, Cynthia. *I Had Seen Castles.* ISBN-13: 9780152053123, 2004

When Pearl Harbor is attacked, John Dante, 17, enlists to avenge his country, despite the protests of his new girlfriend, and experiences the full horrors of war.

Lexile: 950L (Grades 6–10) F

Salisbury, Graham. *Under the Blood-Red Sun.* ISBN-13: 9780440411390, 1995

When Pearl Harbor is attacked, Tomikazu's quiet life on Oahu is turned upside down. He watches as the attacks take place and then sees the frightening aftermath for Japanese Americans. It's worse for those born in Japan—like his father and grandfather, who are both arrested. Salisbury expertly shows the emotions Tomikazu experiences as he deals with the racism, the fear, and the pressures of his father's absence.

Lexile: 640L (Grades 5–8) F

Smith, Frank Dabba, and Mendel Grossman. *My Secret Camera: Life in the Lodz Ghetto.*

ISBN-13: 9781845078928, 2008

Mendel Grossman was a photographer for the ghetto leaders, but he also secretly took thousands of photos documenting the heartbreaking suffering the Jews went through there.

Lexile: N/A (Grades 5–8) NF

Tanaka, Shelley. *Attack on Pearl Harbor: The True Story of the Day America Entered World War II.* ISBN-13: 9780786816620, 2011

This title recounts the events leading up to, during, and immediately after the Pearl Harbor bombing. The book is centered around the accounts of four young men who experienced it firsthand. Lexile: N/A (Grades 5–8) NF

Uchida, Yoshiko. *The Bracelet.*   ISBN-13: 9780698113909, 1996

Japanese Americans are en route to the Japanese internment camps when Emi realizes she's lost a cherished friendship bracelet. She's distraught at first, but then she realizes that she doesn't need it after all because she carries her friend in her heart and her memories.

Lexile: 710L   (Grades K–5)   F

Uchida, Yoshiko. *The Invisible Thread.*   ISBN-13: 9780688137038, 1995

This is a memoir of a girl consigned to a concentration camp by the U.S. government. Yoshiko felt like a normal American girl living a normal American life, until Pearl Harbor. After that, her family and others were rounded up and sent to an internment camp in the desert, along with tens of thousands of other Japanese Americans who had no civil rights and no ability to protest the act.   Lexile: 1060L   (Grades 5–8)   NF

Warren, Andrea. *Surviving Hitler: A Boy in the Nazi Death Camps.*

ISBN-13: 9780060007676, 2002

A Holocaust survivor gives a personal account of his experiences in Nazi prison camps and takes readers into the horrors of the concentration camp. His courage and determination to see his family again got him through the experience.   Lexile: 820L   (Grades 5–9)   NF

Williams, Marcia. *Archie's War.*   ISBN-13: 9780763635329, 2007

This is a fictional scrapbook set in the year 1914, the year the Great War began. Through its pages, readers can see the war through one child's eyes and see the impact it has had on that child's life and on the lives of those whom he writes to on the front and who write him back.

Lexile: N/A   (Grades 4–9)   F

Yolen, Jane. *The Devil's Arithmetic.*   ISBN-13: 9780142401095, 2004

As Hannah opens the door during Passover to welcome the prophet Elijah, she finds herself in a village in 1940s Poland, captured by the Nazis and taken to a death camp. She is befriended by a girl named Rivka, who helps her survive and hold on to her identity. Hannah takes Rivka's place in the gas chamber, but as its door closes she is transported back to her grandparents' home and Passover.   Lexile: 730L   (Grades 4–8)   F

Civil Rights

Adler, David A. *Heroes for Civil Rights.*   ISBN-13: 9780823420087, 2007

Whether marching, speaking, or simply going to school, brave men and women who fought to advance social justice during the Civil Rights movement are highlighted here.

Lexile: IG970L   (Grades K–4)   NF

Armistead, John. *The Return of Gabriel.*   ISBN-13: 9781571316387, 2002

When civil rights workers come to Cooper and Jubal's Mississippi town to try and get the blacks to vote, Cooper finds himself in the middle between Jubal's black family and his own prejudiced white family. In fact, Cooper's father is pressuring him to join the Ku Klux Klan and attend meetings with him.   Lexile: 700L   (Grades 5–8)   F

Birtha, Becky. *Grandmama's Pride.*   ISBN-13: 9780807530283, 2005

Two African American girls from northern states are exposed to the segregated South for the first time, but their mama and grandmama handle it all with quiet dignity and wisdom.

Lexile: AD720L   (Grades K–5)   F

Bridges, Ruby. *Through My Eyes: Ruby Bridges.*   ISBN-13: 9780590189231, 1999

Six-year-old Ruby was the first black student to attend an all-white school in the segregated South. In this title, Ruby tells the story as she remembers it in an account that shows her sweet innocence about what a historic event this was.   Lexile: 860L   (Grades 3–7)   NF

Coleman, Evelyn. *White Socks Only.*   ISBN-13: 9780807589564, 1996

Grandma tells the story about her first trip alone into town during the days when segregation still existed in Mississippi.   Lexile: N/A   (Grades K–4)   F

Curtis, Christopher Paul. *The Watsons Go to Birmingham—1963.*

ISBN-13: 9780440228004, 2000

This is the story of a family living in the 1960s in Michigan. When the eldest brother starts to get into trouble, the family travels to Alabama for him to spend the summer with his grandmother, and they arrive just in time to experience the church bombing known as Birmingham Sunday.   Lexile: 1000L   (Grades 3–8)   F

Draper, Sharon M. *Fire from the Rock.*   ISBN-13: 9780142411995, 2008

Sylvia is honored to have been selected to be one of the first African American students to attend Little Rock's Central High School, but it's 1957 and racial tensions are high. She doesn't aspire to be a hero of the movement. Maybe she should just stay at her black school with her friends.   Lexile: N/A   (Grades 4–8)   F

Farris, Christine King. *March On! The Day My Brother Martin Changed the World.*

ISBN-13: 9780545035378, 2008

The sister of Dr. Martin Luther King, Jr., answers questions about her brother and the 1963 March on Washington, including how he prepared for his well-known "I Have a Dream" speech.   Lexile: N/A   (Grades 1–6)   NF

Freedman, Russell. *Freedom Walkers: The Story of the Montgomery Bus Boycott.*

ISBN-13: 9780823421954, 2008

Most people do not realize the coordination and sacrifice that went into the 381-day Montgomery Bus Boycott. This title combines segments from memoirs, scholarly articles, personal stories, and historical accounts.   Lexile: 1110L   (Grades 3–8)   NF

Giovanni, Nikki. *Rosa.*   ISBN-13: 9780312376024, 2007

This picture book begins with the story of Rosa Parks (who she was and what she did to spark the movement), then moves on to cover other key milestones in the movement.

Lexile: 900L   (Grades K–6)   NF

Hoose, Philip. *Claudette Colvin: Twice Toward Justice.*   ISBN-13: 9780312661052, 2010

Rosa Parks was not the first African American to refuse to give up her seat to a white person. It was 15-year-old Claudette several months prior. Claudette was arrested, but did not become the face of the movement.   Lexile: 1000L   (Grades 6–10)   NF

Johnson, Angela. *Just Like Josh Gibson.*   ISBN-13: 9781416927280, 2007

The legendary Josh Gibson, arguably the best Negro-League player to never make it into the majors, faced many challenges, and no matter how well a girl growing up in the 1940s played the game of baseball, she would have faced equally difficult challenges.

Lexile: 0920L   (Grades K–5)   F

Johnson, Angela. *A Sweet Smell of Roses.*   ISBN-13: 9781416953616, 2007

Two African American sisters sneak out of their house and walk down the street to join folks who are going to march with and listen to Dr. Martin Luther King, Jr. They smell the sweet smell of roses—a metaphor for the scent of freedom.   Lexile: 0710L   (Grades K–5)   F

Lorbiecki, Marybeth. *Sister Anne's Hands.*   ISBN-13: 9780140565348, 2000

It's the early 1960s, and Anna has never seen a person with dark skin—until she meets Sister Anne. At first she is afraid of her new teacher, but she quickly discovers how wonderful Sister Anne is. Then one of Anna's classmates directs a racist remark toward Sister Anne. The teacher's wise way of turning the incident into a powerful learning experience has a profound impact on Anna.   Lexile: 0580L   (Grades Pre-K–4)   F

McKissack, Patricia C. *Goin' Someplace Special.*   ISBN-13: 9781416927358, 2008

Set in 1950s Nashville, this picture book shows the injustices of segregation through the story of Tricia Ann, an African American girl, who's finally allowed to go outside her neighborhood on her own. The laws say she can't be in many of the places white people can, so she goes to the public library, where everybody is welcome.

Lexile: 550L   (Grades Pre-K–3)   F

Pinkney, Andrea Davis. *Boycott Blues: How Rosa Parks Inspired a Nation.*

ISBN-13: 9780060821180, 2008

An uplifting, visually stunning overview of the civil rights movement, starting with Rosa Park's refusal to give up her seat on the bus and then continuing onto Dr. King's boycott speech and the ever-growing movement.   Lexile: 560L   (Grades 3–6)   NF

Pinkney, Andrea Davis. *Sit-In: How Four Friends Stood Up by Sitting Down.*

ISBN-13: 9780316070164, 2010

This book celebrates the 50th anniversary of the Woolworth's lunch counter sit-in, when four college students staged a peaceful protest that became a defining moment in the struggle for racial equality and the growing civil rights movement.

Lexile: AD500L   (Grades 1–4)   NF

Rappaport, Doreen. *The School Is Not White! A True Story of the Civil Rights Movement.*

ISBN-13: 9780786818389, 2005

This is a true story about heroes of the civil rights movement—the Carters, who sent their seven children to an all-white school because it had better resources, and had to endure violent threats as well as losing their home and jobs.   Lexile: AD850L   (Grades 2–5)   NF

Ringgold, Faith. *If a Bus Could Talk: The Story of Rosa Parks.*   ISBN-13: 9780689856761, 2003

In this book a bus does talk, and on her way to school a girl named Marcie learns why Rosa Parks is the mother of the Civil Rights movement.   Lexile: 0790L   (Grades K–4)   F

Robinet, Harriette. *Walking to the Bus-Rider Blues.*   ISBN-13: 9780689838866, 2002

In this mystery set during the Alabama bus boycott, 12-year-old Alfa and his sister try to find out who is stealing Grandma's rent money. They begin cleaning houses to help pay the rent, and when they are wrongly accused of theft, Alfa discovers that whites have money problems too.   Lexile: 0550L   (Grades 5–8)   F

Rodman, Mary Ann. *Yankee Girl.*   ISBN-13: 9780312535766, 2008

Alice's family has just moved to Mississippi, where her father's job is to protect civil rights workers and African Americans registering to vote. Alice has a hard time making friends at school because of her father's job. When the school is integrated by two black girls, Alice struggles with whether she should befriend the girls and be further ostracized by the popular but racist girls at her school.   Lexile: 550L   (Grades 4–8)   F

Shelton, Paula Young. *Child of the Civil Rights Movement.*   ISBN-13: 9780375843143, 2009

Poignant, moving, and hopeful, this is an intimate look at the birth of the Civil Rights Movement.   Lexile: AD960L   (Grades K–3)   NF

Uhlberg, Myron. *Dad, Jackie, and Me.*   ISBN-13: 9781561453290, 2005

A young boy shares the excitement of Robinson's rookie season with his deaf father.

Lexile: 610L   (Grades K–4)   F

Weatherford, Carole Boston. *Freedom on the Menu: The Greensboro Sit-Ins.*

ISBN-13: 9780142408940, 2007

There were signs all throughout town telling eight-year-old Connie where she could and could not go. But when Connie sees four young men take a stand for equal rights at a Woolworth's lunch counter in Greensboro, North Carolina, she realizes that things may soon change.   Lexile: N/A   (Grades K–4)   F

Wiles, Deborah. *Freedom Summer.*   ISBN-13: 9780689878299, 2005

Joe and John Henry are a lot alike, but there's one important way they're different: Joe is white and John Henry is black. In the South in 1964, that means John Henry isn't allowed to do everything his best friend can. Then a law is passed that forbids segregation and opens the town pool to everyone, but they realize it takes more than a new law to change people's hearts.   Lexile: 0460L   (Grades Pre-K–3)   F

Williams-Garcia, Rita. *One Crazy Summer.*   ISBN-13: 9780060760908, 2011

What Delphine and her sisters really want is to get to know their estranged mother, who they are visiting in Oakland during the summer of 1968. But their mother is cold to them and sends them to a local day camp run by the Black Panthers to get them out of her hair. While there, the girls learn about racial injustice and black power.

Lexile: N/A   (Grades 3–8)   F

Vietnam War

Antle, Nancy. *Lost in the War.*   ISBN-13: 9780141308364, 2000

Lisa's father was killed in the Vietnam War, and now her mother is depressed and having nightmares about her time as a nurse in the war. When Lisa's history teacher assigns the students a project on Vietnam, Lisa refuses. She is tired of the war, tired of Vietnam and how it tore apart her family. In time, however, she comes to accept the past and with the help of supportive people, her family begins to heal.

Lexile: 1010L   (Grades 4–8)   F

Brown, Jackie. *Little Cricket.*   ISBN-13: 9780786818525, 2004

When North Vietnamese soldiers destroy the village of 12-year-old Kia, they almost destroy her family too. Her father disappears and the rest of them flee to a refugee camp. Eventually Kia, her brother, and her grandfather immigrate to America.   Lexile: 1010L   (Grades 4–8)   F

Bunting, Eve. *The Wall.*   ISBN-13: 9780395629772, 1992

A boy and his father visit the Vietnam War Memorial to look for his grandfather's name. His father says he is proud that his dad's name is there, but the boy says he would rather his grandpa was there with them.   Lexile: AD270L   (Grades 1–4)   F

Caputo, Philip. *10,000 Days of Thunder: A History of the Vietnam War.*

ISBN-13: 9780689862311, 2005

An exploration of the 10,000 day-long Vietnam War is presented in this book. The background for the conflict, the main battles, the key players, and the impact back home are all covered in these pages.   Lexile: 1210L   (Grades 6–12)   NF

Dean-Myers, Walter. *Patrol: An American Soldier in Vietnam.*   ISBN-13: 9780060731595, 2005

A young soldier's feelings of fear and exhaustion are captured in verse in this powerful story-poem about his experiences in Viet Nam.   Lexile: 0280L   (Grades 4–12)   F

Dowell, Frances O'Roark. *Shooting the Moon.*   ISBN-13: 9781416979869, 2009

Jamie's father is a colonel in the army, and she's thrilled and envious when her brother enlists and goes to Vietnam. When she starts to get rolls of film from him, she sees the horrors of what he has experienced, and her view of the world changes.

Lexile: 890L   (Grades 5–8)   F

Kadohata, Cynthia. ***Cracker! The Best Dog in Vietnam.*** ISBN-13: 9781416906384, 2008

This story is about the bond between an army canine unit dog named Cracker and his handler Rick during the Vietnam War. Together, they spend their days searching for booby traps. The story is told via their alternating viewpoints and shows that Cracker looked after Rick just as much as Rick looked after Cracker.

Lexile: 0730L   (Grades 5–8)   F

Warren, Andrea. ***Escape from Saigon: How a Vietnam War Orphan Became an American Boy.*** ISBN-13: 9780374400231, 2008

In 1975, Operation Babylift brought eight-year-old Long from Vietnam to an adoptive family in America. This photo-essay tells Long's story, including his abandonment, the kindness of orphanage workers, his escape under fire, his sadness at leaving Vietnam, and his efforts to become American. Lexile: 0930L   (Grades 6–12)   NF

Reference

Jarolimek, John. (1990). *Social Studies in Elementary Education.* New York: Macmillan.

13

Math

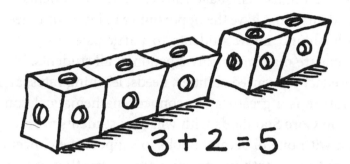

$$3 + 2 = 5$$

Using children's literature has long been a basis of classroom instruction. Literature invites children into the world of various curricular areas, including math. Books on relatable math topics can engage mathematical imaginations in ways that textbooks and workbooks often cannot. Such books help show how math can be exciting, imaginative, and accessible. Students who struggle with math can learn to see it in a new way, especially those who love to read but find math is not their best subject. Teachers who do not enjoy teaching math but include literature into their math lesson planning and instruction build off their strengths in reading and language arts instruction and boost their own enthusiasm for teaching math.

Using books for math lessons is effective for teaching important and basic mathematics concepts and skills, motivating students to think and reason mathematically, and engaging kids in problem-solving experiences, while building an appreciation for both mathematics and literature. The following lists offer a handful of math topics and related literature to use as read-alouds to open math units, provide students choices for reading on their own, and serve as academic time fillers for those students who tend to finish their work early.

With the Common Core Standards (http://www.corestandards.org/Math) being implemented across the nation, it's important to note them and consider ways in which you can incorporate literature to support the Common Core Standards for Mathematical Practice, which describe expertise that mathematics educators should seek to develop in their students. The standards begin with eight general criteria for mathematical practice:

1. Make sense of problems and persevere in solving them.
2. Reason abstractly and quantitatively.
3. Construct viable arguments and critique the reasoning of others.
4. Model with mathematics.
5. Use appropriate tools strategically.

6. Attend to precision.
7. Look for and make use of structure.
8. Look for and express regularity in repeated reasoning.

Important as they are, the standards do not define the intervention methods or materials necessary to support students, especially those who are well below or well above grade-level expectations. It is also beyond the scope of the standards to define the full range of supports appropriate for English language learners and for students with special needs. At the same time, all students must have the opportunity to learn and meet the same high standards. The standards should allow students to participate fully along with appropriate accommodations to ensure maximum participation of all students. No set of grade-specific standards can fully reflect the varied abilities, needs, learning rates, and achievement levels of all students. Literature is a great way to connect mathematical concepts and skills discussed in the Common Core Standards with what the students are studying in class. Opening a unit or a lesson with one or several books to support the concepts offers these varied learners opportunities to see math in engaging and interesting ways that often connect to real-life examples. To do just that, this chapter provides you with several titles related to specific mathematical concepts.

Addition, Subtraction, Multiplication, and Division

Bridges, Margaret Park. *Now . . . for My Next Number! Songs for Multiplying Fun.*   ISBN-13: 9780915556380, 2007
> The easy-to-memorize and fun-to-sing songs each focus on a number, telling a story that teaches the number's multiples in memorable, rhyming lyrics.   Lexile: N/A   (Grades Pre-K–3)   NF

Cleary, Brian P. *The Action of Subtraction.*   ISBN-13: 9781580138437, 2008
> Educational rhyming text is paired with cartoon cats and other animals. Together they teach about basic subtraction and provide ample instructive examples.
>
> Lexile: 410L   (Grades 1–3)   NF

Cleary, Brian P. *The Mission of Addition.*   ISBN-13: 9780822566953, 2007
> These playful rhymes and silly illustrations make this a fun book on addition for kids.
>
> Lexile: N/A   (Grades Pre-K–2)   NF

Demi. *One Grain of Rice: A Mathematical Folktale.*   ISBN-13: 9780590939980, 1997
> An Indian folktale about a clever young girl who outsmarts the greedy king through her knowledge of the power of doubling. When Rani does a good deed, the raja offers to reward her, but all she asks for is one grain of rice, doubled each day for 30 days. The raja is happy to comply, not realizing it will amount to enough rice to feed her entire village.
>
> Lexile: N/A   (Grades Pre-K–2)   F

Dodds, Dayle Ann. *Minnie's Diner: A Multiplying Menu.*   ISBN-13: 9780763633134, 2007

The McFay brothers don't want to do their chores, so one by one, they sneak over to Minnie's Diner to eat. Since Minnie thinks each brother looks about twice the size of the one just younger than him, she gives each brother twice the amount of food.

Lexile: N/A   (Grades K–8)   F

Fromental, Jean-Luc. *365 Penguins.*   ISBN-13: 9780810944602, 2006

A family is baffled when their uncle, an ecologist, keeps sending them a penguin a day. They quickly become overwhelmed trying to care for the increasing number of penguins and finally use multiplication to organize, feed, and care for them.

Lexile: N/A   (Grades 1–4)   F

Leedy, Loreen. *Mission: Addition.*   ISBN-13: 9780823414123, 1999

Miss Prime and her class are learning addition facts via a variety of scenarios, such as taking a survey, figuring out the total on a lunch bill, and pretending to be detectives and adding up clues.   Lexile: 410L   (Grades Pre-K–3)   F

Leedy, Loreen. *Subtraction Action.*   ISBN-13: 9780823417643, 2002

Miss Prime is back, this time teaching basic subtraction concepts, such as defining difference, writing an equation, regrouping, and more. A trip to the school fair then provides fun practical applications.   Lexile: 410L   (Grades Pre-K–3)   F

Losi, Carol A. *The 512 Ants on Sullivan Street.*   ISBN-13: 9780439798549, 2006

As a little girl and her companion lay out their food for a picnic, one ant sees them through a telescope. Before long, two ants are on the scene, then four, and so on until 512 ants are enjoying the great feast.   Lexile: N/A   (Grades Pre-K–3)   F

McElligott, Matthew. *The Lion's Share: A Tale of Halving Cake and Eating It Too.*

ISBN-13: 9780802723604, 2012

The lion has baked a cake for his friends, but each of his greedy friends takes half the cake when it's passed to them, leaving the lion with only a crumb. Ant feels bad and offers to bake another cake. The others hear this, and not wanting to look bad, each offers to likewise bake cakes for the lion. But they each try to outdo the other, promising twice the cakes promised by the previous guest. Soon, hundreds of cakes are being promised, and the result is quite comical.   Lexile: AD550L   (Grades Pre-K–3)   F

Mills, Claudia. *7 × 9 = Trouble!*   ISBN-13: 9780374464523, 2004

Third-grader Wilson struggles with multiplication, especially timed tests. His kindergartener brother Kipper surprises him when he comes to the rescue!

Lexile: 590L   (Grades 2–4)   F

Murphy, Stuart J. *Animals on Board.*   ISBN-13: 9780064467162, 1998

In the story, a truck driver named Jill keeps seeing vehicles drive past with all sorts of animals on board. As they pass, Jill adds up the animals she sees on each truck. At the end, the animals' surprise destination is finally revealed: they are going to be part of a carousel under construction.   Lexile: 270L   (Grades 1–5)   F

Murphy, Stuart J. *Elevator Magic.* ISBN-13: 9780064467094, 1997

Ben and his mother are in a skyscraper and must make a few stops on their way to the ground floor. Since Ben wants to be the one to push the elevator buttons, he must use subtraction to decide what floor they are going to next. Lexile: 240L (Grades 1–4) F

Murphy, Stuart J. *Mall Mania.* ISBN-13: 9780060557775, 2006

The Parkside Mall is holding a "Mall Mania" day, and, to celebrate, the 100th person to enter the mall will win a large assortment of prizes. It's the job of a group of friends to add up the shoppers as they enter one of the four doors of the mall. Throughout the day, they share their numbers via walkie-talkies, with each update employing a range of addition strategies. Lexile: N/A (Grades 1–5) F

Murphy, Stuart J. *Monster Musical Chairs.* ISBN-13: 9780064467308, 2000

Bouncy rhymes and adorable monsters keep the mood light and fun in teaching subtraction. Lexile: 170L (Grades Pre-K–1) F

Murphy, Stuart J. *Shark Swimathon.* ISBN-13: 9780064467353, 2000

The Ocean City Sharks need money to participate in the state swim meet, so a local bank offers to sponsor them if they swim 75 laps by the end of the week. To meet their challenge, they swim every day and use subtraction to figure out how many laps are left to go. Lexile: 380L (Grades 3–6) F

Neuschwander, Cindy. *Amanda Bean's Amazing Dream.* ISBN-13: 9780590300124, 1998

Amanda Bean loves to count things but isn't interested in learning multiplication. Her teacher says it will speed up the process, but Amanda can't see how. Lexile: AD290L (Grades Pre-K–2) F

Pallotta, Jerry. *The Hershey's Kisses Subtraction Book.* ISBN-13: 9780439337793, 2002

This book makes for some fun subtraction lesson plans (although we know using real candy has obvious downsides). Lexile: AD340L (Grades Pre-K–2) NF

Shaskan, Trisha Speed. *If You Were a Minus Sign.* ISBN-13: 9781404847880, 2008

This book features illustrations and clear explanations about what a minus sign is and how it works. Pages have examples of subtraction problems in text, pictures, and number equations. Lexile: 530L (Grades Pre-K–2) NF

Slade, Suzanne. *What's New at the Zoo? An Animal Adding Adventure.*

ISBN-13: 9781934359938, 2009

Each spread presents a detailed zoo scene paired with a rhyme and number equation that leads the reader to solve an addition problem. Lexile: 80L (Grades K–3) NF

Tang, Gregory. *The Best of Times.* ISBN-13: 9780439210447, 2002

This book sets aside memorization and rules when teaching multiplication. It demonstrates the relationships between numbers and how that can help with learning and performing multiplication. Lexile: AD130L (Grades 3–6) NF

Tang, Gregory. *The Grapes of Math.* ISBN-13: 9780439598408, 2004

There are 16 spreads posing math problems that challenge readers to think creatively and conceptually when solving the problem, rather than simply trying to count the items. The aim is to help the transition from addition to multiplication.

Lexile: N/A (Grades 2–6) NF

Tang, Gregory. *Math for All Seasons.* ISBN-13: 9780439755375, 2004

This title shows the power of thinking creatively when solving addition problems. The riddles depict the seasons and ask the reader to determine "how many" using clues that encourage creative problem solving. Lexile: N/A (Grades 2–6) NF

Tang. Gregory. *Math-terpieces: The Art of Problem-Solving.* ISBN-13: 9780439443883, 2003

In this creative math concept book, 12 masterpieces of art help children see the benefits of grouping when adding or subtracting. Lexile: NPL (Grades 2–5) NF

Wise, William. *Ten Sly Piranhas: A Counting Story in Reverse.*

ISBN-13: 9780142400746, 2004

A rhythmic tale of piranhas who outmaneuver and eat each other, making this a fun and effective early lesson in subtraction. Finally, a crocodile comes along, and "then there were none." Lexile: NPL (Grades 2–5) F

Time

Adam, Winky. *Telling Time.* ISBN-13: 9780486407944, 2000

Meant for preschool and early school-age children, this book explains how to read a clock, describe the two hands, tell how minutes are counted, explain how many minutes make up an hour, and much more. Lexile: N/A (Grades Pre-K–2) NF

Appelt, Kathi. *Bats Around the Clock.*

ISBN-13: 9780688164690, 1999

It's fun to tell time as readers dance around the clock on a 12-hour rock-and-roll extravaganza with Click Dark as the host. Lexile: 640L (Grades 3–6) F

Butterfield, Moira. *Learning Clock.* ISBN-13: 9780760719169, 2000

This children's introduction to telling time combines a traditional clock with digital numbers and time in words. Lexile: N/A (Grades Pre-K–2) NF

Cuyler, Margery. *Tick Tock Clock.* ISBN-13: 9780061363115, 2012

The story of twin girls and their grandmother are told through each hour of the day as they engage in a variety of activities. Lexile: N/A (Grades Pre-K–1) F

Harris, Trudy. *The Clock Struck One: A Time-Telling Tale.*   ISBN-13: 9780822590675, 2008

This book starts with the familiar phrase, but "hickory dickory dock" takes an interesting turn when the grandfather clock strikes two. The book goes through the next time-telling rhyme where each of the hours draws another animal or person into the chase.

Lexile: N/A   (Grades 3–6)   F

Heling, Kathryn. *Midnight Fright.*   ISBN-13: 9780545044448, 2008

Each hour something exciting happens in the Halloween-themed title, and the countdown continues all the way to midnight.   Lexile: N/A   (Grades Pre-K–1)   F

Jenkins, Steve. *Just a Second: A Different Way to Look at Time.*

ISBN-13: 9780618708963, 2011

This book explores time in the framework of the natural world—from seconds all the way up to the history of the universe.   Lexile: 870L   (Grades Pre-K–3)   NF

Nagda, Ann Whitehead. *Chimp Math: Learning About Time from a Baby Chimpanzee.*

ISBN-13: 9780805066746, 2002

Follow Jiggs as he grows from a wobbly infant to a wild and wonderful toddler. Along the way you can learn about clocks, calendars, timelines, and other ways of keeping time records.   Lexile: N/A   (Grades 2–6)   NF

Older, Jules. *Telling Time.*   ISBN-13: 9780881063974, 2000

With a sense of humor, this book shows kids why telling time is important. It covers large chunks of time, like months, years, and millenniums, as well as seconds and minutes. The book explains both digital and analog clocks. A poem at the end reminds children how many seconds are in a minute, how many minutes are in an hour, and so on.

Lexile: AD330L   (Grades Pre-K–1)   NF

Pyle, Howard. *The Wonder Clock.*   ISBN-13: 9780765342669, 2003

Twenty-four stories, one for every hour of the day, are described.

Lexile: N/A   (Grades 5–10)   F

Sweeney, Joan. *Me Counting Time: From Seconds to Centuries.*

ISBN-13: 9780440417514, 2001

This introduction to time "from seconds to centuries" is told by a young girl approaching her seventh birthday.   Lexile: 170L   (Grades Pre-K–2)   NF

Updike, John. *A Child's Calendar.*   ISBN-13: 9780823417667, 2002

This collection of 12 poems describes the activities in the life of a multicultural family and the changes in the weather that surrounds them throughout each month of the year.

Lexile: NPL   (Grades K–6)   NF

Wells, Robert E. *How Do You Know What Time It Is?*   ISBN-13: 9780807579404, 2002

This book provides an age-appropriate depiction of the history of measuring time—from simply observing the movement of the sun to using shadow-stick clocks to our modern atomic and quartz clocks. The book also covers time zones, meridians, and more.

Lexile: 870L   (Grades 3–6)   NF

Wright, Marsha Elyn. *Telling Time Games: Using the Judy Clock.*

ISBN-13: 9780768227215, 2002

This resource requires the use of the Judy Clock to provide a simple introduction and additional practice in learning about time. It introduces young learners to basic time concepts and then engages them in challenging games that reinforce the concepts.

Lexile: N/A   (Grades Pre-K–1)   NF

Fractions

Adler, David A. *Fraction Fun.*   ISBN-13: 9780823413416, 1996

This simple, hands-on book is clear and concise. The simple definition of a fraction, that it is a part of something, is introduced with a pizza pie that is divided, studied, and compared. Weighing coins determines how many make one ounce and what the fractional value of each coin is.   Lexile: 580L   (Grades 2–4)   NF

Adler, David A. *Working with Fractions.*   ISBN-13: 9780823422074, 2009

This fun math book shows how fractions are everywhere, even at a child's birthday party! Party games, food, and the actions of a performing clown and a magician help present different scenarios involving fractions.

Lexile: 0690L   (Grades 1–4)   NF

Bussell, Linda. *Pizza Parts: Fractions!*   ISBN-13: 9780836893885, 2008

Elena is throwing a pizza party for her birthday. Her friends like different toppings, so they will have to use fractions to make sure that they all get their favorite slices.

Lexile: 610L   (Grades 2–4)   F

Dodds, Dayle Ann. *Full House: An Invitation to Fractions.*   ISBN-13: 9780763660901, 2012

Miss Bloom runs the Strawberry Inn, and she absolutely loves visitors. Throughout the day, she welcomes a cast of hilarious characters, from a duchess to a dog trainer, until all the rooms are taken. It's a full house! But in the middle of the night, Miss Bloom realizes that something is just not right—and sure enough, downstairs the guests are eating her cake.

Lexile: N/A   (Grades 1–4)   F

Greenberg, Dan. *Funny and Fabulous Fraction Stories.*   ISBN-13: 9780590965767, 1996

These are hilarious fractions stories with follow-up problems that reinforce essential fraction skills.   Lexile: N/A   (Grades 3–6)   F

McElligott, Matthew. *The Lion's Share: A Tale of Halving Cake and Eating It Too.*

ISBN-13: 9780802723604, 2012

Lion has baked a cake for his friends, but each of his greedy friends takes half the cake when it's passed to them, and the lion is left with a crumb. Feeling bad, they offer to bake new cakes, each trying to outdo the former offer. Soon hundreds of cakes are being promised.

Lexile: 0550L   (Grades Pre-K–3)   F

Mills, Claudia. *Fractions = Trouble!*   ISBN-13: 9781250003362, 2012

Wilson Williams is finding fractions impossible. His parents hire a math tutor for him, but he is determined to make sure that no one finds out.   Lexile: AD490L   (Grades 2–6)   F

Nagda, Ann Whitehead, and Cindy Bickel. *Polar Bear Math: Learning About Fractions from Klondike and Snow.*   ISBN-13: 9780312377496, 2007

Readers will follow Klondike and Snow as they grow from fragile newborns to large, lively bears, and along the way they'll learn about fractions.   Lexile: N/A   (Grades Pre-K–2)   NF

Pallotta, Jerry. *Apple Fractions.*   ISBN-13: 9780439389013, 2003

The author uses a variety of different apples to teach kids all about fractions in this book. Playful elves demonstrate how to divide apples into halves, thirds, fourths, and more. Readers will also learn about varieties of apples, including Golden and Red Delicious, Granny Smiths, Cortlands, and Asian pears.   Lexile: AD490L   (Grades 2–4)   NF

Pallota, Jerry. *Hershey's Milk Chocolate Fractions Book.*   ISBN-13: 9780439135191, 1999

This book teaches multiplication with a Hershey's milk chocolate bar. With its 3 horizontal rows and 4 vertical columns, totaling 12 sections in all, children can easily begin to understand the concept and process of multiplication.   Lexile: AD460L   (Grades 2–6)   NF

Souder, Taryn. *Whole-y Cow! Fractions Are Fun.*   ISBN-13: 9781585364602, 2010

With the guidance of a likable cow, readers are guided in the basics of fractions, like parts of a group, parts of a whole. Each spread shows the cow in a different scenario and asks related fraction questions (e.g., "What fraction of the cow is white?"). Written by an elementary math teacher, this book really does make fractions fun.

Lexile: AD600L   (Grades 1–4)   NF

Sterling, Kristin. *Fractions.*   ISBN-13: 9780822588474, 2008

Learn fractions by dividing a pizza among your friends.

Lexile: N/A   (Grades 2–4)   NF

Counting

Baker, Keith. **Potato Joe.**   ISBN-13: 9780152062309, 2008

Spunky leader Potato Joe and his nine spud pals count to 10 and then back down, making it a great book for young ones learning numbers.

Lexile: N/A   (Grades Pre-K–4)   NF

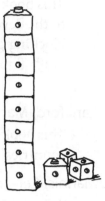

Cronin, Doreen. **Click, Clack, Splish, Splash.**

ISBN-13: 9780689877162, 2006

In this title, Duck and friends are on a rescue mission, but readers don't find out exactly who is being rescued until the end. Each step in the mission involves increasing numbers.

Lexile: AD300L   (Grades Pre-K–1)   F

Dobson, Christina. **Pizza Counting.**   ISBN-13: 9780881063394, 2003

This book introduces kids to counting and fractions using decorated pizzas. Kids can make a grinning pizza face with varying numbers of vegetables and learn how many pizzas it would take to circle the earth at the equator.   Lexile: AD930L   (Grades 2–4)   NF

Falconer, Ian. **Olivia Counts.**   ISBN-13: 9780689850875, 2002

The spunky pig Olivia is teaching numbers 1 through 10.   Lexile: N/A   (Grades Pre-K–1)   F

Grossman, Bill. **My Little Sister Ate One Hare.**   ISBN-13: 9780517885765, 1998

This rhyming tale is about a little girl who won't eat anything nutritious but has no problem eating disgusting items as part of her magic act. The little girl eats an ever-increasing numbers of items.   Lexile: 0380L   (Grades Pre-K–2)   F

Jaffe, Elizabeth Dana. **Dominoes: Games Around the World.**   ISBN-13: 9780756501327, 2002

This book sets down the dominoes, shuffles them, and sorts them out on the way to explaining important aspects of the game. Sidebars offer information throughout. The history of dominoes and games from America, Spain, and Hungary are included.

Lexile: N/A   (Grades Pre-K–2)   NF

Jay, Alison. **1 2 3: A Child's First Counting Book.**   ISBN-13: 9780525478362, 2007

A little girl dreams that she travels to a magical fairyland and encounters popular fairy tale characters like three little pigs, four frog princes, six gingerbread men, and eight running rats. Each spread is devoted to a number from 1 to 10 and back again.

Lexile: N/A   (Grades Pre-K–2)   F

Jenkins, Emily. **Five Creatures.**   ISBN-13: 9780374423285, 2005

A little girl sorts and counts the five members of her household based on various characteristics, interests, talents, and even food choices.   Lexile: 0130L   (Grades Pre-K–2)   F

Johnson, Stephen T. **City by Numbers.**   ISBN-13: 9780140566369, 2003

This title is stunning and features highly realistic paintings of the numerals 1 to 21 that are depicted in various urban scenes.   Lexile: N/A   (Grades Pre-K–3)   NF

Kelley, Jennifer. *The Little Giant Book of Dominoes.*   ISBN-13: 9781402749865, 2003

This book shows learners what makes up a suit, how to score, and how to add your domino to the developing structure. It also analyzes entire games and offers a variety of variations: blocking games like Latin American Match; scoring ones, such as Merry-Go-Round and Sniff; Trumps and Tricks, including Nel-O and Plunge; and several solitaire versions.

Lexile: N/A   (Grades Pre-K–2)   NF

Lankford, Mary D. *Dominoes Around the World.*   ISBN-13: 9780688140519, 1998

This book offers a clear explanation of domino basics, along with versions of the game from countries as diverse as Mexico, Vietnam, and France.   Lexile: N/A   (Grades Pre-K–2)   NF

Mannis, Celeste. *One Leaf Rides the Wind.*   ISBN-13: 9780756952136, 2005

A young Japanese girl explores a temple garden and counts the various items that she sees.

Lexile: N/A   (Grades 1–4)   F

Morales, Yuyi. *Just a Minute: A Trickster Tale and Counting Book.*

ISBN-13: 9780811837583, 2003

When Death pays Grandma Beetle a visit, she delays going with him with one "just a minute" after another. She first must complete her party preparations; each involves an increasing number of items.   Lexile: 540L   (Grades Pre-K–3)   F

Oringel, Sandy. *Math Activities with Dominoes.*   ISBN-13: 9781574520279, 1997

Children sort, classify, compare, and do arithmetic as they deal with pattern recognition, number theory, probability, and logic. Directions are simple and a game board is provided.

Lexile: N/A   (Grades Pre-K–2)   NF

Seeger, Laura Vaccaro. *One Boy.*   ISBN-13: 9781596432741, 2008

Die cuts on full-page flaps make this counting book full of discovery and imagination. Each number has two different looks on each set of pages.   Lexile: N/A   (Grades Pre-K–2)   NF

Yolen, Jane. *How Do Dinosaurs Count to Ten?*   ISBN-13: 9780007251162, 2009

This book describes how a little dinosaur counts from 1 to 10, using the toys and other things around him.   Lexile: 0480L   (Grades Pre-K–2)   F

Graphs and Charts

Bader, Bonnie. *Penguin Young Readers: Family Reunion.*

ISBN-13: 9780448428963, 2003

Gary doesn't want to go to his family reunion, so he asks if he can stay home and complete his graphing homework. Gary's mom suggests he bring it along. Once there, Gary really gets into the project and uses data about family members at the reunion to make pie, bar, and line graphs.   Lexile: N/A   (Grades K–3)   F

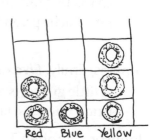

Harris, Trudy. *Tally Cat Keeps Track.*   ISBN-13: 9780761344513, 2010

Tally McNally loves using tally marks to keep track during contests with his friends, but thanks to his sneaky tactics, Tally always wins every contest he competes in. Then one day, Tally gets into a jam during a contest.   Lexile: 570L   (Grades K–3)   F

Leedy, Loreen. *The Great Graph Contest.*   ISBN-13: 9780823420292, 2006

Best friends Gonk the Toad and Beezy the Lizard compete to see who can make the best graph, and in the process, they explore both data-collection methods such as surveys and tallies, and also graphing methods such as line graphs, bar graphs, etc.

Lexile: N/A   (Grades K–3)   F

Murphy, Stuart J. *Lemonade for Sale.*   ISBN-13: 9780064467155, 1997

Four friends start a lemonade business, using graphs to chart their growing sales. Sales are improving until a boy down the street starts a juggling act for money.

Lexile: 380L   (Grades 1–5)   F

Murphy, Stuart J. *Tally O'Malley.*   ISBN-13: 9780060531645, 2004

The O'Malley family is on their way to the beach, but the drive is long and boring. So they decide to pass the time with short tallying competitions—first with cars, then with T-shirts, and finally with train cars.   Lexile: N/A   (Grades K–3)   F

Nagda, Ann Whitehead. *Tiger Math: Learning to Graph from a Baby Tiger.*

ISBN-13: 9780805071610, 2002

TJ is a tiger who was born at the Denver Zoo but sadly became an orphan shortly thereafter. The zoo's veterinary staff takes over for his mother, feeding him by hand until he is able to eat on his own.   Lexile: 810L   (Grades 2–5)   NF

Measurements

Adler, David. *How Tall, How Short, How Far Away.*

ISBN-13: 9780823413751, 1999

A lively introduction to measurement, starting with Egyptian methods and progressing all the way to modern inch/pound and metric systems. Activities include measuring your height, making a metric ruler, and determining distances in kilometers.

Lexile: 0480L   (Grades 2–6)   NF

Cleary, Brian P. *On the Scale, a Weighty Tale.*   ISBN-13: 9780822578512, 2008

This book presents weights and measures through age-appropriate examples in English and metric units.   Lexile: 780   (Grades 1–3)   NF

Clement, Rod. *Counting on Frank.*   ISBN-13: 9780395703939, 1994

Frank loves to ask questions about ordinary things like peas, pens, and his dog Frank, and then answer them with math. This is a fun book for teaching measurement and estimation.

Lexile: N/A   (Grades 3–6)   NF

Jenkins, Steve. *Actual Size.* ISBN-13: 9780547512914, 2011

This title depicts 18 animals and insects in actual size. It illustrates the diversity of our world and the role of measurement, comparison, and observation in scientific knowledge.

Lexile: 1080L (Grades Pre-K–3) NF

Leedy, Loreen. *Measuring Penny.* ISBN-13: 9780805065725, 2000

Lisa's homework is to measure something as many ways as she can, and she selects her dog. Once she starts, she catches the spirit of it and seemingly can't stop measuring.

Lexile: AD500L (Grades 2–4) F

Murphy, Stuart J. *Super Sand Castle Saturday.* ISBN-13: 9780064467209, 1998

On a sunny beach day, three friends compete to see who can build the tallest sand castle, deepest moat, and longest wall. When they're done, the lifeguard measures to pick a winner and then explains the benefits of standard measurements. Lexile: 410L (Grades 1–4) F

Neuschwander, Cindy. *Pastry School in Paris: An Adventure in Capacity.*

ISBN-13: 9780805083149, 2009

While in Paris, Matt and Bibi visit the pastry academy *Les Jumelles Coccinelle* and are put in charge of liquids. Their adventures offer a lesson on American standard and metric liquid measurements. Lexile: N/A (Grades 2–6) F

Schwartz, David M. *Millions to Measure.* ISBN-13: 9780060848064, 2006

Marvelosissimo the Magician teaches the history of measurement, including distance, weight, volume, and the metric system. Lexile: 0470L (Grades K–6) F

Wells, Robert E. *Is a Blue Whale the Biggest Thing There Is?* ISBN-13: 9781619131163, 2012

This book takes measurement and comparison to the extremes of imagination, starting with a whale and progressing up to the universe. Lexile: N/A (Grades 3–6) NF

Money

Adams, Barbara Johnston. *The Go-Around Dollar.*

ISBN-13: 9780027000313, 1992

Experience a day in the life of a dollar bill as it travels from person to person, starting with Matt, who finds the dollar on the way home from school. He uses it to buy shoelaces from Eric, who then uses the dollar to buy bubble gum. The dollar's journey continues until finally, it is put in a picture frame as the first dollar earned at a new store. Lexile: 680L (Grades K–3) F

Adler, David A. *Money Madness.* ISBN-13: 9780823422722, 2010

What would life be like without money? Readers will consider this possibility and the problems it would create, and then trace the history of our monetary system from hunting/gathering and the barter system to paper/coin currency. Lexile: 0770L (Grades K–3) NF

Clements, Andrew. *Lunch Money.*   ISBN-13: 9780689866852, 2007

Twelve-year-old Greg, who has always been good at moneymaking projects, is surprised to find himself teaming up with his lifelong rival, Maura, to create a series of comic books to sell at school.   Lexile: N/A   (Grades 3–6)   F

Flake, Sharon. *Money Hungry.*   ISBN-13: 9781423132493, 2009

Thirteen-year-old Raspberry thinks of ways to make money so that she and her mother never have to worry about living on the streets again.   Lexile: N/A   (Grades 5–12)   F

Glass, Julie. *A Dollar for Penny.*   ISBN-13: 9780679889731, 2000

It's summer and Penny sets up a lemonade stand. At first she sells her lemonade for a penny, then two pennies, then a nickel. Slowly the money builds up in her coin jar, and the total jumps when Grandma spends ten cents and a few customers even spend a quarter.

Lexile: 150L   (Grades K–2)   F

Greenstein, Elaine. *Ice Cream Cones for Sale!*   ISBN-13: 9780439327282, 2003

This book presents the great debate over who invented the ice cream cone. Only one man holds the patent for the first cone-making machine, though, and his claims top them all.

Lexile: AD790L   (Grades 2–6)   NF

Leedy, Loreen. *Follow the Money!*   ISBN-13: 9780823417940, 2003

Written from the point of view of a quarter, this book follows the quarter's path on a day that includes the Federal Reserve, a local bank, a grocery store, a child's piggy bank, and so on. A lot happens to the quarter over the course of the day, resulting in numerous money-related math problems.   Lexile: AD130L   (Grades K–3)   NF

Murphy, Stuart J. *Less Than Zero.*   ISBN-13: 9780060001261, 2003

Penguin Perry wants an ice scooter, but needs nine clams to buy one. He decides to do odd jobs to earn the money and uses a line graph to track his progress. Unfortunately, he seems to lose and spend as much as he earns.   Lexile: 0620L   (Grades 3–6)   F

Murphy, Stuart J. *The Penny Pot.*   ISBN-13: 9780064467179, 1998

The face painting booth at the school fair provides plenty of opportunities to count combinations of coins adding up to 50.   Lexile: 240L   (Grades 2–6)   F

Schwartz, David M. *If You Made a Million.*   ISBN-13: 9780688136345, 1994

This book teaches money in a funny, accessible way, bringing confusing financial concepts down to a level that children will understand. Topics include saving and spending, writing checks, interest, the relationship between accomplishing tasks and getting paid, and more.

Lexile: 0810L   (Grades K–3)   NF

Viorst, Judith. *Alexander, Who Used to Be Rich Last Sunday.*

ISBN-13: 9780689711992, 1987

Although Alexander and his money are quickly parted, he comes to realize all the things that can be done with a dollar.   Lexile: AD570L   (Grades K–3)   F

Williams, Rozanne Lanczak. *The Coin Counting Book.*   ISBN-13: 9780881063264, 2001

Children will enjoy counting and adding while learning the names and denominations of all of the U.S. coins.   Lexile: N/A   (Grades K–3)   NF

Worth, Bonnie. *One Cent, Two Cents, Old Cent, New Cent: All About Money.*

ISBN-13: 9780375828812, 2008

This title provides an introduction to the history of money, from bartering to modern money systems, plus information about how coins are made, what banks are for, and so on.   Lexile: N/A   (Grades K–3)   NF

Geometry and Shapes

Adler, David A. *Shape Up! Fun with Triangles and Other Polygons.*   ISBN-13: 9780823416387, 2000

This book provides a hands-on introduction to basic geometry concepts, like triangles, angles, and polygons—all via fun, interactive exercises that incorporate small food items like cheese, pretzels, pieces of bread, and so on.   Lexile: 0560L   (Grades Pre-K–3)   NF

Burns, Marilyn. *The Greedy Triangle.*   ISBN-13: 9780590489911, 1995

Dissatisfied with its shape, a triangle keeps asking the local shapeshifter to add more lines and angles until it doesn't know which side is up.   Lexile: AD580L   (Grades Pre-K–3)   F

Burns, Marilyn. *Spaghetti and Meatballs for All!*   ISBN-13: 9780545044455, 2008

Mr. and Mrs. Comfort are holding a family reunion and have planned every detail—from the delicious spaghetti dinner to the perfect seating arrangements with enough tables and chairs for all. But when their relatives arrive, they move everything around, ensuring a frantic Mrs. Comfort that there'll be plenty of room. Mrs. Comfort knows and understands area and perimeter, so she knows better.   Lexile: 0420L   (Grades Pre-K–3)   F

Dodds, Dayle Ann. *Shape of Things.*   ISBN-13: 9781564026989, 1996

Shapes are everywhere, and this book will help young children identify shapes in the world around them. A square is just a square until it becomes a house; a circle becomes a spinning Ferris wheel; and when some string and a tail are added to a diamond shape, it becomes a kite flying high in the sky.   Lexile: NP   (Grades Pre-K–3)   NF

Ellis, Julie. *Pythagoras and the Ratios.*   ISBN-13: 9781570917769, 2010

Young Pythagoras and his friends want to win a music contest, but their instruments are out of tune. In puzzling over the problem, Pythagoras uncovers mathematical relationships in the sounds.   Lexile: N/A   (Grades 3–12)   F

Ellis, Julie. *What's Your Angle, Pythagoras?*　　　　ISBN-13: 9781570911507, 2004

This is a fictionalized story about how a curious boy named Pythagoras first learned about right angles and then through experimentation and observation discovered his famous theorem.　　　　　　　　　　　　Lexile: N/A　(Grades 3–12)　F

Ernst, Lisa Campbell. *Tangram Magician.*　　　　ISBN-13: 9781593541064, 2005

Tangram Magician brings this ancient Chinese puzzle to readers. As the work of the magician unfolds, the reader can make the designs using the seven puzzle pieces provided with the book.　　　　　　　　　　　　Lexile: N/A　(Grades K–4)　NF

Lasky, Kathryn. *The Librarian Who Measured the Earth.*　　　ISBN-13: 9780316515269, 1994

The first section of this book paints a lovely picture of life in the ancient world and of Eratosthenes' early years and how he rose to prominence. The second half focuses on how he calculated the circumference of the earth so long ago.　　　Lexile: AD840L　(Grades 1–5)　NF

Leech, Bonnie Coulter. *Triangles.*　　　　ISBN-13: 9781404234956, 2006

Readers will be introduced to things of three, polygons, parts of a triangle, naming triangles, triangles classified by sides, triangles classified by angles, sum of the angles in a triangle, the perimeter and the area of triangles, triangles around us, and more.

Lexile: N/A　(Grades 3–6)　NF

Maccarone, Grace, and Marilyn Burns. *Three Pigs, One Wolf, and Seven Magic Shapes.*

ISBN-13: 9780590308571, 1997

This is a parody of the tale about three little pigs and the hungry wolf. In this story, the pigs meet magic animals that give them seven magic shapes to help them find their fortune. These shapes form a tangram.　　　　　　Lexile: 630L　(Grades K–3)　F

Marsh, Valerie. *Story Puzzles: Tales in the Tangram Tradition.*

ISBN-13: 9780917846595, 1996

The author suggests the use of an enhanced set of tangram puzzle pieces to create visual images of a story. The book offers some clever ideas for using the technique in libraries and classrooms. It also includes a number of stories from selected folklore traditions, as well as some interesting material with history and science content.

Lexile: N/A　(Grades K–6)　NF

Martin, Joshua Rae. *3-D Fort Shapes.*　　　　ISBN-13: 9781429668453, 2011

From treasure hunting in an attic to planting a garden, kids will have fun and discover many shapes and dimensions. They will see how they use math every day, sometimes without even realizing it.　　　　　　　Lexile: IG450L　(Grades 2–4)　NF

Millington, Jon. *Pentominoes.*　　　　ISBN-13: 9780906212578, 1997

If you take five squares of the same size and join them edge-to-edge, the resulting shape is called a pentomino. This book shows some of the possibilities, poses some problems, and suggests fruitful lines of investigation of pentominoes.　　Lexile: N/A　(Grades 2–6)　NF

Millington, Jon. *Tangrams.*   ISBN-13: 9780906212561, 1997

This colorful book shows that when a square is cut into seven pieces, you can construct a large variety of different images and patterns.   Lexile: N/A   (Grades Pre-K–3)   NF

Murphy, Stuart J. *Racing Around.*   ISBN-13: 9780064462440, 2001

Three siblings want to participate in a 15-kilometer bike race, but the older two insist it's too long for young Mike. To gauge how long 15 kilometers is, they ride around a field and then a zoo, and then they calculate the perimeter of each.   Lexile: N/A   (Grades 1–4)   F

Neuschwander, Cindy. *Mummy Math: An Adventure in Geometry.*

ISBN-13: 9780805075052, 2005

The Zills family is summoned to Egypt to help find the hidden burial chamber of an ancient pharaoh. With only the geometric hieroglyphics on the walls to help them, they use their math skills to locate the burial chamber—and the way out.   Lexile: 530L   (Grades 4–8)   F

Onyefulu, Ifeoma. *Triangle for Adaora: An African Book of Shapes.*

ISBN-13: 9781845077389, 2007

When Adaora's cousin promises to find a triangle for her, he doesn't realize just how difficult the task will be. As they search, the cousins encounter heart-shaped *akwukwo ede* leaves, round elephant drums, and crescent-shaped plantains, everything but the shape they seek.   Lexile: 0400L   (Grades Pre-K–3)   F

Pollack, Pam. *Chickens on the Move.*   ISBN-13: 9781575651132, 2002

Tom, Gordon, and Anne learn all about perimeter when they help make a chicken coop.

Lexile: 270L   (Grades Pre-K–3)   F

Reisberg, Joanne. *Zachary Zormer, Shape Transformer.*   ISBN-13: 9781570918766, 2006

Zachary always forgets to bring in an object for the weekly math show-and-tell. But the quick-thinking boy manages to use ordinary items to demonstrate geometric concepts (e.g., a flashlight to teach the area of a rectangle or scraps of paper to teach perimeter).

Lexile: N/A   (Grades Pre-K–3)   F

Smith, A. G. *Cut and Assemble 3-D Geometrical Shapes.*   ISBN-13: 9780486250939, 1990

Complete step-by-step instructions and diagrams for assembling 10 full-color geometric solids, tetrahedron, octahedron, cube, trapezohedron, icosahedron, and simple and intricate variations of dodecahedrons.   Lexile: N/A   (Grades 3–6)   NF

Sundby, Scott. *Cut Down to Size at High Noon.*   ISBN-13: 9781570911682, 2000

Set in the Old West in the fictional town of Cowlick, this is the story of a big-scale drawing show-down between tough-talking newcomer Buzzsaw Bart and the town's much-loved barber.   Lexile: AD800L   (Grades 3–6)   F

Tompert, Ann. *Grandfather Tang's Story.*   ISBN-13: 9780517885581, 1997

Drawing on a Chinese form of storytelling with seven shapes cut from a square of paper, the author recounts the tale of two fox fairies as they create tangram designs.

Lexile: AD660L   (Grades K–4)   F

14

Science

Children's literature is important for incorporating meaningful and engaging classroom instruction. It invites children into the world of science in a way they might not have been comfortable with before. Books on relatable science topics can engage scientific imaginations in ways that textbooks and workbooks aren't always able to do. They help show how science is inquiry based and also accessible. Students who struggle with science or don't enjoy the subject area learn to see it in a new way. Teachers who do not enjoy teaching science or lack confidence in teaching it can include literature in their science planning and instruction to build from their strengths in reading and language arts instruction and boost their own enthusiasm for teaching science-related topics.

Using children's books for science is effective for teaching important and basic research skills, doing investigations, and engaging kids in problem-solving experiences, while building an appreciation for both science and literature. The following provide a handful of science-related topics and corresponding literature to use as read-alouds to open science units, to offer students choices for reading on their own, and to serve as academic time fillers for those students who tend to finish their work early.

Astronomy and Space

Aldrin, Buzz. ***Reaching for the Moon.***   ISBN-13: 9780060554477, 2008

This is a picture-book autobiography of astronaut Buzz Aldrin, recounting the events in his early years that led him to take part in the *Apollo* mission.

Lexile: 0860L   (Grades 1–5)   NF

Aston, Dianna Hutts. ***The Moon Over Star.***   ISBN-13: 9780803731073, 2008

A young narrator reflects on witnessing the first moon landing and the air of excitement and anticipation that surrounded it.

Lexile: N/A   (Grades K–4)   F

Bang, Molly. ***My Light.***   ISBN-13: 9780439489614, 2001

An exploration of light and energy is narrated by the sun.

Lexile: AD490L   (Grades 1–5)   NF

Brown, Don. ***One Giant Leap: The Story of Neil Armstrong.***   ISBN-13: 9780618152391, 2001

This is the story of the first moon landing.   Lexile: N/A   (Grades 1–3)   NF

Carle, Eric. ***Papa, Please Get the Moon for Me.***   ISBN-13: 9780887080265, 1991

A simple story about a girl who wants to play with the moon, and a father's efforts to make that possible.   Lexile: 0310L   (Grades K–3)   F

Coffelt, Nancy. ***Dogs in Space.***   ISBN-13: 9780152010041, 1996

Equipped with jet packs, five brightly colored dogs soar through the solar system, discovering facts about each of the planets they visit.   Lexile: N/A   (Grades K–2)   F

Cole, Joanna. ***The Magic School Bus: Lost in the Solar System.***

ISBN-13: 9780590414296, 1992

On a special field trip in the Magic School Bus, Ms. Frizzle's class goes into outer space and visits each planet in the solar system.   Lexile: 480L   (Grades 1–3)   F

Crelin, Bob. ***There Once Was a Sky Full of Stars.***   ISBN-13: 9781931559379, 2007

This book looks at a serious problem for astronomy: light pollution.

Lexile: N/A   (Grades K–6)   NF

Driscoll, Michael. ***A Child's Introduction to the Night Sky.***   ISBN-13: 9781579123666, 2004

The story of the stars, planets, and constellations and how to find them in the sky. This is an introduction to astronomy and stargazing.   Lexile: NC1120L   (Grades 4–6)   NF

Fletcher, Ralph. ***Hello, Harvest Moon.***   ISBN-13: 9780618164516, 2003

Poetic prose describes a full autumn moon and the magical effect it has on the earth, plants, animals, and people around it.   Lexile: N/A   (Grades Pre-K–3)   F

Florian, Douglas. ***Comets, Stars, the Moon and Mars.***   ISBN-13: 9780152053727, 2007

This is a collection of short poems, each devoted to different aspects of the cosmos (planets, a comet, etc.).   Lexile: NPL   (Grades 1–6)   NF

Gibbons, Gail. *The Moon Book.* ISBN-13: 9780823413645, 1998

This is an introduction to our planet's cosmic companion, the moon. It includes explanations about the moon's orbit, phases, impact on tides, and more.

Lexile: 740L   (Grades 1–4)   NF

Karas, G. Brian. *On Earth.* ISBN-13: 9780142410639, 2008

This book is an illumination of the earth's orbit, rotation, and tilt.

Lexile: 0660L   (Grades K–3)   NF

Leedy, Loreen. *Postcards from Pluto: A Tour of the Solar System.*

ISBN-13: 9780823420650, 2006

Dr. Quasar gives a group of children a tour of the solar system, describing each of the planets from Mercury to Pluto. The kids send postcards home whenever they stop. Each postcard contains details about the planet visited.   Lexile: 0490L   (Grades 1–3)   F

McNulty, Faith. *You Decide to Go to the Moon.* ISBN-13: 9780590483599, 2005

This is a travel manual for visiting the moon, including how to prepare, the journey en route, what to expect once there, and the final return home.

Lexile: AD690L   (Grades K–2)   F

Mitton, Jacqueline. *Zoo in the Sky: A Book of Animal Constellations.*

ISBN-13: 9780792259350, 2006

Each constellation is made of shiny metallic stars in the formation of the creature it is named after. Simple explanations accompany each illustration.

Lexile: 0750L   (Grades Pre-K–3)   NF

O'Brien, Patrick. *You Are the First Kid on Mars.* ISBN-13: 9780399246340, 2009

This is a step-by-step itinerary for those about to embark on a four-month trip to Mars.

Lexile: N/A   (Grades K–3)   F

Pollock, Penny. *When the Moon Is Full: A Lunar Year.* ISBN-13: 9780316713177, 2001

This book uses Native American names for the moon in 12 moving poems for each month's full moon.   Lexile: N/A   (Grades K–3)   NF

Rabe, Tish. *There's No Place Like Space: All About Our Solar System.*

ISBN-13: 9780679891154, 1999

Dr. Seuss's Cat in the Hat introduces Sally and Dick to the planets, stars, and moons in our solar system.   Lexile: N/A   (Grades Pre-K–3)   NF

Rey, H. A. *Find the Constellations.* ISBN 13: 9780547131788, 1976

This classic book has star charts, a guide to the constellations for kids, and details about seasons and the movement of the objects we see in the sky.   Lexile: N/A   (Grades 4–6)   NF

Rylant, Cynthia. *Long Night Moon.* ISBN-13: 9780689854262, 2004

Text and illustrations depict the varied seasonal full moons that change and assume personalities of their own throughout the year.   Lexile: N/A   (Grades Pre-K–1)   NF

Simon, Seymour. **Comets, Meteors, and Asteroids.**   ISBN-13: 9780688158439, 1998

Whether they appear as distant specks in an astronomer's telescope or shoot across the sky, comets, meteors, and asteroids have fascinated sky gazers throughout history.

Lexile: 1050L   (Grades 1–5)   NF

Simon, Seymour. **Destination: Space.**   ISBN-13: 9780060877231, 2006

This book explains new discoveries about the universe made possible by the Hubble Telescope.   Lexile: N/A   (Grades 1–5)   NF

Simon, Seymour. **Galaxies.**   ISBN-13: 9780688109929, 1991

This book identifies the nature, locations, movements, and different categories of galaxies and examines the Milky Way and other known examples.

Lexile: 1010L   (Grades 1–5)   NF

Simon, Seymour. **Stars.**   ISBN-13: 9780060890018, 2006

This book discusses the stars, their composition and characteristics, and includes actual photographs.   Lexile: 0830L   (Grades 1–5)   NF

Simon, Seymour. **The Sun.**   ISBN-13: 9780688092368, 1989

This is about the center of our solar system—our sun. It describes the nature of the sun, its origin, source of energy, layers, atmosphere, sunspots, and activity.

Lexile: N/A   (Grades K–3)   NF

Simon, Seymour. **The Universe.**   ISBN-13: 9780060877255, 2006

This book describes the expansion of the universe as a result of the Big Bang.

Lexile: 0980L   (Grades 1–5)   NF

Sweeney, Joan. **Me and My Place in Space.**   ISBN-13: 9780517885901, 1999

A child describes how the earth, sun, and planets are part of our solar system, which is just one small part of the universe.   Lexile: N/A   (Grades Pre-K–2)   NF

Chemical Reactions

Blakey, Nancy. **Lotions, Potions, and Slime: Mudpies and More!**

ISBN-13: 9781883672218, 1996

Every activity, craft, or recipe in this book includes a wet or gooey stage. This is a collection of creative activities involving science, art, and cooking.

Lexile: N/A   (Grades Pre-K–2)   NF

Daly, Kathleen. **The Good Humor Man.**   ISBN-13: 9780375832802, 2005

The Good Humor Man brings walnut whizzes and dairy dizzies while gathering friends together in this book.   Lexile: N/A   (Grades Pre-K–1)   F

Elder, Vanessa. *Disney's Flubber: My Story.*   ISBN-13: 9780786842001, 1997

A professor invents a goo that makes cars fly and he thinks it will make him a fortune.

Lexile: N/A   (Grades 2–5)   F

Erlback, Arlene. *Peanut Butter.*   ISBN-13: 9780822597094, 1995

This book describes how peanut butter is made, from the cultivation of peanuts through filling the jars.   Lexile: N/A   (Grades 2–5)   NF

Henkes, Kevin. *Wemberly's Ice-Cream Star.*   ISBN-13: 9780060504052, 2003

Wemberly has issues with her red, white, and blue ice-cream star. Fortunately all it takes is two bowls, two spoons, two napkins, and a little patience.   Lexile: N/A   (Grades Pre-K)   F

Kline, Suzy. *Horrible Harry and the Green Slime.*   ISBN-13: 9780590439435, 1989

Horrible Harry is never boring. Readers will follow the school activities of second-graders Harry and Doug as they participate in a secret mission to celebrate *Charlotte's Web*, learn how to make green slime, and role-play the dangers of smoking.

Lexile: 470L   (Grades 2–5)   F

Seuss, Dr. *Bartholomew and the Oobleck.*   ISBN-13: 9780394800752, 1976

Green oobleck was not what the king had in mind when he ordered something special from his royal magicians, but this story shows the steps of a cool chemical reaction when oobleck comes to fruition.   Lexile: 500L   (Grades K–4)   F

Wake, Susan. *Butter.*   ISBN-13: 9780876144275, 1990

This book includes details showing the differences between butter and margarine, cane and beet sugar, and varieties of rice.   Lexile: N/A   (Grades Pre-K–3)   NF

Dinosaurs and Fossils

Aliki. *Fossils Tell of Long Ago.*

ISBN-13: 9780064450935, 1990

This book explains how fossils are formed and what they tell us about the past.

Lexile: 480L   (Grades Pre-K–3)   NF

Allen, Judy. *Flip the Flaps: Dinosaurs.*   ISBN-13: 9780753464960, 2011

With their sharp teeth, massive size, and otherworldly shapes, dinosaurs are an endlessly fascinating topic for children. By starting with children's most common questions, this book's accessible approach lets them uncover all kinds of extraordinary facts about favorite topics like feeding and nesting, fighting, defense, and adaptation.

Lexile: N/A   (Grades K–2)   NF

Barrows, Annie. *Ivy and Bean Break the Fossil Record.*   ISBN-13: 9780811862509, 2007

World-record fever grips the second grade, and soon Ivy and Bean are trying to set their own record by becoming the youngest people to have ever discovered a dinosaur.

Lexile: 0520L   (Grades 1–5)   F

Berkowitz, Jacob. *Jurassic Poop: What Dinosaurs (and Others) Left Behind.*

ISBN-13: 9781553378679, 2006

The premise of this book for kids is that dinosaur doo-doo is actually a priceless artifact, full of information about how dinosaurs lived, what they ate, and more.

Lexile: N/A   (Grades 3–6)   NF

Florian, Douglas. *Dinothesaurus.*   ISBN-13: 9781416979784, 2009

This is a collection of poetry about iguanadons, plesiosaurs, brachiosaurs, and more! The Glossarysaurus helps separate the fact from the fiction.   Lexile: N/A   (Grades K–4)   NF

French, Vivian. *T. Rex.*   ISBN-13: 9780763631772, 2006

On a visit to the natural history museum, a boy and his grandfather discuss the life cycle of the T. Rex on display.   Lexile: AD640L   (Grades Pre-K–2)   F

Harcourt. *Fossils.*   ISBN-13: 9780153620799, 2006

Readers will learn all about fossils.   Lexile: N/A   (Grades 4–8)   NF

Harrison, Carol. *Dinosaurs Everywhere!*   ISBN-13: 9780590000895, 1998

This book discusses the probable structure and behavior of dinosaurs and describes such individual species as the *Tyrannosaurus*, *Maiasaura*, and *Seismosaurus*.

Lexile: AD750L   (Grades Pre-K–3)   NF

Jenkins, Steve. *Prehistoric Actual Size.*   ISBN-13: 9780618535781, 2005

This book introduces prehistoric creatures from tiny to gigantic including the ones where only a small portion of the enormous creature is visible on the page.

Lexile: IG1130L   (Grades Pre-K–5)   NF

MacLeod, Elizabeth. *What Did Dinosaurs Eat? And Other Things You Want to Know About Dinosaurs.*   ISBN-13: 9781553374602, 2002

Dinosaurs roamed the Earth millions of years ago, but they still fascinate us today. Questions remain: were they big, small, fast, or slow? Meat-eaters, plant-eaters—or both? By carefully studying fossils, scientists have been able to answer many interesting questions about the lives of these "terrible lizards."   Lexile: 0600L   (Grades Pre-K–3)   NF

Rohmann, Eric. *Time Flies.*   ISBN-13: 9780517885550, 1997

This wordless picture book is about a bird who flies into the open gallery of a natural history museum, then circles around and through the dinosaurs on display. Over the course of several pages, the dinosaurs begin to "come to life" and the background of the museum fades into a real, open-air prehistoric environment.   Lexile: N/A   (Grades Pre-K–5)   F

Zoehfeld, Kathleen. *Fossil Fever.*   ISBN-13: 9780307556233, 2010

Jeff's Uncle Roy runs a museum. That means he's always zooming off to strange places to find ruins and treasure. But Jeff has never gone along—until now. They're headed to the Sahara Desert to search for dinosaur fossils. And Jeff knows he'll find the bones of the biggest meat-eater ever.   Lexile: N/A   (Grades 1–4)   F

Human Body

Arnold, Tedd. *Parts.* ISBN-13: 9780140565331, 2000

A neurotic little boy panics when he notices distressing things about this body, like losing hair, peeling skin, belly-button lint, and "boogers." His parents come along and explain that the body's "lost parts" renew themselves.

Lexile: N/A (Grades K–2) F

Balestrino, Philip. *The Skeleton Inside You.*

ISBN-13: 9780064450874, 1989

This introduction to the human skeletal system explains how the 206 bones of the skeleton join together, how they grow, how they help make blood, what happens when they break, and how they mend. Lexile: 600L (Grades Pre-K–3) NF

Barner, Bob. *Dem Bones.* ISBN-13: 9780811808279, 1996

This is an exploration of the human skeletal system, using the well-known folk song "Dem Bones." Each page is devoted to a line of the song, with the featured bone highlighted in red and relevant information about that bone clearly explained.

Lexile: AD930L (Grades 2–4) F

Berger, Melvin. *Why I Sneeze, Shiver, Hiccup, and Yawn.* ISBN-13: 9780064451932

What child hasn't wondered why they sneeze when in a dusty room or yawn when they are tired or shiver when they are cold? Lexile: 480L (Grades K–2) NF

Cole, Joanna. *The Magic School Bus: Explores the Senses.* ISBN-13: 9780590446983, 2001

Assistant principal Mr. Wilde gets behind the wheel instead of Ms. Frizzle. Join the gang as they travel through the senses of various living beings—a police officer's eye, a dog's nose, a child's ear, and even Ms. Frizzle's mouth. Lexile: 490L (Grades 2–5) F

Cole, Joanna. *The Magic School Bus: Inside the Human Body.* ISBN-13: 9780590414272, 1990

The Magic School Bus takes Ms. Frizzle's class and shrinks down to explore the inside of a classmate who has just swallowed them. The bus travels into a blood vessel for a view of plasma and red and white blood cells. Students climb up bones, follow nerves to see how muscles work, and so on. Lexile: AD520L (Grades 1–4) F

Jenkins, Steve. *Bones: Skeletons and How They Work.* ISBN-13: 9780545046510, 2010

This book takes a look at the human skeletal system. It compares various human skeletal segments to those of other animals (e.g., the difference between a man's hand and a spider monkey's hand), showing the similarities and difference among skeletal structures of many living creatures. Lexile: N/A (Grades 3–6) NF

Macaulay, David. *The Way We Work: Getting to Know the Amazing Human Body.*

ISBN-13: 9780618233786, 2008

This book covers all the major functions and parts of the human body in stunning illustrations that are paired with detailed descriptions. Lexile: N/A (Grades 6–12) NF

Roy, Ron. *A to Z Mysteries: The School Skeleton.*   ISBN-13: 9780375813689, 2003

An entire school becomes involved in a mystery when Mr. Bones, the skeleton in the nurse's office, disappears.   Lexile: 500L   (Grades K–4)   F

Schoenberg, Jane, and Steven Schoenberg. *My Bodyworks: Songs About Your Bones, Muscles, Heart, and More!*   ISBN-13: 9781566565837, 2005

This picture book and 12-song CD teaches about the parts of the human body, from muscles and movement to how the senses work to why we pass gas.   Lexile: N/A   (Grades K–2)   NF

Seuling, Barbara. *From Head to Toe: The Amazing Human Body and How It Works.*

ISBN-13: 9780823416998, 2002

This book about the human body teaches how each body part performs its daily functions, from bones, muscles, and organs, to skin, hair, and nails.   Lexile: 810L   (Grades 2–4)   NF

Showers, Paul. *A Drop of Blood.*   ISBN-13: 9780060091101, 2004

A charming vampire and his sidekick teach all about blood and how vital it is to different bodily functions—healing, fueling the body, breathing.   Lexile: 480L   (Grades K–3)   F

Showers, Paul. *What Happens to a Hamburger?*   ISBN-13: 9780064451833, 2001

This title takes readers on a journey through the digestive system, from when food enters the mouth and moves down the gullet to what happens in the stomach and the small and large intestines. Along the way, readers learn what each organ does to transform the food they eat into fuel for their bodies, and what happens to food that their body can't use.

Lexile: 520L   (Grades K–2)   NF

Sweeney, Joan. *Me and My Amazing Body.*   ISBN-13: 9780375806230, 2000

A young narrator guides readers through a tour of the human body, including parts of the human body that can be seen and parts that cannot. She explains how different parts of her body work, such as her skin, brain, heart, stomach, bones, muscles, and so on.

Lexile: NC710L   (Grades Pre-K–2)   NF

Magnets, Batteries, and Electricity

Branley, Franklyn M. *What Makes a Magnet?*

ISBN-13: 9780064451482, 1996

This book explains the properties and behavior of magnets. Hands-on activities include making a magnet and a compass.

Lexile: 640L   (Grades Pre-K–4)   NF

Carmi, Rebecca. *Amazing Magnetism.*   ISBN-13: 9780439314329, 2002

This book takes you on a journey when Ms. Frizzle's class challenges Mr. Order's class to a science contest, where the topic of the contest is magnetism.   Lexile: 570L   (Grades K–3)   F

Flaherty, Michael. *Electricity and Batteries.*   ISBN-13: 9780761332565, 2004

This book provides an introduction to practical application and experimentation using batteries that can easily be made by the reader.   Lexile: N/A   (Grades K–4)   NF

Gardner, Robert. *Electricity and Magnetism Science Fair Projects: Using Batteries, Balloons, and Other Hair-Raising Stuff.*   ISBN-13: 9780766021273, 2004

This book introduces the secrets of circuits, batteries, and magnets and offers ideas for science fair projects.   Lexile: N/A   (Grades 5–12)   NF

Holderness, Jackie. *Why Does a Battery Make It Go?*   ISBN-13: 9780761318415, 2002

Learn from a variety of experiments how batteries can make things work.

Lexile: 580L   (Grades K–4)   NF

Lauw, Darlene, and Lim Cheng Puay. *Magnets.*   ISBN-13: 9780778706090, 2001

This book is about how to use magnets and what their different purposes are.

Lexile: 470L   (Grades 2–5)   NF

Rosinsky, Natalie M. *Magnets: Pulling Together, Pushing Apart.*

ISBN-13: 9781404800144, 2002

This book describes how magnets work and includes experiments that children can try, such as testing various objects in the room to find out which are attracted by magnets.

Lexile: 0780L   (Grades K–4)   NF

Schreiber, Anne. *Magnets.*   ISBN-13: 9780448431499, 2003

This introduces different kinds of magnets, how they work, and some of the ways in which they are used.   Lexile: 0760L   (Grades 1–3)   NF

Still, Darlene. *Electricity: Bulbs, Batteries, and Sparks.*   ISBN-13: 9781404802452, 2004

This book shows how your house is powered by electricity.

Lexile: 650L   (Grades 2–5)   NF

Stillinger, Doug. *Battery Science: Make Widgets That Work and Gadgets That Go.*

ISBN-13: 9781591742517, 2003

This book includes a Klutz alkaline battery, a buzzer, a propeller, a lightbulb, a motor, and other items for eight projects.   Lexile: N/A   (Grades Pre-K–3)   NF

Insects, Worms, and Butterflies

Arnosky, Jim. *Creep and Flutter: The Secret World of Insects and Spiders.*

ISBN-13: 9781402777660, 2012

This book brings out the beauty and the "yuck" factors of hundreds of insects and spiders.   Lexile: N/A   (Grades 1–5)   NF

Aston, Dianna Hutts. *A Butterfly Is Patient.*   ISBN-13: 9780811864794, 2011

From swallowtails and orange monarchs to the world's tiniest butterfly and the world's largest, a variety of butterflies are celebrated here in all of their beauty and wonder.

Lexile: AD1040L   (Grades K–3)   NF

Berger, Melvin. *Chirping Crickets.*   ISBN-13: 9780064451802, 1998

This book describes the physical characteristics, behavior, and life cycle of crickets while giving particular emphasis to how they chirp.   Lexile: 590   (Grades Pre-K–3)   NF

Fredericks, Anthony D. *On One Flower: Butterflies, Ticks and a Few More Icks.*

ISBN-13: 9781584690870, 2006

A goldenrod flower attracts many things. A butterfly sipping nectar, a ladybug snacking on aphids—and look out for the ambushbug.   Lexile: NPL   (Grades Pre-K–5)   NF

French, Vivian. *Yucky Worms.*   ISBN-13: 9780763658175, 2012

Readers will find out where worms live, see how they move, and understand why gardeners consider them friends with the help of this humorous and informative look at these little creatures.   Lexile: 0620L   (Grades K–3)   NF

Himmelman, John. *A Mealworm's Life.*   ISBN-13: 9780516272863, 2001

This book is great for the teacher raising mealworms as a class project.

Lexile: 580L   (Grades K–3)   NF

Kerz, Anna. *The Mealworm Diaries.*   ISBN-13: 9781551439822, 2009

Mealworms are small creatures that live in dark secret places. Jeremy is a bit like that when he leaves his home and moves to Toronto with his mother. Lots of things keep him from enjoying his new life, but when his mealworm project yields some surprising results, Jeremy is finally able to talk through his problems and gain compassion for others.

Lexile: 640L   (Grades 3–8)   F

Loewen, Nancy. *Garden Wigglers: Earthworms in Your Backyard.*

ISBN-13: 9781404817579, 2006

This book describes the physical characteristics, life cycle, and behavior of earthworms. It includes an anatomy diagram and activity.   Lexile: N/A   (Grades K–3)   NF

Markle, Sandra. *Insects.*   ISBN-13: 9781590788721, 2011

Here are 21 six-legged wonders from around the world, including the 22-inch-long giant stick insect of Borneo and North America's Western pygmy blue butterfly, with a wingspan of just a half inch.   Lexile: N/A   (Grades 1–3)   NF

Mason, Adrienne. *Mealworms: Raise Them, Watch Them, See Them Change.*

ISBN-13: 9781550745061, 2001

This book includes easy-to-follow experiments and examines such topics as the common characteristics of insects, metamorphosis, life cycles, habitats, and animals' responses to their environments.   Lexile: N/A   (Grades 2–5)   NF

Mortenson, Lori. *In the Trees, Honeybees.* ISBN-13: 9781584691143, 2009

This inside-the-hive view of a wild colony of honeybees offers close-up views of the queen, the cells, and even bee eggs. Lexile: AD650L (Grades K–5) NF

Nelson, Robin. *Worms.* ISBN-13: 9780761340645, 2009

This book provides a basic overview of the life cycle of a worm.

Lexile: 400L (Grades Pre-K–3) NF

Pfeffer, Wendy. *Wiggling Worms at Work.* ISBN-13: 9780064451994, 2003

This book explains how earthworms eat, move, and reproduce and how they help plants grow. Lexile: 0740L (Grades K–3) NF

Rockwell, Anne. *Bugs Are Insects.* ISBN-13: 9780064452038, 2001

This book introduces common backyard insects and explains the basic characteristics of these creatures. Lexile: AD590L (Grades K–3) NF

Rosinsky, Natalie. *Dirt: The Scoop on Soil.* ISBN-13: 9781404803312, 2006

Sand, silt, clay, and humus—what are they? Dig deep into this book about soil to discover the world beneath your feet. Lexile: N/A (Grades K–3) NF

Schaffer, Donna. *Mealworms.* ISBN-13: 9780736802093, 1999

Kids learn about each stage of the mealworm metamorphosis process, and they see pictures of the eggs, larva stage, pupa, and finally the adult mealworm, which is a beetle.

Lexile: 620L (Grades 2–4) NF

Simon, Seymour. *Butterflies.* ISBN-13: 9780061914935, 2011

Learn where to find butterflies and moths, how to observe them in nature, and how to plant your very own butterfly garden. Lexile: N/A (Grades 1–5) NF

Singer, Marilyn. *Caterpillars.* ISBN-13: 9780979745577, 2010

Caterpillars attract children to their shapes, colors, and locomotion styles, and they are impossible to resist. Lexile: NC930L (Grades 1–5) NF

Stewart, Melissa. *A Place for Butterflies.* ISBN-13: 9780439024846, 2007

Butterflies have lived on the earth for 140 million years. Find out what you can do to make sure there is always a place for butterflies. Lexile: N/A (Grades K–3) NF

Taylor, Barbara. *Insects.* ISBN-13: 9780753459331, 2006

This book presents information on the physical characteristics and habits of some insects, such as dragonflies and wasps, and some arachnids, such as snails and scorpions.

Lexile: N/A (Grades K–3) NF

Wallace, Karen. *Flip the Flaps: Creepy-Crawlies.* ISBN-13: 9780753467398, 2012

Pouncing spiders, industrious ants, buzzing bees, and beautiful butterflies scuttle, zoom and swoop within the pages of this book. Lexile: N/A (Grades K–3) NF

Weller, Alan. **Insects.** ISBN-13: 9780486997520, 2008

This book comes with a helpful CD-ROM filled with more than 200 images celebrating the diversity of insects with patterns, ornamental motifs, and natural renderings in styles ranging from 17th-century drawings to Art Nouveau motifs. Lexile: N/A (Grades 6–12) NF

Woodward, John. **Insects.** ISBN-13: 9781607100270, 2010

This book presents the thousands of tiny lenses found in a fly's compound eye, the feathery antennae that a moth uses to sniff out food, and many more microscopic marvels.

Lexile: N/A (Grades 2–8) NF

The Seasons

Berger, Samantha, and Pamela Chanko. **It's Spring!**

ISBN-13: 9780439442381, 2003

This simple rhyming story about spring is for the very youngest ages. Lexile: 310L (Grades K–2) F

Bernard, Robin. **A Tree for All Seasons.**

ISBN-13: 9780792266747, 2001

This book looks at a tree throughout the year to see how it changes with the seasons.

Lexile: 420L (Grades Pre-K–3) NF

Birnbaum, A. **Green Eyes.** ISBN-13: 9780375862014, 2011

An updated edition of the classic 1953 Caldecott Honor book on seasons, this title features a curious little kitten that ventures outside the safety of his red box to greet each new season and discover what makes them unique. Lexile: N/A (Grades Pre-K–3) F

Bruchac, Joseph. **Thirteen Moons on Turtle's Back: A Native American Year of Moons.**

ISBN-13: 9780698115842, 1997

This book celebrates the seasons of the year through poems from the legends of such Native American tribes as the Cherokee, Cree, and Sioux. Lexile: 0960L (Grades Pre-K–3) NF

Carr, Jan. **Splish, Splash, Spring.** ISBN-13: 9780823417544, 2002

Three children and a dog go out in the wet weather and go outside to enjoy spring. After raindrops, puddles, and the sun coming out, they take off their raincoats and fold up their umbrellas. They also find baby robins and help the mother birds dig up worms.

Lexile: N/A (Grades K–2) F

Gibbons, Gail. **The Reasons for Seasons.** ISBN-13: 9780823412389, 1996

This book covers solstices, equinoxes, the earth's tilt and orbit . . . all the basics.

Lexile: AD620L (Grades Pre-K–3) NF

Locker, Thomas. *Sky Tree: Seeing Science Through Art.*   ISBN-13: 9780064437509, 2001

A tree stands on a hill by a river, and the glorious illustrations in this book show how changeable the tree can be depending on the weather and the season.

Lexile: N/A   (Grades Pre-K–3)   NF

Schutte, Sarah L. *Let's Look at Spring.*   ISBN-13: 9780736867078, 2007

How do we know it's spring? The sun shines and rain falls. Baby animals are born, and flowers bloom.

Lexile: 180L   (Grades Pre-K–2)   NF

Sidman, Joyce. *Red Sings from Treetops: A Year in Colors.*   ISBN-13: 9780547562131, 2009

This collection of poems about seasons takes a unique approach, exploring each season in relation to the colors and senses that the seasons conjure up in the author's mind (i.e., old leaves and crushed berries smell "purple").

Lexile: N/A   (Grades Pre-K–3)   NF

Zolotow, Charlotte. *When the Wind Stops.*   ISBN-13: 9780064434720, 1997

A young boy asks his mother a series of questions about wind, clouds, seasons, and other parts of the cycle of life.

Lexile: AD490L   (Grades Pre-K–3)   F

Seeds and Plants

Anthony, Joseph. *The Dandelion Seed.*   ISBN-13: 9781883220679, 1997

A surprisingly touching story of a dandelion seed that won't let go because it's afraid of the world. Soon the winds blow it free, and it learns that the world is full of challenge, wonder, and beauty. Eventually, it lands, grows, casts its own seeds, and eventually finds itself reassuring one scared little seed that the sun, the wind, and the rain will take care of it.

Lexile: AD490L   (Grades K–4)   F

Anthony, Joseph. *In a Nutshell.*   ISBN-13: 9781883220983, 1999

This is a moving story about the stages of life and the circle of life. An acorn drops from a great oak and grows. Animals nibble at it and a fire threatens it, but the little acorn overcomes many challenges and eventually grows tall enough to tower over the forest and observe the changing landscape below.

Lexile: AD540L   (Grades K–4)   F

Aston, Dianna Hutts. *A Seed Is Sleepy.*   ISBN-13: 9780811855204, 2007

Each page is devoted to a specific quality of the seed, with a short phrase like "A seed is sleepy," a few paragraphs of text explaining why this is the case, and detailed sketches.

Lexile: AD750L   (Grades 1–4)   NF

Bang, Molly, and Penny Chisholm. *Living Sunlight: How Plants Bring the Earth to Life.*

ISBN-13: 9780545044226, 2009

This title tackles photosynthesis. Narrated by the sun, the text explains what is happening at a molecular level and why it matters on a broad scale.

Lexile: AD610L   (Grades 2–5)   NF

Bash, Barbara. *Ancient Ones: The World of the Old Growth Douglas Fir.*

ISBN-13: 9781578050819, 2002

This is a look at the world of the old-growth Douglas fir forest habitat of the Pacific Northwest. It portrays a vibrant forest full of life that is interconnected, living in niches within the forest, and part of the overall cycle of decay and rejuvenation. Double-page spreads feature animals in various parts of the forest, from the forest floor to high in the canopy, from inside a fallen log to deep beneath the tree bark. Lexile: N/A (Grades 2–6) NF

Bash, Barbara. *Tree of Life: The World of the African Baobab.* ISBN-13: 9780316083225, 1994

This book gives a look at the stately and very unique African baobab tree, which can grow to more than 1,000 years old, 60 feet tall, and 40 feet wide, and looks as if it was planted upside down. This title depicts not only the stages of growth and other scientific details about the tree, but also its interactions with the surrounding environment.

Lexile: AD1040L (Grades 2–6) NF

Batten, Mary. *Hungry Plants.* ISBN-13: 9780375825330, 2004

Readers learn all about carnivorous plants, particularly the Venus flytrap, the sundew, the pitcher plant, and the bladderwort (i.e., the structure of the plant, how it captures insects, etc.). Lexile: N/A (Grades 4–8) NF

Bulla, Clyde Robert. *A Tree Is a Plant.* ISBN-13: 9780064451963, 2001

Through the example of an apple tree, readers learn how a tree grows, how it is nourished from the sun and water, how water travels up from the root system, and so on.

Lexile: AD290L (Grades Pre-K–3) NF

Burnie, David. *Eyewitness Plant.* ISBN-13: 9780756660352, 2011

Sharp, close-up photographs of leaves, flowers, seeds, fruits, and more help show the basics of plant anatomy and growth. This title covers a wide range of plant topics, such as how flowers attract insects and defend themselves, how a plant can climb, and why some plants have no seeds. Lexile: N/A (Grades 4–7) NF

Carle, Eric. *The Tiny Seed.* ISBN-13: 9780689842443, 2001

This book gives the description of a flowering plant's life cycle through the seasons.

Lexile: 440L (Grades Pre-K–2) NF

Cole, Henry. *Jack's Garden.* ISBN-13: 9780688152833, 2001

This title follows the growth of a boy's backyard flower garden.

Lexile: N/A (Grades Pre-K–2) F

Cole, Joanna. *The Magic School Bus Plants Seeds.* ISBN-13: 9780590222969, 1995

All aboard the Magic School Bus, as Ms. Frizzle's class shrinks down and explores the inside of a flower and learns about the basic parts of a plant, how plants grow, and more.

Lexile: 420L (Grades K–2) F

Crum, Shutta. *Who Took My Hairy Toe?*   ISBN-13: 9780807559727, 2001

Old Tar Pockets was a greedy old man who took things that weren't his. One Halloween he dug up a huge hairy toe, but later that night something big and scary came in search of its missing toe.   Lexile: 550L   (Grades K–4)   F

Ehlert, Lois. *Red Leaf, Yellow Leaf.*   ISBN-13: 9780547328584, 2010

A young child observes the life cycle of a maple tree, from a fallen seed that sprouts in the woods to being transplanted and sold at a nursery to being replanted and cherished in a new home.   Lexile: AD680L   (Grades K–3)   F

Florian, Douglas. *Poetrees.*   ISBN-13: 9781416986720, 2010

A collection of 18 poems and illustrations celebrate all that is wonderful about trees.

Lexile: N/A   (Grades 2–6)   NF

Hiscock, Bruce. *The Big Tree.*   ISBN-13: 9780689315985, 1991

This title illustrates the long lifespan of trees and illuminates their general stages of growth, all told through the story of one maple tree from its beginnings as a seed that sprouted during the American Revolutionary War to the towering tree that provides shade to picnickers during a modern Fourth of July celebration.   Lexile: AD730L   (Grades 1–4)   NF

Jordan, Helene. *How a Seed Grows.*   ISBN-13: 9780064451079, 1992

This book describes the simple steps for turning a packet of seeds into your own garden.

Lexile: AD400L   (Grades Pre-K–1)   NF

Kudlinski, Kathleen V. *What Do Roots Do?*   ISBN-13: 9781559719803, 2007

The book uses a question-and-answer format and covers nine different types of plants.

Lexile: N/A   (Grades K–3)   NF

Locker, Thomas. *Sky Tree: Seeing Science Through Art.*   ISBN-13: 9780064437509, 2001

This book depicts a single tree as it transforms with the arrival of each new season.

Lexile: 490L   (Grades Pre-K–3)   NF

Lyons, Dana. *The Tree.*   ISBN-13: 9780970190710, 2002

An ancient Douglas fir shares the experiences of its life and a plea for conservation. The book reminds the reader of the connections between all living things on Earth.

Lexile: N/A   (Grades K–3)   F

Richards, Jean. *A Fruit Is a Suitcase for Seeds.*   ISBN-13: 9780822559917, 2006

After a few introductory pages about seeds, each double-page is devoted to a different type of seed, like fruits with pits (avocado, peaches), fruits with seeds on the outside (strawberries), fruits with a clearly visible seed inside (apples), fruits with seeds that are hard to see (kiwi), and vegetables that are actually fruits (tomatoes).

Lexile: N/A   (Grades Pre-K–2)   NF

Rockwell, Anne. ***One Bean.*** ISBN-13: 9780802775726, 1999

This is a book about planting and observation, and it discusses a plant's growth cycle, step-by-step from planting the bean in a paper cup to the end results. It describes what happens to a bean as it is soaked, planted, watered, repotted, and then produces pods with more beans inside. Lexile: 510L (Grades Pre-K–1) NF

Rockwell, Thomas. ***How to Eat Fried Worms.*** ISBN-13: 9780440421856, 1977

Two boys set out to show that eating 15 worms in 15 days can make delicious meals in this hilarious novel that is great for reading aloud. Lexile: 0650L (Grades 2–5) F

Schaefer, Lola M. ***Pick, Pull, Snap! Where Once a Flower Bloomed.***

ISBN-13: 9780688178345, 2003

This title provides a basic introduction to plant growth (flowering, pollination, maturation) in clear explanations; rhythmic, poetic text; and stunning photo-realistic illustrations.

Lexile: 1040L (Grades K–3) NF

Swanson, Susan. ***To Be Like the Sun.*** ISBN-13: 9780152057961, 2008

A young girl plants a sunflower seed and then eagerly watches it grow through the different seasons. Lexile: N/A (Grades Pre-K–1) F

Worth, Bonnie. ***Oh Say Can You Seed? All About Flowering Plants.***

ISBN-13: 9780375810954, 2001

The Cat in the Hat examines the parts of plants, seeds, and flowers; basic photosynthesis and pollination; and seed dispersal. Lexile: AD530L (Grades K–3) NF

Volcanoes and Earthquakes

Bauer, Marion Dane. ***Earthquake!***

ISBN-13: 9781416925514, 2009

What causes an earthquake is deep beneath the earth's surface. This book will help you find out what causes this destructive natural disaster.

Lexile: N/A (Grades Pre-K–1) NF

Bauer, Marion Dane. ***Volcano!*** ISBN-13: 9781416925491, 2008

The earth as we know it was partly created by volcanoes. Many are still active today. Learn how volcanoes form and what is going on when they erupt.

Lexile: N/A (Grades Pre-K–1) NF

Branley, Franklyn M. ***Earthquakes.*** ISBN-13: 9780064451888, 2005

This book discusses why earthquakes happen, what their sometimes devastating effects can be, where the danger zones are, and what measures people can take to safeguard themselves.

Lexile: 0690L (Grades Pre-K–3) NF

Branley, Franklyn M. *Volcanoes.* ISBN-13: 9780060280116, 2008

When Mount Vesuvius blew up in AD 79, ash, cinders, and stones buried a great city below the mountain. Volcanoes can be dramatic. There are thousands of them all over the earth. This book explores the subject of volcanoes, how they form and erupt, where they are found, and when you can expect a volcano to blow its top.   Lexile: 0590L   (Grades Pre-K–3)   NF

Gonzales, Doreen. *Earthquakes.* ISBN-13: 9781448874422, 2012

This book talks about why earthquakes happen, what the effects can be, where the danger zones are, and what people can do to take precautions.   Lexile: N/A   (Grades 3–6)   NF

Hamilton, James. *Volcano: Nature and Culture.* ISBN-13: 9781861899170, 2012

This book explores the cultural history generated by the violence and terrifying beauty of volcanoes. The author describes the reverberations of early eruptions of Vesuvius and Etna in Greek and Roman myth. He also examines the depiction of volcanoes in art—from the earliest known wall painting of an erupting volcano in 6200 BCE to the distinctive colors of Andy Warhol and Michael Sandle's exploding mountains.

Lexile: N/A   (Grades 5–12)   NF

Herman, Gail. *The Magic School Bus Blows Its Top.* ISBN-13: 9780590508353, 1996

Ms. Frizzle's class goes beneath the ocean's surface to explore an underwater volcano.

Lexile: 540L   (Grades K–3)   F

Moores, Eldridge M. *Volcanoes & Earthquakes.* ISBN-13: 9780760750735, 2003

This reference book for children has atmospheric illustrations, photographs, and descriptions to encourage readers to discover for themselves a part of the world's exciting story. The book is meant to engage through imagination and to stimulate curiosity.

Lexile: N/A   (Grades 3–6)   NF

Nirgiotis, Nicholas. *Volcanoes: Mountains That Blow Their Tops.*

ISBN-13: 9780448411439, 1996

Find out how volcanoes erupt, what lava is, and what happens when it cools, as well as where the world's biggest volcanoes are located.   Lexile: 0310L   (Grades 2–5)   NF

Osborne, Mary Pope. *Earthquake in the Early Morning.* ISBN-13: 9780679890706, 2001

The magic tree house takes Jack and Annie to San Francisco in 1906, in time for them to experience one of the biggest earthquakes the United States had ever known.

Lexile: 350L   (Grades 1–3)   F

Prager, Ellen J. *Earthquakes!* ISBN-13: 9781426300905, 2007

You will find out what causes earthquakes, where they happen most, and what you should do if you feel the earth shake.   Lexile: N/A   (Grades K–3)   NF

Prager, Ellen J. *Volcano!* ISBN-13: 9781426300912, 2007

How do volcanoes erupt? What is lava, and what happens when it cools? Where are the world's biggest volcanoes?   Lexile: N/A   (Grades K–3)   NF

Simon, Seymour. *Earthquakes.*   ISBN-13: 9780060877156, 2006

This book examines the phenomenon of earthquakes, describing how and where they occur, how they can be predicted, and how much damage they can inflict.

Lexile: 1010L   (Grades K–4)   NF

Simon, Seymour. *Volcanoes.*   ISBN-13: 9780060877170, 2006

This book explains, in simple terms, the characteristics of volcanoes and describes some famous eruptions and their aftermath.   Lexile: 0880L   (Grades K–4)   NF

Tarshis, Lauren. *I Survived the San Francisco Earthquake, 1906.*

ISBN-13: 9780545206990, 2012

Early one spring morning, everything changes and Leo's world is literally shaken as he finds himself stranded in the middle of San Francisco while it crumbles and burns to the ground.

Lexile: 610L   (Grades 2–5)   F

Walker, Sally M. *Earthquakes.*   ISBN-13: 9780822567356, 2007

This book describes the forces that cause earthquakes; famous earthquakes in history; the possible environmental effects, such as global warming; and earthquake predictions and precautions.   Lexile: 640L   (Grades 3–6)   NF

Wood, Lily. *Volcanoes.*   ISBN-13: 9780439295857, 2001

This book on volcanoes offers a look at the past and present, how and why they erupt, and the scientists that study them.   Lexile: N/A   (Grades Pre-K–3)   NF

Woods, Michael. *Earthquakes.*   ISBN-13: 9780822547112, 2006

This book looks at earthquakes, describing how and where they occur, how they can be predicted, and how much damage they can impose.   Lexile: N/A   (Grades 2–6)   NF

Weather and Climate

Beard, Darleen Bailey. *Twister.*

ISBN-13: 9780374480141, 2003

Two children are playing outside when Mama sees a storm brewing and rushes them to the safety of the storm shelter. A little extra sus-

pense is added when Mama must leave the shelter to help an elderly neighbor, and the two children must ride out the twister alone.   Lexile: AD300L   (Grades Pre-K–3)   F

Branley, Franklyn M. *Flash, Crash, Rumble, and Roll.*   ISBN-13: 9780064451796, 1999

This introduction to thunderstorms turns a scary experience into something less mysterious and more understandable.   Lexile: 500L   (Grades Pre-K–4)   NF

Crum, Shutta. *Thunder-Boomer!*   ISBN-13: 9780618618651, 2009

A big storm rolls in and cools everything down on a hot summer day on the farm.

Lexile: AD490L   (Grades K–2)   F

Dorros, Arthur. *Feel the Wind.* ISBN-13: 9780064450959, 1990

This book answers questions about the wind. Readers learn how the wind impacts weather, what causes wind, and even how we can use it. Lexile: AD600L (Grades K–2) NF

Hesse, Karen. *Come on, Rain!* ISBN-13: 9780590331258, 1999

A young girl pleads with the sky for rain to end the sweltering heat of summer. Her whole city neighborhood is waiting and melting! Then when clouds roll in and the rain pours down, everyone dances for joy and readers can't help but feel the refreshment vicariously and remember the last time they experienced a lovely summer rainstorm.

Lexile: AD780L (Grades Pre-K–3) F

Kaner, Etta. *Exploring the Elements Series.*

Children share what they like about snow, sun, wind, or rain, plus ask related questions that are then answered in fold-outs on the right-hand pages.

Who Likes the Rain?	ISBN-13: 9781553378419, 2007
Who Likes the Snow?	ISBN-13: 9781553378426, 2006
Who Likes the Sun?	ISBN-13: 9781553378402, 2007
Who Likes the Wind?	ISBN-13: 9781553378396, 2006

Lexile: N/A (Grades Pre-K–2) NF

Rabe, Tish. *Oh Say Can You Say, What's the Weather Today? All About Weather.*

ISBN-13: 9780375822766, 2004

Take a hot-air balloon ride with Cat in the Hat and friends, and experience various types of weather like rain, snow, thunder, even tornadoes. Lexile: N/A (Grades Pre-K–2) NF

Singer, Marilyn. *On the Same Day in March: A Tour of the World's Weather.*

ISBN-13: 9780064435284, 2001

Readers will check out what the weather is like on March 17 in many places throughout the world. Readers learn that even though it's cold in the arctic on March 17, it's sunny on the Caribbean island of Barbados, windy in Australia, and so on. The weather in certain weather zones, including what residents wear, eat, and do each day, are shared.

Lexile: AD540L (Grades K–3) NF

Wiesner, David. *Hurricane.* ISBN-13: 9780395629741, 1992

In the first half of the book, a family is warm in their home, waiting out a large hurricane. Then the next day, the two brothers find that their big elm tree has fallen in the storm, and with the help of their imaginations, they are whisked off on a series of exotic adventures.

Lexile: AD460L (Grades K–2) F

15

Literature for Holidays

Children's literature is a powerful medium. Through fictional stories and nonfiction texts we can explore controversial issues, a diversity of cultures, and a multitude of historical perspectives. Because of the critical role that children's literature plays in the classroom and in young people's lives, it's imperative that titles in your classroom and school libraries are selected with foresight and care. You will always want to review children's and young adult books that focus on history, culture, or other curricular areas as they relate to your grade level and standards.

Since many of the major holidays occur during the school year, it is important not to skip over them. However, in choosing books for your library for these topics, it is also important that teachers veer away from choosing only the "cutesy" kinds of books that offer activities for the holidays. Rather, focus more on the historical and cultural context of the holidays, while also incorporating the fun and artistic lessons. This is also important, given that teachers must be cognizant of families who do not want their children to participate in some of the holiday activities often celebrated at schools. The books in this chapter offer readers an opportunity to learn about the background of holidays that are usually recognized in schools.

Martin Luther King Day

Bader, Bonnie. *Who Was Martin Luther King, Jr.?*

ISBN-13: 9780756989354, 2008

The famous civil rights leader Dr. Martin Luther King, Jr., spoke out against racial and economic injustice until his death from an assassin's bullet in 1968.

Lexile: 0750L   (Grades 3–6)   NF

Bray, Rosemary L. *Martin Luther King.*   ISBN-13: 9780688152192, 1996

This introduction to the life of King starts with his early years in the American South, his exposure to segregation and racism, his schooling, and his family life and then discusses his civil rights experiences.   Lexile: 890L   (Grades K–5)   NF

Deutsch, Stacia. *King's Courage.*   ISBN-13: 9781416912699, 2005

It's another exciting Monday for Abigail, Zack, Jacob, and Bo—they are going to jump back to the past to meet Dr. Martin Luther King, Jr.! The kids need to convince Dr. King not to get discouraged and to lead one of his famous voting rights marches.

Lexile: 620L   (Grades 2–5)   F

Farris, Christine King. *My Brother Martin.*   ISBN-13: 9780689843884, 2002

Martin Luther King, Jr., embarks on a journey that would change the course of American history.   Lexile: 970L   (Grades K–4)   NF

Marzollo, Jean. *Happy Birthday, Martin Luther King.*   ISBN-13: 9780439782241, 2006

This is an introduction to a great civil rights leader.   Lexile: 800L   (Grades K–3)   NF

McNamara, Margaret. *Martin Luther King Jr. Day.*   ISBN-13: 9781416934943, 2007

When Mrs. Conner's class learns about a great man, they discover their own dreams and hopes for a better world.   Lexile: 600L   (Grades Pre-K–2)   F

McWhorter, Diane. *A Dream of Freedom.*   ISBN-13: 9780439576789, 2004

This book focuses on the significant events that occurred between 1954 (the year of *Brown vs. the Board of Education*) and 1968 (the year that Dr. King was assassinated).

Lexile: 1220L   (Grades 4–8)   NF

Medearis, Angela Shelf. *Singing for Dr. King.*   ISBN-13: 9780439568555, 2004

This story follows third-grader Sheyann Webb and her friend Rachel West in 1965 as they help change America by singing and marching for civil rights with Dr. Martin Luther King, Jr.   Lexile: 660L   (Grades K–4)   F

Moore, Johnny Ray. *The Story of Martin Luther King Jr.*   ISBN-13: 9780824941444, 2001

This book tells the story of Dr. King's life.   Lexile: N/A   (Grades Pre-K–1)   NF

Rappaport, Doreen. *Martin's Big Words: The Life of Dr. Martin Luther King, Jr.*

ISBN-13: 9781423106357, 2001

This picture book weaves the words of Dr. King into a narrative to tell the story of his life.

Lexile: N/A (Grades K–6) NF

Ringgold, Faith. *My Dream of Martin Luther King.*

ISBN-13: 9780517885772, 1998

The author recounts the life of Martin Luther King, Jr., in the form of her own dream.

Lexile: N/A (Grades 1–3) NF

Chinese/Lunar New Year

Bouchard, David. *The Dragon New Year: A Chinese Legend.* ISBN-13: 9781561452101, 1999

On Chinese New Year's eve a little girl can't sleep because of all the noise from the fireworks. Her grandmother comforts her by telling her the story of how the dragon became a central figure in Chinese culture, and the young girl finally falls asleep amid all the noise.

Lexile: AD540L (Grades K–3) F

Chang, Monica. *Story of the Chinese Zodiac.* ISBN-13: 9789573221494, 1994

This is a humorous version of how the 12 animals of the zodiac were chosen.

Lexile: N/A (Grades 4–8) F

Chinn, Karen. *Sam and the Lucky Money.* ISBN-13: 9781880000533, 1997

This is a story with a socially conscious message that helps children realize the value of all that they have. Sam is excited to receive his red envelopes of money for Chinese New Year, until he goes to Chinatown with his mother to spend it and realizes he can't buy very much with four dollars. Then he meets a homeless Chinese man with no shoes in the middle of winter, and he gives away his red envelopes so that the man can at least buy some socks.

Lexile: AD660L (Grades K–2) F

Demi. *Happy, Happy Chinese New Year!* ISBN-13: 9780375826429, 2003

In this book, the reader learns about various traditional activities for celebrating the Chinese New Year.

Lexile: N/A (Grades Pre-K–2) NF

Holub, Joan. *Dragon Dance: A Chinese New Year.* ISBN-13: 9780142400005, 2003

In this tale, readers will discover that there are so many fun things to do on Chinese New Year, such as shopping at the outdoor market for fresh flowers, eating New Year's dinner with the whole family, and receiving red envelopes before watching the Chinese New Year's parade.

Lexile: N/A (Grades Pre-K–2) NF

Hoyt-Goldsmith, Diane. *Celebrating Chinese New Year.* ISBN-13: 9780823413935, 1999

This story depicts a San Francisco boy and his family preparing for and enjoying their celebration of the Chinese New Year.

Lexile: 940L (Grades K–3) F

Lin, Grace. *Dim Sum for Everyone.* ISBN-13: 9780440417705, 2003

A child describes the various little dishes of dim sum that she and her family enjoy on a visit to a restaurant in Chinatown. Lexile: N/A (Grades Pre-K–2) F

Lin, Grace. *Fortune Cookie Fortunes.* ISBN-13: 9780440421924, 2006

After a young Chinese American girl opens fortune cookies with her family, she notices that the fortunes seem to come true. Lexile: N/A (Grades Pre-K–2) F

Rattigan, Jama Kim. *Dumpling Soup.* ISBN-13: 9780316730471, 1998

A young girl, Marisa, gets to help make dumplings to celebrate the New Year, but she worries if anyone will eat her funny-looking dumplings. Lexile: 500L (Grades K–3) F

Simonds, Nina. *Moonbeams, Dumplings, and Dragon Boats.* ISBN-13: 9780152019839, 2002

This book presents background information, related tales, and activities for celebrating five Chinese festivals—Chinese New Year, the Lantern Festival, Qing Ming, the Dragon Boat Festival, and the Moon Festival. Lexile: N/A (Grades 3–6) NF

Vaughan, Marcia K. *The Dancing Dragon.* ISBN-13: 9781572551343, 1996

This book tells the story, in rhyme, of preparing for Chinese New Year and attending the parade in Chinatown. Lexile: NC590L (Grades K–3) F

Waters, Kate. *Lion Dancer.* ISBN-13: 9780590430470, 1990

Six-year-old Ernie Wan celebrates his first Lion Dance on the streets of New York, and readers will also learn about other Chinese traditions. Lexile: 540L (Grades K–3) F

Wong, Janet S. *This Next New Year.* ISBN-13: 9780374355036, 2000

A family prepares to celebrate the Lunar New Year and looks forward to the good luck they hope it will bring. Lexile: N/A (Grades Pre-K–3) F

Yep, Laurence. *When the Circus Came to Town.* ISBN-13: 9780064409650, 2004

An Asian cook and a Chinese New Year celebration help a 10-year-old girl regain her confidence after smallpox scars her face. Lexile: 530L (Grades K–4) F

Groundhog Day

Arno, Iris Hiskey. *The Secret of the First One Up.*
ISBN-13: 9781559718677, 2003

After a long winter's sleep, a young groundhog named Lila wakes up before anyone else in her family, goes outside, and learns about her important role in predicting the arrival of spring. Lexile: 540L (Grades K–3) F

Cuyler, Margery. *Groundhog Stays Up Late.* ISBN-13: 9780802797322, 2007

Groundhog refuses to hibernate, even though his friends warn that he'll be hungry, cold, and lonely. He has fun running and playing in the snow, until he realizes that without anyone else around to play with, he really does get hungry, cold, and lonely. Then he has a brilliant idea! He'll announce an early spring. Lexile: 0570L (Grades Pre-K–3) F

Fleming, Denise. *Time to Sleep.*   ISBN-13: 9780805067675, 2001

When Bear notices that winter is nearly here, he hurries to tell Snail, after which each animal tells another until finally the already sleeping Bear is awakened in his den with the news.   Lexile: AD310L   (Grades Pre-K–3)   F

Freeman, Don. *Gregory's Shadow.*   ISBN-13: 9780142301968, 2003

Gregory Groundhog and his shadow look for each other after they become separated from one another just before their annual appearance on Groundhog Day.

Lexile: 0180L   (Grades Pre-K–1)   F

Hill, Susanna Leonard. *Punxsutawney Phyllis.*   ISBN-13: 9780823420407, 2006

Phyllis, a brightly clad groundhog, loves to be outdoors in all types of weather. Her uncle is Punxsutawney Phil, and she dreams of one day taking over his job, even though everyone tells her that she can't because she is a girl.   Lexile: N/A   (Grades K–3)   F

Korman, Susan. *Wake Up, Groundhog!*   ISBN-13: 9780307988485, 1998

Anxious to know if spring will soon be sprung, the friends of Gregory Groundhog arrive one by one to wake him from his burrow on Groundhog Day, with very surprising results.

Lexile: N/A   (Grades K–3)   F

Koscielniak, Bruce. *Geoffrey Groundhog Predicts the Weather.*

ISBN-13: 9780395883983, 1998

When Geoffrey Groundhog pops out of his hole to predict the weather, he is blinded by television cameras and lights and is unable to see if he has a shadow. No one in town knows how to proceed, so Geoffrey needs help fast.   Lexile: 550L   (Grades Pre-K–2)   F

Kroll, Steven. *It's Groundhog Day.*   ISBN-13: 9780590446693, 1991

Worried that an early spring will ruin his ski lodge business, Roland Raccoon takes drastic steps to prevent Godfrey Groundhog from looking for his shadow on Groundhog Day.

Lexile: 460L   (Grades Pre-K–2)   F

Levine, Abby. *Gretchen Groundhog, It's Your Day!*   ISBN-13: 9780807530597, 1998

When she has to take over the job of appearing in Piccadilly on Groundhog Day to look for her shadow, Gretchen Groundhog is worried and nervous and threatens not to come out.

Lexile: 0380L   (Grades K–3)   F

McMullan, Kate. *Fluffy Meets the Groundhog.*   ISBN-13: 9780439206723, 2001

Groundhog Dog inspires the class to celebrate Groundpig Day with their guinea pig Fluffy, and Fluffy gets to help an unhappy groundhog.   Lexile: 150L   (Grades Pre-K–1)   F

McNamara, Margaret. *Groundhog Day.*   ISBN-13: 9781416905073, 2005

It's Groundhog Day in Mrs. Connor's class, but instead of watching a real groundhog, the first graders wait to see if Chester the hamster will see his shadow.

Lexile: 430L   (Grades Pre-K–1)   F

Miller, Pat. ***Substitute Groundhog.***　　　　ISBN-13: 9780807576441, 2010

It's almost Groundhog Day, but Groundhog is not feeling well. Dr. Owl diagnoses him with the flu and orders two days of bed rest. Then Groundhog has an idea: he can hire a substitute. Maybe Squirrel can be the substitute, or Eagle, or Bear.　　Lexile: N/A　(Grades K–3)　F

Pickford, Susan T. ***It's Up to You, Griffin!***　　　　ISBN-13: 9780870334467, 1993

Delighted when Mother Nature asks him to help her by announcing the arrival of spring, Griffin the groundhog overcomes his fears and accepts this great responsibility.

Lexile: N/A　(Grades Pre-K–1)　F

Swallow, Pamela Curtis. ***Groundhog Gets a Say.***　　　　ISBN-13: 9780142408964, 2007

Groundhog has decided it's time to tell the world the Hog truth. With the help of a few of his fans, Groundhog is ready to tell everything about himself, from how loud he can whistle (loud), to how fast he can run (not fast), to how many things he uses his teeth for (a lot).

Lexile: N/A　(Grades Pre-K–3)　F

Valentine's Day

Giff, Patricia Reilly. ***Valentine Star.***　　ISBN-13: 9780307548658, 2009

Valentine's Day approaches and her class gets busy making cards, but Emily is worried about her fight with Sherri, who tells her, "You'll be sorry. . . ."　　Lexile: N/A　(Grades Pre-K–2)　F

Landau, Elaine. ***Valentine's Day: Candy, Love and Hearts.***

ISBN-13: 9780766017795, 2002

Children love the Valentine's Day holiday and will learn the historical background of this holiday. The tradition of cards, how we celebrate the holiday in our country, and unusual weddings that have occurred on the holiday are shared in this book.

Lexile: N/A　(Grades Pre-K–2)　NF

Maitland, Barbara. ***The Bookstore Valentine.***　　　　ISBN-13: 9780756912055, 2002

With Valentine's Day coming, Mr. Brown's bookstore is so busy that he hires Miss Button for the job. Mr. Brown and Miss Button begin to like one another, but they're both too shy to say so.　　　　　　　　　　Lexile: N/A　(Grades K–2)　F

Marney, Dean. ***How to Drive Your Family Crazy . . . on Valentine's Day.***

ISBN-13: 9780439158497, 2001

Lizzie, Scott, Sybil, and their teacher are all sucked into the class Valentine Box—and swept to another world!　　　　　　Lexile: N/A　(Grades Pre-K–1)　F

O'Connor, Jane. ***Fancy Nancy Heart to Heart.***　　　　ISBN-13: 9780061235962, 2009

It's Valentine's Day and Fancy Nancy has a mystery on her hands: Who sent her the extra special Valentine? Join Nancy as she follows the clues and solves the mystery.

Lexile: AD360L　(Grades Pre-K–2)　F

Park, Barbara. *Junie B. Jones and the Mushy Gushy Valentime* (Junie B. Jones Series #14).

ISBN-13: 9780307754806, 2010

On February 14, "Valentime's" Day, as Junie B. calls it, she can't wait to see all the valentimes she'll get. But she never expected a big, mushy card from a secret admirer!

Lexile: N/A   (Grades 1–3)   F

Pearson, Susan. *Slugs in Love.*

ISBN-13: 9780761462484, 2012

Shy slug Marylou uses her slime trail to write love poems to Herbie the slug, who responds with a rhyme of his own. But a series of unfortunate circumstances prevents her from finding his responses. Desperate to meet her, he composes one final message on a tomato plant. At last, Marylou sees it; the two slugs meet and fall in love.

Lexile: AD590L   (Grades Pre-K–2)   F

Rau, Dana Meachen. *Valentine's Day.*

ISBN-13: 9780516273464, 2001

The history of Valentine's Day is shared in this picture book.

Lexile: 810L   (Grades Pre-K–1)   NF

Rosenthal, Amy Krouse. *Plant a Kiss.*

ISBN-13: 9780061986758, 2011

Little Miss planted a kiss. One small act of love blooms into something bigger and more dazzling than Little Miss could have ever imagined in this epic journey about life, kindness, and giving.

Lexile: N/A   (Grades Pre-K–3)   F

Rylant, Cynthia. *If You'll Be My Valentine.*

ISBN-13: 9780060092719, 2005

A little boy creates Valentines for all the loved ones in his life—his pets, family, and even his teddy bear—describing how they could spend time together "if you'll be my valentine."

Lexile: N/A   (Grades Pre-K–3)   F

Sabuda, Robert. *Saint Valentine.*

ISBN-13: 9780689824296, 1999

A Valentine's Day kids' book about the origins of the holiday. It started in ancient Rome when a doctor named Valentine restored sight to a young, poor blind girl and then sent her a secret message that she didn't receive until after Valentine was executed.

Lexile: N/A   (Grades 1–3)   NF

Scotton, Rob. *Love, Splat.*

ISBN-13: 9780062077769, 2011

Splat has a crush on a fluffy white cat, but so does Spike, who informs Splat that his Valentine for her is much better than Splat's. Discouraged, Splat tosses his Valentine into the trash, but the kitten finds it and surprises Splat with an extra special pink Valentine just for him.

Lexile: AD700L   (Grades Pre-K–2)   F

Willard, Eliza. *Totally Crushed.*

ISBN-13: 9780545028141, 2008

Annabel is excited to find a red carnation at her locker on Valentine's Day, but it's from her best guy friend Sam, whom her best friend Phoebe likes. Annabel's perfect Valentine's Day turns into a disaster.

Lexile: 540L   (Grades 3–6)   F

President's Day

Davis, Kenneth C. *Don't Know Much About the Presidents.*

ISBN-13: 9780061718236, 2009

This book helps readers learn all about the presidents' important political achievements, their nicknames, hobbies, and even what kind of foods they ate.   Lexile: N/A   (Grades 3–8)   NF

Deutsch, Stacia, and Rhody Cohon. *Lincoln's Legacy.*

ISBN-13: 9780689042096, 2005

Abigail loves Mondays when Mr. Caruthers asks them questions about history. An important one, "What if Abraham Lincoln never freed the slaves?" gave Abigail and her friends an opportunity to travel back in time. Mr. C needs their help because it looks like President Lincoln might quit and never free the slaves.   Lexile: N/A   (Grades 3–8)   F

DiPucchio, Kelly S. *Grace for President.*   ISBN-13: 9781423139997, 2012

When Grace's teacher reveals that the United States has never had a female president, Grace decides to be the first. And she immediately starts off her political career as a candidate for the school's mock election. But soon she realizes that she has entered a tough race. Her popular opponent claims to be the "best man for the job" and seems to have captured all the male votes—but Grace concentrates on being the best person.

Lexile: N/A   (Grades 1–3)   F

Ditchfield, Christin. *Presidents' Day.*   ISBN-13: 9780516227849, 2003

Presidents' Day elaborates on the lives of Washington and Lincoln, including the stories of Washington's escape in a battle during the French and Indian War and why Lincoln grew a beard.   Lexile: N/A   (Grades 3–8)   NF

MacMillan, Dianne M. *Presidents Day.*   ISBN-13: 9780894908200, 1997

This book provides brief accounts of the lives of two prominent U.S. presidents and describes the holiday that was established in their honor.   Lexile: N/A   (Grades 3–8)   NF

Piven, Hanoch. *What Presidents Are Made Of.*   ISBN-13: 9781442444331, 2012

Focusing on 17 U.S. presidents, each entry begins with the same phrase ("Presidents are made of . . ."), includes an interesting anecdote showing the human side of that individual, and presents a collage caricature made of bits of realia that extend the metaphors of the text.

Lexile: N/A   (Grades 2–6)   NF

Rockwell, Anne. *Presidents' Day.*   ISBN-13: 9780060501969, 2009

Mrs. Madoff's class celebrates Presidents' Day by putting on a play and then voting for class president.   Lexile: N/A   (Grades Pre-K–1)   F

St. George, Judith. *So You Want to Be President?*   ISBN-13: 9780399243172, 2004

This lighthearted, humorous roundup of anecdotes and trivia is cast as a handbook of helpful hints to aspiring presidential candidates.   Lexile: N/A   (Grades Pre-K–8)   NF

Stier, Catherine. *If I Ran for President.*   ISBN-13: 9780807535448, 2007

Six children take turns explaining the election process as if they were running for president. They discuss their decision to run, campaigning, primaries and conventions, debating, being interviewed, meeting the public, voting, and being sworn in on Inauguration Day.

Lexile: N/A   (Grades 1–3)   NF

Wade, Mary Dodson. *Presidents' Day.*   ISBN-13: 9780766022348, 2004

Presidents' Day is celebrated on the third Monday in February in the United States. First meant to honor George Washington and Abraham Lincoln, this holiday now honors all the presidents of the United States.   Lexile: N/A   (Grades 3–8)   NF

St. Patrick's Day

Bateman, Teresa. *Fiona's Luck.*   ISBN-13: 9781570916434, 2009

Using the background of the Irish potato famine, this story weaves a tale of Irish history and leprechauns, with some optimism, cleverness, and luck thrown in. At one time, luck was in abundance in Ireland until the leprechaun king got angry at the humans for soaking it all up. Using a spell, he steals it away. The people fall on hard times, and Fiona uses her wits to get it back from the wily king.   Lexile: N/A   (Grades K–5)   F

Burton, Martin Nelson. *Dear Mr. Leprechaun.*   ISBN-13: 9780966649000, 2003

This is a true account of a magical exchange of letters between a boy and a "leprechaun," including the original childhood notes and the sweet, fatherly replies that he received from "Mr. Leprechaun."   Lexile: N/A   (Grades K–3)   NF

Calamari, Barbara. *Green with Envy.*   ISBN-13: 9780689845833, 2002

Angela wears her new orange jacket while everyone else in her class is wearing disgusting green. Too bad Angela just found out that it is Saint Patrick's Day and those who don't wear green suffer the consequences.   Lexile: 720L   (Grades K–3)   F

dePaola, Tomie. *Patrick: Patron Saint of Ireland.*   ISBN-13: 9780823410774, 1994

This biography integrates both the tones and design elements of Celtic art and relates the familiar and not-so-familiar details of Patrick's life, such as that March 17 is the date of his death, not birth.   Lexile: N/A   (Grades K–4)   NF

Freeman, Dorothy Rhodes. *St. Patrick's Day.*   ISBN-13: 9780766030466, 1992

This book describes the celebration of Saint Patrick's Day, which honors the patron saint of Ireland.   Lexile: N/A   (Grades K–3)   NF

Landau, Elaine. *St. Patrick's Day.*   ISBN-13: 9780766017771, 2002

The story of St. Patrick is told, with legend and fact. The significance of the color green, shamrocks, four-leaf clovers, and pots of gold are explained. Parades, festivals, athletic events, and special foods are also discussed.   Lexile: N/A   (Grades 1–4)   NF

McDermott, Gerald. *Tim O'Toole and the Wee Folk: An Irish Tale.*

ISBN-13: 9780140506754, 1992

When the evil McGoons trick Tim O'Toole out of his fortune, he teams up with his benefactors, the Little People, to regain his treasure. Lexile: N/A (Grades K–3) F

Nolan, Janet. *St. Patrick's Day Shillelagh.*

ISBN-13: 9780807573457, 2002

A family retells the story of the shillelagh that was whittled from a tree when escaping Ireland to America during the potato famine. Lexile: N/A (Grades 1–4) NF

Rockwell, Anne. *St. Patrick's Day.*

ISBN-13: 9780060501976, 2010

Mrs. Madoff's class is celebrating St. Patrick's Day with gusto—wearing green, dancing Irish dances, writing reports, and acting in a play. And Evan, who is of Irish ancestry, shows pictures of his visit to Ireland to see his grandparents. Lexile: N/A (Grades K–3) F

Rue, Nancy. *Sophie's Irish Showdown.*

ISBN-13: 9780310707592, 2005

A new girl in class is assigned to Sophie's drama group, and Sophie wants to get to know her. Sophie learns to accept her new friend's culture. Lexile: N/A (Grades K–3) F

Wing, Natasha. *The Night Before St. Patrick's Day.*

ISBN-13: 9780448448527, 2009

It's the night before St. Patrick's Day, and Tim and Maureen are setting traps to catch a leprechaun! When they wake the next morning to the sound of their dad playing the bagpipes and the smell of their mom cooking green eggs, they're shocked to find that they've actually caught a leprechaun. Lexile: N/A (Grades K–3) F

Wojciechowski, Susan. *A Fine St. Patrick's Day.*

ISBN-13: 9780385736404, 2008

Two towns compete in a St. Patrick's Day decorating contest, and each year the town of Tralee loses! Determined to win this year, they've decided to paint the entire town green. In the midst of the decorating, a small, pointy-eared man arrives and asks for their help in getting his cows unstuck from the mud. Only the people of Tralee offer to help and are delighted the next morning to find that the little stranger had painted the town green while they were sleeping as a thank-you. Lexile: N/A (Grades K–3) F

Easter

Balian, Lorna. *Humbug Rabbit.*

ISBN-13: 9781932065404, 2004

While Granny searches for eggs to decorate for Easter, the Rabbit children become convinced that their father is the Easter Bunny. Lexile: N/A (Grades K–3) F

Barth, Edna. *Lilies, Rabbits, and Painted Eggs.*

ISBN-13: 9780618096480, 2001

This book traces the history of Easter symbols from their Christian and pagan origins to such present-day additions as rabbits and new clothes. Lexile: N/A (Grades 3–6) F

Brown, Margaret Wise. *Home for a Bunny.*

ISBN-13: 9780307930095, 2012

A bunny searches the springtime forest for a home of his own.

Lexile: N/A (Grades K–2) F

Carlson, Melody. *The Easterville Miracle.*   ISBN-13: 9780805426809, 2004

A little boy named Sam and a man named Henry remind the town of Easterville of the true meaning of Easter and that it's not just about Easter bonnets, baskets, colored eggs, candy, and decorations.   Lexile: N/A   (Grades K–3)   F

Henkes, Kevin. *Owen's Marshmallow Chick.*   ISBN-13: 9780060010126, 2002

Owen's Easter basket is full of sweet treats like jelly beans, gumdrops, buttercream eggs, a big chocolate bunny, and a little marshmallow chick. He happily gobbles each treat one by one.   Lexile: AD150L   (Grades Pre-K–1)   F

Korman, Justine. *The Grumpy Easter Bunny.*   ISBN-13: 9780439635950, 2004

Hopper is a grumpy Easter bunny who works all year making chocolate eggs, filling marshmallow chicks, and rolling thousands of jelly beans. Then he hops all over the place to deliver the goodies.   Lexile: N/A   (Grades K–3)   F

Lewison, Wendy Cheyette. *Easter Bunny's Amazing Egg Machine.*

ISBN-13: 9780375812637, 2002

When Easter Bunny's egg-coloring machine goes haywire, his friends are there to help.

Lexile: N/A   (Grades Pre-K–3)   F

Maier, Paul L. *The Very First Easter.*   ISBN-13: 9780758606273, 2000

This is the true Easter story that answers the real questions children ask about Easter.

Lexile: N/A   (Grades K–3)   NF

Milhous, Katherine. *The Egg Tree.*   ISBN-13: 9780689715686, 1992

Katy's Easter morning discovery renews the tradition of the Easter egg tree.

Lexile: 560L   (Grades K–3)   NF

Polacco, Patricia. *Chicken Sunday.*   ISBN-13: 9780698116153, 1998

After being initiated into a neighbor's family by a solemn backyard ceremony, a young Russian American girl and her African American brothers determine to buy their gramma Eula a beautiful Easter hat. But their good intentions are misunderstood, until they discover just the right way to pay for the hat that Eula has had her eye on.

Lexile: 0650L   (Grades K–6)   F

Polacco, Patricia. *Rechenka's Eggs.*   ISBN-13: 9780698113855, 1996

An injured goose rescued by Babushka, having broken the painted eggs intended for the Easter Festival in Moscva, lays 13 marvelously colored eggs to replace them and then leaves behind one final miracle in egg form before returning to her own kind.

Lexile: 0780L   (Grades Pre-K–3)   F

Sanders, Nancy I. *Easter.*   ISBN-13: 9780516277776, 2003

This book explores the history of Easter and how Easter is celebrated differently in different parts of the world.   Lexile: 740L   (Grades K–4)   NF

Tangvald, Christine Harder. *The Best Thing About Easter.*   ISBN-13: 9780784720004, 2007

Easter is eggs, candy, and getting dressed up on a very special holiday, but the real reason we celebrate Easter is the resurrection of Jesus.   Lexile: N/A   (Grades Pre-K–3)   NF

Tegen, Katherine. *The Story of the Easter Bunny.*   ISBN-13: 9780060507114, 2005

A little rabbit watches an old couple paint eggs, make chocolate, and braid baskets for the village children at Easter, and he eventually becomes the Easter Bunny.

Lexile: N/A   (Grades Pre-K–3)   F

Wilhelm, Hans. *Bunny Trouble.*   ISBN-13: 9780590450423, 1991

Ralph is one soccer-loving bunny. But when his soccer high jinks almost land him in the farmer's stewpot, he discovers he needs the help of his brave sister—and lots of Easter eggs—to get him safely home again.   Lexile: N/A   (Grades Pre-K–3)   F

Wing, Natasha. *The Night Before Easter.*   ISBN-13: 9780448418735, 2011

Two siblings witness the nighttime arrival of the Easter Bunny.

Lexile: AD550L   (Grades K–2)   F

Wood, A. J. *The Golden Egg.*   ISBN-13: 9780811828376, 2000

Little Duck is hunting for a very special Easter egg. She searches high and low with the help of her forest friends, but where will they find the golden egg?

Lexile: N/A   (Grades Pre-K–3)   F

Zolotow, Charlotte. *The Bunny Who Found Easter.*   ISBN-13: 9780618111275, 2001

A lonely rabbit searches for others of his kind from summer through winter, until spring arrives and he finds one special bunny.   Lexile: N/A   (Grades Pre K–3)   F

Zolotow, Charlotte. *Mr. Rabbit and the Lovely Present.*   ISBN-13: 9780064430203, 1977

Mr. Rabbit helps a little girl find a lovely present for her mother, who is especially fond of red, yellow, green, and blue.   Lexile: 280L   (Grades Pre-K–3)   F

April Fool's Day

Bateman, Teresa. *April Foolishness.*

ISBN-13: 9780807504055, 2004

This is about a grandpa who sits calmly in the farmhouse despite all his grandchildren coming to warn him of some disaster or the other. Thinking himself to be the wisest one he is determined not to be fooled by the young ones on this April Fool's Day. However, as it turns out, the grandma has the last laugh.

Lexile: 0440L   (Grades K–2)   F

Brown, Marc. ***Arthur's April Fool.*** ISBN-13: 9780316112345, 1985

This is a story about a young boy named Arthur who turns the table against Binky Barnes, a big bully at school. Binky is a nasty boy who steals Arthur's favorite pen while he is rehearsing his magic act for the school April Fool's Day assembly. Despite all the nightmares and Binky being made his assistant, Arthur manages to make Binky an April Fool and tackles the situation with flying colors. Lexile: 400L   (Grades K–2)   F

Hill, Susanna Leonard. ***April Fool, Phyllis!*** ISBN-13: 9780823422708, 1990

It might be April Fools' Day, but Punxsutawney Phyllis knows that winter isn't over yet.

Lexile: AD500L   (Grades K–2)   F

Kroll, Steven. ***It's April Fool's Day.*** ISBN-13: 9780590443487, 1990

On April Fool's Day, Alice gets tired of Horace's pranks and teaches him that good friends can have fun together without mean tricks. Lexile: N/A   (Grades K–2)   F

Maguire, Gregory. ***A Couple of April Fools.*** ISBN-13: 9780618274741, 2004

The students at Joshua Fawcett Elementary School plan their practical jokes for April Fool's Day, but their pranks fall flat when it is discovered that their beloved teacher, Miss Earth, has gone missing. They know that the clock is ticking, and they must find the answer—and their teacher—before it is too late. Lexile: 800L   (Grades 2–4)   F

Modell, Frank. ***Look Out, It's April Fools' Day!*** ISBN-13: 9780688040161, 1985

This story is about two boys, Marvin and Milton. Marvin keeps trying to fool Milton while taking a walk on April Fool's Day. But he fails continuously until their mutual kidding leads to a funny situation where both the boys fool each other unconsciously.

Lexile: N/A   (Grades 2–4)   F

Roy, Ron. ***A to Z Mysteries: The School Skeleton.*** ISBN-13: 9780375813689, 2003

At Green Lawn Elementary, the school becomes involved in a mystery when Mr. Bones, the skeleton in the nurse's office, disappears. Lexile: 500L   (Grades K–3)   F

Schiller, Melissa. ***April Fool's Day.*** ISBN-13: 9780516279428, 2003

This book introduces the history of April Fool's Day and explains how it is observed today.

Lexile: N/A   (Grades K–3)   NF

Smith, Dian G. ***World's Greatest Practical Jokes.*** ISBN-13: 9781402710209, 2004

This book is full of April Fool's tricks, including school tricks, body parts, bathroom humor, and more. Lexile: N/A   (Grades K–5)   NF

Earth Day

Ansary, Mir Tamim. ***Earth Day.*** ISBN-13: 9781403488978, 2001

This book introduces Earth Day, explaining what causes air pollution, how a river caught fire in 1969, and what can be done to help the earth every day. Lexile: N/A   (Grades K–5)   NF

Cherry, Lynne. *The Great Kapok Tree: A Tale of the Amazon Rain Forest.*

ISBN-13: 9780152026141, 2000

A man chopping down a great kapok tree in the Brazilian rain forest puts down his ax to nap. As he does, the animals who live in the tree ask him not to destroy their world.

Lexile: 670L   (Grades K–8)   NF

Hiaasen, Carl. *Hoot.*   ISBN-13: 9780440419396, 2004

Roy, who is new to his small Florida community, becomes involved in another boy's attempt to save a colony of burrowing owls from a proposed construction site.

Lexile: 760L   (Grades 5–8)   F

Lowery, Linda. *Earth Day.*   ISBN-13: 9781575056203, 2003

Lowery addresses the concerns that eventually brought about Earth Day and the laws and programs that have come about due to its establishment in 1970.

Lexile: 670L   (Grades 2–4)   NF

Murphy, Stuart J. *Earth Day—Hooray!*   ISBN-13: 9780060001292, 2004

A drive to recycle cans on Earth Day teaches the children of the Maple Street School Save-the-Planet Club about place value.   Lexile: N/A   (Grades 3–6)   NF

Nelson, Robin. *Earth Day.*   ISBN-13: 9780822513209, 2003

This book introduces readers to the history of Earth Day.   Lexile: N/A   (Grades 2–4)   NF

Roop, Peter. *Let's Celebrate Earth Day.*   ISBN-13: 9780761316909, 2001

Using a question-and-answer format, this book introduces the history and importance of Earth Day.   Lexile: N/A   (Grades K–3)   NF

Schnetzler, Pattie. *Earth Day Birthday.*   ISBN-13: 9781584690535, 2004

Set to the familiar music of "The Twelve Days of Christmas," the verses describe different animals that illustrate the wonders of the wild world. It includes a factual section about Earth Day and ways to celebrate it.   Lexile: N/A   (Grades K–5)   NF

Sensel, Joni. *The Garbage Monster.*   ISBN-13: 9780970119520, 2003

When Jo is slow to take out the trash one evening, the garbage comes to life and hauls her outside instead. This book brings to life the benefits of recycling and the hazards of a wasteful attitude.   Lexile: N/A   (Grades Pre-K–3)   F

Seuss, Dr. *The Lorax.*   ISBN-13: 9780394823379, 1971

The Once-ler describes the results of the local pollution problem.

Lexile: 560L   (Grades K–6)   F

Wallace, Nancy Elizabeth. *Recycle Every Day!*   ISBN-13: 9780761451495, 2003

A busy family of rabbits demonstrates the three R's of recycling.

Lexile: N/A   (Grades Pre-K–3)   NF

Arbor Day

Ansary, Mir Tamim. *Arbor Day.* ISBN-13: 9781403488824, 2001

Readers will see what North America looked like 500 years ago and learn why trees are important, why some states do not celebrate Arbor Day on the same date, and more.

Lexile: N/A   (Grades 2–4)   NF

Beaty, Sandy. *Champion of Arbor Day: J. Sterling Morton.*

ISBN-13: 9780966447019, 1999

This text chronicles the life of an early environmentalist who promoted the idea of a day dedicated to trees and motivated Nebraskans who plant one million trees on the first Arbor Day in 1872.

Lexile: N/A   (Grades 1–5)   NF

Bennett, Kelly. *Arbor Day.* ISBN-13: 9780516277547, 2003

J. Sterling Morton was worried about the many trees that were being cut down, and, because of him, the holiday came about. Arbor Day is the last Friday in April, but the celebration varies depending on the best time of year to plant trees in different areas.

Lexile: 290L   (Grades 1–4)   NF

Brimner, Larry Dane. *What Good Is a Tree?* ISBN-13: 9780516264141, 1999

When a boy wonders, "What good is a tree?" he and his sister come up with a lot of answers, from using it as a fort to making it second base. Lexile: N/A   (Grades 1–3)   F

Bulla, Clyde Robert. *A Tree Is a Plant.* ISBN-13: 9780064451963, 2001

A tree is the biggest plant that grows. Trees can live for a very long time, and they are alive all year long, even when they look dead in winter. Lexile: AD290L   (Grades Pre-K–3)   NF

Cooper, Jason. *Arbor Day.* ISBN-13: 9781589522176, 2003

This text is about the history, purpose, and observance of Arbor Day. The book explains how the earth is fragile, and if we don't take care of it, it will not be a good place for plants, animals, or people. More important is the lesson about how trees are essential to the ecosystem, they offer cooling shade, help remove pollutants from the air, provide homes for animals and food, and their roots keep the soil in place.

Lexile: IG830L   (Grades 2–6)   NF

Gibbons, Gail. *Nature's Green Umbrella.* ISBN-13: 9780688154110, 1997

This book describes the climatic conditions of the rain forest as well as the different layers of plants and animals that comprise the ecosystem. Lexile: 880L   (Grades K–3)   NF

Muldrow, Diane. *We Planted a Tree.* ISBN-13: 9780375864322, 2010

This book celebrates the life and hope that every tree—from Paris to Brooklyn to Tokyo—brings to our planet. Lexile: AD620L   (Grades K–3)   NF

Silverstein, Shel. *The Giving Tree.*   ISBN-13: 9780060256654, 1964

"Once there was a little tree . . . and she loved a little boy." Every day the boy would come to the tree to eat her apples, swing from her branches, or slide down her trunk, and the tree was happy. But as the boy grew older, he wanted more from the tree, and the tree gave and gave and gave.   Lexile: 530L   (Grades K–3)   F

Mother's Day

Balian, Lorna. *Mother's Mother's Day.*

ISBN-13: 9781932065398, 2004

Hazel the mouse goes to visit her mother on Mother's Day, but finds she has gone to visit her mother.

Lexile: N/A   (Grades Pre-K–3)   F

Bernhard, Emery and Durga. *A Ride on Mother's Back:*
A Day of Baby Carrying Around the World.

ISBN-13: 9780152008703, 1996

This book explores the ways that people from a variety of cultures carry their young ones, and it describes what children see and learn as they are carried.

Lexile: 940L   (Grades Pre-K–3)   NF

Carrick, Carol. *Mothers Are Like That.*   ISBN-13: 9780618752416, 2007

Mothers care for their babies in all kinds of ways. The connection between mother and child emanates from every word in this book.   Lexile: 80   (Grades Pre-K–1)   NF

Eastman, P. D. *Are You My Mother?*   ISBN-13: 9780394800189, 1960

A baby bird, fallen from his nest, sets out to find his mother.

Lexile: 80   (Grades Pre-K–3)   F

Evans, Edie. *I Love You, Mommy!*   ISBN-13: 9780307995070, 2001

Moms are thanked for all the fun things they do with their children in this book that shows the various activities moms do with their kids.   Lexile: N/A   (Grades Pre-K–2)   F

Joosse, Barbara. *Mama, Do You Love Me?*   ISBN-13: 9780877017592, 1991

This story is of a child living in the Arctic who learns that a mother's love is unconditional.

Lexile: AD420L   (Grades Pre-K–6)   F

Lasky, Kathryn. *Before I Was Your Mother.*   ISBN-13: 9780152058425, 2007

A mother tells her own daughter what she was like and what she used to do when she was a little girl.   Lexile: N/A   (Grades Pre-K–3)   F

Melmed, Laura Krauss. *I Love You as Much.*   ISBN-13: 9780060002022, 1998

This lullaby rhyme is a book about the celebration of the bond between mothers and their babies.   Lexile: N/A   (Grades Pre-K–2)   F

Munsch, Robert. *Love You Forever.*   ISBN-13: 9780920668368, 1995

A young woman holds her newborn son and looks at him lovingly. Softly she sings to him: "I'll love you forever, I'll like you for always, As long as I'm living, My baby you'll be."

Lexile: AD780   (Grades Pre-K–1)   F

Parr, Todd. *The Mommy Book.*   ISBN-13: 9780316608275, 2002

This book celebrates mothers by highlighting the many things moms do for their families.

Lexile: N/A   (Grades Pre-K–2)   F

Rockwell, Anne. *Mother's Day.*   ISBN-13: 9780060513740, 2004

This picture book is a tribute to all the mothers, grandmothers, and mothers-to-be.

Lexile: N/A   (Grades Pre-K–2)   NF

Memorial Day

Cotton, Jacqueline S. *Memorial Day.*   ISBN-13: 9780516273693, 2002

This book introduces the basic facts about Memorial Day, including the development of the holiday and how it is celebrated today. It also includes holiday games, traditions, crafts, and foods.

Lexile: 600L   (Grades K–5)   NF

Golding, Theresa. *Memorial Day Surprise.*

ISBN-13: 9781590780480, 2004

This book shares the meaning of Memorial Day through historical fiction. It's the story of a boy, Marco, and his mother as they leave for the Memorial Day parade. At the parade, they see Marco's grandfather in his army uniform and his medals across his chest.   Lexile: N/A   (Grades 2–5)   F

Hamilton, Lynn. *Memorial Day.*   ISBN-13: 9781605967714, 2004

The origins and customs of Memorial Day are explained in this book. A description of the Civil War details the origins of various memorial ceremonies. A map of the United States shows where and how different regions celebrate Memorial Day.

Lexile: N/A   (Grades K–5)   NF

Nelson, Robin. *Memorial Day.*   ISBN-13: 9780822513179, 2003

This title presents very basic information about this holiday. Each page has a photograph or reproduction and one line of text.   Lexile: N/A   (Grades K–2)   NF

Father's Day

Bauer, Marion Dane. ***The Very Best Daddy of All.***

ISBN-13: 9781416927365, 2007

Some animal daddies comfort their babies, hold them tight, or face every danger for them. But the narrator of this loving picture book knows his daddy does all of that and more for him.

Lexile: N/A   (Grades Pre-K–2)   F

Braun, Sebastien. ***I Love My Daddy.***   ISBN-13: 9780060543112, 2004

A father bear and his cub spend the whole day together.

Lexile: N/A   (Grades K–3)   F

Bridges, Margaret Park. ***If I Were Your Father.***   ISBN-13: 9780688151928, 1999

A boy tells his father all the special things he would do for him if their positions were reversed and he was the father.   Lexile: N/A   (Grades Pre-K–2)   F

Browne, Anthony. ***My Dad.***   ISBN-13: 9780374351014, 2001

A child describes the many wonderful things about "my dad," who can jump over the moon, swim like a fish, and be as warm as toast.   Lexile: BR   (Grades K–3)   F

Bunting, Eve. ***A Perfect Father's Day.***   ISBN-13: 9780395664162, 1993

In this story a four-year-old takes her father from one activity to the next. He gets to eat kid food, climb monkey bars, and buy her a red balloon. Readers will enjoy this book and think about ways they can spend Father's Day with their dads.

Lexile: 430L   (Grades Pre-K–2)   F

Callahan, Sean. ***A Wild Father's Day.***   ISBN-13: 9780807522936, 2009

When his children present him with a card that says, "Have a wild Father's Day!" the dad suggests that they act like animals all day. First, they jump on the bed like kangaroos, then they stretch like cats, run like cheetahs, swing like monkeys, wrestle like bears, and so on.

Lexile: N/A   (Grades K–2)   F

Capucilli, Alyssa Satin. ***Biscuit Loves Father's Day.***   ISBN-13: 9780060094638, 2004

As she rises from bed, Biscuit's human companion tells Biscuit that they are "going to spend an extra-special day with Dad" since it is Father's Day. She makes a card and helps Dad make sandwiches.   Lexile: AD370L   (Grades Pre-K–2)   F

Clements, Andrew. ***Because Your Daddy Loves You.***   ISBN-13: 9780547237640, 2009

When things go wrong during a day at the beach, like a ball that drifts away or a gooey ice cream mess, a father could do a lot of things but always picks the loving one.

Lexile: N/A   (Grades Pre-K–2)   F

Clements, Andrew. ***The Secret Father's Day Present.***   ISBN-13: 9780689833595, 2000

Sarah and James are busy making their best Father's Day present ever.

Lexile: N/A   (Grades Pre-K–2)   F

Gaiman, Neil. *The Day I Swapped My Dad for Two Goldfish.* ISBN-13: 9780060587031, 2006

After trading his father for two goldfish, a boy and his little sister go on a rollicking adventure around town to get him back. Lexile: N/A (Grades Pre-K–2) F

Guettier, Bénédicte. *The Father Who Had 10 Children.* ISBN-13: 9780140568318, 2001

Every day the father who had 10 children made them breakfast, helped them get dressed, drove them to school, cooked them dinner, gave them a bath, and put them to bed. Finally he needed a rest! So he left his brood with Grandma and set off on a 10-day, or maybe 10-month, vacation. But after just one peaceful day, it seemed like something was missing, something times 10. Lexile: 0380L (Grades Pre-K–2) F

Gutman, Anne. *Daddy Kisses.* ISBN-13: 9780811839143, 2003

Animal and human fathers kiss in different ways, but they all show love.

Lexile: AD240 (Grades Pre-K–1) F

Mayer, Mercer. *Happy Father's Day!* ISBN-13: 9780060539658, 2007

Father's Day is just around the corner, and Little Critter and Little Sister have decided to plan a big surprise for Dad and Grandpa. Join them as they make cards, cook a special breakfast together, and put on a magic show. Lexile: N/A (Grades K–2) F

Rusackas, Francesca. *Daddy All Day Long.* ISBN-13: 9780060502850, 2004

Owen Pig and his daddy count the ways they love each other from one to ten and a million zillion more—all day long. Lexile: N/A (Grades Pre-K–2) F

Steptoe, Javaka. *In Daddy's Arms I Am Tall: African Americans Celebrating Fathers.*

ISBN-13: 9781584300168, 2001

This collection of poems celebrates African American fathers.

Lexile: N/A (Grades Pre-K–2) NF

Wing, Natasha. *The Night Before Father's Day.* ISBN-13: 9780448458717, 2012

It's the night before Father's Day, and Mom and the kids have a plan to surprise Dad with a special gift. When Dad goes for a bike ride, everyone gets to work. Dad wakes up the next day to find his garage newly organized and his car sparkly clean. So of course, he celebrates by taking everyone for a spin! Lexile: N/A (Grades Pre-K–2) F

Wood, Douglas. *What Dads Can't Do.* ISBN-13: 9780689826207, 2000

This book describes how dads show love by explaining all the things that they cannot do, such as sleeping late, keeping their ties clean, and reading books by themselves.

Lexile: AD460L (Grades Pre-K–3) F

Independence Day

Giblin, James Cross. *Fireworks, Picnics, and Flags: The Story of July Symbols.* ISBN-13: 9780899191744, 2001

This book looks at our national birthday and explores the stories behind the familiar symbols of the Fourth of July and tells how they have come to be associated with the holiday.

Lexile: 990L   (Grades Pre-K–3)   NF

Dalgliesh, Alice. *Fourth of July Story.* ISBN-13: 9780684131641, 1972

This story goes back to revolutionary times, back to the colonists' desire for freedom and the creation of the Declaration of Independence. Lexile: N/A   (Grades K–3)   NF

Murray, Julie. *Independence Day.* ISBN-13: 9781591975885, 2005

This is the story of how the Declaration of Independence came to be.

Lexile: N/A   (Grades K–5)   NF

Nardo, Don. *History of the World: Declaration of Independence.*

ISBN-13: 9780689718021, 2003

This book traces the history of the Declaration of Independence.

Lexile: N/A   (Grades 3–6)   NF

Nelson, Robin. *Independence Day.* ISBN-13: 9780822512745, 2003

This book is full of interesting facts about Independence Day.

Lexile: N/A   (Grades Pre-K–2)   NF

Osborne, Mary Pope. *Happy Birthday, America.* ISBN-13: 9781596430518, 2005

This is a warm family story showing three generations enjoying parades, popcorn, "Yankee Doodle," and fireworks. Lexile: N/A   (Grades Pre-K–3)   F

Pingry, Patricia A. *The Story of America's Birthday.* ISBN-13: 9780824941703, 2000

This book is a wonderful place to start to teach children how the Fourth of July came to be.

Lexile: N/A   (Grades Pre-K–2)   NF

Roberts, Bethany. *Fourth of July Mice!* ISBN-13: 9780618313662, 2004

Four energetic mice enjoy a parade and other festivities on Independence Day.

Lexile: N/A   (Grades K–2)   F

Wardlaw, Lee. *Red, White, and Boom!* ISBN-13: 9780805090659, 2012

In this book, readers will move across the country for a city parade, a beach picnic, and fireworks in the park for this celebration of the many cultures and traditions that make up this great holiday. Lexile: N/A   (Grades Pre-K–3)   F

Wong, Janet S. *Apple Pie 4th of July.*   ISBN-13: 9780152057084, 2006

This book shows that this holiday can be celebrated in many ways, including a trip through a Chinese buffet after a parade. The young girl doubts anyone will want Chinese food on such an American holiday, but her father points out that fireworks are Chinese.

Lexile: N/A   (Grades Pre-K–3)   F

Labor Day

Ansary, Mir Tamim. *Labor Day.*   ISBN-13: 9781403489012, 1998

This book reminds readers that the labor-union movement brought about laws to keep children out of the workplace and in school.   Lexile: N/A   (Grades Pre-K–3)   NF

Bartoletti, Susan Campbell. *Black Potatoes: The Story of the Irish Famine, 1845–1850.*   ISBN-13: 9780618548835, 2005

The story of men, women, and children who defied landlords and searched empty fields for scraps of harvested vegetables and edible weeds to eat, who walked several miles each day to hard-labor jobs for meager wages and to soup kitchens for food, and who committed crimes just to be sent to jail, where they were ensured a meal. All this came about after the start to the 1845 disaster that struck Ireland destroying the only real food of nearly six million people.

Lexile: N/A   (Grades 2–6)   NF

Bredeson, Carmen. *Labor Day.*   ISBN-13: 9780516263120, 2007

This book explains the development of the holiday and how it is celebrated today. It includes holiday games, traditions, crafts, and foods.   Lexile: 320L   (Grades K–6)   NF

Hamilton, Lynn. *Labor Day.*   ISBN-13: 9781590361290, 2004

This book explains the development of the holiday and how it is celebrated today.

Lexile: N/A   (Grades K–3)   NF

Schuh, Mari C. *Labor Day.*   ISBN-13: 9780736816533, 2003

This book presents the history of Labor Day.   Lexile: N/A   (Grades K–3)   NF

Walker, Robert. *Labor Day.*   ISBN-13: 9780778749363, 2010

This book explains the development of the holiday and unions.

Lexile: N/A   (Grades K–3   NF

Ramadan

Addasi, Maha. *The White Nights of Ramadan.*

ISBN-13: 9781590785232, 2008

This story of a young girl in Kuwait tells how her family celebrates Girgian, three days under the full moon in the middle of the holy month of Ramadan: the traditions; the special clothing, foods, and crafts; and the meaning of the holiday.

Lexile: N/A   (Grades 2–8)   F

Douglass, Susan L. *Ramadan.*   ISBN-13: 9781575055848, 2003

This is a good basic introduction to the holy month of Ramadan as observed by the Muslim community. It covers the unique calendar, fasting, appropriate dress, and more.
Lexile: N/A   (Grades K–3)   NF

Heiligman, Deborah. *Celebrate Ramadan and Eid Al-Fitr with Praying, Fasting, and Charity.*   ISBN-13: 9781426304767, 2006

Ramadan, the Muslim holy month of fasting, and Eid Al-Fitr, which marks the fast's end, are sacred times for millions throughout the world. This book examines the reasons for the monthlong dawn-to-dusk fast and observes some of the different celebrations at the end of the fast worldwide.
Lexile: N/A   (Grades K–5)   NF

Hoyt-Goldsmith, Diane. *Celebrating Ramadan.*   ISBN-13: 9780823417629, 2002

This book discusses the Muslim holy month of Ramadan as a time of fasting and reflection. It begins with the sighting of the new moon and, because of the Islamic lunar calendar, gradually rotates through all of the seasons. It concludes with a three-day feast called Eid al-Fitr, a welcome celebration after a month of total fasting from sunrise to sunset every day.
Lexile: 990L   (Grades K–5)   NF

Jalali, Reza. *Moon Watchers: Shirin's Ramadan Miracle.*   ISBN-13: 9780884483212, 2010

This is a story about a young Muslim girl and her family at Ramadan as they weave together the traditional observance and its meaning.   Lexile: 990L   (Grades K–5)   F

Kahn, Hena. *Golden Domes and Silver Lanterns: A Muslim Book of Colors.*

ISBN-13: 9780811879057, 2011

This informative picture book celebrates Islam's beauty and traditions.
Lexile: N/A   (Grades K–5)   NF

Kahn, Hena. *Night of the Moon: A Muslim Holiday Story*   ISBN-13: 9780811860620, 2000

Yasmeen, a seven-year-old Pakistani American girl, celebrates the Muslim holidays of Ramadan.   Lexile: 780L   (Grades 1–5)   F

Sievert, Terry. *Ramadan: Islamic Holy Month.*   ISBN-13: 9780736869355, 2006

This is an accurate discussion of the basic practices and beliefs around Ramadan. This book also offers a small glossary, resource list, and simple index.

Lexile: N/A   (Grades K–5)   NF

Whitman, Sylvia. *Under the Ramadan Moon.*   ISBN-13: 9780807583050, 2011

This book celebrates the coming of Ramadan and shows a family's activities taking place "under the moon, under the moon, under the Ramadan moon."

Lexile: N/A   (Grades K–2)   F

Zucker, Jonny. *Fasting and Dates: A Ramadan and Eid-ul-Fitr Story.*

ISBN-13: 9780764126710, 2004

This book describes the activities of typical families as parents and children celebrate this cultural holiday.   Lexile: N/A   (Grades K–5)   NF

Columbus Day

Dorris, Michael. *Morning Girl.*

ISBN-13: 9780786813582, 1999

Morning Girl, who loves the day, and her younger brother Star Boy, who loves the night, take turns describing their life on an island in pre-Columbian America.

Lexile: 980L   (Grades 4–8)   F

Fritz, Jean. *Around the World in a Hundred Years: From Henry the Navigator to Magellan.*   ISBN-13: 9780698116382, 1998

This book tells 10 true tales of 15th-century European explorers—from Bartholomew Diaz and Christopher Columbus to Juan Ponce de Leon and Vasco Núñez de Balboa.

Lexile: 1050L   (Grades 4–8)   NF

Murray, Julie. *Columbus Day.*   ISBN-13: 9781591975878, 2005

This is the story of Columbus Day.   Lexile: N/A   (Grades K–2)   NF

Yolen, Jane. *Encounter.*   ISBN-13: 9780152013899, 1996

When Christopher Columbus landed on the island of San Salvador in 1492, he discovered the Taino Indians. This is a story told from the point of view of a young Taino boy who tried to warn his people against welcoming the strangers, who seemed interested in things other than friendship.   Lexile: 0760L   (Grades 2–6)   F

Halloween

Bunting, Eve. *The Bones of Fred McFee.*   ISBN-13: 9780152054236, 2005

This book tells the story of an unsuspecting brother and sister who bring a toy skeleton home from the harvest fair, name it Fred McFee, and hang it from a sycamore tree. But soon, eerie things begin to happen.   Lexile: N/A   (Grades K–2)   F

Crimi, Carolyn. ***Where's My Mummy?***　　ISBN-13: 9780763643379, 2009

Little Mummy wants to play just one more game of hide-and-shriek with his Mama Mummy before going to bed, but the dark night is full of friendly creatures. Who will comfort Little Mummy if someone gives him a scare?　　Lexile: N/A　(Grades Pre-K–1)　F

Crum, Shutta. ***Who Took My Hairy Toe?***　　ISBN-13: 9780807559727, 2001

This rendition of a folktale recounts the "ruination" of sticky-fingered Old Tar Pockets after he digs up a monster's furry toe in his neighbor's garden one Halloween.

Lexile: 370L　(Grades K–4)　F

Desmoinaux, Christel. ***"Hallo-what?"***　　ISBN-13: 9780689847950, 2003

Marceline is being ignored by everyone. She goes to her grandmother to find out why. Her grandmother explains that it is time for Halloween and everybody is getting ready for it.

Lexile: N/A　(Grades K–2)　F

Donaldson, Julia. ***Room on the Broom.***　　ISBN-13: 9780142501122, 2003

The witch and her cat are happily flying through the sky on a broomstick when the wind picks up and blows away the witch's hat, then her bow, and then her wand. Luckily, three helpful animals find the missing items, and all they want in return is a ride on the broom. But . . . will there be room on the broom?　　Lexile: AD720L　(Grades K–3)　F

Estes, Eleanor. ***The Witch Family.***　　ISBN-13: 9780152026103, 2000

Two little girls who love to draw witches build an elaborate world around the imaginary Old Witch and her family.　　Lexile: N/A　(Grades 3–6)　F

Evans, Cambria. ***Bone Soup.***　　ISBN-13: 9780618809080, 2008

This is a Halloween-themed rendition of the popular folktale *Stone Soup.*

Lexile: N/A　(Grades K–3)　F

Howitt, Mary. ***The Spider and the Fly.***　　ISBN-13: 9781442454545, 2002

In this title, Mary Howitt's 1829 poem *The Spider and the Fly* remains the same and teaches the same vital message about how kind words can sometimes be used to mask less-than-kind intentions.　　Lexile: N/A　(Grades 1–5)　F

Johnston, Tony. ***The Vanishing Pumpkin.***　　ISBN-13: 9780698114142, 1983

A 700-year-old woman wakes up and realizes that it is Halloween, so she decides to make a pumpkin pie. She and her husband go outside to pick their pumpkin and discover that it is missing. Out looking for it, they encounter a ghoul, a rapscallion, and a varmint. They discover that the wizard has made it into a jack-o-lantern. To thank the old couple, the wizard makes pumpkin pie.　　Lexile: N/A　(Grades K–2)　F

Kline, Suzy. ***Horrible Harry at Halloween.***　　ISBN-13: 9780141306759, 2002

Horrible Harry and his classmates wear costumes to school, and each year Harry shocks his classmates with his scary costume.　　Lexile: 370L　(Grades K–2)　F

Krosoczka, Jarrett. *Annie Was Warned.* ISBN-13: 9780385753418, 2011

Annie was warned not to go into creepy Montgomery mansion . . . and maybe she wouldn't have if her best friend hadn't dared her. But Annie isn't afraid of anything—not bats, not spiders, and certainly not some haunted house. Lexile: 220L (Grades Pre-K–3) F

Leuck, Laura. *My Monster Mama Loves Me So.* ISBN-13: 9780060088606, 2002

In cute and clever rhyming verse, this title describes all the many ways that monster mamas love their little ones. Lexile: 890L (Grades Pre-K–3) F

Lies, Brian. *Bats at the Beach.* ISBN-13: 9780618557448, 2006

Pack your blankets and moon-tan lotion for this fun story of bats playing at the beach. Lexile: 720L (Grades Pre-K–3) F

Lies, Brian. *Bats at the Library.* ISBN-13: 9780618999231, 2008

Join the fun at the public library with these book-loving bats, who roam aisles, frolick in the fountain, and even settle for story time. Lexile: 720L (Grades Pre-K–3) F

McGhee, Alison. *Only a Witch Can Fly.* ISBN-13: 9780312375034, 2009

One little girl *wants* to fly—more than anything. So on a special night, with the moon shining bright and her cat by her side, she gathers herself up, she grips her broom tight, and she tries. And she fails. But she's brave. So she tries again. Lexile: AD950L (Grades K–4) F

McGhee, Alison. *A Very Brave Witch.* ISBN-13: 9780689867316, 2011

On the far side of town in a big dark house lives a brave little witch. She has heard lots and lots about that very human holiday Halloween. Although she thinks she knows what humans are like, she has never seen Halloween for herself until this adventure.

Lexile: N/A (Grades K–3) F

Minor, Wendell. *Pumpkin Heads!* ISBN-13: 9780590521383, 2007

Detailed illustrations present a range of jack-o-lantern faces, from cowboys to witches to snowmen. Lexile: 130L (Grades Pre-K–1) F

Pilkey, Dav. *The Hallo-wiener.* ISBN-13: 9780439079464, 1999

Oscar is a dachshund who is tired of being made fun of by the other dogs. The criticism gets worse when he shows up to trick-or-treat wearing a hot-dog costume, but one brave act shows what a hero he really is. Lexile: 580L (Grades Pre-K–3) F

Rex, Adam. *Frankenstein Makes a Sandwich.* ISBN-13: 9780547576831, 2011

Being a monster isn't just about frightening villagers and sucking blood. Monsters have their trials, too. Poor Frankenstein's cupboard is bare, Wolfman is in need of some household help, and it's best not to get started on Dracula's hygiene issues.

Lexile: AD670L (Grades 3–6) F

Rex, Adam. *Frankenstein Takes the Cake.* ISBN-13: 9780547850627, 2012

Poems about the secret trials of being a monster like poor Frankenstein just wants a happy wedding to his undead bride, but best man Dracula is freaking out about the garlic bread.

Lexile: AD670L (Grades 3–6) NF

Rylant, Cynthia. *Moonlight: The Halloween Cat.*　　　ISBN-13: 9780064438148, 2003

Moonlight the cat loves everything about Halloween, from pumpkins to children to candy.

Lexile: N/A　(Grades K–2)　F

Seinfeld, Jerry. *Halloween.*　　　ISBN-13: 9780316706254, 2002

This book captures the hilarity of Halloween from Superman costumes that look like pajamas to getting bad trick-or-treat candy.　　Lexile: N/A　(Grades K–3)　F

Silverman, Erica. *Big Pumpkin.*　　　ISBN-13: 9780689801297, 1995

The witch has grown a huge pumpkin and wants to make a pumpkin pie, but it's so big she can't get it off the vine. The ghost can't move it either, or the vampire, or the mummy.

Lexile: AD350L　(Grades Pre-K–2)　F

Singer, Marilyn. *Monster Museum.*　　　ISBN-13: 9781423121008, 2009

In the Monster Museum you will meet the werewolf, Count Dracula, the mummy, and some of their slimy, screaming, slithering friends.　　Lexile: N/A　(Grades Pre-K–2)　F

Thomas, Valerie. *Winnie the Witch.*　　　ISBN-13: 9780061173127, 2009

Everything in Winnie's house is black—the carpet, the chairs, the bed and the sheets, the pictures on the walls, and even the bathtub! And of course her cat, Wilbur, is black too—all except for his bright-green eyes. Whenever poor Wilbur closes his eyes and tries to take a catnap, Winnie stumbles right over him or accidentally sits on top of him. One day, Winnie gets a brilliant idea: what if Wilbur were a different color?　　Lexile: 6448L　(Grades K–3)　F

Ziefert, Harriet. *On Halloween Night.*　　　ISBN-13: 9780140568202, 2001

Emily struggles to decide what costume to wear for Halloween.

Lexile: N/A　(Grades K–3)　F

Day of the Dead

da Coll, Ivar. *El dia de muertos.*　ISBN-13: 9781933032436, 2003

Rhyming verse describes the good food, decorations, and stories when the grandmother arrives for the annual celebration of the Mexican holiday, Day of the Dead.

Lexile: N/A　(Grades K–3)　F

Goldman, Judy. *Uncle Monarch and the Day of the Dead.*　ISBN-13: 9781590784259, 2008

Lupita and her family get ready for the holiday. When the first of November arrives, the family will go to the cemetery to honor the memories of their loved ones. But this year is different—Lupita's uncle cannot join them. Now Lupita learns the true meaning of the celebration.　　Lexile: N/A　(Grades 2–5)　F

Johnston, Tony. *Day of the Dead.*　　　ISBN-13: 9780152024468, 2000

This book introduces the traditions of Day of the Dead as two children notice all the food being cooked, the flowers being gathered, and the special packages bought at the bakery that they long to taste, smell, and investigate.　　Lexile: N/A　(Grades K–3)　NF

Keep, Richard. *Clatter Bash! A Day of the Dead Celebration.*   ISBN-13: 9781561453221, 2004

This book honors both the memorial and festive aspects of this Mexican holiday.

Lexile: N/A   (Grades K–3)   NF

Lowery, Linda. *Day of the Dead.*   ISBN-13: 9781575055817, 2003

This text speaks about the Mexican holiday that celebrates the cycle of life.

Lexile: N/A   (Grades K–3)   NF

Luenn, Nancy. *Gift for Abuelita/Un regalo para Abuelita: Celebrating the Day of the Dead/En Celebración del Día de los Muertos.*   ISBN-13: 9780873586887, 1998

After her beloved grandmother dies, Rosita hopes to be reunited with Abuelita as she prepares a gift to give her when her family celebrates the Day of the Dead.

Lexile: N/A   (Grades 1–3)   F

Muller, Birte. *Felipa and the Day of the Dead.*   ISBN-13: 9780735820111, 2005

In the Andes Mountains, Felipa misses her grandmother Abuelita and goes in search of her soul, only to find the celebration of the Day of the Dead to be the perfect way to feel close to Abuelita again.   Lexile: N/A   (Grades 1–3)   F

San Vicente, Luis. *Festival of the bones / El festival de las Calaveras.*

ISBN-13: 9780938317678, 2002

This book describes the Day of the Dead, or *el Día de los muertos*, a holiday celebrated in Mexico from October 31 to November 2.   Lexile: N/A   (Grades K–3)   F

Election Day

Battle-Lavert, Gwendolyn. *Papa's Mark.*

ISBN-13: 9780823416509, 2004

This is the story about the historical scope referencing blacks' hesitancy about voting, as they fear trouble from angry whites.   Lexile: 430L   (Grades K–3)   NF

Bausum, Ann. *With Courage and Cloth: Winning the Fight for a Woman's Right to Vote.*

ISBN-13: 9780792276470, 2004

This book explains how support for women's suffrage grew, leading to the passage of the 19th Amendment in 1919, and the battle to get it ratified by three-fourths of the nation's 48 states. The story of how half the U.S. population earned voting rights is an important part of American history, and it is told in a straightforward way.

Lexile: 1080L   (Grades 5–12)   NF

Christelow, Eileen. *Vote!*   ISBN-13: 9780547059730, 2004

Using a town's mayoral election as a model, this book introduces voting and covers every step in the process, from the start of the campaign all the way to the voting booth.

Lexile: N/A   (Grades 2–5)   NF

McNamara, Margaret. *Election Day.*   ISBN-13: 9780689864254, 2004

It's Becky's first day at Robin Hill School. She thinks she would make a great class president, but she's new and has no friends yet. But since it's election day, she goes for it anyway.

Lexile: 350L   (Grades 2–5)   F

Nobleman, Marc Tyler. *Election Day.*   ISBN-13: 9780756509583, 2004

This book teaches what and when Election Day is.

Lexile: IG760L   (Grades 2–5)   NF

Veteran's Day

Crew, Gary. *Memorial.*   ISBN-13: 9781894965088, 2004

A young boy tells the moving story of a particular tree planted as a memorial to soldiers killed in World War I, as related to him by his great grandfather, grandfather, and father, each of whom has participated in wars over the years.

Lexile: N/A   (Grades 2–5)   F

Henry, Heather French. *Pepper's Purple Heart.*

ISBN-13: 9780970634108, 2003

Through the eyes of a little girl named Claire and her friend Robbie, children learn about this nation's veterans and why we honor them on Veterans Day.

Lexile: N/A   (Grades 2–5)   F

Landau, Elaine. *Veterans Day: Remembering Our War Heroes.*

ISBN-13: 9780766017757, 2002

Learn about Veterans Day and how we celebrate those who have fought for this country.

Lexile: N/A   (Grades K–4)   NF

Rissman, Rebecca. *Veterans Day.*   ISBN-13: 9781432940720, 2010

This book explains what happens on this holiday and the festivals that are celebrated in association with it.   Lexile: 460L   (Grades Pre-K–1)   NF

Sorenson, Lynda. *Veterans Day.*   ISBN-13: 9781571030702, 1994

This book teaches readers about this important holiday.   Lexile: N/A   (Grades K–2)   NF

Walker, Robert. *Veterans Day.*   ISBN-13: 9780778747857, 2010

This book teaches readers about the elements that make up the importance of this holiday.

Lexile: NC930L   (Grades 1–4)   NF

Thanksgiving

Allegra, Mike. *Sarah Gives Thanks: How Thanksgiving Became a National Holiday.*   ISBN-13: 9780807572399, 2012

During the 19th century, Sarah Josepha Hale dedicated her life to making Thanksgiving a national holiday, all while raising a family and becoming a groundbreaking writer and women's magazine editor.

Lexile: AD730L   (Grades 2–5)   NF

Bunting, Eve. *How Many Days to America?*   ISBN-13: 9780395547779, 1990

After the police come, a family is forced to flee their Caribbean island and set sail in a small fishing boat toward America where they have a special reason to celebrate Thanksgiving.

Lexile: 460L   (Grades 2–5)   F

Corey, Shana. *Milly and the Macy's Parade.*   ISBN-13: 9780439297554, 2006

Concerned that the immigrant employees of New York City's Macy's department store are homesick at Christmas, a young girl inspires the store's head to hold the first Macy's Parade. Based on a true story, this book includes a historical note.

Lexile: 0420L   (Grades Pre-K–3)   NF

Cowley, Joy. *Gracias: The Thanksgiving Turkey.*   ISBN-13: 9780439769877, 1998

When Papa sends a turkey to be fattened up for Thanksgiving, Miguel takes a liking to the friendly bird. But it's not a pet—he's supposed to be a meal.   Lexile: 470L   (Grades 2–5)   F

Grace, Catherine O'Neill. *1621: A New Look at Thanksgiving.*

ISBN-13: 9780792261391, 2004

This book puts aside that myth and takes a new look at American history. It questions what we know and recovers lost voices of the Wampanoag people.

Lexile: N/A   (Grades 2–5)   NF

Herman, Charlotte. *The Memory Cupboard: A Thanksgiving Story.*

ISBN-13: 9780807550557, 2003

When Katie breaks a gravy boat at Thanksgiving dinner, her grandmother shows her that love is more important than objects.   Lexile: N/A   (Grades 1–4)   F

Kamma, Anne. *If You Were at the First Thanksgiving.*   ISBN-13: 9780439105668, 2001

Nearly half of the 52 Pilgrims at the First Thanksgiving were children age 16 and younger. This book is written from a child's perspective and discusses life in the new settlement of Plymouth.   Lexile: N/A   (Grades 2–5)   NF

Markes, Julie. *Thanks for Thanksgiving.*   ISBN-13: 9780060510985, 2008

At Thanksgiving time, children express their gratitude for the people and things in their lives.   Lexile: N/A   (Grades Pre-K–3)   NF

Pomeranc, Marion Hess. *The Can-Do Thanksgiving.*   ISBN-13: 9780807510544, 1998

A young girl, Dee, experiences excitement and satisfaction when she helps prepare and serve food for the needy at a church on Thanksgiving.   Lexile: N/A   (Grades K–3)   F

Chanukah (Hanukkah)

Alko, Selina. *Daddy Christmas and Hanukkah Mama.*

ISBN-13: 9780375860935, 2012

Holiday time at Sadie's house means golden gelt sparkling under the Christmas tree, candy canes hanging on eight menorah branches, voices uniting to sing carols about Maccabees and the manger, and latkes on the mantel awaiting Santa's arrival.   Lexile: N/A   (Grades K–3)   F

Da Costa, Deborah. *Hanukkah Moon.*   ISBN-13: 9781580132442, 2007

An unusual Hanukkah story with a multicultural focus, this title celebrates a little-known custom of the Latin-Jewish community.   Lexile: 6448L   (Grades Pre-K–3)   F

Glaser, Linda. *The Borrowed Hanukkah Latkes.*   ISBN-13: 9780807508428, 1997

A young girl finds a way to include her elderly neighbor in her family's Hanukkah celebration.   Lexile: N/A   (Grades K–3)   F

Glaser, Linda. *Mrs. Greenberg's Messy Hanukkah.*   ISBN-13: 9780807552988, 2004

When Rachel makes latkes with her friend Mrs. Greenberg, the project turns out to be a very messy one.   Lexile: N/A   (Grades 1–4)   F

Heiligman, Deborah. *Celebrate Hanukkah with Light, Latkes, and Dreidels.*

ISBN-13: 9781426302930, 2006

This book shares the holiday celebrated by Jewish communities around the world. Also included are a latke recipe, Hanukkah blessings, and a Hanukkah song.

Lexile: N/A   (Grades K–3)   NF

Rosen, Michael J. *Chanukah Lights Everywhere.*   ISBN-13: 9780152056759, 2006

A young boy counts the candles on the family menorah and the lights he sees in the world around him on each night of Hanukkah.   Lexile: N/A   (Grades K–3)   NF

Schotter, Roni. *Hanukkah!*   ISBN-13: 9780316034777, 2003

This is a first step to discovering Hanukkah traditions.   Lexile: N/A   (Grades Pre-K–2)   NF

Yolen, Jane. *How Do Dinosaurs Say Happy Chanukah?*   ISBN-13: 9780545416771, 2012

From holiday candles in the menorah to family gatherings, these dinosaurs celebrate the Festival of Lights. But in their excitement for Chanukah, misbehavior can occur.

Lexile: 0570L   (Grades Pre-K–2)   F

Christmas

Alko, Selina. *Daddy Christmas and Hanukkah Mama.*

ISBN-13: 9780375860935, 2012

Holiday time at Sadie's house means golden gelt sparkling under the Christmas tree, candy canes hanging on eight menorah branches, voices uniting to sing carols about Maccabees and the manger, and latkes on the mantel awaiting Santa's arrival.

Lexile: N/A   (Grades K–3)   F

Anaya, Rudolfo. *The Farolitos of Christmas.*

ISBN-13: 9780786800605, 1995

It's Christmas in San Juan, New Mexico, and young Luz worries that with her grandfather sick and her father in the hospital, wounded from the war, they will not have their usual Christmas celebration. Then Luz decides to make her own little lanterns, or *farolitos*, to light the path for the oncoming celebration and for her father, who returns home in time for the holiday.

Lexile: 410L   (Grades Pre-K–6)   F

Freeberg, Jane. *The Scallop Christmas.*   ISBN-13: 9781934031254, 2009

Times were tough in the small New England fishing village where Marcie lived. No one had any money, and work was hard to find. So the villagers rejoiced one glorious fall when an unexpected bounty of scallops filled their little bay. For young Marcie, a week of harvesting scallops also brought an unexpected adventure and a lesson about love that she would never forget.

Lexile: N/A   (Grades Pre-K–3)   F

Henry, O., illustrated by P. J. Lynch. *The Gift of the Magi.*   ISBN-13: 9780763635305, 2008

Della sacrifices to buy a Christmas present for her husband, Jim, as she considers selling her long, beautiful hair. Jim makes his own sacrifice for Della that is no less difficult. As they exchange gifts on Christmas Eve, they discover what each has done and realize that the true gifts of Christmas can be found more readily around them.

Lexile: 0870L   (Grades 5–9)   F

Jeffers, Susan. *Nutcracker.*   ISBN-13: 9780060743864, 2007

This lovely text is based on the classic ballet.   Lexile: 6448L   (Grades Pre-K–3)   F

Litwin, Eric. *Pete the Cat Saves Christmas.*   ISBN-13: 9780062110626, 2012

In this spin on the traditional tale *The Night Before Christmas*, Pete the Cat gives his all in the spirit of Christmas.   Lexile: N/A   (Grades Pre-K–3)   F

Moore, Clement C. *The Night Before Christmas.*   ISBN-13: 9781604332377, 2011

This traditional Christmas poem includes a modern take on the illustrations and Santa's tools, though he still has reindeer.   Lexile: N/A   (Grades Pre-K–2)   F

Mora, Pat. *A Piñata in a Pine Tree: A Latino Twelve Days of Christmas.*

ISBN-13: 9780618841981, 2009

In this version a little girl receives gifts from a secret *amiga*, whose identity is a sweet surprise at the book's conclusion. There are things to find and count in Spanish on every page, with pronunciations provided right in the pictures, and a glossary and music following the story. Lexile: N/A (Grades Pre-K–2) F

Polacco, Patricia. *Christmas Tapestry.* ISBN-13: 9780399239557, 2012

A tapestry that is being used to cover a hole in a church wall at Christmas brings together an elderly couple who were separated during World War II.

Lexile: 0490L (Grades Pre-K–3) F

Polacco, Patricia. *Welcome Comfort.* ISBN-13: 9780698119659, 2002

Welcome Comfort, a lonely foster child, is assured by his friend the school custodian that there is a Santa Claus, but he does not discover the truth until one wondrous and surprising Christmas Eve. Lexile: 0520L (Grades Pre-K–3) F

Primavera, Elise. *Auntie Claus.* ISBN-13: 9780547406220, 2010

When her eccentric Auntie Claus leaves for her annual business trip, Sophie stows away in her luggage, travels with her to the North Pole, and discovers that her aunt is really Santa's sister and helper. Lexile: N/A (Grades Pre-K–2) F

Primavera, Elise. *Auntie Claus and the Key to Christmas.* ISBN-13: 9780152024413, 2002

When Chris expresses doubt about the existence of Santa Claus, his older sister Sophie reveals that their aunt is really Santa's sister and helper and then sends him on a strange journey. Lexile: 400L (Grades Pre-K–2) F

Robinson, Barbara. *The Best Christmas Pageant Ever.* ISBN-13: 9780064402750, 1997

The six Herdman children are the meanest, toughest kids in town. But when they experience the Christmas story for the first time, they help everyone else rediscover its true meaning. Lexile: 930L (Grades 3–6) F

Van Allsburg, Chris. *The Polar Express.* ISBN-13: 9780395389492, 2009

A young man tells a story of his childhood and how his belief in Santa comes to life one snowy Christmas Eve. Lexile: 520L (Grades K–5) F

Yolen, Jane. *How Do Dinosaurs Say Merry Christmas?* ISBN-13: 9780545416788, 2012

From decorating the tree to wrapping presents, these dinosaurs celebrate Christmas. But with the spirit of Christmas, they struggle going to sleep with all the excitement. How can they calm down and behave? Lexile: 0570L (Grades Pre-K–2) F

Kwanzaa

Ford, Juwanda G. *Together for Kwanzaa.*

ISBN-13: 9780375803291, 2000

A perfect introduction to Kwanzaa, this book will teach children all about the traditions and practices that make it special. Lexile: N/A   (Grades Pre-K–2)   NF

Katz, Karen. *My First Kwanzaa.*   ISBN-13: 9780805070774, 2003

This introduction to the African American holiday is told through the eyes of a young girl celebrating with her family. Lexile: N/A   (Grades Pre-K–2)   F

Morninghouse, Sundaira. *Habari Gani? What's the News?*   ISBN-13: 9780940880399, 1992

December 26 to January 1 will never be the same for seven-year-old Kia and her family. The Edwards are celebrating Kwanzaa, the only indigenous, non-heroic African American holiday in the United States. "Habari Gani," replaces "Hi." As each day unfolds, Kia experiences the seven principles of Kwanzaa woven into her family and community life and learns that Kwanzaa is a cultural and political celebration of the African American experience.

Lexile: N/A   (Grades K–4)   F

Otto, Carolyn B. *Celebrate Kwanzaa: With Candles, Community, and the Fruits of the Harvest.*   ISBN-13: 9781426307058, 2010

This book celebrates African American culture and helps us understand and appreciate this special holiday. Lexile: N/A   (Grades Pre-K–2)   NF

Tokunbo, Dimitrea. *The Sound of Kwanzaa.*   ISBN-13: 9780545018654, 2009

For each of the seven nights of the celebration, a candle is lit, symbolizing one of the principles of the holiday. Lexile: N/A   (Grades Pre-K–2)   NF

New Year's

Lewis, Paul Owen. *P. Bear's New Year's Party: A Counting Book.*   ISBN-13: 9781883672997, 1999

A polar bear has a New Year's party and invites all of his animal friends. As each party animal arrives, children learn to count and tell time.

Lexile: N/A   (Grades Pre-K–1)   F

Martin, Bill, Jr. *The Happy Hippopotami.*

ISBN-13: 9780152333829, 1992

The happy hippopotami enjoy a merry holiday at the beach, wearing pretty beach pajamas, dancing the maypole, or battling with water guns. Lexile: N/A   (Grades Pre-K–1)   F

Marx, David F. *New Year's Day.* ISBN-13: 9780516271569, 2000

This text teaches readers about how New Year's is celebrated on different days by different cultures.

Lexile: N/A   (Grades Pre-K–1)   NF

Perry, Marie Fritz. *Cecil's New Year's Eve Tail.* ISBN-13: 9780975567524, 2007

When Cecil the snake is invited to a New Year's Eve ball in New York City, his insecurities almost prevent him from enjoying the evening with his friends. Along the way, he learns an important lesson about acceptance and friendship.   Lexile: N/A   (Grades Pre-K–3)   F

Ruelle, Karen Gray. *Just in Time for New Year's! A Harry and Emily Adventure.*

ISBN-13: 9780823418428, 2004

Harry and his sister Emily want to stay up for New Year's Eve. Dad agrees, and the two have three nights to practice. Their attempts to stay up until midnight don't seem to work. They decide that noise is the answer to keeping them awake.   Lexile: N/A   (Grades Pre-K–2)   F

16

Linking Books Across the Curriculum and the Common Core

The Common Core State Standards provide a consistent, clear understanding of what students are expected to learn, so teachers and parents know what they need to do to help them. The standards are designed to be robust and relevant to the real world, reflecting the knowledge and skills that our young people need for success in college and careers. With American students fully prepared for the future, our communities will be best positioned to compete successfully in the global economy.

—http://www.corestandards.org/

The Common Core Standards have been unveiled across the nation and will connect subject areas in a variety of ways. Considering the previously mentioned Mission Statement about the Common Core, teachers need to continue to prepare themselves to adjust their current curriculum to be more "robust and relevant to the real world, reflecting the knowledge and skills that our young people need for success in college and careers." When considering the use of children's and young adult books in the English language arts (ELA) curriculum, finding ways to link these books across curricular areas makes for opportunities to show real-life connections to the stories and how they can be used within the other subject areas.

When thinking about the ELA standards, the requirements are not only for ELA but also for teaching *literacy* in history and social studies, science, and technical subjects. Students must learn to read, write, speak, listen, and use language effectively in a variety of content areas to show literacy skills and understanding required for college and career readiness in multiple disciplines.

Literacy standards for single-subject areas are predicated on teachers of ELA, history and social studies, science, and technical subjects, using their content area expertise to help students meet the particular challenges of reading, writing, speaking, listening, and language in their respective fields. The literacy standards in history and social studies, science, and technical subjects are not meant to replace content standards in those areas but rather to supplement them: secondary teachers still need to adhere to their subject-specific standards while incorporating literacy standards into their planning as well.

Students who meet the standards undertake attentive reading that is at the heart of understanding complex works of literature. They then can perform critical analysis when moving through the vast amount of information in print and digital forms. Given these skills, they can also actively seek high-quality literary and informational texts. This will help students build knowledge, enlarge experiences, and broaden worldviews. Students who meet the standards develop the skills in reading, writing, speaking, and listening that are the foundation for any creative and purposeful expression in language, no matter the subject area.

Being able to plan lessons while incorporating great books into the curriculum will help prepare students who are college and career ready in reading, writing, speaking, listening, and language. The following are not standards in themselves but offer a portrait of students who meet the standards. As students advance through the grades and master the standards in reading, writing, speaking, listening, and language, they are able to exhibit with increasing fullness and regularity these capacities of the literate individual, which cross over into all subject areas. The ELA standards take on a huge responsibility for helping prepare students in the other subject areas. According to the Common Core website (http://www.corestandards.org/), the ELAs help students:

- **Demonstrate independence.** Students comprehend and evaluate complex texts across a range of types and disciplines, construct effective arguments, and convey intricate or multifaceted information.
- **Build strong content knowledge.** Students become proficient in new areas through research to gain both general knowledge and discipline-specific expertise. They refine and share their knowledge through writing and speaking.
- **Respond to the varying demands of audience, task, purpose, and discipline.** They set and adjust purpose for reading, writing, speaking, listening, and language use as warranted by the task.
- **Comprehend as well as critique.** Students understand precisely what an author or speaker is saying, but they also question an author's or speaker's assumptions and premises and assess the veracity of claims and the soundness of reasoning.

- **Value evidence.** Students cite specific evidence when offering an oral or written interpretation of a text, make their reasoning clear to the reader or listener, and constructively evaluate others' use of evidence.
- **Use technology and digital media strategically and capably.** Students employ technology thoughtfully to enhance their reading, writing, speaking, listening, and language use.
- **Come to understand other perspectives and cultures.** Students understand other diverse experiences, perspectives, and cultures through reading and listening, and they are able to communicate effectively with people of varied backgrounds. Through reading great classic and contemporary works of literature representative of a variety of periods, cultures, and worldviews, students inhabit worlds and appreciate experiences much different than their own.

Incorporating a wide variety of rich and interesting literature into the K–12 curriculum will support these connections and critical learning. The last item mentioned in the previous list, that students come to understand other perspectives and cultures, is likely one of the most important when it comes to choosing relevant books for the ELA curriculum. Books that offer all students an opportunity to know more about their peers and develop connections between them are the ones you should seek for your classroom and library bookshelves. Additionally, titles that can support the subject areas in which teachers have expertise ought to be considered.

This chapter introduces you to several age- and grade-appropriate books as witness to how one title can be linked across the curriculum in many subject areas for not only secondary-grade levels but also for the elementary grades. You will want to think about how the key features of the ELA standards serve as the core in which all other subject areas can follow as these features lend themselves to any subject that requires the following:

- **Reading:** text complexity and the growth of comprehension
- **Writing:** text types, responding to reading, and research
- **Speaking and listening:** flexible communication and collaboration
- **Language:** Conventions, effective use, and vocabulary

The lesson ideas offered in this chapter for each book title will help you start planning for any appropriate grade-level book. Somewhat general in nature, these ideas can be used for most books related to the given grade- and subject-specific content and can be tweaked based on the books you choose for your students' use.

Kindergarten

Top Books for Kindergarten

Actual Size by Steve Jenkins (Houghton Mifflin, 2004).

Bee-Bim Bop by Linda Sue Park, illustrated by Ho Baek Lee (Clarion Books, 2005).

The Boy Who Wouldn't Share by Mike Reiss (Harper Collins, 2008).

Chicka Chicka Boom Boom by Bill Martin, Jr., and John Archambault, illustrated by Lois Ehlert (Simon and Schuster, 1989).

Cleversticks by Bernard Ashley, illustrated by Derek Brazell (Dragonfly Books, 1995).

David Goes to School by David Shannon (Blue Sky Press, 1999).

The Giving Tree by Shel Silverstein (Harper Collins, 2004).

I Can Read with My Eyes Shut by Dr. Seuss (Random House, 1978).

Knuffle Bunny Too: A Case of Mistaken Identity by Mo Willems (Hyperion Books for Children, 2007).

The Lorax by Dr. Seuss (Random House Books for Young Readers, 1971)

My Five Senses by Aliki (Collins, 1989)

Mama Panya's Pancakes: A Village Tale from Kenya by Mary and Richard Chamberlin, illustrated by Julia Cairns (Barefoot Books, 2006).

One Potato, Two Potato by Cynthia DeFelice, illustrated by Andrea U'Ren (Farrar, Straus & Giroux, 2006).

The True Story of the 3 Little Pigs! by Jon Scieszka, illustrated by Lane Smith (Penguin Putnam Inc. 1996).

Lesson Ideas

Dr. Seuss. *One Fish, Two Fish, Red Fish, Blue Fish.*
(1960). Random House Children's Books.   ISBN-13: 9780756921330

This is a book of rhyming adventures in a fantasy world. It taps into simple rhyming patterns with real and nonsensical words. Children love the illustrations, and it is easy to learn rhyming patterns.   Lexile: 0180L   (Pre-K–3)

Reading

- *One Fish, Two Fish, Red Fish, Blue Fish* is the perfect book to read aloud to younger children. Read aloud the story once, all the way through, not stopping but changing the lilt in your voice as the rhyming patterns shift. Then, read it aloud a second time, stopping along the way to point out rhyming patterns. If you have access to this book from the classroom or

school library as a big book, be sure to point out the words as you read them aloud. If you have access to an overhead projector, you can also post the book onto the whiteboard and read it aloud this way so all students can see the words. Again, be sure to track the words with a ruler or pointer as you read them aloud.

Writing

- As a whole class, have students help you create nonsensical poems. Use excerpts from the book as a guide by writing one or two on the board for students to follow.
- Using words from the text in the book, make a word list or wall of numbers (*one, two, three, four, . . . eleven*), colors (*blue, red, yellow,* etc.), and directions (*here, there, everywhere, far, high, low,* etc.). Have students use these words to help you write nonsensical poems.
- Teach students what antonyms are by using examples from the book. Show corresponding pictures so students can "see" the antonyms (*longer, shorter, old, new, near, far, fast, slow, high, low,* etc.).
- To teach adjectives, specifically in regard to physical attributes (*fat, old, new, sad, glad, little, bad, thin,* etc.) use examples from the book and have students tap into these as you work on the nonsensical poems.
- To teach the use of rhyming words, use combinations from the story (*fear, ear, dear, mouse, house, old, gold, hold, cold, book, hook, nook, cook, swish, fish, dish, wink, drink, ink, pink, wet, pet,* etc.) and then have students come up with as many rhyming words as they can. Transcribe these onto the board.

Math

- To teach counting, use the numbers 1 to 11 from the book to teach counting. Write these numbers on the board and see if students can continue counting as far as 30. As they say the numbers out loud, write them on the board. Take this further and have them help you count by 2s. Place a circle around the 2s as students call them out. Continue to do this for 5s and 10s.
- Teach students directions by using words from the book (*here, there, far, near, high, low,* etc.), and then have students stand up and respond to directions as you call them out. For example, "Stand far away from your desk," "Stand near your best friend," "Get down low to the floor," "Stand up high on your toes," and so on. You may want two to four volunteers at a time for this activity, rather than the whole class.

Science

- Teach students the difference between fish and land animals. One way to do this is to compare and contrast body parts. For example, fish have gills, fins, a tail, and so on, while land animals have four legs, a tail, and so on.
- Using weather discussed in the book, have students give examples of what a day would be like if there were sunlight, rain, snow, wind, and so on. Then have them divide a piece of paper into four quadrants and draw a weather example in each quadrant. You may want to model how to draw the weather examples you discuss and then label them.
- Using the illustrations from the text, describe what it means to push and pull. Have volunteers come up and demonstrate the correct way to push and to pull objects.
- Review the five senses (see, smell, taste, hear, feel) with the students. This works well if you have a variety of items (horn, piece of fuzzy material, vanilla candle, M&Ms, bright colored paper), which can contribute to a specific sense. Have students go through each sense for several items and explain what they are seeing, feeling, tasting, smelling, and hearing.

History and Geography

- The book discusses several modes of transportation (air, land, sea). Show pictures of a plane, a car, a bicycle, a boat, a train, and so on, and have students share the types of transportation they have used before. Then have students illustrate two modes of transportation they haven't experienced before.
- In the book, students are introduced to several diverse people, some real and some made-up. A simple way to teach diversity (individual differences) is to talk about how different we all are and have students help you create a list of the ways we are all the same and all different. Remind them not to use names of friends or family but just to share attributes they see as the same and different (hair color, glasses, short, tall, and more).
- Using a world map, have students decide if they would have to take a train, plane, car, or bike or walk to get from one location to another as you point out the locations on the map. Note distances and the need to cross water so they can connect boats to water and distance to air travel, and so on.

Art

- Have students choose their favorite snippet and drawing from the book and illustrate it on their own. They can use the picture from the book as a guide, but encourage them to get creative.
- Draw any of the numbers from the book (1 to 11), and have students create a monster out of the number they choose. Be sure to model this for them. Use lots of color and character.

First Grade

Top Books for First Grade

Alexander and the Terrible, Horrible, No Good, Very Bad Day by Judith Viorst, illustrated by Ray Cruz (Aladdin, 1987).

The Apple Pie That Papa Baked by Lauren Thompson, illustrated by Jonathan Bean (Simon & Schuster, 2007).

Clementine by Sara Pennypacker, illustrated by Marla Frazee (Hyperion, 2006).

Dad, Jackie, and Me by Myron Uhlberg, illustrated by Colin Bootman (Peachtree Publishers, 2005).

The Empty Pot by Demi (Henry Holt, 1996).

How I Became a Pirate by Melinda Long, illustrated by David Shannon (Harcourt Children's Books, 2003).

M Is for Music by Kathleen Krull, illustrated by Stacy Innerst (Harcourt Brace, 2003).

Miss Smith's Incredible Story Book by Michael Garland (Dutton, 2003).

The New Girl . . . and Me by Jacqui Robbins, illustrated by Matt Phelan (Simon & Schuster, 2006).

Reduce and Reuse by Sally Hewitt (Franklin Watts, 2011)

Stuff! Reduce, Reuse, Recycle by Steven Kroll, illustrated by Steve Cox (Crabtree Publishing, 2008).

The Very Hungry Caterpillar by Eric Carle (Philomel Books, 1987).

Wheels! by Annie Cobb (Random House Books for Young Readers, 1986).

Widget by Lyn Rossiter McFarland, illustrated by Jim McFarland (Square Fish, 2006).

Lesson Ideas

Eric Carle. *The Very Hungry Caterpillar.* (1986). Penguin Group.   ISBN-13: 9780399226236

This is one of the most well-known Eric Carle stories on classroom and library shelves. It is funny and full of colorful illustrations, written in narrative form about a hungry caterpillar that grows up to be a beautiful butterfly.   Lexile: AD460L   (Pre-K–3)

Reading

- *The Very Hungry Caterpillar* is a book to read aloud, stopping along the way to ask students to explain what is going on (summarizing) and what is going to happen next (predicting). If you have access to this book from the classroom or school library as a big book, use a ruler or pointer to track the words as you read them aloud. If you have access to a document reader, you can also project the book onto the whiteboard and read it aloud this way so all students can see the words. Again, be sure to track the words with a ruler or pointer as you read them aloud.

Writing

- Create a flipbook with the students to show the sequence of the story. You will want to start off by modeling this on the board with large construction paper so the students can see what you expect of them. They will use regular white paper, which you will need to prepare in advance. Choose at least five events from the story, illustrate each event, and label them for the students to use as a guide when they illustrate their own. Don't forget to have the front be the title page. Hand out the premade flipbooks and ask the students to create their own, using yours as a guide.
- Have the students write a sequel for the butterfly. After reading the book aloud, ask the students to come up with a variety of ideas about what happens to the butterfly. Where does it go? Where does it live? What does it eat? Who are its friends? You may even want to include a geography lesson, showing on the world map where specific types of butterflies are common.
- The students can also write a letter to the hungry caterpillar with your help. Have students contribute ideas as you demonstrate how to write a friendly letter to the caterpillar. Talk about the adventures he has had, all the food he ate, what it must be like to form a chrysalis or cocoon, and ask if the caterpillar is excited or scared to turn into a butterfly.
- After reading the story, it might be fun to review the story again, page by page, and create a list of all the foods that the caterpillar ate. Have students include additional food items they might have wanted to eat if they were caterpillars.
- A different way to sequence the story might be to cut out a handful of circles from construction paper. On each circle, students can draw and label the part of the story it belongs to and then paste the circles together in sequence. They can add a face and legs as well.

Math

- To review counting, have students count the number of holes punched out for each of the days the caterpillar eats through foods. Then for Saturday, have the students count the different types of foods the caterpillar ate.

- Using the text from the book, teach students to compare greater than and less than, by asking the students questions such as, "Did the caterpillar eat more or less on Tuesday than on Friday?"
- Have students sequence the story by using ordinal numbers (*first, second, next, last*).

Science

- Review the life cycle of the butterfly by using pictures from the story. You may even want to photocopy the pictures that show the stages of the life cycle.
- Since this book focuses on healthy foods and unhealthy foods, introduce the food pyramid/food plate. Then using the foods mentioned in the book, decide which part of the food pyramid the food items would fit into. To take this a step further, have each student share a favorite food and decide where it would fit on the pyramid. You may want to graph this with the students.

History and Geography

- Discuss with the students all the people within the community who are needed to meet the nutritional needs of their community. People you might want to consider would include a farmer, baker, chef, grocery store employee, doctor, nutritionist, and more. Make a list of the ways in which these people contribute to the health needs of a community.
- Use the Internet to look up various types of butterflies around the world, then visit places on the world map to show where these places are.

Art

- Butterflies have many colors. To teach children how to make new colors by using primary colors, have them layer tissue paper. For instance, lay one on top of another, such as blue and yellow to make green, red and blue to make purple, orange and red to make yellow, and so on.
- Using the collage and torn art of Eric Carle's style, have students make caterpillars or butterflies with torn construction paper and glue. You may have to tear some of the paper for them in advance, but it's OK if they do this on their own, so long as you model it for them first.

Second Grade

Top Books for Second Grade

Baseball Saved Us by Ken Mochizuki, illustrated by Dom Lee (Lee & Low Books, 1995).

Chig and the Second Spread by Gwenyth Swain (Yearling, 2005).

Children Just Like Me by Anabel Kindersley (DK Children, 1995).

Cloudy with a Chance of Meatballs by Judi Barrett, illustrated by Ronald Barrett (Atheneum, 1978).

Dear Max by Sally Grindley, illustrated by Tony Ross (Simon & Schuster, 2006).

Diary of a Worm by Doreen Cronin, illustrated by Harry Bliss (Harpers Childrens, 2003).

A Fine, Fine School by Sharon Creech, illustrated by Harry Bliss (Joanna Cotler, 2001).

Gator Gumbo by Candace Fleming, illustrated by Sally Anne Lambert (Farrar Straus Giroux, 2004).

Mr. George Baker by Amy Hest, illustrated by Jon J. Muth (Candlewick, 2004).

Sam and the Lucky Money by Karen Chinn, illustrated by Cornelius Van Wright and Ying-Hwa Hu (Lee & Low Books, 1997).

Sneakers, the Seaside Cat by Margaret Wise Brown, illustrated by Anne Mortimer (HarperTrophy, 2005).

Why the Sky Is Far Away: A Nigerian Folktale by Mary-Joan Gerson, illustrated by Carla Golembe (Little, Brown, 1995).

Lesson Ideas

Judith Viorst. *Alexander and the Terrible, Horrible, No Good, Very Bad Day.* (2009). Simon & Schuster.   ISBN-13: 9781416985952

This story is about a boy named Alexander who starts his day off in a terrible way and it only gets worse. Readers are taken through a series of humorous events that create a terrible, horrible, no good very bad day for Alexander. Children can relate to the comical events of this story.   Lexile: AD970L   (K–3)

Reading

- Read this story aloud with a focus on repetition. The book repeats, "It was a terrible, horrible, no good, very bad day." Allow the students to chime in when this line occurs. If using a big book to read this story, point to each of the words in this repetitive line and instead of saying it out loud with the students, let them say it as you point to each word.

Writing

- Take students through sequencing the story by choosing four of the most important events from the story.
- Students can write about how they can relate to this very bad day by writing about their worst day.
- Students can write a letter to Alexander sympathizing with him.
- Students can rewrite the ending to the story or write a story about Alexander's wonderful, perfect, super good day.

Math

- To review the number events in the story, have them go through the text and count how many times Alexander runs into trouble. This will help students in their writing as well as give them an idea of how many events to write about in their own essay for their very bad day or for Alexander's best day.
- Have students use the storyline and items presented in this book to create story problems (e.g., lima beans).

Science

- Using any lima bean lesson plan from the Internet or teacher resource books, have students grow lima beans. This is obviously more accessible if you are serving as a long-term sub.

History and Geography

- Teaching character traits such as persevering, sportsmanship, and getting along with others is perfect after reading a story like this.

Art

- Have students create a new book jacket that shows an event from the story.
- To share students' favorite events from the story, give students a paper plate. Have them draw a cross through the plate to make four quadrants and then have them illustrate four events. Ask them to add text to explain the illustration in each quadrant.

Third Grade

Top Books for Third Grade

I Love Saturdays y domingos by Alma Flor Ada, illustrated by Elivia Savadier (Atheneum, 2002).

La Mariposa by Francisco Jiménez, illustrated by Simón Silva (Houghton Mifflin, 1998).

My Name Is Maria Isabel by Alma Flor Ada, illustrated by K. Dyble Thompson (Aladdin, 1995).

The Quiltmaker's Journey by Jeff Brumbeau, illustrated by Gail de Marcken (Orchard, 2005).

The Rag Coat by Lauren Mills (Little, Brown Young Readers, 1991).

Stellaluna by Janell Cannon (Harcourt Children's Books, 1993).

The Story of Ruby Bridges by Robert Coles, illustrated by George Ford (Scholastic, 2010).

Thank You, Mr. Falker by Patricia Polacco (Philomel, 1988).

Lesson Ideas

Shel Silverstein. *The Giving Tree* (40th Anniversary Edition). (2004). Harper Collins.

ISBN-13: 9780060586751

In this book, students are exposed to the gift of giving and the notion of love. Readers are taken on a journey throughout the life of a boy who grows to be a man and a tree that selflessly and generously gives him her bounty throughout the years.

Lexile: 530L   (Ages 6 to 10 years old)

Reading

- *The Giving Tree* is actually considered a chapter book but can easily be read within a 20-minute time period. It is suggested that you read it aloud one time through and then revisit sections in the book that show the boy taking and the tree giving. Have students consider sections from the book where this occurs; perhaps designate a couple of students as recorders to take notes while the book is read aloud. You may want to post sticky notes throughout to remind you where these sections are.

Writing

- As a whole class, develop a cause-and-effect graphic organizer.
- One way to sequence a story such as this is to discuss each of the events and list them in order on the board. Then have the students fold a piece of paper into six or eight sections so they can illustrate and label the order of events from the story.
- An important part of this story is the fact that the boy has taken so much from the tree. It would be a nice thing to have the students act as the boy and write an apology letter to the tree.

- Using the haiku poetry structure, have students write two to three Haiku poems about different trees they have studied for this book.

Math

- Teach students about measurement, specifically diameter, by measuring the diameter of a tree outside on the playground. Take this further once in the class and have students measure the width and length of two-, three-, or four-edged objects and add them together to find the perimeter.
- Have students go outside and collect twigs from a tree. Once inside, have them sort leaves by color, texture, size, and so on. Afterward, have students combine their leaves by similarities and show them how to graph them.

Science

- Have students go to the computer lab or use the computers in the classroom to study trees (deciduous vs. coniferous). This will lend itself to the activity on finding locations of indigenous trees for the geography activity.
- Students can study the life cycle of a seed and then illustrate and label each stage.
- Teach students about what kind of natural resources are available to them, and then how to conserve natural resources.
- Have students research the forest as a habitat for animals and trees.

History and Geography

- Teach students about the economic aspect of the use of trees. Have them share ideas about what materials they know are made from trees. Discuss how trees go from being cut down and made into something tangible and sold to the consumer. Talk about what can happen if too many trees are cut down and not enough are planted.
- Teach students about character traits such as empathy, kindness, selfishness versus selflessness, friendship, and more.
- Have the students do research and note different types of trees that are indigenous to certain locations (states, habitats, etc.) throughout the United States.

Art

- Using watercolors, white construction paper, and a variety of pictures as guides, have students paint trees using several watercolors. If you have time to pull some pictures from magazines or the Internet to project from your laptop, this will help students as they begin their own paintings.

- Take clipboards or paper and books outside to the school yard to pencil sketch trees. Go for a walking field trip in the yard or on the playground, and have students collect a variety of natural resources for creating an artistic piece of found objects (leaves, twigs, grass).

Fourth Grade

Top Books for Fourth Grade

Centerfield Ballhawk by Matt Christopher, illustrated by Ellen Beier (Little, Brown and Company, 1994).

A Chair for My Mother by Vera B. Williams (Econo-Clad Books, 1999).

Crickwing by Janell Cannon (Voyager Books, 2005).

Grandfather Counts by Andrea Cheng, illustrated by Ange Zhang (Lee & Low, 2003).

How Much Is a Million? by David M. Schwartz, illustrated by Steven Kellogg (HarperTrophy, 2004).

Math Curse by Jon Scieszka, illustrated by Lane Smith (Viking, 1995).

The Misadventures of Maude March by Audrey Couloumbis (Yearling, 2007).

The Patchwork Quilt by Valerie Flournoy, illustrated by Jerry Pinkney (E. P. Dutton, 1985).

Radio Man: A Story in English and Spanish by Arthur Dorros (HarperTrophy, 1997).

Sadako and the Thousand Paper Cranes by Eleanor Coerr, illustrated by Ronald Himler (Puffin, 2004).

Lesson Ideas

Marcia Brown. ***Stone Soup.*** (1997). Scholastic Press. ISBN-13: 9780689711039

Lexile: AD480L (Ages 4 to 10 years old)

Jon J. Muth. ***Stone Soup.*** (2003). Simon & Schuster. ISBN-13: 9780439339094

Lexile: 480L (Ages 4 to 10 years old)

In this story, soldiers march down the road toward a village. The peasants see them coming and suddenly become very busy. The villagers know that soldiers are usually hungry, so they hide their food. When the soldiers begin to make stone soup, the curious villagers begin to share their ingredients, such as add a carrot, some meat, and so on until a real pot of soup comes to life. This community of people comes together in the end.

Reading

- This text has a complicated storyline that allows perfect opportunities for you to stop and summarize, clarify, and predict as you read the book aloud. If several copies are available, do this as a shared reading where you read the text out loud while the students follow along. Otherwise, you can read the book aloud from start to finish, taking the time to stop to incorporate the previously mentioned reading strategies. Be sure to have a discussion about teamwork and coming together as a community after the story has been read.

Writing

- This book lends itself to retelling it as a play. Have student volunteers or randomly called students choose roles (list the roles on the board), and then have these students retell (act out) the story for the rest of the class.
- Have students rewrite the ending where the community remains selfish and does not share their goods.
- Have students create a comic strip using the characters from the story and the events from the storyline.
- Students can get creative with illustrations and short sentences, using a storyboard to sequence the events of the story. You can have them do this by folding a piece of paper into six or eight sections, depending on how much time you have or how many events you want them to use. The first section on the storyboard should include the title and author of the book as well as the student's name and date.

Math

- Pretend to cook stone soup. Have students work in small groups to get creative and come up with fractional measurements and instructions for pulling together their version of stone soup. Encourage students to make it fun even if it's nonsensical. To challenge them, have students explain how to double and triple the recipe as well.

Science

- After reading this book, students will have thoughts of stones and rocks in their minds. If you have access to a variety of rocks, as many fourth-grade classrooms do, have students use the rocks to test their observational skills. They can sort them by color, texture, size, shape, and so on, and they can illustrate and describe the physical characteristics of a handful of them. They can fold a piece of construction paper in half two times to make four quadrants, where they can illustrate and describe their rocks.

History and Geography

- This story is a good example of cooperation and teamwork within a community and coming together for a common goal. Even though this story is similar to a trickster tale, it is still a great example of people working together to make something happen.

- The storyline offers many opportunities to teach students about trade. Have students get together in small groups and create their own lists of personal possessions they have that they would be willing to trade with others for something equal or better. Once the students create their own lists, have them talk about what they would trade with one another if they were allowed to do so. Remind them that this is pretend only.

Art

- Ask the students to draw their favorite scene from story.

Fifth Grade

Top Books for Fifth Grade

The Blue and the Gray by Eve Bunting, illustrated by Ned Bittinger (Scholastic, 1996).

The Butter Man by Elizabeth Alalou & Ali Alalou, illustrated by Julie Klear Essakalli (Charlesbridge, 2008).

Chronicle of America: American Revolution 1700–1800 by Joy Masoff (Scholastic Reference, 2000).

The Declaration of Independence by Elaine Landau (Children's Press, 2008).

First Day in Grapes by L. King Pérez, illustrated by Robert Casilla (Lee and Low Books, 2002).

Going Home by Nicholasa Mohr (Puffin, 1999).

The Happiest Ending by Yoshiko Uchida (Margaret McElderry, 1985).

Indian Shoes by Cynthia Leitich Smith (HarperCollins, 2002).

It Doesn't Have to Be This Way / No tiene que ser así: A Barrio Story / Una historia del barrio by Luis J. Rodriguez, illustrated by Daniel Galvez (Children's Book Press, 1999).

The Jacket by Andrew Clements (Simon & Schuster, 2002).

My Diary from Here to There; Mi diario de aquí hasta allá by Amada Irma Pérez, illustrated by Maya Christina Gonzalez (Children's Book Press, 2002).

Nettie's Trip South by Ann Turner, illustrated by Ronald Himler (Alladin, 1995).

One Green Apple by Eve Bunting, illustrated by Ted Lewin (Clarion, 2006).

Taking Sides by Gary Soto (Harcourt Brace, 1992).

Lesson Ideas

Eve Bunting. *The Blue and the Gray.* (1996).   ISBN-13: 9780590601979

The families of two friends, one black and one white, are building new houses on a field where a Civil War battle took place. One boy's father describes the battle to the two boys, and these scenes are put side-by-side with calm settings of the present. After hearing these stories, the boys say that they'll remember what took place in those fields.

Lexile: 620L   (Ages 9 to 12)

Reading

- If enough copies are available (one copy for every two to three students), this would be a great book to use in literature circles. Have the students break into groups of five and read the book aloud within their group. After the read aloud, each student takes one literature circle role in his or her group:
  - **Summarizer:** This person summarizes the story.
  - **Vocabulary finder:** As the story is read, this person writes down words that might be new to the group and then defines the words after the story has been read.
  - **Illustrator:** This person illustrates one to three scenes from the story.
  - **Travel tracer:** This person describes the settings that come up in the story.
  - **Responder:** This person helps with each of the other roles and then shares out loud for the whole class.
- If literature circles are not feasible, read the story aloud to the class, stopping to predict, review, clarify, and summarize. Once this has been done, talk about the main idea of the story and then write on the board any words that might have been new to the students. Next, have students break into groups of four and carry out some of the literature circle roles (summarizer, illustrator, vocabulary finder, and responder).

Writing

- In the computer lab or using classroom computers, have the students team up and do some research on the Civil War. Ask students to note at least 8 to 10 key events of the Civil War. They will use this information to create a timeline on construction paper.
- Students can compare and contrast the present and the past, by creating a mini-book with opposing pages. They should use the story to create this present and past book.

Math

- Because much of the book is based on measurement, such as building a house, it will be a helpful discussion point when the students are first learning about area and perimeter. Talk with the students about how important it is to know these terms when it comes to building a structure. Have them share reasons for this, especially in terms of acquiring the appropriate amount of supplies and materials for the space that has been measured.

Science

- In this book, you will see a variety of seasons. Fifth graders can revisit the seasons, and at this level they can be more detailed and articulate about what each season entails. This could begin with a discussion about the basics such as weather, appropriate clothing, and food eaten at these times of year, and then move to the more abstract. This might include discussions about weather in different time zones, differences in seasons across the world at the same time of year, weather patterns, how to read the weather, crops that survive best at certain times of year, and more.

- In this book, many of the illustrations are done using watercolor. Many show the blending of colors. Art chromatography is a method to separate the components of a substance for analytical purposes and can be demonstrated by using a black nonpermanent felt pen, a coffee filter, scissors, and a small glass of water. Take a felt pen and draw a horizontal line in the middle of a coffee filter. Put the filter into the water, but make sure your felt-pen line is above the water level. The coffee filter sucks the water up slowly. When the water rises above the point where the felt-pen line is, the water will take parts of the ink with it. The lighter parts of the ink will rise quickly with the water, toward the upper edge of the filter stripe, while the heavy parts of the ink stay where they are. That's the principle of chromatography. Remove the coffee filter from the glass just before the water reaches its top edge. Put it on a piece of newspaper and let it dry.

History and Geography

- This book clearly lends itself to studying the Civil War. In the computer lab or using classroom computers, have students team up and do some research on the causes and effects of the Civil War. Ask students to note at least 8 to 10 key events of the Civil War and then list them on chart paper. Have the small groups compare their key events and teach one another about the causes and effects of the Civil War.

- Teach the students about friendship and teamwork. In so doing, you may also want to tap into the effects of not having won the war, depending on your role in it.

- Have students work in pairs or small groups to trace the battles on a map.

Art

- If you have access to watercolors and paintbrushes, as well as strong construction paper, have students paint their favorite scene from the story or one of their own that wasn't there but relates to the storyline.

- Students can create an American flag using torn construction paper or newspaper.

Sixth Grade

Top Books for Sixth Grade

Baseball Fever by Johanna Hurwitz (Camelot, 2000).

The Breadwinner by Deborah Ellis (Groundwood, 2001)

The Day of Ahmed's Secret by Florence Parry Heide and Judith Heide Gilliland, illustrated by Ted Lewin (HarperTrophy, 1995).

Eagle Song by Joseph Bruchac, illustrated by Dan Andreasen (Puffin, 1999).

Hello, My Name Is Scrambled Eggs by Jamie Gilson (Pocket Books, 1992)

A Jar of Dreams by Yoshiko Uchida (Aladdin, 1993)

Millions to Measure by David M. Schwartz (Harper Collins, 2006)

Music from a Place Called Half Moon by Jerrie Oughton (Laurel Leaf, 1997)

Music for Alice by Allen Say (Lorraine/Houghton, 2004)

Samir and Yonatan by Daniella Carmi (Blue Sky Press, 2002)

Walk Two Moons by Sharon Creech (HarperTrophy, 1996)

Lesson Ideas

Dr. Seuss. *The Lorax.* (1971). Random House.   ISBN-13: 9780394823379

In this story, students will meet the Once-ler and see how his greedy actions destroy a beautiful and thriving environment. Readers will enjoy the characters and rhyming verse but will also understand the subtle messages about the negative effects of deforestation, habitat destruction, and air and water pollution.   Lexile: 560L   (Ages 6 to 12)

Reading

- As you read this story aloud, focus on the cadence and rhyme but also stop along the way to clarify any of the subtle messages that some children might miss. This book lends itself to summary and visualization. So while you are reading, watch for an organic place to stop to do this and have students participate in the discussion.

Writing

- This kind of book is full of verse and rhyme and a great way to model how to write poetry.
- Students would benefit from the experience of writing to a public official about an aspect of conservation in the community (e.g., recycling at school, conserving natural resources, using less water, etc.).

- Have students write a proposal to the Lorax to solve his problem with the greedy Once-ler.
- Write a persuasive letter to stop the deforestation by the Once-ler.

Math

- There is a specific scene in the book where the Once-ler discusses his product and how much he'll make for each one. Have students come up with their own product and talk about the materials needed to make it and how much it would cost to produce. Let students work in teams to do this. Then have them share with the rest of the class. Let the class vote on the best product and the one that uses the least amount of natural resources to develop.

Science

- This is the perfect book to teach students about the environment and the direct impact of using all of our natural resources without replenishing them in some way. Have students work in teams to devise a plan of action for helping the Lorax save the forest.
- Have students discuss habitat destruction and what happened to the wildlife in the book as a result of all the trees being cut down.
- Have students discuss air and water pollution and what happened to the wildlife and plants and water in the book as a result of all the trees being cut down.

History

- Have students share how they would feel if nearby orange tree fields, strawberry fields, or redwood forest were going to be cut down or taken out to build another mall or housing project. Then break the class into groups, those for the idea and those against. Give groups time to come up with an argument in favor of the new mall or housing project and an argument against it. Hold a class debate for and against the idea. It's helpful if you assign roles to group members so everyone can contribute ideas.

Art

- This is a great opportunity for students to create a recycling poster. Have small groups work on one poster per group and then share them with the rest of the class.

Seventh and Eighth Grades

Top Books for Seventh and Eighth Grades

Are You There God? It's Me, Margaret by Judy Blume (Random House Children's Books, 1986)

Bridge to Terabithia by Katherine Paterson (HarperCollins Publishers, 1987)

Catching Fire by Suzanne Collins (Scholastic, Inc., 2009)

Dead End in Norvelt by Jack Gantos (Farrar, Straus and Giroux, 2011)

Flipped by Wendelin Van Draanen (Random House Children's Books, 2003)

The Giver by Lois Lowry (Random House Children's Books, 2002)

Hatchet by Gary Paulsen (Simon & Schuster Books for Young Readers, 2007)

Holes by Louis Sachar (Random House Children's Books, 2001)

The Hunger Games by Suzanne Collins (Scholastic, Inc., 2010)

Island of the Blue Dolphins by Scott O'Dell (Houghton Mifflin Harcourt, 2010)

Mockingjay by Suzanne Collins (Scholastic, Inc. 2010)

Okay for Now by Gary D. Schmidt (Houghton Mifflin Harcourt, 2013)

Out of My Mind by Sharon M. Draper (Atheneum Books for Young Readers, 2012)

The Outsiders by S. E. Hinton (Penguin Group [USA] Incorporated, 1997)

Roll of Thunder Hear My Cry by Mildred D. Taylor (Penguin Group [USA] Inc., 2002)

Stargirl by Jerry Spinelli (Random House Children's Books, 2004)

Walk Two Moons by Sharon Creech (HarperCollins Publishers, 1996)

The Wednesday Wars by Gary D. Schmidt (Houghton Mifflin Harcourt, 2009)

When You Reach Me by Rebecca Stead (Random House Children's Books, 2010)

Wonder by R. J. Palacio (Random House Children's Books, 2012)

Lesson Ideas

Francisco Jiménez. *The Circuit.* (1999). Houghton Mifflin Harcourt.   ISBN-13: 9780395979020

This book is an honest and powerful account of a family's journey to the fields of California, and to a life of constant moving, from strawberry fields to cotton fields, from tent cities to one-room shacks, from picking grapes to topping carrots and thinning lettuce. Seen through the eyes of a boy who longs for an education and the right to call one place home, this is a story of survival, faith, and hope. It is a journey that will open readers' hearts and minds.

Lexile: 0880L   (Ages 11 to 16)

Reading

- Discussion: Prior to doing any writing or adding to the ongoing timeline, discuss the story using the basics: who (main character/s), what (summary), when (sequence the events of the chapter), where (setting), and why (author's or character's purpose). Then before adding to the whole class or individual timelines, describe three to five of the most important events from each chapter for the summary.

- Literature circles: Each day, have the students break into small groups and read aloud the chapter. After the reading, have students take a literature circle role such as the following (see the chapter on reading strategies for specific definitions and other roles):
  - **Summarizer:** This person summarizes the story.
  - **Vocabulary finder:** As the story is read, this person writes down words that might be new to the group and then defines the words after the story has been read.
  - **Illustrator:** This person illustrates one to three scenes from the story.
  - **Travel tracer:** This person describes the settings in the story.
  - **Responder:** This person helps with each of the other roles and then shares out loud for the whole class.

Writing

- **Word bank:** Throughout the book, readers will come across unfamiliar words in both English and Spanish. Using a word wall or journal as a word bank, have students note these words by showing (illustrate), saying (speak out loud), explaining (define the word), expanding (use it in a sentence), or buzzing about the word briefly (talk about its meaning with a partner). This should be done each time a chapter is completed either individually or as a whole class.

- **Sequence on a timeline:** After reading each chapter, have students or small groups of students note the chapter's setting(s), main character(s) and a brief summary on an ongoing timeline (whole class or individual).

- **Literature connection (personal):** Have students respond with a "quick write" or short essay at the end of each chapter. Design questions related to the content of each chapter so students can see personal connections to the novel. Begin the unit with the following questions: Did you ever travel from one city to another, or have you remained in the same city all your life? If yes, was your travel meant to visit family or friends or to take a vacation? Explain. If you traveled to move from one city, state, or country to another, what do you remember most from the experience? Explain.

- **Autobiographical essay:** Students will write an autobiographical essay similar to the format from *The Circuit* by Francisco Jimenez. It should guide readers through students' early years up to the current day. Students should organize their data on a personal timeline, which they can reference for writing their autobiography. They can also use the writing prompts that follow each chapter as models for formulating their ideas and paragraphs.

History and Geography

- Build background knowledge: Using a world map, have students identify the following Mexican cities, as these will be discussed in the beginning of the book: Guadalajara, Mexicali, Jalisco, and Moreles. As other locations, such as the Californian cities of Santa Clara, Santa Rosa, Santa Maria, Fowler, Corcoran, Fresno, and Orosi as well as the San Joaquin Valley, are introduced throughout the book, be sure to note them on the class map so all the students can include them in their map research.

- Each time a new location is introduced throughout the novel, take students on a virtual tour of the area via an online map such as Google Maps or MapQuest. This will give them a more concrete image of the location and surrounding area without actually visiting the location.

Science

- **Study crops:** Individually or in small groups, students will choose a crop that is known to grow well in California. Using the Internet and other resources, students will discover the history of the crops, develop a timeline from planting to harvesting, and determine who works the fields, where the fruit or plants go after they are picked (grocery stores, farmers' markets, etc.), and who and how many people benefit from the harvesting of said crops.

Art

- **Diorama:** Students will choose one of the labor camps to re-create in the form of a shoebox diorama.

Research

- **Map locations:** Students will work in pairs or small groups to develop a map showing the Jimenez family as they travel throughout the novel. The groups will use the Internet (or other resource if applicable) to research states, cities, and distances. Every couple of days, the students will add to their own map, with the end product of an 11-by-17-inch map (or size to be determined).

- **Virtual tour:** Take students on a virtual tour of Santa Clara University. Once they see all of the elements associated with this university, have them choose a different California university to explore on their own. Offer students a list of elements to research such as location, fields of study, student life, demographics, financial aid options, etc.

Ninth and Tenth Grades

Top Books for Ninth and Tenth Grades

Animal Farm by George Orwell (Penguin Group, 2006)

Black Boy by Richard Wright (HarperCollins Publishers, 2007)

Bless Me, Ultima by Rudolfo Anaya (Grand Central Publishing, 1994)

Brave New World by Aldous Huxley (HarperCollins Publishers, 2006)

The Catcher in the Rye by J. D. Salinger (Little, Brown & Company, 1991)

Esperanza Rising by Pam Muñoz Ryan (Scholastic, Inc., 2002)

The Glass Castle by Jeanette Walls (MTV Books, 2012)

Go Ask Alice by Beatrice Soarks (Simon Pulse, 2005)

The House of the Spirits by Isabel Allende (Random House Publishing Group, 2005)

I Am the Messenger by Markus Zusak (Random House Children's Books, 2006)

The Joy Luck Club by Amy Tan (Penguin Group, 2006)

The Kite Runner by Khaled Hosseini (Penguin Group, 2011)

Lord of the Flies by William Golding (Penguin Group, 1959)

The Lovely Bones by Alice Sebold (Little, Brown & Company, 2009)

Night by Elie Wiesel (Farrar, Straus and Giroux, 2006)

The Perks of Being a Wallflower by Stephen Chbosky (MTV Books, 2012)

Running with Scissors by Augusten Burroughs (Picador, 2003)

Snow Falling on Cedars by David Guterson (Knopf Doubleday Publishing Group, 1995)

Thirteen Reasons Why by Jay Asjer (Penguin Group, 2011)

Woman at Point Zero by Nawal El Saadawi (Zed Books, 2007)

A Yellow Raft in Blue Water by Michael Dorris (Picador, 2003)

Lesson Plans

Sandra Cisneros. *The House on Mango Street*. (1984). Knopf Doubleday.

ISBN-13: 9780679734772

This is the story of a young girl, Esperanza Cordero, growing up in the Latino section of Chicago. Her neighborhood is one of harsh realities and harsh beauty. Esperanza doesn't want to belong to her rundown neighborhood nor the low expectations the world has for her. Esperanza's story is that of a young girl coming into her power and inventing for herself what she will become.

Lexile: 0870L   (Ages 14 to 18)

Reading

- In small groups, students will discuss how Cisneros tells her story in a series of vignettes. Have students consider the following questions as they move through their dialogue: Was this format effective? Could she have told the story another way that might have improved it? Imagine that you were telling a friend about this book. What would you say?

Writing

- Students will write a poem about Mango Street as Esperanza might write one. Each line should begin with the words "I Come From." Leave it open to interpretation but have them consider statements about where they're from regionally, ethnically, religiously, and so on; memories from different points in their life; interests and hobbies; mottos or credos; favorite phrases; family traditions and customs; and whatever else defines who they are. This activity allows the teacher and other classmates to learn about one another and to note similarities and differences among them.

- Helping students relate to a main character is useful in keeping them engaged. For this activity, students will organize their thoughts while comparing themselves to Esperanza. Have them fold a paper in half the long way, and then fold it in half twice to make eight boxes, four on each side of the paper. Next, have students label the boxes on the left as My Goals, My Values, My Traditions, Where I Live. On the right-hand side, have the students label the boxes to correspond with those on the left: Esperanza's Goals, Esperanza's Values, Esperanza's Traditions, Esperanza's Home. On the back, have the students write about ways that they and Esperanza are similar and ways in which they are different, using the table as their reference point. This is also a helpful tool in writing the "I Come From" poem.

- Students will analyze the main characters, their relationships with one another, and any distinct characteristics they may have and then transcribe those thoughts into a graphic organizer. Students can fold a piece of paper the long way into thirds. Then have students list characters' names as they come up in the novel, their relationship to the main character, and any defining characteristics about these characters. Students can use these to make connections among the characters in the book and consider ways in which they can relate to the characters as well.

- Students will create a graphic organizer that will help students study the story's setting, problem, and solution. Fold a piece of paper in half and then fold it in half again. In one of the four boxes, students will write Character (who), Setting (time, place, where), Problem (conflict), and Solution (resolution). Throughout the novel, students can complete these and save them to use later for a novel test, quiz, or essay.

History and Geography

- Americans of Spanish or Latin American descent comprise a major ethnic group in the United States often referred to as Hispanic, Latino/Latina, or Chicano/Chicana. Students will research and write about one of these groups. They may want to consider some of the following questions: From what countries does this ethnic group come? In which areas of the United States are Hispanic, Latino/Latina, or Chicano/Chicana populations concentrated? How well are they able to enter the mainstream?

- American culture incorporates the customs and traditions of many of the large ethnic groups that have settled here. Students will find out how the cultures of people from Spanish and Latin American descent have found a place in the overall culture of the United States. Consider aspects such as food, language, and specific events. They can present their information through the use of a chart, chant or song, essay, PowerPoint presentation, and so on.

- Esperanza Cordero was very sure of where she came from. Students will research their heritage and then look for classmates with the same background.

- On a world map, use small stick-on flags or a small picture of each student to note where each student and his or her family originally came from.

Art

- In English, Esperanza means "hope." On blank white paper, using colored pencils, magazine cutouts, or other forms of multimedia, students will create a collage of what their name means to them.

- In diorama format or on large poster board, students will consider whether or not the house on Mango Street was the kind of house Esperanza always wanted. In their discussion, they will talk about what kind of house they would want and in what kind of neighborhood. They will then create their presentation.

Eleventh and Twelfth Grades

Top Books for Eleventh and Twelfth Grades

All She Was Worth by Miyuki Miyabe (Houghton Mifflin Harcourt, 1999)

Big Girl Small by Rachel DeWoskin (Picador, 2012)

Bone Black: Memories of a Girlhood by Bell Hooks (Holt, Henry & Company, Inc., 1996)

Color of the Sea by John Hamamura (Knopf Doubleday Publishing Group, 2007)

Daughter of Fortune by Isabel Allende (HarperCollins Publishers, 2006)

Eat, Pray, Love by Elizabeth Gilbert (Penguin Group, 2007)

Flowers for Algernon by Daniel Keyes (Houghton Mifflin Harcourt, 2004)

The Glass Castle by Jeanette Walls (Scribner, 2006)

How I Understood Israel in 60 Days or Less by Sarah Glidden (DC Comics, 2011)

If I Stay by Gayle Forman (Penguin Group, 2010)

In Zanesville by Jo Ann Beard (Little, Brown & Company, 2012)

The Kids Are All Right: A Memoir by Diana Welch (Crown Publishing Group, 2010)

The Last Song by Nicholas Sparks (Grand Central Publishing, 2010)

Little Scarlet by Walter Mosley (Grand Central Publishing, 2005)

A Long Way Gone by Ishmael Beah (Farrar, Straus and Giroux, 2008)

March by Geraldine Brooks (Penguin Group, 2006)

Me Talk Pretty One Day by David Sedaris (Little, Brown & Company, 2001)

Nineteen Minutes by Jodi Picoult (Pocket Books, 2013)

One Hundred Years of Solitude by Gabriel García Márquez (HarperCollins Publishers, 2006)

The Road by Cormac McCarthy (Knopf Doubleday Publishing Group, 2007)

The Scrapbook of Frankie Pratt by Caroline Preston (HarperCollins Publishers, 2011)

Speak by Laurie Halse Anderson (Square Fish, 2011)

The Taliban Shuffle: Strange Days in Afghanistan and Pakistan by Kim Barker (Knopf Doubleday Publishing Group, 2012)

The Talk-Funny Girl: A Novel by Roland Merullo (Crown Publishing Group, 2012)

The Time Traveler's Wife by Audrey Niffenegger (Houghton Mifflin Harcourt, 2004)

This Lullaby by Sarah Dressen (Penguin Group, 2004)

A Thousand Splendid Sons by Khaled Hosseini (Penguin Group, 2008)

To Kill a Mockingbird by Harper Lee (Grand Central Publishing, 1988)

What's Eating Gilbert Grape by Peter Hedges (Simon & Schuster, 1999)

Lesson Ideas

Harper Lee. *To Kill a Mockingbird.* (1988). Grand Central.   ISBN-13: 9780446310789

Lawyer Atticus Finch defends the real mockingbird, Tom Robinson, a black man charged with the rape of a white woman. Through the eyes of Atticus's children, Scout and Jem Finch, the book explores the irrationality of adult attitudes toward race and class in the Deep South of the 1930s.   Lexile: 0870L   (Ages 14 to 18)

Reading

• Following each chapter, hold a "two, four, share some more" class discussion (this can be found in Chapter 4 on group strategies). The teacher poses prompts, questions, ideas, or problems from the book or chapter. Two students discuss this with one another, then those two students join another group of two, and, finally, the small group of four share with the whole class. Responses can be transcribed to a chart, poster, or the like to use as reference later. Topics from this book such as the following can be considered for this:

1. Why is Boo Radley such a mystery?
2. What is the significance of the hole in the tree?
3. Who is the protagonist and who is the antagonist in the novel? How does the opposition of these two characters help develop the drama of the story?
4. The only time Atticus describes "sin" to his children is when he advises Scout and Jem to avoid shooting mockingbirds. Why does the mockingbird become a central symbol of the novel? How does this warning relate to the other people and events of the story?
5. Which characters in the story change their views, and in what ways do they do this?
6. Why did Lee choose this title?
7. How is literacy a theme of the novel?
8. Have students identify the most important turning points in the novel.
9. Does the novel make a final statement about how race should affect our treatment of others? Explain.
10. Discuss the meaning of Scout's concluding comment, "Well, it'd be sort of like shootin' a mockingbird, wouldn't it?"

- Have a whole-class discussion about how this story would be narrated, in the third person, from the point of view of Dill's imagination. Have the class brainstorm and outline a new version of the novel told from this perspective.

Writing

- The novel begins with, "Lawyers, I suppose, were children once." Have students consider why they think Lee chose this quote to begin her novel. Then have them write two paragraphs on how this statement relates to what they have learned about Lee's life.
- The protagonist's journey is enriched by characters who hold differing beliefs in a story. One such character type, a foil, has traits that contrast with the protagonist's and highlight important features of the main character's personality. The most important foil, the antagonist, opposes the protagonist, barring or complicating his or her success. Divide the class into groups to examine the role of foils in the novel. Assign each group two secondary characters: Calpurnia, Boo Radley, Tom Robinson, Miss Maudie, Aunt Alexandra, Uncle Jack, Francis, or Miss Caroline. Ask students to review the first ninety-nine pages of the novel. Have each group list key attributes of their characters and prepare a document with moments when these characters bring out reactions from Scout and identify how their personalities help Scout learn about herself.
- This novel hinges on occasions in which adults act like children and children act like adults. To argue for racial equality, Lee must demonstrate situations in which narrow-minded prejudice can realistically yield to an expanded moral sensibility. On what occasions do you wish a character might have acted more maturely? On what occasions are you surprised that a character acted very maturely? Explain.

- As a class, map a timeline that depicts the development of the story. This map should include the most significant turning points but also examine the lesser events that build tension. As students develop their maps, they should define the beginning, middle, and end of the novel.
- Rewrite the novel's ending as if Tom Robinson was acquitted.

Math

- Give students a list of items that were available during the time of the Great Depression (i.e., coffee, bread, tires, movie tickets, boots) and how much they would generally cost today. Have students find out how much these items would have cost back then.

History and Geography

- Cultural and historical contexts are at the center of this novel. Studying details of the time and place help readers understand the motivations of the characters. *To Kill a Mockingbird* is set in the mid-1930s during the Great Depression. Throughout the decade jobs were hard to find, food lines were long, and movies were cheap. This time period left an impression on Harper Lee. As a novel quiz, and after some discussion and research, have students write a one-page, in-class essay on how the book reflects historical realities.
- Have students research and discuss significant features of the Civil Rights movement and then write a one-page, in-class essay on how the main characters might be reflecting similar tensions of the Civil Rights movement.
- Throughout the novel the subject of race comes up. Students should keep a journal noting at what points in the story different characters make remarks about race.
- Scout is described at the beginning of the novel as a tomboy. She becomes more feminine as the novel closes. Respond to the following questions: How does Scout deal with her gender role? Does she redefine femininity? How does this relate to the rest of the story? In what ways do others encourage or discourage her growth? Does this reflect on other decades from the twentieth and twenty-first centuries? How so?

Science

- To further explore mockingbirds, have students do research on them. They will need to answer the following questions: Do mockingbirds have other natural features that relate to the story?

Art

- Individually or in small groups, students will refer to the text and then use construction paper or chart paper to illustrate the town square on the day the trial began.
- Have students explain how their names might serve as symbols of something. Have them illustrate their names in block letters in ways that reflect their namesakes.

Research

- Since some events in the novel mirror circumstances in Harper Lee's life such as her experience as a lawyer's daughter and as a tomboy growing up in a small Southern town during the Great Depression, have students use the Internet to research Harper Lee's life by identifying five to eight significant events that they think influenced her writing *To Kill a Mockingbird*.